Roads to Recovery

362.2   Moore, Jean   2148
             Roads to recovery

$17.95

DATE			

IMPERIAL PUBLIC LIBRARY
P.O. BOX 307
IMPERIAL, TEXAS 79743

© THE BAKER & TAYLOR CO.

Roads to Recovery

A NATIONAL DIRECTORY OF ALCOHOL AND DRUG ADDICTION TREATMENT CENTERS

Edited by Jean Moore

Foreword by LeClair Bissell, M.D.

Collier Books

Macmillan Publishing Company

New York

Collier Macmillan Publishers

London

Copyright © 1985 by Jean Moore

Foreword copyright © 1985 by LeClair Bissell, M.D.

All rights reserved. No part of this book may be reproduced or transmitted in any form or by any means, electronic or mechanical, including photocopying, recording or by any information storage and retrieval system, without permission in writing from the Publisher.

Macmillan Publishing Company
866 Third Avenue, New York, N.Y. 10022
Collier Macmillan Canada, Inc.

Library of Congress Cataloging-in-Publication Data
Moore, Jean.
  Roads to recovery.
    Bibliography: p.
    1. Alcoholism—Hospitals—United States—Directories.
2. Narcotic habit—Hospitals—United States—
Directories. I. Title.
RC564.73.M66 1985   362.2'9'02573   85-19538
ISBN 0-02-059470-4

Macmillan books are available at special discounts for bulk purchases for sales promotions, premiums, fund-raising, or educational use. For details, contact:

Special Sales Director
Macmillan Publishing Company
866 Third Avenue
New York, N.Y. 10022

10 9 8 7 6 5 4 3 2 1

Designed by Jack Meserole

Printed in the United States of America

Contents

Foreword by LeClair Bissell, M.D.   vii

How to Use This Directory   xi

EASTERN TREATMENT CENTERS

CONNECTICUT, 3
DELAWARE, 14
DISTRICT OF COLUMBIA, 16
FLORIDA, 17
GEORGIA, 36
MAINE, 45
MARYLAND, 49
MASSACHUSETTS, 54
NEW HAMPSHIRE, 60
NEW JERSEY, 64
NEW YORK, 69
NORTH CAROLINA, 85
PENNSYLVANIA, 90
RHODE ISLAND, 103
SOUTH CAROLINA, 106
VERMONT, 109
VIRGINIA, 113
WEST VIRGINIA, 124

CENTRAL/SOUTHERN TREATMENT CENTERS

ALABAMA, 129
ARKANSAS, 136
ILLINOIS, 139
INDIANA, 153
IOWA, 163
KANSAS, 169
KENTUCKY, 175
LOUISIANA, 179
MICHIGAN, 188
MINNESOTA, 194
MISSISSIPPI, 207
MISSOURI, 214
NEBRASKA, 220
NORTH DAKOTA, 225
OHIO, 229
OKLAHOMA, 239
SOUTH DAKOTA, 242
TENNESSEE, 244
TEXAS, 250
WISCONSIN, 265

WESTERN TREATMENT CENTERS

ALASKA, 275
ARIZONA, 278
CALIFORNIA, 284
COLORADO, 324
HAWAII, 332
IDAHO, 335
MONTANA, 339
NEVADA, 341
NEW MEXICO, 343
OREGON, 350
UTAH, 355
WASHINGTON, 358
WYOMING, 368

Appendix 370
NATIONAL ASSOCIATIONS, ORGANIZATIONS AND GOVERNMENT AGENCIES, 370
STATE ALCOHOL AND DRUG AGENCIES, 371

Suggested Reading List 376
Glossary of Terms 378
Index of Treatment Centers with Programs for Specific Groups 380

ADOLESCENTS, 380
BLACKS, 383
GAYS/LESBIANS, 383
HEARING-IMPAIRED/DEAF, 383
HISPANIC, 383
IMPAIRED PHYSICIANS AND HEALTH PROFESSIONALS, 383
MEN ONLY, 384
NATIVE AMERICANS, 384
OLDER ADULTS, 384
PRIESTS, NUNS, BROTHERS, 384
RETREAT CENTER FOR ADDICTION WORKERS, 384
WOMEN ONLY, 384

Foreword
by LeClair Bissell, M.D.

The years since the passage of Sen. Harold Hughes's 1970 landmark legislation addressing the problems of alcoholism on a federal level and establishing the National Institute on Alcohol Abuse and Alcoholism have been marked by a proliferation of treatment possibilities. Part of the change resulted from the experience of Alcoholics Anonymous. The successful recovery of thousands and thousands of its members led to a growing and realistic optimism. Alcoholics can and do recover. So do people addicted to other drugs. Techniques and approaches used successfully by AA were borrowed and integrated into other treatment methods. AA is careful not to call what it does "treatment" and insists that it is simply a fellowship of men and women who share experiences, strengths and hopes with one another. It does, however, hold to several basic beliefs: Once it is clear that an individual is alcoholic, a return to controlled drinking is not a realistic goal. The substitution of another mood-altering drug in an attempt to replace alcohol is usually unwise and more likely to lead to a second addiction rather than to solve the drinking problem. People working together at a common problem can do things that no one of them could do in isolation. These convictions are also common to the "Minnesota Model" of alcoholism treatment, sometimes referred to as the treatment of "chemical dependency." This model also embraces the notion that alcoholism is a primary illness in its own right, not merely a symptom of something else.

As this approach gained wider acceptance, more people did recover. Often they went on to become advocates for those still in trouble and in need of help. Many got involved in offering treatment themselves. While most residential facilities provided little more than a structured drug- and alcohol-free environment and an introduction to AA, they were swiftly followed by increasingly sophisticated programs. A host of additional services for both patient and family were added. With that often came much better care and improved treatment outcome, but with it also came the need for larger staffs with more diversified skills and increased expenses.

Recent years have finally seen the development of health insurance coverage for the treatment of alcoholism and other drug addictions. This has not occurred in an orderly, or even a rational, way. It varies widely by state and by population group. Federal employees, for instance, frequently have no such benefits. Medicare has paid for the most expensive part of treatment detoxification in a general hospital at full hospital day rates while denying care in the less expensive and often more effective freestanding facilities. Blue Cross is not a single company but is composed of many separate and independent companies, each with its own policies and benefit packages. A Blue Cross subscriber may have excellent coverage for alcoholism treatment in a variety of settings and in more than one state or may have no protection at all. Every individual in need of help will have to check out his or her own particular situation with someone who can look into a variety of possibilities before deciding what may be feasible.

As the availability of treatment monies increased, an old problem was rapidly replaced by a new one. The profit motive, always present when the patient is affluent, now appeared in different garb. Underutilized hospital beds were discovered as a place to put alcoholics. This could help them, and the financially troubled hospital as well. Frequently it did, and some of these hospital-based units are excellent. Some are not. In many cases, freestanding treatment facilities also received insurance coverage. Most of these are more reasonably priced than hospitals and offer comparable treatment for the addictive illnesses, even though they are not designed primarily to deal with the more complex medical complications. Some of them are far too expensive and more likely to promote themselves on the basis of physical plant and country club amenities than by the quality of treatment.

To add to the intricacy of all this, the availability of treatment has often outstripped demand, and the treatment facilities are found hiring large numbers of people to market for them. Not only do they solicit business from a variety of referral sources, but they also are producing a variety of radio and television messages designed to reach the alcoholic and affected family members and invite them to come *directly* into treatment. Given the traditional reluctance of many health professionals to diagnose and confront alcohol and drug problems, this is not a bad idea, but it does leave the unsophisticated person at something of a loss as to what is needed and where best to find it.

Since so many of the treatment facilities are new, it isn't at all feasible to rely only on those places of proven reliability over the years. There simply has not been time for a great many quite deserving places to build a reputation and to be judged by their results. Eventually one hopes to make decisions that way rather than by the quality of a brochure or by the cleverness of a public relations firm in getting a given facility mentioned frequently in the press.

Price itself tells us very little. Some of the very best are some of the least expensive. One of the most widely publicized as catering to celebrities is among the more reasonable.

Yet another problem that will not be solved either by time or by a book like this is that treatment facilities, like people, change with time. Many are at their best when very new, when hopes and enthusiasms are high and the honeymoon is at its peak. Others begin badly with inexperienced staff and inadequate planning, but they may persist and learn and eventually become excellent. Still others will reflect the personalities of one or more particularly talented individuals and will change character altogether if there is staff turnover and several of the key people leave. Treatment staff, like families, go through periods of getting along together and working smoothly for the benefit of patients only to go through other periods of turmoil that will make them relatively ineffective. Therapists, like patients, are human beings who tend to do the best they can at a given time and in a given place. At times they are successful, at other times not.

This book attempts to introduce some order into how to go about finding a residential treatment facility. It does not attempt to list outpatient services, which must, of necessity, be physically located near enough to the patient or family to make regular visits reasonable and which should be explored locally. The yellow pages of most large telephone directories can usually help. So can local councils of alcoholism, many of which are affiliated with the National Council on Alcoholism, 12 West 21st Street, New York, New York 10010.

Information given in this directory cannot be totally comprehensive, since not every facility invited to submit information did so, some omitted some factual data, and others may be unknown to the editor. Each facility has described itself and made its own claims. There is no way in which they could all have been visited and the information they provided verified.

This volume remains, however, the most complete and most accurate directory of its kind of which I am aware.

The greatest challenge when referring someone to residential treatment is to individualize that treatment as much as possible, to make as good a match between place and patient as possible. I am a firm believer that the disease of alcoholism is much the same, whether it affects a king or a charwoman, a celebrity or a library clerk, an adolescent or a recent retiree. I don't think there is black alcoholism or gay alcoholism or women's alcoholism. There are alcoholic people—some black, some gay, some women. I don't think we need to create little islands of specialness and difference on which to put each person. At the same time there are individuals who do better in one kind of setting than in another. Some are comfortable only with other women or where there are significant numbers of their own ethnic or age group, and decisions will have to include these concerns. At other times there will be choices forced upon people by restrictions of insurance coverage, law or policies set by employers and colleagues. People who are deaf will need to know about the rehabilitation facility and the halfway house where American Sign Language is used. Those lacking a familiarity with English will need help in their own language.

This directory will provide a beginning for anyone trying to sort out the many residential settings now available. It will help. It will not provide the last word, and some of the information on cost and staff will change and become out of date. Once I might have bemoaned that fact. Now I feel it is a welcome problem, since what we have now is so much better than what we had available only a few years ago. There is every reason to believe that the future will be brighter still.

How to Use This Directory

There may be some people in today's world whose lives have not in some way been touched by the disease of alcohol and drug addiction . . . but if such people exist they are few and far between! It is for the rest of us, the wives and husbands of alcoholics, the parents and children of victims of chemical dependency, the physicians, counselors and employers of victims of addictive disease, that this directory has been compiled.

The bewilderment, anger and feeling of powerlessness that grip any one of us tied by affection or professional responsibility to an individual whose life has become unmanageable through dependence on alcohol or drugs can be erased if we have information at hand that can lead toward recovery. There are outpatient programs available in almost every part of the country; there are AA and NA meetings in nearly every city and town; and there are residential treatment facilities all across the country. All of these can offer support to any victim who has come to the point of accepting his or her need for help. Although residential programs very often promise the most intensive and effective push along the long road to recovery, it has, in the past, been difficult, if not impossible, to make an informed choice as to the best facility for the particular individual in need of treatment. And it is an important choice, since residential treatment involves a major commitment of time, money and hope on the part of the patient, and on the part of the family members and business associates involved. There is, as Dr. LeClair Bissell has said in her eloquent introduction, no feasible way of accurately evaluating the effectiveness of the residential programs listed in this directory. There is just no valid process of awarding four-star or three-star designations as if these rehabilitative programs were restaurants or hotels that can be graded on tenderness of the sirloin or promptness of room service. Rehabilitative programs are all alike in their focus on addiction, but each one is different in the particular approach to rehabilitation they choose. The most effective way to get the "feel" of each facility, therefore, is to read the descriptions of their programs very carefully, since these descriptions have been adapted from the literature they sent in and have been checked and approved by the facility. If the "feel" of the facility matches, as well as it can, the particular needs of the chemical abuser with whom you are concerned, then this directory has, in fact, performed the service for which it was designed.

WHERE TO BEGIN

Recovery, for those who have found, in the words of the Twelve Steps of Alcoholics Anonymous, "that their lives have become unmanageable," begins on the day and the moment when they can make that admission and come to the realization that they can take steps toward getting control of their lives again. But for those of us who stand on the sideline, willing and wanting the alcoholic or drug abuser to come to that moment of decision, there are steps that we can also be taking, as we wait, that can help *us* to help when the moment of acceptance finally comes. That moment can come unexpectedly. Sometimes it comes as a result of some particularly destructive incident that can convince the victim, perhaps still under the influence of the last drinking binge or drug episode, that enough is now, finally, enough. Or sometimes it comes as the result of a planned "confrontation" performed by family, friends or associates who come together to give witness to the repeated lapses in judgment and performance that, recited as he or she listens, can convince the victim of addiction that there is no more room for denial. Or sometimes it is a decision made by the individual alone, out of fatigue, or despair, or the tiny glimmerings of hope. But whenever or however that life-and-death decision is finally made, it is essential to have instantly available the needed information on where, how and when treatment can be started, since delay between the decision to accept help and becoming involved in a program can destroy that hard-won resolve. *Someday* is another word for *never* in the vocabulary of addiction, and when the person you are concerned with finally says, "I'm willing to get help today," you must have the answers he or she needs instantly available.

If you are now involved, by family ties or professional responsibility, with someone approaching the moment of decision, you must equip yourself with all the information he or she will need to follow that life-giving decision with constructive action. Your job is to review the outpatient and AA services available in your area, and if residential programs are appropriate, review those available and suitable *before* the moment of decison on the part of the addicted individual has been made. The following are some of the details that will affect your decision.

Where Is the Facility?

So far as the patient is concerned, whether the center he or she attends is ten minutes or ten hours travel time away from home is relatively unimportant, since the trip, for him, will be made only once to get there and once to come home. But the location of the facility is enormously important for the family members, since, as those in the field are becoming increasingly, and belatedly, aware, family involvement is an essential part of recovery. Family education and understanding are vital, not only of the disease their spouse, father, mother or child is afflicted by, but of the disease they themselves have contracted from having lived with an alcoholic or drug abuser. All good rehabilitative programs offer family programs, sometimes on weekends, sometimes for five-day or longer residential stays near the end of the full rehabilitation program. Remember, therefore, if families are to visit the center on a regular basis, it must be near enough to make those visits possible and practical for those who stay at home.

Is He Sober? Is She Drug-free?

Almost all of the facilities listed in this directory offer detoxification but some of them do not. And although almost all chemical abusers make their decision to accept treatment when they are sober or temporarily straight, some come to the point of decision at a time when they are still under the influence of the alcohol and/or drugs. If the person you care about decides, on some haggard and hung-over morning that he is ready —right now—to do something about his habit, it would be disastrous to be prepared only with a facility that asks for a period of drug-free time before admission. Be ready to recommend a facility that will accept patients who are drunk or high if that is the condition in which they will agree to go.

How Much Does the Program Cost?
Will the Abuser's Insurance Apply?

Again, this is the kind of information you will want to have checked before the decision to go for treatment has been made. Both costs and insurance coverage vary widely from state to state, and from facility to facility. Call two or three suitable treatment centers beforehand to be sure that financial capability will not interfere with admission. If neither funds nor insurance is available, there are state-operated programs—you will find the state offices listed in the appendix of this directory—that can offer programs at reduced or subsidized rates.

Does the "Personality" of the Program Fit the Needs of the Individual?

Study the program descriptions of each facility with respect to the individual needs of the person you are trying to help. If, for example, he or she is drug- or poly-addicted, then locate a facility that is geared to meet those needs. Many, if not most, of the centers listed here, deal with chemical dependency on alcohol, marijuana, cocaine, sedatives, amphetamines, narcotic analgesics and hallucinogens, as well as those suffering from cross-addiction to any of these. Some centers offer treatment only to those whose primary addiction is alcohol, and some treat only alcoholism. Although some offer treatment for the special complications involved in heroin, methadone and morphine addiction, you will want to query the centers prior to request for admission if you have doubts about the program they offer for addictions of that kind.

Will the Facility Have Space Available?

The best insurance you can have that there will be an available bed for your sufferer on the day he or she is willing to go for help is to select a handful of centers that meet the criteria. If the moment of decision seems close at hand, call them to check on the availability of a room so that you can be sure to avoid disappointment that could be fatal to the patient's resolve.

Ask yourself these questions, along with particular ones you know of in connection with the alcoholic and/or drug abuser you are involved with, and select several centers that would seem to meet the needs. Every facility listed in this directory is willing to answer inquiries and to send you their brochures, complete descriptions of programs and answers to your specific questions. Write or call them to provide yourself, and the prospective patient, with all the information possible to prepare for involvement in the program.

Many of the centers will also, as you will find in the text, be willing to offer intervention service performed by staff members who understand this delicate and often very effective process. In addition, many centers provide an assessment and evaluation service, which can be of real value, particularly for adolescents, in selection of the most appropriate mode of treatment. Again, call or write to the centers if you feel they can help with the individual you have in mind or to get their advice as to how you, yourself, can arrange for the confrontation that may help the alcoholic or addict choose the help he or she needs.

The following are steps you can follow to bring the addict/alcoholic/sufferer to the rehabilitative services he or she so desperately needs, and that you, sometimes with equal desperation, want to offer:

1. Once you decide that residential treatment is an option, select several that fit the geographic, financial and programmatic requirements you feel apply to the individual involved.
2. Call or write to get further information, and to ascertain willingness to accept the individual addicted, and the availability of space in the program.
3. Arrange an intervention process, if it seems appropriate, that may speed the patient to an acceptance of his or her illness.
4. Accept the fact that leading a horse to water does not, as we all know, guarantee that he will drink, and that leading an alcoholic and/or drug abuser to treatment carries the same caveat. In the words of AA's Serenity Prayer, remember that your duty is not only to "have the courage to change the things that you can change," but also to "accept those things that you cannot change." It is possible for you to point the way to recovery to those whose fatal illness of addiction makes them turn to you for help. But remember that they must walk that path themselves, and they must walk it alone.

The editor of this volume wishes to express her gratitude for the cooperation and help of all the facilities listed in this directory. Although it is important to note that none of these facilities pays for inclusion in the directory, each one of the centers has been involved in the preparation and approval of the material that describes the program, and I wish to thank them for their time and their effort.

It is also important to express the even broader gratitude we feel, along with the hundreds of thousands of alcohol- and/or drug-damaged men, women and young people whom they have helped, for the caring, the compassion and the concern that the many staff members of the many facilities listed in this directory bring to the all-important work they do.

EASTERN TREATMENT CENTERS

Connecticut

REID TREATMENT CENTER

121 West Avon Road
Avon, Connecticut 06001

(203) 673-6115

Director: John Reid

Average Patient Census: 30
Minimum Duration of Treatment: 10-day minimum; 28-day program
Cost: $125 per day. Insurance eligible.
Detoxification Offered: Yes
Accreditation: State of Connecticut

Reid Treatment Center offers a three-part program.

Acute Care: Detoxification by a staff of qualified physicians, nurses and therapists who will assist the patient during this crucial period. Personnel are employed around the clock to assure the comfort and safety of each patient.

Intensive Care Program: Individual and group counseling, family group therapy, psychotherapy, therapeutic community (patient government), occupational therapy, relaxation therapy, recreational therapy, awareness groups and AA meetings, both on and off the premises.

Aftercare Program: Follow-up group therapy sessions, family counseling. Family groups are held weekly.

Admissions 24 hours a day and free patient transportation statewide are offered.

THE BLUERIDGE CENTER

1095 Blue Hills Avenue
Bloomfield, Connecticut 06002

(203) 243-1331

Director: Mona L. Bloomfield
Average Patient Census: Capacity, 45 patients
Minimum Duration of Treatment:
Inpatient, 21 days; no minimum acute care

Cost: Preadmission screening, no charge; inpatient program including evaluation, acute care, 21 days; inpatient treatment and 12 weeks aftercare, $5,460 inclusive. Insurance eligible.
Detoxification Offered: Yes
Accreditation: In process

BlueRidge recognizes that alcoholism is a progressive disease. As such, methods of treatment vary with the severity of the illness and the particular needs of the patient and the patient's family. The ability to match the needs of patients with particular services is central to effective treatment.

The comprehensive range of treatment services at BlueRidge is designed to assure a maximum number of individualized treatment plans. BlueRidge is dedicated to treating alcoholism with the least restrictive methods. In every case, restoring the individual to health is the result of a multidisciplinary approach and the association of AA as the long-term support system for continued sobriety. All too often, alcoholics seeking treatment are limited to two alternatives—hospitalization or AA. BlueRidge attempts to broaden these options by integrating its services with AA in a range of treatment modalities based on the long-term commitment to AA.

Since many alcoholics suffer from the disease without any significant prior psychological illness, but others may have emotional problems that also require professional attention, BlueRidge emphasizes a team treatment approach, assuring that these varied treatment needs be evaluated and met appropriately.

The treatment team at this facility is particularly concerned with issues of confidentiality and is committed to protecting all patient information.

The range of services includes: Acute Care and Evaluation, Intensive Inpatient Rehabilitation, a Partial Hospitalization Program, Day and Evening Hospitalization Services, Outpatient Services, Aftercare and Family Treatment Services, both for families of patients and for families of those who are not willing to seek treatment.

ALCOHOL AND DRUG ABUSE TREATMENT CENTER
John Dempsey Hospital

University of Connecticut Health Center
Farmington, Connecticut 06032

(203) 674-3422

Director: Ronald Kadden, Ph.D.

Average Patient Census: 20
Minimum Duration of Treatment: 21 days
Cost: Hospital rates. Insurance eligible.
Detoxification Offered: Yes
Accreditation: JCAH

The University of Connecticut Health Center encompasses the University Medical School and its many ancillary services, including the John Dempsey Hospital, a full-service teaching institution. The Alcohol and Drug Abuse Treatment Center is located on the third floor of this hospital. Directed by the Department of Psychiatry and staffed by experienced and highly trained people, the unit offers an intense 21-day inpatient program and long-term outpatient aftercare.

Men and women age 18 and older presenting with substance abuse problems, with the exception of heroin addiction, are eligible for admission. Access to the many sophisticated services of the hospital and medical school allows for the treatment of patients with concomitant physical and/or psychiatric illness if they are ambulatory and able to comprehend the content of the program.

For each patient, the program includes detoxification if needed, a complete medical and psychological assessment, education on the many aspects of substance abuse and group and individual counseling. There is also a structured family program. AA, Al-Anon and NA are integral elements of both inpatient care and aftercare. Each patient receives assessment of aftercare needs and works with the treatment team to develop the most appropriate long-term care plan.

Prospective patients may be referred by themselves, a family member, physician, AA sponsor, community agency, employer, clergy or other responsible party.

THE GREENWICH HOSPITAL ALCOHOLISM RECOVERY CENTER

Perryridge Road
Greenwich, Connecticut 06830

(203) 869-7000, ext. 335

Director: Phillip Hurley

Average Patient Census: 13
Minimum Duration of Treatment: 28 days
Cost: $207 per day. Insurance eligible.
Detoxification Offered: Yes
Accreditation: JCAH

The treatment philosophy at the Alcoholism Recovery Center at Greenwich Hospital derives from the belief that chemical dependency is a complex, chronic, progressive physical illness, with serious emotional and spiritual consequences.

A complete medical evaluation—physical examination and laboratory tests—is ordered and interpreted by the patient's private physician, or the medical director of ARC. Payment for these services can be arranged with the individual physician. Detoxification, if required, is offered under the supervision of the medical director or private physician, with assurance of protection of the confidentiality of treatment, since no one is advised of a patient's admission without written authorization from the patient.

Each patient requires individual consideration and a treatment plan that reflects his or her special needs. Daily program is scheduled from 8:00 A.M. to 10:00 P.M., and includes educational films and lectures, group sessions, art therapy, physical therapy and a minimum of four AA meetings each week.

Family participation includes individual family/patient meetings with the assigned family counselor/social worker, as well as Family Group Sessions. Lectures on the disease of alcoholism are offered, as well as films. Al-Anon meetings are held on Thursday evenings.

Upon discharge from the program, patients are expected to participate in a Sobriety Counseling Group 12-week program designed to facilitate the patient's transition into an appropriate and effective ongoing support system, AA.

THE INSTITUTE OF LIVING

400 Washington Street
Hartford, Connecticut 06106

(203) 278-7950

Director: Thomas J. Conklin, M.D.

Average Patient Census: 375
Minimum Duration of Treatment: None
Cost: $178–229 per day. Insurance eligible.
Detoxification Offered: Yes
Accreditation: JCAH

The Institute of Living is a private, nonprofit, tertiary-care institution for the treatment of nervous and mental disorders. Therapeutic programs are offered to patients with mental disorders, including those whose symptoms are excessive use of alcohol or drugs.

Patients are accepted on recommendations of a physician, and the Institute requests, before they make definite arrangements for admission, a report from the patient's doctor on clinical history and current level of adjustment, using that information to determine whether or not they might be best able to help.

The Institute offers, upon admission, thorough physical and neurological examinations, including appropriate laboratory studies. Complete psychiatric studies are then undertaken, and an individualized multidisciplinary treatment program is developed for each patient. Alcohol-dependent patients are actively encouraged to participate in the AA program offered on the grounds.

The rehabilitation program places emphasis upon dynamic psychotherapy, along with active involvement in educational, physical, social and recreational programs. The therapeutic program is varied, individualized and based on the staff's full knowledge of the patient's needs.

Facilities include an accredited high school for younger patients who can pursue their studies, obtaining credits toward graduation. The charge for this school program is $174 to $188 per week.

The Institute requests that on admission the patient be accompanied by some person(s), usually a family member(s), who can arrange to remain in the Hartford area for at least 24 hours in order to provide sufficient time for staff to obtain as much background information as possible.

Evening Intensive Alcoholism Clinic: The Institute of Living offers a partial hospitalization program for the treatment of alcoholism as a primary disease. Admission can be arranged through family, friend, employer, physician or self-referral.

During Phase I the program meets 4 hours per night, three times per week for 6 weeks. This is followed, in Phases II and III, by weekly sessions for 4½ months and then monthly sessions.

Emphasis on sobriety and active involvement in AA is an important part of the treatment program. The cost of the program is approximately $1,500 for Phase I.

HIGH WATCH FARM

Box 206
Kent, Connecticut 06757

(203) 927-3772

Director: Frank Jackman

Average Patient Census: 35
Minimum Duration of Treatment: 2 weeks
Cost: $180 per week, payable on admission. Insurance eligible.
Detoxification Offered: No

High Watch Farm offers a program built upon the principles of AA and the techniques toward rehabilitation employed by AA. Qualifications for admission are a diagnosis of alcoholism only and a desire to stop drinking on the part of the applicant. Formal family counseling is not offered.

SILVER HILL FOUNDATION

P.O. Box 1177
Valley Road
New Canaan, Connecticut 06840

(203) 966-3561

Director: Carlotta L. Shuster, M.D.
Average Patient Census: 25 in substance abuse program

Minimum Duration of Treatment: 4 weeks
Cost: $2,500 per week approximately. Admission deposit, $2,500 with no insurance, $1,500 with insurance, $500 with Medicare. Insurance eligible.
Detoxification Offered: Yes
Accreditation: JCAH

Silver Hill Foundation is a general psychiatric hospital of 77 beds, with four different programs and offers an alcoholism and substance abuse program. This program consists of an intensive and specialized course of treatment, including a brief period of detoxification if necessary, individual therapy, group therapy, AA meetings, films, lectures and discussion groups focused on the subject of alcoholism and substance abuse. Silver Hill emphasizes family involvement from day of admission. Aftercare is available. Admissions must be arranged in advance.

PARKSIDE LODGE OF CONNECTICUT

P.O. Box 668
Route 7
North Canaan, Connecticut 06018

(203) 824-5426

Director: John Reese

Average Patient Census: 44
Minimum Duration of Treatment: 30 days
Cost: $170 per day. Insurance eligible.
Detoxification Offered: Yes
Accreditation: JCAH

Parkside Lodge offers treatment for both adult and adolescent substance abuse in a residential setting. Initially, all patients are admitted to the program's medical unit for comprehensive medical workup and detoxification. Following this phase, patients are admitted to the structured Rehabilitation Program. The program includes small groups, community meetings, lectures, AA meetings, recreational therapy and specialized groups. In addition, youth are involved in an educational program.

Aftercare following treatment is provided both at the facility and at satellite offices.

Family members are involved in the treatment program at all levels. In addition, families are encouraged to participate in a specialized Three-Day Family Recovery Program.

STONINGTON INSTITUTE

Box 216
Swantown Hill Road
North Stonington, Connecticut 06359

(203) 535-1010

Director: Robert Fox

Average Patient Census: 35
Minimum Duration of Treatment: Detox, 1 week; intensive rehab, 4 weeks
Cost: $180 per day. Insurance eligible.
Detoxification Offered: Yes, medical examination
Accreditation: JCAH

Available programs at Stonington Institute for the treatment of alcoholism are as follows:

1. The acute treatment and evaluation-detoxification program is a 1-week program for medical management. Diagnosis, evaluation, medical treatment for detox and therapy are provided.
2. Intensive treatment-therapy program is a multiweek program with individual diagnosis and treatment plan developed with the patient's participation. Extensive orientation to AA, group therapy and indi-

vidual counseling are basic treatment modalities, with emphasis on psychosocial planning and activities leading toward recovery. Many employers require this program for their employees suffering from the disease of alcoholism, since it ensures the highest level of success in arresting the disease. Audiovisual aids are utilized, and informal discussions are an important part of the intensive daily program.
3. Family therapy includes individual and multifamily counseling and is encouraged as an essential element of total treatment.

Staff includes physicians, psychiatrists, psychologists, therapy counselors and staff nurses. The relationship of staff to patients of over one to one has proven to have a significant effect within the recovery program.

Aftercare and continuity-of-care programs are arranged prior to discharge.

STONEHAVEN

325 Main Street
Portland, Connecticut 06480

(203) 342-1774

Director: Diane Tokarz

Average Patient Census: 24
Minimum Duration of Treatment: 28 days
Cost: $3,000. Insurance eligible.
Detoxification Offered: Yes
Accreditation: JCAH

At Stonehaven, alcohol and drug users get plain talk as a sign of love and hope, an attitude of treatment based on the understanding at this facility of the fact that when someone is addicted, it may be impossible to talk sense to them in a gentle way.

Substance abusers have many-sided problems, and for this reason, Stonehaven helps them work through their problems using a many-sided approach, offering highly individualized programs directed by a team of certified, experienced chemical dependency specialists: physician, psychologist, social workers, nurses, dietician and admission, therapy and aftercare coordinators.

Following detoxification, when necessary, each patient is asked to agree to complete the 4- to 6-week program. Thereupon the staff develops a "problem list" and "treatment goals" for each patient. The primary focus of the treatment that follows is on communication, and on discussing, analyzing and learning. The patient learns in groups and individually, in counseling, in family and marital therapy and as a member of a therapeutic community. The Stonehaven program is consistent with the philosophies of AA and NA, and every effort is made in treatment to educate each person in the Twelve-Step way of continuing recovery. Family Education Group meetings are held 2 nights per week.

Admission to Stonehaven, the chemical dependency treatment division of Elmcrest, can be arranged for anyone 18 years or older by individuals themselves, families or concerned others.

EAGLE HILL REHABILITATION CENTER

Alberts Hill Road
P.O. Box 836
Sandy Hook, Connecticut 06482

(203) 426-8085

Director: William Moriarty

Average Patient Census: 50
Minimum Duration of Treatment: Detox, average 4 days; rehab, 28 days
Cost: $185 per day. Insurance eligible.
Detoxification Offered: Yes
Accreditation: JCAH

Eagle Hill offers a residential alcoholism treatment program that includes an initial period of detoxification and medical evaluation averaging 4 days, followed by a 28-day intensive rehabilitation program. The therapy program includes individual and group counseling, didactic lecture sessions for alcoholism information, family therapy, activities therapy and active participation in AA. The patient is also referred after inpatient treatment to an active aftercare system, which is provided by Eagle Hill and other outside support services in the client's home area.

Individuals seeking admission should call the admissions office to make arrangements. Admissions are accepted 24 hours a day, 7 days a week, after an initial phone call to the facility. To be considered for admission, the primary problem must be alcoholism, although individuals using other drugs similar to alcohol can be accepted. The individual must not be suffering from any acute medical or psychiatric problems. Insurance must be verified or other financial arrangements made prior to admission.

GAYLORD HOSPITAL ALCOHOLISM REHABILITATION PROGRAM

Gaylord Farms Road
Wallingford, Connecticut 06492

(203) 269-3344, ext. 240

Director: Nancy R. Winialski, R.N., M.S.

Average Patient Census: 20
Minimum Duration of Treatment: 28-day average, option of shorter term
Cost: $130 per day. Insurance eligible.
Detoxification Offered: Yes
Accreditation: JCAH

The Gaylord Hospital, with a long record of rehabilitation service for victims of traumatic brain injuries, spinal cord injuries, pulmonary disease and others, offers a logical extension of its work in a comprehensive program for the rehabilitation of alcoholic men and women.

The program includes education about alcoholism, individual counseling and group therapy. A strong emphasis is placed on AA and its Twelve-Step life program. Relaxation therapy, assertiveness training and leisure counseling are also offered. Cooperation with other services at the rehabilitation center permits delivery of the physical medicine therapies, respiratory rehabilitation and psychology as needed.

A four-session family program of alcoholism education and Al-Anon involvement stresses help for family members and interested others.

Prospective patients should be 18 years of age or older. A preadmission visit may be requested by prospective patients or by the program staff.

NATCHAUG HOSPITAL INC.

189 Storrs Road
Willimantic, Connecticut 06226

(203) 423-2514, 423-5429

Director: Lorraine Hediger, M.A., A.C.S., C.A.C.
Average Patient Census: 55–60

Minimum Duration of Treatment: 1 week (adolescent rehab, 1–3 months; adult rehab, 4–6 weeks)
Cost: Approximately $6,000 for 4 weeks. Insurance eligible.
Detoxification Offered: Yes
Accreditation: JCAH

The Alcohol and Drug Abuse Service at Natchaug Hospital is within the psychiatric units. There are services for both adolescents and adults: active, multifaceted treatment and aftercare for persons with the problem of severe alcohol and/or drug abuse providing a special experience in community living and group interaction.

The goal of the adolescent program is to return each youngster to health and well-being within his family and community as quickly and as simply as possible. The patient meets regularly in individual sessions with his or her primary therapist, who coordinates all aspects of the treatment program, with patient participation in establishing goals. Family involvement is strongly encouraged, with a parents' group in the planning phase to support parents and therapeutic passes home that may become an integral part of the program. All adolescents on the Unit are required to attend the on-grounds school, and an educational diagnosis is developed for each patient. The Unit is in a wing of the hospital, designed and staffed expressly to meet the needs of children 12 to 18 years of age.

The adult program includes medical detox, psychiatric evaluation and a complete rehabilitation program of education; group, individual, family and marital therapy; and AA meetings, both in-hospital and community. Aftercare arrangements include counseling, therapy or return to referring physician or agency.

Natchaug Hospital also offers both day and evening outpatient programs.

Delaware

LOWER KENSINGTON ENVIRONMENTAL CENTER, INC.
Delaware Addictive Services

Governor Beacon Health Center
Delaware City, Delaware 19706

(302) 834-9201

Director: Joseph S. Allmond

Average Patient Census: 29 (31-bed capacity)
Minimum Duration of Treatment: 28 days
Cost: $45 per day. Insurance eligible.
Detoxification Offered: Yes
Accreditation: JCAH

Lower Kensington Environmental Center, Delaware Addictive Services is a private, not-for-profit firm providing a residential alcoholism program under contract with the State of Delaware's Division of Alcoholism, Drug Abuse and Mental Health. The program is located on the grounds of the Governor Beacon Health Center in Delaware City, in a spacious, modern one-story building formerly used as a school. A gymnasium and the grounds adjacent to the program offer ample recreational areas.

The program is designed for people with a primary problem of alcoholism. Persons with a secondary drug problem will also be considered for admission; however, persons with a primary drug problem or who have psychiatric problems are best treated at another facility. All applicants must be at least 18 years of age and state a willingness to voluntarily enter the program and abide by the program's rules. All applicants must be free from any mood-changing drugs or psychoactive medications and must be cleared by a medical doctor prior to admission. Referrals to the residential program are accepted from all sources and are screened by admission into the detoxification unit prior to acceptance into the longer-term program.

During the course of the 28-day program, the client receives 160 hours of structured therapy, including educational lectures, group therapy sessions, specialized groups for men, women and youths and reading/reflection groups. Additionally, each client receives individual counseling and aftercare placement services. A follow-up of the client's progress is made 6 months after discharge. The program also works closely with many local AA groups, including 5 meetings per week in the facility. A family education group and an Al-Anon meeting are held each weekend during visiting hours.

The clinical staff includes five alcoholism counselors, the clinical director and support personnel. All clinical staff are certified alcoholism counselors. The overall project is coordinated by the project director, and all services are reviewed on an ongoing basis by the program's quality assurance director to ensure a high level of quality treatment.

District of Columbia

SETON HOUSE AT PROVIDENCE HOSPITAL

1053 Buchanan Street, N.E.
Washington, D.C. 20017

(202) 269-7777

Director: Jean Genson
Average Patient Census: 26

Minimum Duration of Treatment: Detox, 7 days; rehab, 21 days
Cost: Hospital-fixed costs, covered by most insurance plans. Insurance eligible.
Detoxification Offered: Yes
Accreditation: JCAH

Seton House at Providence Hospital offers a comprehensive alcoholism and drug addiction treatment program. The staff of professionals at Seton House recognize alcoholism to be a chronic and, if left untreated, potentially fatal disease and believe that abstinence is the only route to recovery.

A broad-based treatment structure is offered at Seton House, which includes a 21-day intensive inpatient treatment program that begins with detoxification under medical supervision and individual case management, including liaison with a person's employer or EAP representative. There is a multidisciplinary approach to treatment involving medicine, nursing, counseling, both group and individual, as well as social services, pastoral care, dietary aid and access to all hospital services when necessary. Aftercare includes a 15-week treatment and counseling program and a 1-year follow-up after discharge.

Weekly men's and women's rap sessions, structured intervention when appropriate, and a 7-day detoxification-only program are also available. An outpatient program is also offered by Seton House.

Florida

THE CENTER FOR RECOVERY
JFK Memorial Hospital

4800 South Congress Avenue
Atlantis, Florida 33462

(305) 433-3600

Director: Ivan Goldberg
Average Patient Census: 36 beds

Minimum Duration of Treatment: alcoholism, 28 days; dual-drug addiction, 42 days
Cost: Available on request. Insurance eligible.
Detoxification Offered: Yes
Accreditation: JCAH

Located on Four West at JFK Memorial Hospital, the Center for Recovery is a homelike setting with administrative and professional offices, therapy rooms, attractive and comfortable patient accommodations, lounge and kitchen area. Nearby park and beach facilities are used for recreational-program therapy.

Persons who are suffering from alcohol and drug problems or related family problems are eligible for assessment and treatment. The program consists of a hospital-based medical detoxification under physician and nursing supervision and an individual treatment plan based on psychosocial and medical assessments. Elements of the program include individual and group therapy, alcohol and drug education program, exercise therapy, nutritional planning and involvement in AA, NA, Al-Anon and other self-help groups. Emphasis is placed on family involvement, and individual aftercare planning is part of the treatment program.

The Center for Recovery maintains a professionally trained staff of alcohol and drug counselors, nurses, physicians and professional consultants when appropriate. All of these have been carefully selected to provide the love, care and understanding that the Center believes to be the heart of their treatment philosophy.

BOWLING GREEN INN

P.O. Box 337
Bowling Green, Florida 33834

(813) 375-2218

Director: George E. Furnival, M.Div., M.A.

Average Patient Census: 21
Minimum Duration of Treatment: 28 days
Cost: Approximately $4,450. Insurance eligible.
Detoxification Offered: Yes (subacute)
Accreditation: JCAH

Bowling Green Inn offers a short-term intensive residential treatment program for men and women of any age who have an alcohol or drug problem, either psychologically or physically dependent.

Individual treatment goals are established for each resident, and techniques utilized in reaching them include individual counseling, group therapy, psychodrama and didactic groups utilizing audiovisual materials, as well as recreational and social activities, and an introduction to AA. Many different approaches may be used, such as Transactional Analysis, Gestalt, reality therapy, behavior modification, movement therapy and confrontation.

A particular program for the spouse is offered, including 1 or 2 weeks conjointly with the mate in treatment. In addition, for the recovering alcoholic who has achieved physical sobriety but desires greater self-awareness and understanding, they offer a 28-day residential program.

Emphasis is placed on discharge planning for aftercare. Bowling Green Inn is licensed by the State of Florida Department of Health and Rehabilitative Services as a Drug Abuse Treatment and Education Center and an Alcoholism Rehabilitation Center.

KOALA CENTER
(FORMERLY WHITE DEER RUN TREATMENT CENTER)

P.O. Box 250
Bushnell, Florida 33513

(904) 793-6000

Director: Dave Heebner
Average Patient Census: 60

Minimum Duration of Treatment: adult, 30 days
Cost: Available on request. Insurance eligible.
Detoxification Offered: Yes
Accreditation: JCAH

Koala Centers and White Deer Centers are part of a network of specialized facilities devoted to the treatment of alcoholism and drug abuse.

Until recently these two respected names in the health care field were separate entities. Now Koala and White Deer have joined forces, enabling them to provide a wider range of services over a broader geographic area. Together, White Deer and Koala are committed to a common goal of continued progress in the development of successful substance abuse treatment programs.

These centers use a multidisciplinary approach to treatment designed to obtain the most positive results. They offer individualized programs that include 4- to 6-week inpatient care for adults and adolescents, outpatient services and an intensive family program. The centers work closely with employers and unions, physicians, school systems, parent groups, court officials and clergy, as well as with other groups who become involved in the problems of alcohol or drug abuse.

HORIZON HOSPITAL

11300 U.S. Highway 19 South
Clearwater, Florida 33546

(813) 541-2646, ext. 232

Director: John Toms, Program Coordinator

Average Patient Census: 17
Minimum Duration of Treatment: Varies with disorder
Cost: $295 per day plus ancillary and physician fees. Insurance eligible.
Detoxification Offered: Yes
Accreditation: JCAH

Horizon Hospital is a 200-bed private psychiatric hospital dedicated to providing quality mental health care. Its sun-coast location allows full use of the environment for outdoor activities and seashore outings as part of the recovery process. All treatment programs at Horizon Hospital are designed to meet the specific needs of each patient. The goal of treatment is to help every patient achieve a productive and happy life when he or she returns to the community.

Horizon Hospital's Alcohol and Chemical Abuse Program of Treatment (ACAPT) is unusual in that, unlike many other alcoholism rehabilitation centers, it is capable of treating the alcoholic who is not only in need of alcoholism counseling but also has severe emotional conflicts that require psychotherapy.

Programs are available for both adults and adolescents. The treatment plan for every patient includes individual and group psychotherapy, family therapy, allied therapies and recreational therapy. With the realization that successful treatment of the disease must include the participation of those who are emotionally involved with the alcoholic/chemical abuser, programs are designed to treat the codependent (those who live with the chemical abuser). The codependent program begins when the patient enters treatment, starting with educational sessions in which the disease concept is explored. Attendance at AA, NA and Al-Anon meetings begins on admission and continues throughout the aftercare program.

Horizon Hospital features modern and attractive facilities, beautiful grounds and a high staff-to-patient ratio, but the essence of the hospital is rooted in its staff of dedicated professionals, who maintain a spirit of hope, compassion and genuine caring.

THE BEACHCOMBER

4493 North Ocean Boulevard
Delray Beach, Florida 33444

(305) 734-1818

Director: James A. Bryan

Average Patient Census: 16
Minimum Duration of Treatment: 4 weeks
Cost: $4,340 for 28 days. Insurance eligible.
Detoxification Offered: Local hospital
Accreditation: JCAH

The Beachcomber describes its program as "updated and uncluttered in a pleasant place." The principles of the AA recovery program and regular AA meetings are an integral part of the therapy. Identifying with sober alcoholics provides those in treatment with the primary requirement for recovery—hope. Both individual and group therapy are part of an intensive program, with one certified therapist for each four patients. In the belief that alcoholism affects the whole family and that understanding is essential to the recovery process, it is expected that family members will participate, separately and jointly, in treatment procedures. A 1-year Aftercare Program is provided for the alcoholic and family members.

Admission may be arranged 24 hours a day, 7 days a week. Five days' sobriety is required for admission. If necessary, detoxification arrangements will be made with a local hospital. Transportation from Palm Beach International Airport will be provided.

BAYSHORE ON THE GULF

1340 Bayshore Boulevard
Dunedin, Florida 33528

(813) 733-0421

Director: N. Sidney Archer, Ed.D., C.A.C.
Average Patient Census: 12 (16 maximum)
Minimum Duration of Treatment:
Alcoholism, 28 days; adolescents, 42 days

Cost: 28 days, $4,480; 42 days, $6,720; codependency, $4,480. Insurance eligible.
Detoxification Offered: No. Referral by consulting physician to a Bayshore hospital if necessary.
Accreditation: State of Florida

Bayshore on the Gulf is a private, cost-contained, freestanding therapeutic community for chemically dependent people and their families, located on Saint Joseph Sound and the Gulf of Mexico. An intimate family atmosphere is emphasized at this facility, and clients share a living room, bedroom and bath in one of ten clustered cottages on Saint Joseph Sound.

Basically, the program follows the Johnson model. There are seven outside NA, AA and Al-Anon meetings per week, as well as one NA and one AA/Al-Anon speaker per week on site.

Family members are encouraged to enter treatment for their primary illness: codependency. This treatment is separate, independent and at a different time than that of the chemically dependent family member. Three evening sessions of family education per week are required.

The aftercare program involves the following: For 2 years clients and family members can participate in any therapeutic experience on site at no additional cost, and clients are encouraged to reenter 1 week of formal treatment for 2 periods: (1) 5 to 7 weeks from discharge date and 5 to 7 months from discharge date.

Staff will meet clients at Tampa International Airport at any time.

COUNTERPOINT CENTER OF FORT LAUDERDALE HOSPITAL

1601 E. Las Olas Boulevard
Fort Lauderdale, Florida 33301

(305) 463-4321

Director: Steve Wells, Adult Program.
John Christianson, Adolescent Program

Average Patient Census: 34 beds
Minimum Duration of Treatment: 28-day program
Cost: Available on request. Insurance eligible.
Detoxification Offered: Yes
Accreditation: JCAH

CounterPoint Center is a Chemical Dependency Program for adults and adolescents. The Center is part of an international network of chemical dependency treatment centers located throughout the United States and Europe.

Chemical dependency is recognized as a primary disorder: chronic, progressive and potentially fatal, and prone to relapse if not properly treated. The disease factor is basic to treatment, which is provided by a multidisciplinary team of skilled professionals, many themselves recovering. All areas of a person's life are affected by chemical dependency. Therefore, the physical, emotional, social and spiritual needs of patients are all addressed through the treatment program.

Detoxification is the first phase of treatment. Following stabilization of acute medical problems, patients begin an intensive program of rehabilitation. The Twelve Steps of AA and NA are emphasized, and patients are expected to have selected an AA or NA group and a temporary sponsor by the time they are to begin the aftercare program. An individualized plan for aftercare is formulated with patient and family during the last week of treatment. Weekly group therapy is provided at no extra cost for 1 year, with a 2-year advisement period.

Family and significant others are included in treatment from the time of admission, with family assessment and couples and family therapy several times each week. Crisis intervention is also available.

For employers, the staff maintains open communications with EAP counselors and supervisors. Employers are included in the treatment process from the beginning, through discharge, and into follow-up care.

CHARTER GLADE HOSPITAL

P.O. Box 06120
6900 Colonial Boulevard, S.E.
Fort Myers, Florida 33906

(813) 939-0403

Director: Arthur ("Chic") Bancroft, C.A.C.

Average Patient Census: 24 beds
Minimum Duration of Treatment: 28 days
Cost: Varies; available on request. Insurance eligible.
Detoxification Offered: Yes
Accreditation: JCAH

The program at Charter Glade Hospital offers medically supervised detoxification, if necessary, and individual, group and family counseling as part of the holistic (multidisciplinary) approach toward effectively treating the disease of addiction. All patients are also encouraged to participate in activities therapy and didactic lectures. These programs are AA/NA based philosophically. The hospital offers both adult and adolescent programs.

Patient and family aftercare services are available at all Charter Medical Addictive Disease units, emphasizing that recovery from this relentless disease is a continuing process affecting both the patient and his or her family.

THE FRIARY

Route 2, Box 174
Gulf Breeze, Florida 32561

(904) 932-9375

Director: Ronald J. Cantanzaro, M.D.
Average Patient Census: 12–15

Minimum Duration of Treatment: 4–6 weeks
Cost: Available on request. Insurance eligible.
Detoxification Offered: Yes
Accreditation: JCAH, State of Florida, Department of Health and Rehabilitative Service

The Friary is a private, freestanding facility secluded on 7 acres overlooking Pensacola Bay. Once used as a retreat for retired Franciscan monks, this serene setting is now used to provide effective specialized help for families affected by alcoholism, drug dependency and depression. The Friary's Familization Therapy has received worldwide recognition for its effectiveness in solving chemical dependency problems. It is based on the belief that alcohol and drug dependency are problems that affect the entire family. Therefore, careful attention has been given to provide a private family setting where family members can share in common purpose and make a positive commitment together.

BROOKWOOD RECOVERY CENTER—ORLANDO

5970 South Orange Blossom Trail
Intercession City, Florida 33848

(305) 841-7071, Crisis Line
(305) 933-5222, Business Line

Director: Bob Hinds

Average Patient Census: 66 beds
Minimum Duration of Treatment: 28–42 days
Cost: Available on request. Insurance eligible.
Detoxification Offered: Yes
Accreditation: JCAH

Brookwood Recovery Center—Orlando believes that people are alcoholics or drug abusers when they repeatedly use alcohol or drugs in a manner that impairs their physical, emotional and mental health and that disrupts their social and economic position.

Brookwood's treatment program is designed to treat the total person, restoring him to a comfortable sobriety in which he is able to resume a healthy, productive way of life. Brookwood does not "cure" alcoholism or drug addiction; rather, it arrests the condition and helps the patient develop a motivation based primarily on reason. In all cases, the goal is to help the patient achieve and maintain total abstinence from alcohol and/or drugs.

To accomplish this, Brookwood uses the therapeutic-community approach, in which every employee, from the groundskeeper to the counselors, plays a part in the physical, mental, emotional, spiritual and economic rehabilitation of the patient. All aspects of Brookwood's programs are supervised by experienced professionals certified in the treatment of alcoholism and chemical dependencies.

Upon admission to Brookwood Recovery Center, patients receive a complete physical examination. Patients are required to be free of all medications except those prescribed to control seizures or other chronic conditions unrelated to the disease of alcoholism or drug addiction. Treatment then begins with medically controlled withdrawal from alcohol or drugs under the care of Brookwood's physicians and nursing staff.

Although Brookwood is not associated in any way with AA or NA, it does recognize the effectiveness of the AA and NA programs, especially for the patient's spiritual growth. Therefore the Center introduces patients to AA and NA, hosts meetings at the center and strongly encourages patients to become members.

Brookwood Recovery Center also offers a family treatment program. Individual counseling, as well as counseling with the patient, ensures that all involved fully comprehend the task that lies ahead.

As part of its never-ending commitment to the patient, Brookwood maintains a 2-year Continuing-Care Program to assist the alcoholic or drug abuser in making a successful return to the home, community and job.

COUNTERPOINT CENTER OF SAINT JOHN'S RIVER HOSPITAL

6300 Beach Boulevard
Jacksonville, Florida 32216

(904) 724-9202

Director: Steve Stevenson, Adult Program. Caroline Noyes, Adolescent Program

Average Patient Census: 33 beds
Minimum Duration of Treatment: 28-day program
Cost: Available on request. Insurance eligible.
Detoxification Offered: Yes
Accreditation: JCAH

CounterPoint Center is a Chemical Dependency Program for adults and adolescents. The center is part of an international network of chemical dependency treatment centers located throughout the United States and Europe.

Chemical dependency is recognized as a primary disorder: chronic, progressive and potentially fatal, and prone to relapse if not properly treated. The disease factor is basic to treatment, which is provided by a multidisciplinary team of skilled professionals, many themselves recovering. All areas of a person's life are affected by chemical dependency. Therefore, the physical, emotional, social and spiritual needs of patients are all addressed through the treatment program.

Detoxification is the first phase of treatment. Following stabilization of acute medical problems, patients begin an intensive program of rehabilitation. The Twelve Steps of AA and NA are emphasized, and patients are expected to have selected an AA or NA group and a temporary sponsor by the time they are to begin the aftercare program. An individualized plan for aftercare is formulated with patient and family during the last week of treatment. Weekly group therapy is provided at no extra cost for 1 year, with a 2-year advisement period.

Family and significant others are included in treatment from the time of admission, with family assessment and couples and family therapy several times each week. Crisis intervention is also available.

For employers, the staff maintains open communications with EAP counselors and supervisors. Employers are included in the treatment process from the beginning, through discharge and into follow-up care.

CAREUNIT OF JACKSONVILLE

1320 Roberts Drive
Jacksonville Beach, Florida 32250

(904) 241-5133

Director: E. A. ("Skip") Mitts
Average Patient Census: adults, 50; adolescents, 34

Minimum Duration of Treatment: Adults, 21–28 days; adolescents, 45–60 days
Cost: Approximately $300 per day. Insurance eligible.
Detoxification Offered: Yes
Accreditation: JCAH

CareUnit of Jacksonville is a facility specializing in the family treatment of alcohol and other drug dependencies for adults and adolescents. Patients undergo a complete physiological and psychological examination and detoxification under the supervision of the medical director of the facility. The treatment program is personalized to fit individual needs and consists of individual and group therapy, participation in specific activities, lectures and films designed to increase the patient's understanding of his or her disease and appropriate ways to enjoy life free from chemical dependency. Families are invited to join in the treatment program, which is designed to free family members from the effects of the disease in areas such as behavior, attitudes and life-styles.

The recovery continues following the patient's discharge. Patients return to the CareUnit for aftercare 2 evenings a week for a specified period following discharge. Family units participate once weekly in the aftercare program. Patients and their families are encouraged to explore other resources, such as AA, Al-Anon, Alateen, NA and others, to which they were introduced during their inpatient stay. Aftercare is free to all patients—for a lifetime, if desired.

CareUnit of Jacksonville also offers an outpatient treatment program.

DELPHOS ALCOHOL AND DRUG TREATMENT CENTER
FLORIDA KEYS MEMORIAL HOSPITAL

5900 West Jr. College Road
Key West, Florida 33040

(305) 294-5531

Director: Ron Ersay

Average Patient Census: 11
Minimum Duration of Treatment: 28 days
Cost: $6,800 approximate. Insurance eligible.
Detoxification Offered: Yes
Accreditation: JCAH

DELPHOS is a medically based, AA-oriented, 4- to 6-week therapy program taking patients from detoxification through to aftercare in a unit within a fully accredited general acute 120-bed hospital. Treatment of alcohol and drug problems recognizes addiction as a total disease involving every area of its victims' lives—mental, physical and spiritual. Therapy is firmly rooted in the Twelve Steps of AA, an approach long proven effective for most people. DELPHOS' team approach involves doctors, nurses and aides, many of whom have themselves recovered from addiction, and all of whom have a deep commitment to helping the suffering drug and/or alcohol abuser.

Detoxification is medically supervised as the first phase of the recovery program. Then the inpatient treatment program, highly structured, consists of classroom instruction, individual and group therapy, AA and NA meetings in the community, stress reduction therapy, case conferences, psychological testing where indicated and pastoral counseling upon request.

The program is divided into four phases. During the first, patients identify their problems, develop with the staff a treatment plan and learn about addiction. During the second, they learn the basic principles of recovery. During the third, a self-analysis is accomplished and, in the last phase, patients begin to restructure their lives and set goals for their continuing recovery with the development of an aftercare plan.

DELPHOS also has a family component as part of their program. Their aftercare services for the following year are included in the cost of treatment. Additionally, they offer outpatient services, as well as special outreach programs for impaired professionals and lesbian and gay alcoholics and addicts.

CHEMICAL DEPENDENCY UNIT
Lakeland General Hospital

P.O. Drawer 448
Lakeland, Florida 33802-0448

(813) 687-1112, 1-800-622-HOPE

Director: Kenneth L. Wegman, M.A.
Average Patient Census: 34

Minimum Duration of Treatment:
Tailored to patient needs
Cost: $5,700 plus physician's fee of approximately $450. Insurance eligible.
Detoxification Offered: Yes
Accreditation: JCAH

The treatment philosophy at the Lakeland General Hospital CDU draws heavily on the therapeutic program of AA. Therapy is directive and didactic. Goals are to teach the patient basic coping skills and the essential steps of recovery from alcoholism and chemical dependency.

Each patient is assigned a primary counselor, who is one of four on the staff, who supervises the individual's recovery. Each patient is interviewed and evaluated by the unit director, who is a clinical psychologist. It is not necessary for the patient to be referred by a physician. Patients are admitted by a physician on the staff of Lakeland General.

A program of therapy and education for family members is held each Saturday. This program comprises approximately 12 hours of the patient's stay.

The unit is a nonmedical unit. It is also drug-free. Alcoholism and chemical dependency respond best to a therapy that maximizes the patient's inner coping skills and minimizes reliance on medications. When it is medically appropriate, medication is used for chronic or acute conditions not related to alcoholism.

PALMVIEW HOSPITAL

2510 North Florida Avenue
Lakeland, Florida 33805

(813) 682-6105

Director: Lawrence H. Pomeroy
Average Patient Census: 10

Minimum Duration of Treatment: 30–90 days
Cost: Approximately $250 per day plus physician fees. Insurance eligible.
Detoxification Offered: Yes, as part of total program
Accreditation: JCAH

Palmview Hospital offers an Adolescent Chemical Dependency Program for short-term, intensive treatment of 12- to 18-year-olds. This highly structured program incorporates a multidisciplinary approach, stressing family involvement and AA/NA participation. An aftercare program is provided to maintain a chemically free life-style.

The program is housed in one wing of a 66-bed hospital, which provides relaxed and pleasant surroundings. The facility includes a swimming pool and recreation room.

TWELVE OAKS

Route 1, Healthcare Avenue
Mary Esther, Florida 32569

(904) 932-9279

Director: Michael V. Robertson, M.P.H.

Average Patient Census: 20
Minimum Duration of Treatment: 28 days
Cost: $9,991. Insurance eligible.
Detoxification Offered: Yes
Accreditation: JCAH

Twelve Oaks is a private, 36-bed, alcohol and drug recovery center located on the Gulf coastline of Florida, midway between Pensacola and Fort Walden Beach. The 5-acre campus offers a serene environment in which someone addicted to alcohol or drugs can learn to overcome the addiction and recover from the disease.

The program features an eclectic approach, individualized for the special needs of each patient. Twelve Oaks has a multidisciplinary team of credentialed professionals and people who have personally recovered from addiction. The Twelve Steps of AA are used as the program base, and maximum exposure to AA and NA is provided during the patient's stay.

The program provides a continuum of care that begins with the detoxification component, continues into the rehabilitation phase and follows through with an extended aftercare program. The various components of treatment are supervised by the center's medical director and implemented by a team of professionals in substance abuse rehabilitation, with skilled counselors as primary therapists. Components available include individual and group therapy, medical and psychiatric support for coexisting problems, personality testing and psychosocial evaluation, recreational and activity services, an intensive family involvement plan, pastoral counseling upon request and vocational counseling as necessary.

The explicit family and peer-oriented aftercare program assists patients in their return to the home and in their maintenance of a chemical-free life.

Twelve Oaks offers treatment for chemically dependent men, women and adolescents, providing a residential program that serves as an alternative to intensive hospitalization and provides personalized attention in an environment conducive to the recovery process.

THE RECOVERY CENTER
HIGHLAND PARK GENERAL HOSPITAL

1660 N.W. Seventh Court
Miami, Florida 33136

(305) 326-7008

Director: Louise Mehrman Goodman
Average Patient Census: 15

Minimum Duration of Treatment: alcoholism, 4 weeks; drug or poly-addicted, 6 weeks
Cost: $149 per day. Insurance eligible.
Detoxification Offered: Yes, as part of total program
Accreditation: JCAH

The Recovery Center at Highland Park General Hospital offers a multidisciplinary approach that integrates medical, social and counseling services for the treatment of chemical dependency. Treatment options include in-hospital detoxification, comprehensive inpatient counseling that is AA and NA oriented and specially designed programs for both families and employers. The Center also offers strong outpatient and aftercare programs for the chemically dependent and their families.

To qualify for admission a patient must be over 18 years of age, willing to make a commitment to the program, have no active psychosis and have the willingness and ability to pay for treatment.

In addition to providing direct treatment services, the Recovery Center offers Employee Assistance Program services to local industry, including consultation, program design, supervisory training, diagnosis and referral.

In 1984 the Recovery Center opened a Primary Outpatient Rehabilitation at Suite 303, Capital Plaza II, 8900 S.W. 107 Avenue, Miami, Florida 33176, (305) 271-5577. The basic cost of this 6-week program is $1,500 and is insurance eligible.

This evening program is designed to allow chemically dependent persons to live at home and continue to work while undergoing intensive treatment. Codependents are expected to attend all counseling sessions and to engage actively in the treatment process. The program consists of therapy conducted in groups of up to eight families and is based on the disease concept and philosophy of AA and NA. Rebuilding relationships that have been damaged by chemical dependency is a priority treatment. Criteria for admission are that the patient be drug-free on admission and able and willing to remain so during treatment, functional at work or home and living in an environment supportive to sobriety.

NAPLES RESEARCH AND COUNSELING CENTER

9001 Tamiami Trail East
Naples, Florida 33962

(813) 775-4500

Director: Marcus P. Zillman

Average Patient Census: 92 beds
Minimum Duration of Treatment: 4 weeks
Cost: Available on request. Insurance eligible.
Detoxification Offered: Yes
Accreditation: JCAH

The Naples Research and Counseling Center (NRCC) has been designed for the residential treatment of alcoholism, drug dependency, food addiction and other stress-related problems. Ambulatory persons 18 years and older are eligible for assessment and treatment. Patients' family members are also eligible for the programs and are strongly encouraged to participate as inpatients for 1 week during the patient's treatment.

NRCC's program is centered around the concept of Familization Therapy. The therapeutic family, which is the fundamental working element in this approach, consists of patients and copatients who join together in the treatment experience to help themselves as well as one another. By becoming part of this family in residence, each patient and copatient learns how individual behaviors affect family functioning.

NRCC offers all the basic modalities of treatment from intensive medical and psychiatric evaluation and individualized treatment plans to nutritional and physical awareness programs, as well as a minimum of 1 year aftercare with a written aftercare plan, weekly support group, contacts with appropriate self-help groups and recharge and recovery renewal planning.

Special programs at NRCC include the following: a newly developed Comprehensive Drug Program for persons addicted to cocaine, narcotics, tranquilizers or multiple drugs; Extended Care for patients who have completed treatment but who are in need of transitional care services prior to full discharge; Recovery Renewal Program, which involves short-term problem-specific counseling for individuals and families focusing on life-adjustment problems that often occur after discharge; and a Co-Addiction Program, designed to help those living with a family member who is suffering from addiction.

Recreational amenities at NRCC include a pool, tennis and handball courts, a heart trail and exercise room with Nautilus, Jacuzzi and saunas. Other available recreational facilities include a championship golf course and private beach.

THE CLOISTERS AT PINE ISLAND

P.O. Box 1616
Pineland Road
Pineland, Florida 33945

(813) 283-1019

Director: Michel G. Doherty, M.H.S., C.A.C.
Average Patient Census: 32

Minimum Duration of Treatment: Cross-addiction or drug addiction (women and adolescent programs), 42 days; alcoholism only, 28 days
Cost: 28 days, $5,460; 42 days, $8,190. Insurance eligible.
Detoxification Offered: Yes
Accreditation: JCAH

The Cloisters at Pine Island is a facility for the treatment of addictive disease, staffed by highly credentialed and certified addiction counselors. Rehabilitation care is comprised of individually planned programs utilizing a range of therapeutic procedures designed to meet the distinct needs of each patient.

An integral part of the treatment is planned follow-up in the patient's home community. Introduction to AA/Al-Anon is incorporated into the treatment process and in every aftercare plan.

Medical services are administered by a team of physicians and 24-hour coverage staffed by registered nurses and certified addiction counselors.

Family counseling is offered and a special family education program is provided every Sunday for 3 hours. Individual counseling for the family is available by the full-time family therapy staff.

PARKSIDE LODGE OF PINELLAS

Metropolitan General Hospital
7950 Sixty-sixth Street North
Pinellas Park, Florida 33565

(813) 541-7548

Director: Daniel J. Kelly

Average Patient Census: 17
Minimum Duration of Treatment: 28 days
Cost: Approximately $5,300. Insurance eligible.
Detoxification Offered: Yes
Accreditation: AOHA

Parkside Lodge of Pinellas offers a short-term intensive residential treatment program for men and women of any age who have an alcohol or drug problem, either psychologically or physically dependent.

In this hospital unit, patients can be accepted who require continuous medical management of other illnesses while they undergo treatment for alcoholism or other drug abuse. Patients receive a complete physical examination and necessary laboratory tests. They are under the direct care of a physician and are served by the hospital staff and the alcoholism treatment unit staff at the same time.

Individual treatment goals are established for each resident, and techniques utilized in reaching them include individual counseling, group therapy, psychodrama and didactic groups utilizing audiovisual materials, as well as recreational and social activities and an introduction to AA. Many different approaches may be used, such as Transactional Analysis, Gestalt, reality therapy, behavior modification, movement therapy, and confrontation.

A particular program for the spouse is offered, including 1 or 2 weeks conjointly with the mate in treatment. In addition, for the recovering alcoholic who has achieved physical sobriety but desires greater self-awareness and understanding, they offer a 28-day residential program.

Emphasis is placed on discharge planning for aftercare. Parkside Lodge of Pinellas is licensed by the State of Florida Department of Health and Rehabilitative Service as a Drug Abuse Treatment and Education Center and an Alcoholism Rehabilitation Center.

BROOKWOOD RECOVERY CENTER—TAMPA

Town and Country Hospital
6001 Webb Road
Tampa, Florida 33615

(813) 884-1904, crisis line
(813) 885-6666, business line

Director: Al Salo

Average Patient Census: 20 beds
Minimum Duration of Treatment:
  Completion of treatment
Cost: Approximately $225 per day.
  Insurance eligible.
Detoxification Offered: Yes
Accreditation: JCAH

Brookwood Recovery Center—Tampa is a hospital-based facility containing 20 private patient rooms. The treatment program at Brookwood is designed to treat the total person and to restore them to comfortable sobriety in which they are able to choose not to drink or use other mood-altering chemicals and are able to resume a healthy, productive way of life. The treatment philosophy of Brookwood Recovery Center—Tampa is based on the fact that the ability to stay sober resides in a group rather than on an individual. Group therapy, along with individual counseling and the philosophy of AA, play an integral part in the recovery process. Therefore, patients attend AA meetings on a daily basis. The goal for the patients is the achievement and maintenance of total abstinence from alcohol and other chemicals. All aspects of the program are supervised by experienced professionals certified in the treatment of alcoholism and chemical dependency.

The Intensive Family Program meets on a weekly basis, with family members attending 4 consecutive Monday afternoon educational sessions, in addition to the 3 consecutive days during Family Week while the patient is a resident. The dynamics include the practice of conjunct multifamily interaction treatment.

Brookwood—Tampa also offers to the public a 4-week education program. Each week is set up as complete within itself, yet fits into the entire learning series. Covering the disease concept, roles of each family member, intervention and recovery, the group seeks to educate the public about the disease of chemical dependency.

As a part of Brookwood's never-ending commitment to the patient, a Continuing-Care Program is maintained to ensure continued assistance and support of the patient through community resources.

CAREUNIT OF TAMPA

3102 East One Hundred Thirty-eighth Avenue
Tampa, Florida 33612

(813) 971-5000

Director: Bob Yost

Average Patient Census: Adults, 80; adolescents, 40
Minimum Duration of Treatment: Adults, 21–28 days; adolescents, 45–60 days
Cost: Approximately $300 per day. Insurance eligible.
Detoxification Offered: Yes
Accreditation: JCAH

CareUnit of Tampa is a facility specializing in the family treatment of alcohol and other drug dependencies for adults and adolescents. Patients undergo a complete physiological and psychological examination and detoxification under the supervision of the medical director of the facility. The treatment program is personalized to fit individual needs and consists of individual and group therapy, participation in specific activities, lectures and films designed to increase the patient's understanding of his or her disease and appropriate ways to enjoy life free from chemical dependency. Families are invited to join in the treatment program, which is designed to free family members from the effects of the disease in areas such as behavior, attitudes and life-styles.

The recovery continues following the patient's discharge. Patients return to the CareUnit for aftercare 2 evenings a week for a specified period following discharge. Family units participate once weekly in the aftercare program. Patients and their families are encouraged to explore other resources such as AA, Al-Anon, Alateen, NA and others, to which they were introduced during their inpatient stay. Aftercare is free to all patients—for a lifetime, if desired.

CareUnit of Tampa also offers an outpatient treatment program.

Georgia

CHARTER BROOK HOSPITAL

3913 North Peachtree Road
Atlanta, Georgia 30341

(404) 457-8315

Director: Sherry Kollmeyer
Average Patient Census: 45 beds

Minimum Duration of Treatment: Individualized
Cost: Varies; available on request. Insurance eligible.
Detoxification Offered: Yes
Accreditation: JCAH

The program at Charter Brook Hospital, which is devoted entirely to adolescent chemical dependency treatment, offers medically supervised detoxification, if necessary, and individual, group and family counseling as part of the holistic (multidisciplinary) approach toward effectively treating the disease of addiction. All patients are also encouraged to participate in activities therapy and didactic lectures. These programs are AA/NA based philosophically.

Patient and family aftercare services are available at all Charter Medical Addictive Disease units, emphasizing that recovery from this relentless disease is a continuing process affecting both the patient and his or her family.

CHARTER PEACHFORD HOSPITAL

2151 Peachford Road
Atlanta, Georgia 30338

(404) 455-3200

Director: Shirley Hodges

Average Patient Census: 75 beds
Minimum Duration of Treatment: 28 days
Cost: Varies; available on request.
Insurance eligible.
Detoxification Offered: Yes
Accreditation: JCAH

The program at Charter Peachford Hospital offers medically supervised detoxification, if necessary, and individual, group and family counseling as part of the holistic (multidisciplinary) approach toward effectively treating the disease of addiction. All patients are also encouraged to participate in activities therapy and didactic lectures. These programs are AA/NA based philosophically. The hospital offers both adult and young adult programs.

Patient and family aftercare services are available at all Charter Medical Addictive Disease units, emphasizing that recovery from this relentless disease is a continuing process affecting both the patient and his or her family.

COUNTERPOINT CENTER OF PARKWOOD HOSPITAL

1999 Cliff Valley Way, N.E.
Atlanta, Georgia 30329

(404) 633-8431

Director: John Gibbons

Average Patient Census: 100 beds
Minimum Duration of Treatment: 28 days
Cost: Varies according to program.
Insurance eligible.
Detoxification Offered: Yes
Accreditation: JCAH

CounterPoint Center is a chemical dependency program for adults. The center is part of an international network of chemical dependency treatment centers located throughout the United States and Europe.

Chemical dependency is recognized as a primary disorder—chronic, progressive and potentially fatal, and prone to relapse if not properly treated. The disease factor is basic to treatment, which is provided by a multidisciplinary team of skilled professionals, many themselves recovering. All areas of a person's life are affected by chemical dependency; therefore, the physical, emotional, social and spiritual needs of patients are all addressed through the treatment program.

Detoxification is the first phase of treatment. Following stabilization of acute medical problems, patients begin an intensive program of rehabilitation. The Twelve Steps of AA and NA are emphasized, and patients are expected to have selected an AA or NA group and a temporary sponsor by the time they are to begin the aftercare program. An individualized plan for aftercare is formulated with patient and family during the last week of treatment. Weekly group therapy is provided at no extra cost for 1 year, with a 2-year advisement period.

Family and significant others are included in treatment from the time of admission, with family assessment and couples and family therapy several times each week. Crisis intervention is also available.

For employers, the staff maintains open communications with EAP counselors and supervisors. Employers are included in the treatment process from the beginning, through discharge and into follow-up care.

WOODRIDGE

P.O. Box 1764
Clayton, Georgia 30525

(404) 782-2803

Director: Louis E. Kuntz

Average Patient Census: 20
Minimum Duration of Treatment: 28 days
Cost: $7,400. Insurance eligible.
Detoxification Offered: Yes
Accreditation: Pending

Woodridge is a private, freestanding treatment facility for the education and treatment of those suffering from the disease of chemical dependency. Woodridge is located on U.S. Highway 76 in the town of Clayton, in the heart of the Blue Ridge Mountains, and convenient to such major cities as Atlanta and Augusta, Georgia; Asheville, North Carolina; Greenville, South Carolina; and Knoxville and Chattanooga, Tennessee.

Woodridge offers a full range of treatment programs including inpatient and outpatient care, as well as partial hospitalization and EAP programs. All treatment programs at Woodridge are based on the principles and programs of AA and NA. Family care is stressed, as well as an Aftercare Program that lasts for approximately 1 to 2 years. Woodridge also sponsors seminars for professionals who work with those suffering from the disease of chemical dependency.

The staff includes physicians, psychiatrists, psychologists, addiction counselors, family counselors, activity therapist, staff chaplain and nurses, all of whom are thoroughly trained in the treatment of chemical dependency.

All programs at Woodridge are housed in a new facility, with beds for thirty-two patients, which is set in beautiful mountain scenery.

BROOKWOOD RECOVERY CENTER—DUBLIN

804 Industrial Boulevard
P.O. Box 1285
Dublin, Georgia 31040

(912) 275-0353
1-800-241-5216 (within Georgia)

Director: Hal Ward

Average Patient Census: 54 beds
Minimum Duration of Treatment: Alcohol (normally), 28 days; drugs (normally), 42 days
Cost: Available on request. Insurance eligible.
Detoxification Offered: Yes
Accreditation: JCAH

The treatment program at Brookwood Recovery Center, designed to treat the total individual as well as his family, is based on the fundamental concepts of AA, Al-Anon and NA and employs the disease model concept. The core of the treatment philosophy is that the power to stay sober resides in a group process rather than left to an individual's own effort and initiative. Two main goals in the treatment process are education and therapy. The individual is taught that he cannot rely on willpower alone and that in order to achieve recovery, a person must change his entire life-style into a new, productive way of living. In the process of therapy, family involvement and therapy are encouraged and provided. The therapeutic-community approach is employed, in which every member of the staff is involved in the individual's treatment. The person's physical, mental, emotional, spiritual, social and economic needs are considered in the process of treatment.

After a patient has received medical evaluation and detoxification, the basic program provides for a minimum of 35 hours a week formalized individual and group counseling. All aspects of the program are supervised by experienced professionals familiar with alcoholism and chemical dependency. It is realized that the intensive portion of therapy in a controlled environment is not sufficient to maintain a lasting sobriety and change of life-style without further reinforcement. Therefore, a 2-year Continuing-Care Program is made available to both patient and family in order to maintain and strengthen the principles learned in the inpatient portion of therapy, and patients and their families are encouraged to participate in AA activities in their local home communities.

Brookwood—Dublin also offers industrial consultation, crisis-line service, intervention counseling, community educational services and assessment.

CHARTER LAKE HOSPITAL

P.O. Box 7067
3500 Riverside Drive
Macon, Georgia 31209

(912) 474-6200

Director: Al Stines

Average Patient Census: 24 beds
Minimum Duration of Treatment: 28 days
Cost: Varies; available on request. Insurance eligible.
Detoxification Offered: Yes
Accreditation: JCAH

The program at Charter Lake Hospital offers medically supervised detoxification, if necessary, and individual, group and family counseling as part of the holistic (multidisciplinary) approach toward effectively treating the disease of addiction. All patients are also encouraged to participate in activities therapy and didactic lectures. These programs are AA/NA based philosophically. The hospital offers both adult and adolescent programs.

Patient and family aftercare services are available at all Charter Medical Addictive Disease units, emphasizing that recovery from this relentless disease is a continuing process affecting both the patient and his or her family.

CHARTER BY-THE-SEA HOSPITAL

2927 Demere Road
Saint Simons Island, Georgia 31522

(912) 638-1999

Director: Judy Herig, C.A.C.

Average Patient Census: 36 beds
Minimum Duration of Treatment: 30 days
Cost: Varies; available on request. Insurance eligible.
Detoxification Offered: Yes
Accreditation: JCAH

Charter By-The-Sea Hospital takes a holistic approach to addiction and addresses the patient's physical, mental, emotional and spiritual needs for treatment. The staff strives to foster personal awareness and growth in each patient, in order to enable him or her to live drug-free. The program, geared for patients 16 and older, begins with thorough medical, psychological, family, recreational and nutritional assessments, which help the staff design an individualized treatment program for each patient.

Charter By-The-Sea Hospital follows AA/NA philosophy and AA/NA Step work, and meeting attendance is integral to treatment. Each patient is assigned a counselor and participates in daily group and individual therapies. Further, recreational therapy addresses the patient's physical deterioration and teaches leisure activities that may continue after treatment. A full-service health and fitness facility adjoins the hospital, offering Nautilus equipment, racquetball, exercise areas and indoor/outdoor swimming.

Since the disease of addiction negatively impacts the patient's family, a highly specialized family program is offered in which a trained family counselor educates the family about the disease of addiction and outlines the steps that must be taken to help the patient live drug-free.

Prior to discharge, each patient meets with the aftercare counselor to design an aftercare contract that will encourage continued recovery, and identifies an AA/NA contact in the patient's hometown to serve as a temporary sponsor. Aftercare counseling is available for 2 years at no additional cost.

Charter By-The-Sea, a 60-bed hospital that also maintains a mental health unit, is located on beautifully serene Saint Simons Island, which lends an aura of peace that aids the healing process.

BRAWNER RECOVERY CENTER

3180 Atlanta Street, Southeast
Smyrna, Georgia 30080

(404) 436-0081

Director: William H. Benson, M.D.
Average Patient Census: 17

Minimum Duration of Treatment: alcoholism, 28 days, drug abuse, 42 days
Cost: $259 per day. Insurance eligible.
Detoxification Offered: Yes
Accreditation: JCAH

Brawner Recovery Center offers a program of rehabilitation that is strongly AA and NA oriented, with rehabilitation training offered following detoxification treatment.

The program includes education regarding the disease concept of addiction. Recovering counselors and physicians offer a well-structured program lasting from 28 to 42 days. The patient is evaluated from the physical, the psychological, the psychiatric and the addiction standpoints. Family therapy is an integral part of the program.

Aftercare extends for a 2-year period. This is structured to maintain continued sobriety and personal growth, and to enhance the probability of complete recovery.

RIDGEVIEW INSTITUTE

3995 South Cobb Drive
Smyrna, Georgia 30080

(404) 434-4567

Director: G. Douglas Talbott, M.D.
Average Patient Census: 100

Minimum Duration of Treatment: 29 days, or extended treatment in hospital or halfway-house setting as needed
Cost: Adults, $245 per day; adolescents, $275 per day. Insurance eligible.
Detoxification Offered: Yes
Accreditation: JCAH

The Ridgeview Institute Chemical Dependence Programs provide specialized treatment for adults, adolescents and impaired health professionals. The interdisciplinary programs seek to provide treatment services to persons suffering from the disease of chemical addiction.

The treatment programs are based on the philosophy that alcohol and/or drug addiction is a chronic, progressive, biochemical, genetic, primary disease that affects the physical, psychological and sociocultural aspects of the life of the addict, as well as those of his or her family. The overall goal, the achievement of chemical-free living, is achieved through a variety of services including group therapy, family therapy, AA and NA, as well as spiritual counseling, education, physical rehabilitation and coping-skills training.

The programs strongly emphasize helping addicted persons return to their families, respective work and educational settings with a minimum of turmoil. Working relationships with Employee Assistance Programs for industry and business are maintained by the facility in order to offer support to those returning to work after rehabilitation.

The Impaired Health Professionals Program, designed specifically for addicted physicians, nurses, pharmacists and dentists, began at Ridgeview Institute.

WILLINGWAY HOSPITAL

P.O. Box 508
311 Jones Mill Road
Statesboro, Georgia 30458

(912) 764-6236

Director: Al J. Mooney, III, M.D.
Average Patient Census: 40
Minimum Duration of Treatment: Single addiction to alcohol, 4–6 weeks; alcoholism with significant drug involvement, 5–8 weeks; drug addiction (narcotics, sedatives, tranquilizers), 2–3 months or longer

Cost: $235 per day; intensive care, $335 per day. Medical evaluation and physician's fees additional. Insurance eligible.
Detoxification Offered: Yes
Accreditation: JCAH

Willingway Hospital specializes in the treatment of alcoholism and drug dependency conditions, offering care designed to achieve total and permanent recovery from addiction.

Two phases of treatment compose Willingway's program. During Phase One, patients are withdrawn from alcohol and/or other mood-changing drugs. Members of the medical staff constantly supervise the detoxification process.

When the patient's physical condition is stabilized, he or she begins Phase Two of the program, an intensive readjustment program of increasing knowledge and activity to prevent relapse. In Unit II's living quarters, patients begin to accept responsibility for a chemical-free life. All activities at Willingway are geared toward recovery; patients can neither make nor receive telephone calls nor receive visitors during their hospitalization.

Activities geared toward recovery include group sessions, sharing meetings, recreation, and self-help group meetings. Patients also attend physician lectures, hear outside speakers, view films and listen to tapes at this time.

The completion of a life history is the patient's major responsibility in Phase Two; its writing is guided by his or her counselor, who is the primary contact for patients during the entire program.

The patient's spouse or another close family member is encouraged to spend the final 5 days of treatment with the patient at Willingway, participating in all program activities as well as special family therapy sessions. This orientation and preparation of the family member is considered vital in the patient's recovery process.

Willingway's aftercare program will follow the patient for an entire year after treatment and is considered "the balancing factor" in recovery. Services offered the patient include 24-hour-a-day telephone contact with the hospital, individual and family counseling, referral services in home areas, provision of schedules for self-help meetings and notification of special hospital events including workshops.

Maine

EASTERN MAINE MEDICAL CENTER ALCOHOL INSTITUTE

489 State Street
Bangor, Maine 04401

(207) 945-7272

Director: Loa J. Sullivan, M.S., Ed.D.

Average Patient Census: 33
Minimum Duration of Treatment: Detox, 1–5 days; treatment, 21 days
Cost: $5,200. Insurance eligible.
Detoxification Offered: Yes
Accreditation: JCAH

Eastern Maine Medical Center's Alcohol Institute provides treatment services for alcoholism and other chemical dependencies. The inpatient program, where intensive treatment occurs in a hospital setting, affords detoxification, assessment and rehabilitation for adolescents and adults.

The rehabilitation component of the program includes individual, group, family and children's counseling and is designed to assist both patient and family begin the process of recovery from the damages caused by alcoholism and chemical dependencies. Aftercare services are provided as part of the continuing recovery process.

MERRYMEETING HOUSE

51 Center Road
Bowdoinham, Maine 04008

(207) 666-5583

Director: Robert Gordon

Average Patient Census: 15 beds
Minimum Duration of Treatment: 28 days
Cost: $5–90, based on sliding fee scale. Insurance eligible.
Detoxification Offered: No
Accreditation: State of Maine.

Merrymeeting House Alcohol and Chemical Dependency Treatment Center recognizes alcoholism as a progressive and potentially fatal illness that shows no preference for sex, social standing or geography. They strive to assist people afflicted with alcoholism and other chemical dependencies to achieve and maintain sobriety in order that they may live happier, more productive and self-sufficient lives.

Treatment is never an easy decision for alcoholics or their families. At Merrymeeting House, a full range of services is provided to help guide the individual and family through the transition to recovery in recognition that recovery requires continual, consistent awareness and effort.

The 28- to 30-day program of intense treatment is designed to present numerous recovery options and methods. Group sessions of both education and therapy, as well as individual counseling, are focused on helping the individual in becoming more responsible for his or her own behavior. Since family involvement in treatment has a profound effect on the course of the disease for the patient, family members are expected to participate to the fullest extent possible and encouraged to attend the Concerned Persons Day that is held each week at Merrymeeting House. AA and Al-Anon meetings are also held at the facility on a regular basis.

Complete aftercare services are provided for former residential clients and their families. Outpatient services, employee assistance services, as well as consultation and evaluation, are also available.

Merrymeeting House is located in a secluded, rural setting that offers clients the tranquility often needed to explore personal issues, and provides a noninstitutional familylike atmosphere for men and women of all ages, including adolescents, who are experiencing problems with alcohol or other similar substances. Referrals are accepted from all sources.

MILESTONE FOUNDATION, INC.

88 Union Avenue
P.O. Box T
Old Orchard Beach, Maine 04064

(207) 934-5231

Director: Paul A. McDonnell

Average Patient Census: 20
Minimum Duration of Treatment: Open-ended residency, but expected length 1 year
Cost: Sliding scale. Not insurance eligible.
Detoxification Offered: No

Milestone Foundation is an extended-care program designed to meet the specialized treatment needs of individuals who can be categorized as being in the final stages of the disease and who have been unsuccessful in maintaining sobriety through existing treatment modalities.

This program is offered to those suffering only from the disease of alcoholism.

CROSSROADS

1040 Main Street
South Windham, Maine 04082

(207) 892-2192

Director: Griffith Matthews
Average Patient Census: 10 (women only)

Minimum Duration of Treatment: 28 days. Extended treatment available.
Cost: $92 per day. Fee based on ability to pay for Maine residents. Insurance eligible.
Detoxification Offered: Yes
Accreditation: JCAH

Crossroads, serving female alcohol and drug abusers only, designs its program particularly to meet the needs of women.

The program provides group counseling, education concerning the disease of alcoholism, assertiveness training and social recreational therapy.

The facility offers a homelike setting, near Maine's largest city, Portland. Nursing staff is on duty at all times, with a physician on call 24 hours per day. A physical examination shortly after admission and second medical rounds ensure medical support to follow through the duration of residential treatment.

A structured and intensive therapy program is offered by trained counselors 6 days per week, while Saturdays are left open for visits from husbands, children and parents. Each client is required to attend AA while in treatment and is strongly encouraged to continue such participation after completion of the program. Additionally, each client is referred to an aftercare component in his or her home community.

Referrals are accepted from all sources, including self-referral, and the appropriateness for treatment is determined through an initial telephone interview, followed by preadmission interview with staff.

KENNEBEC VALLEY COMPREHENSIVE ALCOHOLISM TREATMENT PROGRAM

Seton Unit
Mid-Maine Medical Center
Waterville, Maine 04901

(207) 873-0621, ext. Seton-137

Director: Sylvia V. Lund
Average Patient Census: 25

Minimum Duration of Treatment: 28 days, with extension for those needing more care
Cost: Approximately $190 per day. Insurance eligible.
Detoxification Offered: Yes, offered in the hospital on a separate floor
Accreditation: JCAH

Kennebec Valley Comprehensive Alcoholism Treatment Program offers an intermediate care, hospital-based, inpatient program using group therapy, Steps of AA (the first five) and treatment for the patient's family. The inpatient program is followed by a 2-year aftercare program.

KVCATP also offers outpatient counseling, counseling for DWI offenders, and extensive outreach. KVCATP works closely with New Directions, a program specifically designed for chemically dependent women and their families. An adolescent inpatient program is also offered.

To be admitted to the unit, the patient must be alcoholic or chemically dependent, with a desire for recovery. Patients may be Blue Cross, eligible self-pay, or low-income eligible under state guidelines.

Maryland

SHEPPARD AND ENOCH PRATT ALCOHOL AND CHEMICAL DEPENDENCY PROGRAM

6501 North Charles Street
Baltimore, Maryland 21204

(301) 823-8200

Director: Dr. Sheldon I. Miller

Average Patient Census: 25
Minimum Duration of Treatment: 28 days
Cost: Available on request. Insurance eligible.
Detoxification Offered: Yes
Accreditation: JCAH

The Alcoholism Inpatient Unit at Sheppard Pratt Hospital is a 15-bed, coed hall offering both detoxification and rehabilitation. The multidisciplinary treatment team's sole purpose is to help the patient answer two critical questions: Do I have a drinking problem? and What will I need to achieve abstinence? Operating on the basic premise that alcoholism is a complex, primary, chronic and progressive disease, and that this disease is treatable, the team uses a number of treatment modalities. Frequent attendance at AA meetings and the presence of AA volunteers on the unit is all-important; in addition there are alcohol education, the support of group living, group therapy, spiritual/religious guidance and activity therapy. Other regular activities include physical exercise and/or relaxation training, a Know-Your-Feelings Group and a group on the special problems of the woman alcoholic. Pharmacological treatment is offered when medically advisable during detox, and Antabuse when appropriate.

The family program has three key components: (1) Social Work Services meets with patient and family; (2) 2-day Family Days Program held monthly with specially designed activities and (3) a weekly family group discussion.

The Chemical Dependency Inpatient Treatment Program is a 13-bed, coed hall offering detoxification and rehabilitation to patients who abuse narcotics, sedatives and minor tranquilizers. In addition, patients who are doubly addicted to alcohol and some other chemical are treated on this unit. This program is capable of doing detoxification from narcotics (including methadone), sedative drugs and alcohol. Detox will be brief and make use of social support in lieu of large doses of medication.

The components of the program, which seek to break down the denial system of the addict through the group process, are like those of the Alcoholism Unit, with the addition of NA meetings held in and outside of the hospital. Attendance of a minimum of 8 meetings per week is required.

Aftercare planning on both units begins on the day of admission and involves special group meetings with family and employers as appropriate. A detailed, written aftercare plan is developed and signed by all appropriate parties prior to discharge, and all patients leave the hospital with specific plans and information about attendance at daily meetings of AA and NA. Referral of families is also made to Al-Anon, Alateen and Nar-Anon.

HIDDEN BROOK TREATMENT CENTER

522 Thomas Run Road
Belair, Maryland 21014

(301) 879-1919

Director: Joseph F. Quinn
Average Patient Census: 45

Minimum Duration of Treatment: 30 days
Cost: Comprehensive fee of $5,700 based on a 30-day treatment at $190 per day. Insurance eligible.
Detoxification Offered: Yes
Accreditation: JCAH

Hidden Brook offers a 30-day residential inpatient program designed to include treatment of all phases of alcoholism: physical, emotional, social and spiritual.

The program offers individual and group counseling by certified resident staff members and by a variety of outside professional consultants. Frequent AA meetings introduce the alcoholic to this organization as a cornerstone to recovery. The program places strong emphasis upon physical health through diet, recreation and rest.

Hidden Brook accepts referrals from physicians, clergy and families, as well as from business and industry.

MOUNTAIN MANOR TREATMENT CENTER

Route 15, Box 126
Emmitsburg, Maryland 21727

(301) 447-2361

Director: Charles Roby, M.A.
Average Patient Census: 50

Minimum Duration of Treatment:
Program is based on minimum 30-day stay; does not usually exceed 45 days
Cost: $175 per day; $5,250 for 30-day stay. Insurance eligible.
Detoxification Offered: Yes
Accreditation: JCAH

The 30-day program of residential care at Mountain Manor includes an admission physical, care by nursing staff (24-hour duty) and both individual and group therapy. There is also an educational program on aspects of the disease of alcoholism and involvement in the AA program (2 meetings in community and 3 meetings in-house). Family involvement, nutritional meals and recreational programs are also included.

A 60-day extended-care program, at various Mountain Manor counseling centers or on a contractual basis with local resources, as well as sessions in life skills and group therapy, complete the continuum of care. Ongoing patient involvement in AA is an integral part of the program of therapy.

Transportation to and from Mountain Manor can be arranged. Industrial or professional consultation is also available on request.

MELWOOD FARM, INC.

Box 182
Olney, Maryland 20832

(301) 924-5000

Director: Stuart M. Brownell
Average Patient Census: 20

Minimum Duration of Treatment: 28 days
Cost: $5,600 (all-inclusive) for 28 days, including 12 weeks of aftercare and family programs. Insurance eligible.
Detoxification Offered: Yes
Accreditation: JCAH

Located 10 miles north of Washington, D.C., Melwood Farm Alcoholism Treatment Center offers a 28-day, AA-oriented, rehabilitation program that includes the following: group and individual counseling by alcoholism counselors, lectures, films, art therapy, pastoral counseling and AA meetings in-house and in the community. Twenty-four-hour nursing is provided under the supervision of the medical director (M.D.).

A family program and a 12-week aftercare program are also provided at no additional charge.

Requirements for admission are that the patient be able to take care of personal needs and be 18 years of age or older.

SENECA HOUSE

13025 Riley's Lock Road
Poolesville, Maryland 20837

(301) 948-2412

Director: Peggy McMahon, M.A., C.A.C.
Average Patient Census: 18

Minimum Duration of Treatment: 4–6 weeks
Cost: $137.50 per day; $3,850 for 28 days. Insurance eligible.
Detoxification Offered: Subacute
Accreditation: JCAH

Seneca House was founded in 1971 by a group of recovered alcoholics from metropolitan Washington, D.C., to create a workable, nonprofit rehabilitation program. In its growth and development, Seneca House has continued to highlight the experience, strength and hope offered by the personal recoveries of its staff members and volunteers.

Believing in the disease concept of alcoholism and chemical dependency, and that there is no moral issue or lack of willpower attached to the illness, Seneca House includes the following modalities in its treatment program: medical and nursing supervision 24 hours a day; psychiatric evaluation as needed; individual and group therapy daily; lectures, films and tapes about addiction; intensive orientation to AA and NA and recreational therapy.

Family Care includes family conference at discharge, 12 weeks of group sessions, as well as information and support from full-time Family Care counselors.

Cooperation with employers includes a Back-to-Work conference and progress reports.

Strong support is given through an individualized Aftercare Program including 8 weeks of return visits to share the adjustment period. Emergency crisis intervention during the postdischarge period is available, as well as optional extended Aftercare and Couples Communication groups.

Applicants must be detoxified prior to admission. Most begin at chemical dependency units of local general hospitals for medical supervision of withdrawal.

SAINT LUKE INSTITUTE, INC.

2420 Brooks Drive
Suitland, Maryland 20746

(301) 967-3700

Director: Chris Bowman

Average Patient Census: 24
Minimum Duration of Treatment: 4 months
Cost: $191 per day. Insurance eligible.
Detoxification Offered: Yes
Accreditation: JCAH

Saint Luke Institute is a private, not-for-profit treatment center whose mission is to assist alcoholic and chemically dependent priests, nuns and brothers in attaining peaceful and quality sobriety. The comprehensive treatment reflects the philosophy that alcoholism is a disease that affects the total person and those within that person's environment. Therefore, the concern at Saint Luke Institute is with the individual's development toward acceptance of the disease, the improvement of physical and emotional health, the fostering of more intimate and growth-producing relationships, the strengthening of spirituality and the continuation of the assessment of vocational choices and responsibility. Commitment to the fellowship of AA is essential.

The program starts with Phase One, an extensive 4-day evaluation, including a complete medical workup, psychological and neuropsychological testing, CT scan, EEG, EKG, individual interviews and a feedback session with the Evaluation Team.

Following the evaluation, the patient may be admitted to the inpatient program, where Phase Two, an individualized treatment plan, includes individual and group psychotherapy, educational lectures and AVs, relaxation instruction, biofeedback techniques, pastoral counseling, yoga and exercise, nutritional and vocational programs.

The high staff-to-patient ratio is supportive of individualized attention, and ongoing feedback and evaluation from both the staff's and the resident's perspective are built into the program.

Aftercare, the third phase, which covers 2 years and a Reentry Workshop about a month after discharge, is facilitated by the staff for the individual and significant persons in the home community or diocese.

The Institute also offers Superior's Workshops, which strengthen understanding of chemical dependency and also strategize interventions and continued follow-up.

Located in a suburb of Washington, D.C., the Institute can take advantage of the services offered by theologians, scholars and the many organizations of the area, as well as its creative social and cultural activities.

Massachusetts

NAUKEAG HOSPITAL, INC.

216 Lake Road
Ashburnham, Massachusetts 01430

(617) 827-5115

Director: Donald T. Connors, Sr.
Average Patient Census: 26

Minimum Duration of Treatment: Individual determination in accordance with utilization review procedures
Cost: $135 per day room and board plus physician's fee. Insurance eligible.
Detoxification Offered: Yes
Accreditation: JCAH

Naukeag Hospital is licensed to treat mental illness (mild nervous disorders), alcoholism and drug addiction. The services provided are therapeutic, based on medical, psychiatric and social therapies.

A typical patient stay begins with medical management followed by a rehabilitative program centered around group therapy sessions, which are held daily, and instructional seminars each afternoon. Patients attend outside AA meetings in the community in the evenings. Psychiatric and psychological services are provided. Individual counseling is initiated at intake, and each patient is assigned his or her individual certified addiction counselor.

Group therapy is based upon eliciting motivation toward self-help. Group leaders represent a variety of disciplines and include a counseling staff who are themselves recovering alcoholics.

The chief of the Psychiatric Service supervises the entire therapeutic process, reviewing patients' case histories. It is the feeling of the staff of this hospital that medical management, group therapy and individual counseling are all necessary requirements for a continuing care plan; to that end, they offer referral to appropriate, preferably therapeutic, programs available in the home community.

APPLETON TREATMENT CENTER
McLean Hospital

115 Mill Street
Belmont, Massachusetts 02178

(617) 855-2781

Director: Lance M. Dodes, M.D.
Average Patient Census: 17

Minimum Duration of Treatment: 2 weeks; individuals transferred from other hospital facilities, 30–35 days
Cost: $327 per day. Insurance eligible.
Detoxification Offered: Yes
Accreditation: JCAH

Appleton Treatment Center provides both inpatient and outpatient treatment, as well as extended aftercare for the alcoholic patient. Individual patient appropriateness is assessed before admission. In addition, diagnostic evaluation services for industry are offered, as well as a family program.

The program includes detoxification and rehabilitation and medical evaluation. The rehabilitation program is based upon AA orientation with individual and group therapy, family and couples counseling and psychological testing. It includes relaxation therapy, recreational therapy, occupation therapy and vocational counseling, psychodrama, social services, psychological testing and Antabuse.

Appleton offers in-service training to staff, a training center for social work, psychology and Harvard Medical School students, as well as training, education and consultation for community groups, industrial consultation, employee assistance programming, management and supervisory training and education.

Appleton is licensed by the Massachusetts Department of Public Health, Department of Mental Health.

BEACON HOUSE PROGRAM

Beacon House for Men
53 Beacon Street

Beacon House for Women
153 High Street
Greenfield, Massachusetts 01301

Men (413) 773-8020
Women (413) 774-5378

Director: Ruth Yanka

Average Patient Census: Men, 13; women, 13
Minimum Duration of Treatment: East Spoke, short term; Beacon Houses, up to 12 months
Cost: 50% of weekly net income, not to exceed the rate of $28.25 per day
Detoxification Offered: Yes
Accreditation: Licensed by Massachusetts

The alcohol program of Franklin Medical Center includes an outpatient facility known as The Beacon Clinic, the Beacon House program for men and women and limited inpatient availability on the East Spoke. The East Spoke is a voluntary unit offering special services to persons having a variety of problems including alcoholism and alcohol abuse. The Beacon Clinic provides treatment plans that are highly individualized by the staff. Services may include alcohol education, detoxification, drug therapy, psychological testing, individual and group therapy, psychodrama, occupational therapy, recreation activities and aftercare planning.

The Beacon Houses are transitional group-living residences for those who are motivated to overcome their drinking problem, have a potential for employment and can assume an independent status within 6 months of becoming a resident of the House. This facility treats alcoholism only.

MOUNT PLEASANT HOSPITAL

60 Granite Street
Lynn, Massachusetts 01904

(617) 581-5600

Director: A. Daniel Rubenstein, M.D.

Average Patient Census: 78
Minimum Duration of Treatment: 14 days
Cost: Available on request. Insurance eligible.
Detoxification Offered: Yes
Accreditation: JCAH

Mount Pleasant Hospital offers a comprehensive program for the treatment of alcoholism and polysubstance abuse. Laboratory, EKG and radiological services are available to aid in the medical evaluation of patients referred from industry and other sources. The multidisciplinary approach is used, and the basic therapeutic team consists of a physician, counselor and nurse. Psychological and social services are provided.

The program includes individual counseling, group therapy and pastoral counseling. There is a special program for female patients. In addition, an involvement with AA, Al-Anon and Alateen is an integral part of the program.

CCAIRU PROJECT FOR THE DEAF
Residential, Outpatient and Educational Programs

Route 28A, P.O. Box 719
West Falmouth, Massachusetts 02574

(617) 540-5052 (voice or TDD)

Director: Paul Rothfield, Executive Director; Nancy Rioux, Project Director for the Deaf
Average Patient Census: 25 beds

Minimum Duration of Treatment: Residential, 1 month; outpatient, individually determined
Cost: Adjusted to ability to pay. Insurance eligible for outpatient.
Detoxification Offered: Available in other CCAIRU components
Accreditation: State-licensed

The CCAIRU Project for the Deaf is a comprehensive treatment program for deaf alcoholics and their family members. The program is specifically designed to provide the specialized services so necessary for effective rehabilitation for the deaf. Treatment components include residential, graduate, outpatient, outreach and community education.

The residential program, the Stephen Miller House, is offered in a 25-bed Victorian manor situated near the beach on Cape Cod. The program includes peer counseling, alcoholism awareness classes, group therapy, AA meetings, vocational and recreational therapy classes and training in independent living. All staff members are trained in the special communication and counseling needs of the hearing-impaired/deaf. All are proficient in sign language, with emphasis placed on ASL communication.

The 5-bed Graduate House offers shared apartment living at low rent to enable clients completing the Stephen Miller House program to live independently while involved in employment training, volunteer placement, educational needs and assessment and ultimately employment.

The outpatient/outreach component of the project provides ambulatory treatment throughout Massachusetts for deaf/hearing-impaired alcoholics and their families. Additionally, efforts are made to maintain meaningful contact with Stephen Miller House and Graduate House clients who have returned to their own communities.

An ongoing program of outreach and community education services for individuals and organizations provides alcoholism education, establishment of reliable communication networks and publicity about the availability of alcoholism treatment for the deaf.

This facility treats alcoholism only.

DOCTORS HOSPITAL OF WORCESTER

107 Lincoln Street
Worcester, Massachusetts 01605

(617) 799-9000

Director: David Hillis, President

Average Patient Census: 88
Minimum Duration of Treatment: 21–28 days
Cost: $185 per day. Insurance eligible.
Detoxification Offered: Yes
Accreditation: JCAH

The 21- to 28-day inpatient alcohol and drug program at Doctors Hospital includes detoxification and medical monitoring through the subacute and rehabilitation phases of treatment, the length of treatment varying with individual needs. Daily group and frequent individual counseling sessions, as well as didactic films and presentations, are designed to influence the patient toward a drug-free, constructive life-style.

A formal family-treatment program is available at Doctors Hospital, and concurrent family participation is strongly encouraged in a program with a qualified specialist. Psychiatric consultation and psychotherapy are carried on as needed, and ancillary modalities such as stress management and physical and recreational therapy are incorporated in the treatment plan.

Aftercare is an integral program component. The entire program is strongly oriented toward AA and Al-Anon philosophy and practice.

F.A.I.T.H., INC.

142 Burncoat Street
Worcester, Massachusetts 01606

(617) 853-9496

Director: Barbara L. Dacri
Average Patient Census: 16

Minimum Duration of Treatment: None, but suggest a 6-month commitment
Cost: Sliding scale. Not insurance eligible.
Detoxification Offered: No
Accreditation: State-licensed

The FAITH program is limited to women for the treatment of alcoholism, and entrance is voluntary. Upon acceptance to the residential program, full cooperation and participation in all components is expected. Treatment modalities include AA, individual and group therapy, alcohol education services for enrichment, advocacy recreation, vocational counseling, employment preparation and placement, psychiatric services, sexuality education, and assertiveness training. All of these are determined jointly by the resident and a staff counselor.

Policy on dismissal: "The substance of any sound rehabilitation program is found in the quality of the content it offers both its participants and its staff. Equally important is the respect and cooperation that exists between staff and those who come seeking and receive treatment for alcoholism and its many consequences. Insomuch as FAITH offers a quality program, the following are sufficient reason or cause for dismissal: use or possession of any amount of alcohol, unprescribed medication, drugs of any kind, inappropriate behavior, need for other treatment model, smoking in restricted areas."

FAITH, Inc. has a three-phase treatment plan: (1) orientation to program and assessment of client needs; (2) treatment and vocational planning; and (3) employment achievement and discharge planning.

New Hampshire

BEECH HILL HOSPITAL, INC.

Box 254
Dublin, New Hampshire 03444

(603) 563-8511

Director: John H. Valentine, President

Average Patient Census: 104
Minimum Duration of Treatment:
   Individual treatment plan
Cost: $190 per day. Insurance eligible.
Detoxification Offered: Yes
Accreditation: JCAH

Beech Hill Hospital offers an intense therapeutic program for the treatment of alcoholism and other chemical dependencies. Detoxification is under the supervision of a full-time medical director and a full staff of RNs. Upon admission, each patient is given a complete physical examination, including EKG, chest X ray, serology and other laboratory tests.

After detoxification, the patient is transferred to the intermediate care phase, where an individualized treatment plan, originated on initial entry to the hospital, is put into effect through individual counseling and group therapy, which are utilized to penetrate the denial system of the chemically dependent patient. A staff psychologist and psychiatrist are available. Strong emphasis is placed on orienting the patient to the principles of the AA program as he may apply them to his own life and life problems. Aftercare planning includes scheduled visits to the hospital or its aftercare locations in Manchester, Connecticut; Randolph, Boston, Springfield, Hyannis and Worcester, Massachusetts; Manchester, New Hampshire; or Ottawa, Canada, as well as return visits, attendence at reunions, AA contact and referral to other community resources. Therapy for families of the patient is also available. Every effort is made to assist the patient to achieve a lasting sobriety and an ability to deal with his or her problems upon discharge.

Admissions may be arranged by industry, other agencies and interested parties at any time by telephone.

HAMPSTEAD HOSPITAL

East Road
Hampstead, New Hampshire 03841

(603) 329-5311

Director: Allan Carney

Average Patient Census: 126 beds
Minimum Duration of Treatment: 28 days
Cost: $226 per day. Insurance eligible.
Detoxification Offered: Yes
Accreditation: JCAH

Hampstead Hospital is primarily a crisis-intervention/acute-care facility. Staffing includes psychiatrist, psychologist, registered nurses, L.P.N.'s, counselors, social workers, occupational therapists and certified substance abuse counselors.

Upon arrival, the chemically dependent person is seen by a physician for history, physical examination and assessment of mental status. The family is interviewed by a counselor, who will remain in contact with them throughout the patient's hospitalization.

After detoxification, the recovery program provides a multidisciplinary approach involving medical, psychiatric and psychological care, along with program activities based upon the acknowledged success of AA philosophy. Individual care is coordinated with a structured group program.

SPOFFORD HALL

Route 9-A, P.O. Box 157
Spofford, New Hampshire 03462

(603) 363-4545
N.H. 1-800-451-1717, Northeast 1-800-451-1716

Average Patient Census: 134
Minimum Duration of Treatment: 29 days; average, 31 days
Cost: $189 per day. Insurance eligible.
Detoxification Offered: Yes
Accreditation: JCAH

Director: Stephen F. Kenny, M.H.S.

The treatment program at Spofford Hall incorporates four elements: Primary Care, Intermediate Care, Family Care and Aftercare.

Primary Care offers detoxification, complete medical examination, a process of psychosocial evaluation and a structured daily program.

Intermediate Care is based upon a comprehensive approach to chemical dependence, addressed to each patient's individual needs. The program includes individual, group and family therapy, Twelve-Step AA involvement, special interest groups, educational lectures, peer group discussions, audiovisual presentations and activities therapy. Four Intermediate-Care programs are offered: Chemical Dependence, Chronic Relapse, Crisis Intervention and Cocaine.

The Chronic-Relapse Program is offered to chemically dependent people who have had previous unsuccessful treatment experience and is designed to provide patients with the tools necessary to build a firm foundation for successful recovery. In addition to the standard Intermediate-Care Program activities, patients undergo extensive psychiatric/psychosocial evaluation and assessment and participate in special groups dealing with issues significant to this population.

Family Care consists of a 7-day program offered to families and significant others who, patients in their own right, participate in treatment programs for their own needs. Emphasis is upon recognition of the disease, building of communications patterns, changing roles, self-esteem and discontinuance of enabling behavior. Family patients need not be related to a Spofford Hall chemically dependent patient in order to be admitted to the Family Program. In addition, many patients are adult children of alcoholics who enter the Family Treatment Program to deal with the issues of the alcoholism in their family of origin.

Aftercare is a 2-year program developed for all patients prior to the completion of their treatment program and is designed to consolidate the gains made during their stay. Spofford Hall provides patients with aftercare groups and ongoing therapeutic support through an extensive follow-up program at the facility and satellite offices throughout the New England region.

In addition to the adult programs, Spofford Hall offers an Adolescent Treatment Program. This course of treatment is similar to the adult chemical dependence program, beginning with the initial assessment phase. However, it is tailored to the particular needs of adolescents, age 13 to 18, and includes structured tutorial services. Parental involvement is an essential component in the treatment of adolescents, and their participation in the family segment of this program is mandatory. The 2-year Aftercare Program is provided for the adolescent patient according to the same format as the adult program patient.

SEMINOLE POINT HOSPITAL

Box 1000, Woodland Road
Sunapee, New Hampshire 03782

1-800-633-4000

Director: James F. O'Neill

Average Patient Census: 750 annually
Minimum Duration of Treatment: 30 days
Cost: Posted rate, $250 per day.
Insurance eligible.
Detoxification Offered: Yes
Accreditation: JCAH

At Seminole Point the strong belief is held that there is no moral culpability for having the disease of alcoholism, but there is a moral responsibility to do something about it on the part of both the alcoholics and those around them, and therefore the alcoholic patient is not viewed judgmentally. While alcoholism is emphasized at this facility, there is both experience and interest in treating other substance abusers of prescription and nonprescription drugs.

In subscribing to the disease concept of alcoholism and its multifaceted nature, the program is multidisciplined and ecumenically administered, with equal weight given to all disciplines employed in order to assure holistic treatment and the expression of commitment to complete care.

In recognition of AA as the most effective support mechanism for the alcoholic, Seminole Point emphasizes AA's principles and uses the Twelve Steps as a treatment modality, providing continuity after primary inpatient treatment. Although the steps of AA are the mainstay of the program, other clinical concepts are also employed: reality therapy, Gestalt and Transactional Analysis and special men's, women's and family treatment groups. "Tough Love"—firmness in treatment blended with, but not diluted by, compassion—is also a principal belief at this facility.

There is a strong, caring Continuing Care program that provides support for patients for a full year, with provisions to extend at option.

Seminole Point Hospital is also presently operating two outpatient offices located at 308 Great Road, Littleton, Massachusetts 01460, (617) 486-9392; and 1265 Route 28, South Yarmouth, Massachusetts 02664, (617) 394-6616.

The outpatient clinics are staffed by degreed professionals who are caring and dedicated. The clinics operate on the same principles as the hospital and offer treatment to all members of the dysfunctional family, whether the alcoholic or substance abuser is recovering or not. Treatment includes psychiatric diagnostic evaluations, individual counseling, group counseling, family therapy, adolescent and adult children of alcoholics, individual and groups, and interventions.

New Jersey

CARRIER FOUNDATION ARU/ARP

P.O. Box 147
Belle Mead, New Jersey 08502

(201) 874-4000, ext. 261

Director: Shirley Carnwath

Average Patient Census: 65
Minimum Duration of Treatment: 4 weeks
Cost: Depends on insurance coverage. Insurance eligible.
Detoxification Offered: Yes
Accreditation: JCAH

Carrier Foundation offers detoxification for those suffering from chemical dependencies (excluding heroin and methadone). Following detoxification, there is a structured inpatient intermediate care program, which includes individual counseling, group counseling, social work services, a family program, lectures and involvement in the AA program.

The Foundation will accept individuals with a psychiatric diagnosis in addition to their chemical dependency. Qualifications for admission to the alcoholism treatment program are that patients be ambulatory, voluntary and willing to participate in a structured treatment program.

An alternative to, or continuation of, the ARU (Addiction Recovery Unit), is the Carrier Foundation ARP (Addiction Rehabilitation Program).

The ARP program, up to 4 weeks' duration, provides treatment for the alcoholic patient who does not have a coexisting medical and/or psychiatric disorder and so does not require psychotherapy or psychotropic medication.

The Adolescent Addiction Recovery Unit (AARU) offers 6 weeks' treatment for appropriate 13–17-year-olds who have been prescreened and accepted for admission.

The Outpatient Addiction Treatment Services (OATS) does the prescreening of adolescents and offers a wide range of outpatient services for addicted persons and their families.

The aftercare program is a once-a-week group session for recently discharged patients and families. Referrals from other rehabs are welcome.

LITTLE HILL–ALINA LODGE
Operated by the Little Hill Foundation, Inc.

Box G
Blairstown, New Jersey 07825

(201) 362-6114

Director: Geraldine O. Delaney
Average Patient Census: 60
Minimum Duration of Treatment: 12 weeks minimum with discharge at discretion of executive director

Cost: $2,100 for first 30 days plus $50 for incidentals. Billing every 2 weeks at $70 per day. Insurance eligible.
Detoxification Offered: No
Accreditation: JCAH

Little Hill–Alina Lodge is an intermediate-care facility for the rehabilitation of men and women suffering from the disease of alcoholism. The treatment process relies heavily upon sufficient time away from mood- and mind-changing chemicals and a nonpermissive approach to the treatment of the disease. Little Hill–Alina Lodge has geared itself to the "reluctant to recover" in order to enable them, through training in self-discipline, to live life to the fullest as a nondrinker in a drinking society. Little Hill–Alina also offers treatment for polyaddiction.

Intermediate Care includes a 12-week minimum length of stay, during which time the student attends four educational sessions each day. Group sessions, one-to-one counseling, films, special lectures, good nutrition and good health are also stressed. AA is emphasized and encouraged.

The Family Program includes weekly educational sessions for family members and/or significant others. The intensive In-Residence Program is also offered for family members and/or significant others toward the end of the student's stay. Al-Anon is emphasized and encouraged.

The Aftercare Program assists the student to formulate a plan that is specific to his or her needs and that will foster the gains made during treatment. A period of extended treatment is offered to students upon discharge. During this time the student returns to Little Hill–Alina Lodge for a 1-week period, usually after the third week of discharge. Each aftercare plan ensures that the student will have a contact to ease entry into AA in his or her community.

SEABROOK HOUSE, INC.

Polk Lane, P.O. Box 55
Seabrook, New Jersey 08302

(609) 455-7575

Director: Jerome J. Diehl
Average Patient Census: 60+
Minimum Duration of Treatment: Detox, 3–5 days, intermediate care, 28 days

Cost: Detox, $150 per day; intermediate care, $4,200 per 28 days; $150 for additional days beyond 4-week period. Insurance eligible.
Detoxification Offered: Yes
Accreditation: JCAH

Seabrook House offers detoxification, if medically indicated, as a prelude to intermediate care treatment. Intermediate care is composed of individually planned programs, utilizing a range of comprehensive therapeutic procedures designed to meet the distinctive needs of each patient. Introduction to AA and Al-Anon are integral parts of the treatment process and are incorporated into every aftercare plan.

Medical services are administered by a team of physicians and staffed around the clock by registered nurses and alcoholism counselors.

This facility is committed to the need for an alcoholic's family to receive treatment, and believes it is essential for the family to develop a way of life in which alcohol ceases to be the focal point, and healthy living becomes the primary interest. Family members' education, individual counseling and group therapy are available to children age 8 to 18, as well as to their parents.

Transportation from hospitals, industries, referring agencies or the patient's home is provided by the facility's driver when alternate means are unavailable. This courtesy is extended to New Jersey, New York, Pennsylvania and Delaware referrals. Philadelphia International Airport is close by, but corporate aircraft are encouraged to utilize the convenience of Millville Airport.

Seabrook House offers an outpatient program at 3111 Atlantic Avenue, Atlantic City, New Jersey 08401, (609) 345-3555.

SUNRISE HOUSE

P.O. Box 600
Lafayette, New Jersey 07848

(201) 383-6300

Director: Frank Clisham

Average Patient Census: 45
Minimum Duration of Treatment: 28 days
Cost: $150 per day. Insurance eligible.
Detoxification Offered: Yes
Accreditation: JCAH

Sunrise House is a private, nonprofit facility situated on a beautiful 22-acre tract in rural Sussex County. Licensed by the State of New Jersey to operate 48 treatment beds, there are plans in progress to increase both the size and the scope of programming.

The treatment philosophy at Sunrise House is based on the proven principles of AA, and the concept is multidisciplinary, combining the talents and skills of a wide spectrum of health care professionals. The program is strongly oriented to the principle of total abstinence from all chemicals of abuse. The power of the peer support group is the core modality of the treatment and recovery processes. Medical, psychiatric and professional psychological support components equip Sunrise House to handle most medical and emotional problems associated with the disease of chemical dependency, and close proximity to the New York metropolitan area makes established linkages with other specialized health care systems readily accessible.

Sunrise House recognizes that the patient's family most often has psychological, social and spiritual readjustment needs. Family members are therefore encouraged to participate concurrently in treatment with various treatment options available to them: outpatient, day program, brief-term residential and aftercare. Outpatient and residential intervention services are also available, and all family treatment services are oriented to Al-Anon.

Sunrise House welcomes the opportunity to work closely with professional, industrial and other third-party referral sources.

PRINCETON HOUSE

905 Herrontown Road
Princeton, New Jersey 08540

(609) 734-4631

Director: Gary Van Nostrand

Average Patient Census: 40
Minimum Duration of Treatment: 28 days
Cost: $7,000. Insurance eligible.
Detoxification Offered: Yes
Accreditation: JCAH

Princeton House was established by the Medical Center at Princeton in 1971 to provide the community of central New Jersey with a comprehensive treatment facility for alcoholism and psychiatric problems. The modern 84-bed facility is located on an attractive 10-acre campus 2 miles from the medical center's hospital unit. The program at Princeton House is offered only to those whose primary addiction is alcohol.

In the belief that alcoholism is not a character weakness but a chronic, progressive, fatal disease, Princeton House strives to help the alcoholic with a comprehensive array of services, including detoxification, rehabilitation, family counseling, discharge planning, aftercare and outpatient services. Emphasis is placed on educating the patient about alcoholism with films, tapes, lectures, group discussions and attendance at AA meetings, both in-house and in the community. Programs are planned to meet the special needs of each patient.

The staff includes clinical directors, a consultant psychiatrist, internists and accredited counselors, as well as occupational, creative and recreational therapists, psychiatric social workers and nurses. In addition, each patient is under the care of an attending staff psychiatrist.

Following discharge, AA contacts are arranged for patients in their local communities, and weekly outpatient groups are held at Princeton House for a 12-week period. The family component of the program includes education and introduction to Al-Anon and Alateen, as well as individual appointments with a counselor when needed in order to meet the important need of the family involvement.

Princeton House believes that the recovery rate is high among those who accept their illness and seek treatment.

New York

BRUNSWICK HOUSE ALCOHOLISM TREATMENT CENTER

366 Broadway
Amityville, Long Island, New York
   11701

(516) 789-7361

Director: Barbara L. McGinley, M.P.S.
Average Patient Census: 84
Minimum Duration of Treatment: Detox, 5–7 days; rehab, 21–28 days; aftercare, 1-year follow-up with 25-week elective aftercare group
Cost: Detox, $269 per day; rehab, $232 per day; elective 25-week aftercare, $250 complete. Insurance eligible.
Detoxification Offered: Yes
Accreditation: JCAH

Brunswick House was created in 1975 for comprehensive treatment of the disease of alcoholism. It is part of the Brunswick Hospital Center, a complex of five accredited hospitals, and can therefore accept patients with secondary medical problems.

After medically supervised toxic withdrawal, the patient receives a complete medical assessment and then may enter the residential rehabilitation program, which includes rehabilitative education in the form of lectures, psychodrama, psychological assessment, one-to-one counseling and nutritional support, as well as social services directly concerned with the patient in the area of family, vocational and social crisis. Patients are evaluated at discharge for ongoing supportive therapies, and there is a predesigned periodic follow-up program for each discharged patient.

Brunswick House has developed a specialized program for women, as well as family guidance and educational services. The Early Recovery Guidance Program for discharged patients consists of structured, weekly, 3-hour multisubject sessions in all alcohol-related areas. Groups are conducted on-site at Brunswick House and at its Manhattan satellite location: Hotel Lancaster, Thirty-eighth Street and Madison Avenue, NYC.

As a special service for companies and corporations who do not have occupational alcoholism programs, Brunswick House will send a cost-free information team to assist in setting up a diagnostic and referral plan.

SOUTH OAKS HOSPITAL
The Long Island Home, Ltd.

400 Sunrise Highway
Amityville, Long Island, New York
11701

(516) 264-4000

Director: Pasquale A. Carone, M.D., Executive Director
Sheila B. Blume, M.D., Medical Director, Alcoholism and Compulsive Gambling Programs
Average Patient Census: 90%
Minimum Duration of Treatment: detox, 3 days; rehab, 4–8 weeks
Cost: $362 per day. Insurance eligible.
Detoxification Offered: Yes
Accreditation: JCAH

South Oaks Hospital (The Long Island Home, Ltd.), one of the oldest and largest private psychiatric hospitals in the country, offers comprehensive treatment programs for mental illness, adolescent problems, drug addiction, alcoholism, compulsive gambling and substance abuse.

Treatment services cover inpatient detoxification and rehabilitation, family counseling, outpatient and continuing-care follow-up. The multi-disciplinary treatment team works with each patient to help him or her define conflicts and learn new ways of resolving them. The program includes complete medical and psychiatric services, family counseling, individual and group therapy, lectures, films, occupational and recreational therapy and AA and Al-Anon involvement, as well as comprehensive outpatient and continuing-care programs.

Additionally, the hospital offers a Helpline/Referral Service (call 1-800-732-9808 in New York State, and 516-264-4334 outside New York State), free consultations and evaluations and free alcoholism workshops.

The Institute of Alcohol Studies at South Oaks offers education and training programs for professionals, as well as those interested in entering the field. It also offers a broad range of educational courses for both alcoholics and their families. South Oaks Hospital also offers services to assist companies and corporations in setting up an employee assistance program.

Write to request brochures and information on the various services offered.

RUSH HALL ALCOHOLISM PROGRAM

1263 Delaware Avenue
Buffalo, New York 14209-2497

(716) 886-8200

Director: Robert J. Bertone, C.A.C.

Average Patient Census: 46
Minimum Duration of Treatment: 28 days
Cost: Available on request. Insurance eligible.
Detoxification Offered: Yes
Accreditation: JCAH

The Rush Hall Chemical Dependency Treatment Program offers an inpatient facility in Bry-Lin Hospital, a private psychiatric hospital. Treatment modalities include education, group therapy, individual and conjoint therapy, and family counseling, psychodrama, recreational therapy, group responsibility, introduction to AA, aftercare and follow-up.

Program components include a Detoxification Unit, an Entry-Level Unit and a Three-Week Program Completion Unit.

Qualifications for admission are: primary diagnosis of substance abuse or alcohol addiction, ambulatory and capable self-care, no overt psychosis. Family involvement is a firm requirement in every case. Rush Hall's experienced multidisciplinary team includes alcoholism counselors, physicians, psychiatrists, nurses, social workers and occupational therapists.

ARMS ACRES

Seminary Hill Road
Box X
Carmel, New York 10512

(914) 225-3400
1-800-227-2767 in New York
1-800-431-1268 outside New York

Director: David Cullen

Average Patient Census: 65
Minimum Duration of Treatment: After detox: adults, 28 days; adolescents, 49 days
Cost: Adult, $212 per day; adolescent, $294 per day; plus additional fees for physician, lab, etc. Insurance eligible.
Detoxification Offered: Yes
Accreditation: JCAH

Arms Acres is a 65-bed residential alcoholism treatment facility located on 54 acres of wooded hilltop in the town of Carmel, New York. It is easily accessible from all major cities in New England, New Jersey and Pennsylvania, as well as New York. The staff will arrange transportation for patients from their homes.

The primary purpose of Arms Acres is to provide a comprehensive treatment program for alcoholic patients, their families, friends, employers and significant others. Treating the disease of alcoholism requires physical, mental and spiritual rehabilitation, with the goal of restoring the person to a meaningful and productive role in society.

Arms Acres provides patients with an environment conducive to increased self-awareness, understanding of interpersonal relationships and an education in the diseases of alcoholism and drug dependence. The treatment program is built around the principles and traditions of AA, which are integrated into every aspect of therapy.

The three alcoholism treatment programs at Arms Acres are: Adult Program, Adolescent Program and Family Program.

Arms Acres also offers a Chronic Relapse Program, which is designed especially for those who have experienced failure to achieve sobriety after completing 28-day rehabilitation programs or long-term halfway-house, therapeutic-community or other long-term residential programs; after having gone repeatedly through detoxification programs; or after having participated in outpatient counseling or AA over a period of time.

After detoxification, medical services and orientation to the program, each chronic relapse patient will be evaluated by the staff psychiatrist to determine whether there are any underlying difficulties responsible for failure to maintain long-term sobriety. Special psychosocial assessments and family involvement are also important to the program.

The intermediate-care program for chronic relapse patients, for a minimum of 6 and a maximum of 8 weeks, involves basic-program as well as special chronic-relapse-program components. Aftercare planning begins 2 weeks prior to discharge with attendance at both AA meetings and at an Arms Acres aftercare group.

CLIFTON SPRINGS HOSPITAL ALCOHOLISM REHABILITATION PROGRAM

2 Coulter Road
Clifton Springs, New York 14432

(315) 462-9561

Director: Patricia Bobermin, M.A., C.A.C.
Average Patient Census: 22
Minimum Duration of Treatment: 28–32 days

Cost: $170 for self-pay patients, plus additional fees for physician, psychologist, lab, X ray, etc. Insurance eligible.
Detoxification Offered: For rehabilitation patients only
Accreditation: New York State Division of Alcoholism and Alcohol Abuse

The Alcoholism Rehabilitation Program at Clifton Springs Hospital is a thorough, intense program involving proven, effective techniques of treatment. These include didactic sessions, lectures, individual and group therapy, community meetings and AA meetings and psychological testing. Psychiatric consultations are available when indicated in a patient's treatment program. Included in this care is the application of a philosophy for living patterned after AA but not confined to it.

Counselors at Clifton Springs ARU plan carefully with the patient, his or her family and the referring agency or employer to implement a program of aftercare help through AA and Al-Anon, with additional follow-ups arranged that involve community agencies. Patients living within a 50-mile radius are expected to participate in a 15-session aftercare program at Clifton Springs.

To qualify for admission, patients must have a problem with alcohol and/or drugs if alcohol is the primary dependency. This facility feels that treatment is most successful for those 21 years of age or older. Patients must be able to care for their own needs; the program is not appropriate for those persons who are deaf, have considerable brain damage or are not physically or emotionally able to withstand the rigors of a 14-hour structured day.

FREEPORT HOSPITAL

267 South Ocean Avenue
Freeport, Long Island, New York 11520

(516) 378-0800

Director: Alvan Small, Administrator

Average Patient Census: 40
Minimum Duration of Treatment: 5–7 days
Cost: $245 per day. Insurance eligible.
Detoxification Offered: Yes
Accreditation: JCAH

Freeport Hospital devotes its entire facility to the treatment of the disease of alcoholism and offers detoxification and complete medical treatment as well as individual counseling, group therapy, lectures and discussions, AA meetings and supportive guidance for initiating and maintaining recovery. Special programs for the labor-union-referred patient are offered.

Freeport Medical Associates, P.C., offers aftercare and therapy programs in Freeport and in Manhattan at the office in the New York Penta Hotel, including a 26-week basic group therapy program, as well as intermediate and advanced group therapy sessions. For information, contact: Patricia Lewis, C.S.W., in Freeport (516) 378-1491; Michael Herzlin in Manhattan (212) 279-2727.

Family services offered by Freeport Medical Associates, P.C., include multidimensional programs. For information, call: on Long Island, (516) 378-1499; in Manhattan, (212) 279-2727.

FOUR WINDS HOSPITAL

800 Cross River Road
Katonah, New York 10536

(914) 763-8151

Director: Ann Wright, C.A.C., Director, Alcohol Service

Average Patient Census: 25 beds alcohol/substance abuse
Minimum Duration of Treatment: 6 weeks
Cost: $570 per diem, all-inclusive. Insurance eligible.
Detoxification Offered: Yes
Accreditation: JCAH

Four Winds Hospital is a private psychiatric treatment center for the inpatient care of adolescents and adults. The 100 beds are divided into small, self-contained specialty units, each located in its own residential building with full-time, exclusive treatment teams. The Alcohol and Substance Abuse services, General Adult Service, Adolescent Service, College Service, Eating Disorders Service and Young Adult Chronic Service each constitute almost a "hospital within a hospital" on the 50-acre wooded campus.

Several characteristics distinguish the Four Winds services: The full-time doctor-to-patient ratio is 1 to 6; individual psychotherapy occurs a minimum of 3 times weekly, and more frequently when indicated; group therapy is part of the intensive daily program; family therapy is integral to all treatment; patients live in a small family environment; and the atmosphere of the country estate is very noninstitutional.

The Alcohol Service approaches treatment as "the marriage of alcoholism and psychotherapy." It is designed for those alcoholics who have not been able to maintain sobriety despite previous participation in detoxification or rehabilitation programs or AA. In AA terminology, the Four Winds Alcohol Service patients are addressed as "some sicker than others." It is not a rehabilitation program. The treatment approach combines the principles of AA, active involvement in AA and contemporary psychiatry, which deals with the underlying psychiatric problems that have prevented continued sobriety and the ability to achieve constructive and secure habitation.

CASA SERENA

Watermelon Hill Road
Mahopac, New York 10541

(914) 628-9622

Director: Joseph LoPiccolo, Jr.
Average Patient Census: 43
Minimum Duration of Treatment: 2 weeks or longer

Cost: $300 per week. Includes physicians' fees and any medications. Not insurance eligible. Visa, Mastercharge, cash or check
Detoxification Offered: No
Accreditation: Licensed by the State of New York

Casa Serena offers both dry-out and rehabilitation programs under the direction of Dr. William B. Sibrans, resident physician. Staff is largely made up of recovering alcoholics. There is, in addition, one registered nurse with training in the management of alcoholics.

The program offers one-to-one counseling and is enriched by 2 AA meetings per day. It is open to anyone over the age of 18 suffering from alcohol abuse.

BREAKTHROUGH CONCEPTS, INC.

Gracie Square Hospital
420 East Seventy-sixth Street
New York, New York 10021

(212) 988-4400, ext. 501, 513

Director: Monica Wright
Average Patient Census: 104 beds

Minimum Duration of Treatment: Detox, 5 days; rehab, 28 days. Highly structured alternative tracks to respond to limited insurance coverage.
Cost: $395 per day. Insurance eligible.
Detoxification Offered: Yes
Accreditation: JCAH

Breakthrough at Gracie Square Hospital believes that neither alcoholism nor drug abuse attack in a straight line and that those touched by these diseases, often bewildered and angered at their own powerlessness, may require an intensive regimen in a closed environment.

The programs are designed to help patients change harmful patterns and they contain enough flexibility to address the complex variety of issues and needs that arise for the alcoholic or drug abuser.

Breakthrough's secure and modern physical plant consists of one floor for alcoholics, intranasal cocainists and pill abusers and another floor for intravenous cocaine and heroin addicts and other hard-drug abusers. Both floors include a Phase I unit, where patients pass their first week—a time of detoxification and more, when staff carefully challenge denial, explain the disease and offer hopeful alternatives.

In Phase II the themes are insight and "change," and group counseling is the primary method; autobiographies and peer feedback allow expression of emotions and stresses, as do art, movement and music therapy sessions. Psychiatrists specially trained in chemical dependency meet with each patient at least 3 times per week. Lectures, workshops and AA, NA and PA meetings occur nightly on both floors to acquaint patients with the most effective support known.

Hourglass is a special 7- to 14-day program at Breakthrough for the patient whose stay is limited by personal or medical coverage considerations and is also suited to the patient who is preparing for ambulatory rehab or a rigorous outpatient program.

Pathfinders Aftercare, the Family Program, Educational Consultation Services, and Liaison Response Services, designed to meet the need for information on their client's progress on the part of the referring organization, are all offered by Breakthrough, as well as organizational and community group educational and consultation services.

REGENT HOSPITAL

425 East Sixty-first Street
New York, New York 10021

(212) 935-4984

Director: Michael Leitzes
Average Patient Census: 35 beds

Minimum Duration of Treatment: 4–6 weeks, flexible
Cost: Available on request. Insurance eligible.
Detoxification Offered: Yes
Accreditation: JCAH

Regent Hospital, a modern, private, 35-bed psychiatric hospital, utilizing new treatments developed by their physician researchers at Yale and their sister hospital in New Jersey, Fair Oaks, offers to patients treatment that detoxifies and rehabilitates polydrug abusers and opiate and methadone addicts. This program has developed and implemented new nonopiate treatments for addicts that make drug- and opiate-free living a reality for motivated adult and adolescent patients. Employing special tests for the biological monitoring of patient progress, the specially trained staff provides treatment and works closely with family and referral sources to prevent relapse.

The neuropsychiatric program is designed to provide, within 1 or 2 weeks, a comprehensive neuropsychiatric assessment that results in specific and individualized treatment recommendations for the patient. Neurochemical, psychodiagnostic and neurological testing are combined with a family and psychosocial assessment, as well as extensive clinical diagnostic interviewing based on the most modern methods of classifying psychiatric disorders.

The substance abuse treatment program is designed to build upon these evaluations and recommendations, and treatment of patients is continued with careful observation and monitoring of patient progress, including newly developed laboratory techniques for therapeutic drug monitoring. Interpersonal and psychosocial problems are explored and treated through group, family and individual psychotherapy.

SMITHERS ALCOHOLISM TREATMENT AND TRAINING CENTER

Saint Luke's–Roosevelt Hospital Center
428 West Fifty-ninth Street
New York, New York 10019

(212) 554-6491

Director: Anne Geller, M.D.
Average Patient Census: Detox, 12; rehab, 42

Minimum Duration: Detox, 5–13 days; rehab, 28 days
Cost: Detox, per New York State Law; rehab, $190 per day. Insurance eligible.
Detoxification Offered: Yes
Accreditation: JCAH

Smithers Alcoholism Treatment and Training Center is a comprehensive treatment program for alcohol and drug dependency. Treatment includes an in-house medical detox, a 28-day inpatient rehabilitation unit and a full range of outpatient services, including a Day Program and family and intervention services.

Admission for treatment can be made for anyone 18 years of age or older who has a problem with alcohol, sedatives, stimulants, opiates or hallucinogens. The most frequent drug abuse problem among the patients is still alcohol, but it is very frequently in combination with other categories of drugs. Admission can be made to any one of the three main programs, detox, rehab or outpatient, which each take referrals from other programs.

The primary mode of treatment is the group, augmented by a full range of counseling services, educational lectures and community experience. The goal of the Smithers program is to improve personal functioning through abstinence, restore emotional and physical health and enhance family communications, job performance and quality of life.

Smithers was the first treatment program for the working alcoholic, and continues to offer industry-based EAPs consultation and evaluation services as well as training seminars for management and professionals. Smithers now offers similar programs in consultation and education for interested individuals in the clergy, social service and the mental health field, in addition to its semiannual training course for physicians.

Smithers is a division of Saint Luke's–Roosevelt Hospital Center, a University Hospital of Columbia University College of Physicians and Surgeons.

STUYVESANT SQUARE CHEMICAL DEPENDENCY PROGRAM
BETH ISRAEL MEDICAL CENTER

Nathan D. Perlman Place
New York, New York 10003

(212) 420-2900

Director: Barbara Cooper-Gordon

Average Patient Census: 51
Minimum Duration of Treatment: 28 days
Cost: $325 per day. Insurance eligible.
Detoxification Offered: Yes
Accreditation: JCAH

Stuyvesant Square provides comprehensive treatment to working adults who are dependent on drugs or alcohol, offering a carefully structured, individually tailored treatment program. During the 28 days in evaluation and rehabilitation, patients remain close to home and family while participating in a rigorous schedule of counseling and therapy. Surroundings are new and comfortable. Fellow patients are other working adults with similar objectives: to stop their dependency and start living healthy, productive, integrated lives.

Stuyvesant Square understands the requirements of business, the special concerns of family and the importance of confidentiality. Therefore, intake evaluation appointments are made through a single knowledgeable source. With the patient's consent, treatment counselors keep employers and others informed of the patient's status before, during and after treatment.

The program at Stuyvesant Square is based on a nationally recognized model with a demonstrated record of success: Saint Mary's in Minneapolis, which incorporates the Twelve Steps of AA, group and individual counseling and family involvement, a combination of Saint Mary's experience with the clinical expertise of Beth Israel.

Involvement of the patient's family at key points throughout treatment and aftercare is emphasized. During the midpoint of the inpatient phase, concerned family or friends are enlisted in a week-long family program.

The length of involvement in the aftercare program is individually determined. Typically, it is offered for up to 24 months. The long period of follow-up is one of the most important determinants of sustained treatment success. Self-help programs, such as AA, NA and Al-Anon, are used to supplement this long-term outpatient follow-up care.

The per diem fee for the initial 28-day stay includes the program's physician component, routine ancillary tests and complete family and aftercare programs.

THE RHINEBECK LODGE FOR SUCCESSFUL LIVING

R.D. 1, Milan Hollow Road
Box 306
Rhinebeck, New York 12572

(914) 266-3481

Director: Marie Maher, R.N.
Average Patient Census: 40

Minimum Duration of Treatment: 30 days; 45 days maximum
Cost: $6,570 for 30 days. Insurance eligible.
Detoxification Offered: At affiliated hospitals
Accreditation: JCAH

Rhinebeck Lodge involves the individual in a structured residential treatment program that includes: daily morning meditation; 30 lectures to educate the client about the human being, alcohol and alcoholism; group therapy 5 days a week; relaxation training; individual counseling and therapy; group study periods; recreation; daily AA meetings; nourishing, delicious meals; resident involvement in activities; psychiatrist on staff; aftercare planning and referral.

Patients must be sober for 3 days prior to admission, ambulatory and have no severe medical problems.

Referring counselors are contacted weekly and advised of client progress, as well as involved in the aftercare planning process.

Rhinebeck Lodge treats patients with a primary diagnosis of alcoholism.

CONIFER PARK

150 Glenridge Road
Scotia, New York 12302

(518) 399-6446

Director: John P. Jaquette, Jr.

Average Patient Census: 105
Minimum Duration of Treatment: 28 days
Cost: Available on request. Insurance eligible.
Detoxification Offered: Yes

Conifer Park is a specialized facility created for the treatment of all aspects of chemical dependency, with a wide variety of programs. As part of the Mediplex Group, it provides the individualized care for special populations that its sister facilities, Spofford Hall and Arms Acres, are known for.

Treatment programs include programs for chemical dependency, substance abuse with a special cocaine treatment component, an adolescent program and inpatient family treatment. Special additional foci include grief groups, assertiveness training, gay issues groups and groups for single parents and victims of sexual and physical abuse. Each patient undergoes a complete medical history and physical, and is assessed for psychological services as needed. Additionally, as part of the regular treatment regime, patients participate in lectures, physical activities and self-help discussion groups.

The treatment philosophy at Conifer Park indicates that inpatient rehabilitation is only the beginning of a life of recovery and that the center's primary function is to provide the tools for active participation in self-help recovery programs such as AA, Al-Anon or NA, not as an end in itself. Patients are encouraged to use the community as a resource through which they might identify their spiritual, emotional and relational needs, and to practice their new skills while in treatment.

Although located near Albany and Schenectady, New York, Conifer Park is nestled in a rural, wooded setting. The current capacity is 105 beds, but renovations for a full complement of 195 beds and additional facilities are scheduled for completion in the fall of 1985.

CHEMICAL ABUSE RECOVERY SERVICE (CARES)
BENJAMIN RUSH CENTER

672 South Salina Street
Syracuse, New York 13202

(315) 476-2161

Director: Ronald J. Dougherty, M.D.;
Young Y. Lee, M.D.

Average Patient Census: 30
Minimum Duration of Treatment: 42 days
Cost: $340 per day. Insurance eligible.
Detoxification Offered: Monitor withdrawal
Accreditation: JCAH

CARES, the Chemical Abuse Recovery Service of the Benjamin Rush Center, is based on the concept that chemical abuse is a primary illness that is treatable. The goal of the CARES program is to help those who have become powerless over their addiction not only to live drug-free, but also to realize personal growth in the process.

At the beginning of the 6-week inpatient program, the patient and staff outline specific treatment goals, taking into account individual differences. Program components include group therapy, assertiveness training, individual counseling, education groups and activities therapy. Intensive study of the principles of AA and NA are an integral part of the program, as well as attendance at those meetings each week.

In addition, family education groups, significant-other groups and Al-Anon are part of the CARES program and available to all families.

The CARES unit also offers a program of aftercare for patients and their families who have been through the CARES program in both the Syracuse and the Rochester areas.

The unit will accept patients who have a dual diagnosis of chemical dependency and psychiatric problems, and has the ability to identify, assess and arrange treatment for medical complications that result from the chemical addiction. In brief, the 6-week program at CARES addresses the reality that chemical dependency is a complicated disease requiring a multifaceted treatment program.

SLEEPY VALLEY CENTER

R.D. 4, Box 177
Warwick, New York 10990-9521

(914) 986-2545

Director: Thomas A. Pakenham
Average Patient Census: 20

Minimum Duration of Treatment: 28-day program
Cost: Available on request. Insurance eligible.
Detoxification Offered: Yes, by arrangement with local hospital
Accreditation: JCAH

The 28-day program at Sleepy Valley Center is designed to equip the patient with knowledge and skills to be applied on a daily basis in order to enable abstention from alcohol. The individual learns how to cope productively with living situations that previously triggered drinking episodes.

The program utilizes group and individual therapy, lectures, tapes, films, peer group discussions, milieu therapy, vitamin therapy, plus other educational and recreational activities. Individual counseling focuses attention on problem areas of the home, family, job and interpersonal relationships.

Sleepy Valley Center is located on 6 beautiful acres of wooded land in the rolling hills of Orange County, New York. There are hiking trails, a large swimming pool and indoor and outdoor recreational facilities. Patients attend AA meetings on and off the premises. As part of the family support program, family members and significant others are encouraged to attend family meetings, Al-Anon meetings, Alateen meetings and young people's meetings held on the grounds.

Admission is open to anyone, provided he or she is generally detoxified and capable of participating in the daily program. Referrals are invited from private individuals, business firms, physicians, social workers, clergy, AA members, hospitals and other care facilities. Inspection is invited.

THE NEW YORK HOSPITAL–CORNELL MEDICAL CENTER
WESTCHESTER DIVISION ALCOHOLISM TREATMENT SERVICE

21 Bloomingdale Road
White Plains, New York 10605

(914) 682-9100

Director: Richard J. Frances, M.D.
Average Patient Census: 25

Minimum Duration of Treatment: Detox, 1 week; rehab, 1–3 weeks; 6 weeks average
Cost: $420 per day. Insurance eligible.
Detoxification Offered: Yes
Accreditation: JCAH

The Alcohol Treatment Service, a 25-bed unit within the Division of Acute Treatment Services of New York Hospital–Cornell Medical Center offers an active, multifaceted treatment program and aftercare services for the person with the problem of severe alcohol abuse. It provides a special experience in community living and group interaction in which patients are given skills to help them attain and maintain their sobriety.

The medical detoxification program of 7 days encourages withdrawal for acutely intoxicated patients with limited medical problems, and includes emotional support within a stimulating therapeutic environment, psychiatric evaluation, group therapy and an introduction to AA.

The rehabilitation program, which patients generally elect to continue after detoxification, is an extensive exploratory program in which patients are intensively involved. They are helped to become and remain alcohol-free and to explore their psychological contributions to their drinking and maladaptive patterns of living. The program includes individual, group and family therapy, intensive education in all aspects of alcoholism, AA meetings, activity therapy and marital and multiple couple therapy.

Arrangements are made for aftercare counseling, individual, marital and group and/or individual psychotherapy in the adult outpatient department, or return to the referring physician or agency, and attendance at AA meetings is strongly encouraged.

Patients over 18 years of age are accepted as a rule, but adolescent patients may be admitted when appropriate school arrangements can be made.

PARKVIEW WESTCHESTER

P.O. Box 37, Route 118
Yorktown Heights, New York 10598

(914) 962-5000

Director: Harold Heinrich
Average Patient Census: Adults, 54; family, 16

Minimum Duration of Treatment: 30 days approximate, depending on progress
Cost: Available on request. Insurance eligible.
Detoxification Offered: No
Accreditation: JCAH

Parkview's recovery process is based on five levels of accomplishment: (1) diagnosis, where the patient personally recognizes that a problem exists; (2) awareness, which includes understanding of the disease and its effect on the patient as well as its impact on the entire family system; (3) acceptance of the realities of the disease and the powerlessness it engenders; (4) actualization, which comes when the patient takes responsibility for his or her recovery, and, finally, (5) commitment to a new way of life, using the tools learned through treatment.

Following initial and thorough individual evaluation with definitive observation and medical supervision of withdrawal symptoms, the program begins with education about the nature of chemical dependency and, in the course of the program, includes components such as one-to-one counseling, family counseling, psychological and medical assessments, spiritual consultation, recreation programs, group therapy and aftercare planning and implementation.

Throughout treatment the resident is exposed to in-depth study of AA and the Twelve Steps. Learning, understanding and accepting, the three Rs of Reality, Responsibility and Respect, is a major treatment goal so that the individual will be able to face reality without compromise, with dignity, understanding and love.

North Carolina

APPALACHIAN HALL/WOODHILL TREATMENT CENTER

Caledonia Road, P.O. Box 5534
Asheville, North Carolina 28813

(704) 253-3681, 1-800-438-4871

Director: Dennis F. Moore, Pharm. D.
Average Patient Census: 22
Minimum Duration of Treatment: 28 days following detoxification; longer stays at discretion of patient, staff and family members
Cost: Financial arrangements should be discussed with the Patient Accounts Office. Insurance eligible.
Detoxification Offered: Yes
Accreditation: JCAH

Appalachian Hall offers an active, multidisciplinary treatment program and detoxification, when necessary, accompanied by intensive medical care and treatment.

Following detoxification, patients are offered individual, group and family therapy, plus intensive education in the medical, social, occupational and family aspects of alcoholism.

Activities provided include psychological services, occupational therapy, career guidance, study groups, seminars, leisure counseling and a series of movies and tapes dealing with alcoholism and addiction to other drugs.

Arrangements for aftercare include outpatient counseling; individual, group and couples therapy is available. Patients are encouraged to attend AA meetings in the hospital and in their home community. Aftercare treatment and follow-up lasts from 1 to 2 years, depending on patients' progress and needs.

Appalachian Hall is a private general psychiatric hospital of 100 beds. The 30-bed chemical dependency unit is in a separate wing from the psychiatric unit; however, facilities of the psychiatric hospital are available.

THE ALCOHOLIC REHABILITATION CENTER

Box 1441
Black Mountain, North Carolina 28711

(704) 669-3400

Director: Millard F. Hall, Jr.
Average Patient Census: 87
Minimum Duration of Treatment:
  Generally 28 days in-resident program

Cost: $100 per day (present cost may vary each year, as determined by North Carolina State Budget for ARC). Insurance eligible.
Detoxification Offered: No
Accreditation: JCAH

The therapy program and activities at the Alcoholic Rehabilitation Center are based on the AA fellowship approach to sobriety. Therapy consists of lectures, films, tapes, individual counseling, group interaction sessions, recreational therapy, AA meetings, family services and aftercare planning.

Admission criteria for the residential program include the patient's need for the program, an honest desire for sobriety, mental and physical ability to participate fully in the program and referral by a mental health center or responsible community agency that will render aftercare and follow-up services.

CHARLOTTE TREATMENT CENTER

P.O. Box 240197
Charlotte, North Carolina 28224

(704) 554-8373

Director: James F. Emmert
Average Patient Census: 57
Minimum Duration of Treatment:
  alcoholism, 28 days; drug/alcoholism, 42 days

Cost: 28 days, approximately $4,200; 42 days, approximately $5,900. Insurance eligible.
Detoxification Offered: Yes
Accreditation: JCAH

The program at the Charlotte Treatment Center is an intensive and highly structured "core" program that is individualized for each patient.

Each patient participates in 13 orientation sessions. Other modalities of the program include special lectures, group and individual counseling, physical activity, and film, videotapes and audiotapes. Involvement with AA and NA takes place both at the Center and in the community.

Major expansion plans at the Charlotte Treatment Center include the provision of acute care and adult rehabilitation services, a separate treatment component for young adults and youth, family treatment on campus and facilities for professional education and training.

FELLOWSHIP HALL

P.O. Box 6929
Greensboro, North Carolina 27415

(919) 621-3381

Director: Jack C. Rothrock
Average Patient Census: 46
Minimum Duration of Treatment: 28 days. Overstay may be implemented with involvement of individual and staff.
Cost: $2,975 for 28 days. Insurance eligible.
Detoxification Offered: Yes, in conjunction with 28-day program.
Accreditation: JCAH

During a 28-day stay at Fellowship Hall, a guest receives at least 82 hours of classroom instruction plus individual counseling and group therapy in order to understand his problem with alcohol better. He completes an intensive self-analysis; a follow-up program is implemented on his return home.

The families of guests are permitted to visit twice weekly, excluding the first week of treatment. During each visit they are involved in an educational program. The family comes for intensive therapy for 4 days of the guest's treatment program.

Guests are referred to the Hall by various disciplines: employers, physicians, counselors on alcoholism, mental health agencies, etc.

Admission requirements: (a) The prospective guest must be suffering from the disease of alcoholism; (b) the person being admitted should be able to walk to classes and meals and know where he or she is and why and be willing to accept treatment; (c) a physician's statement of medical history and physical condition, or at least the name and phone number of the person's physician; (d) a deposit upon admission, which is based upon available insurance benefits (in the absence of health insurance, the full admission fee is due and payable upon admission) and (e) a family member, close friend, or other interested person available to accompany the potential admission in order to furnish the staff with an accurate history and make arrangements to participate in aftercare therapy.

WALTER B. JONES ALCOHOLIC REHABILITATION CENTER

Route 1, Box 20-A
Greenville, North Carolina 27834

(919) 758-3151

Director: Thomas L. Reece

Average Patient Census: 69
Minimum Duration of Treatment: 28 days
Cost: $106 per day. Insurance eligible.
Accreditation: JCAH

Qualifications for admission to the Walter B. Jones Alcoholic Rehabilitation Center are residence in one of the thirty-two eastern counties of North Carolina and a primary addiction to alcohol, although some patients abuse other drugs.

Patients must have no major physical or mental impairment or communicable diseases, must be willing to adhere to all the policies of the center and must be motivated toward rehabilitation.

A program for counseling of families is offered.

CHARTER NORTHRIDGE HOSPITAL

400 Newton Road
Raleigh, North Carolina 27609

(919) 847-0008

Director: Tom English

Average Patient Census: 66 beds
Minimum Duration of Treatment: 28 days
Cost: Varies; available on request. Insurance eligible.
Detoxification Offered: Yes
Accreditation: JCAH

The program at Charter Northridge Hospital offers medically supervised detoxification, if necessary, and individual, group and family counseling as part of the holistic (multidisciplinary) approach toward effectively treating the disease of addiction. All patients are also encouraged to participate in activities therapy and didactic lectures. These programs are AA/NA based philosophically. The hospital offers both adult and adolescent programs.

Patient and family aftercare services are available at all Charter Medical Addictive Disease units, emphasizing that recovery from this relentless disease is a continuing process affecting both the patient and his or her family.

This hospital is a freestanding chemical dependency facility.

CHARTER MANDALA CENTER

3637 Old Vineyard Road
Winston-Salem, North Carolina 27104

(919) 768-7710

Director: Jackie Camden, C.A.C.

Average Patient Census: 24 beds
Minimum Duration of Treatment: 21 days
Cost: Varies; available upon request. Insurance eligible.
Detoxification Offered: Yes
Accreditation: JCAH

The program at Charter Mandala Center offers medically supervised detoxification, if necessary, and individual, group and family counseling as part of the holistic (multidisciplinary) approach toward effectively treating the disease of addiction. All patients are also encouraged to participate in activities therapy and didactic lectures. These programs are AA/NA based philosophically. The hospital offers only an adult program.

Patient and family aftercare services are available at all Charter Medical Addictive Disease units, emphasizing that recovery from this relentless disease is a continuing process affecting both the patient and his or her family.

Pennsylvania

GATEWAY REHABILITATION CENTER

R.D. 2, Moffett Run Road
Aliquippa, Pennsylvania 15001

(412) 378-4461, (412) 766-8700

Director: Kenneth S. Ramsey
Average Patient Census: 75

Minimum Duration of Treatment: 28-day program
Cost: $120 per day; $3,360 for 28-day program. Insurance eligible.
Detoxification Offered: Yes
Accreditation: JCAH

Gateway Rehabilitation Center has a heavy commitment to the AA approach to recovery; 30% of the staff are recovering alcoholics. The staff includes eleven registered nurses and three part-time physicians.

The Center offers 5 hours of therapy each day, including group sessions, and arranges for attendance in outside NA and AA meetings in the community. There is a recreational program under the direction of a full-time recreational therapist. Patients are expected to participate in the care of their own rooms, as well as some community tasks.

Family counseling is offered, and a special family program is offered for 6 hours every Saturday for the 4-week treatment period, plus individual counseling offered by the full-time family therapy staff. A residential family program is available.

Biofeedback, stress management, consultation services and special programs for women are also available.

WHITE DEER RUN TREATMENT CENTER AT ALLENWOOD, A KOALA CENTER

Devitts Camp Road
Allenwood, Pennsylvania 17810

(717) 538-2567

Director: A. Scott Cowan
Average Patient Census: 90

Minimum Duration of Treatment: inpatient, 28 days; adolescent inpatient 45–60 days.
Cost: Available on request. Insurance eligible.
Detoxification Offered: Yes
Accreditation: JCAH

White Deer Run offers an individually designed course of treatment based on physical examination, medical history and psychosocial evaluation offered at the time of admission.

Requirements for admission are that the client be over 13 years of age, ambulatory, nonpsychotic and chemically free for 5 days prior to admission. Admissions are arranged by phone, with admission interviews required only if there is doubt that White Deer Run is the appropriate facility for an individual patient. Transportation service is offered; patients will be picked up and escorted to Allenwood.

The program provides individual therapy, milieu therapy, group therapy and family education programs on weekends. Each patient is expected to take part in work assignments directed toward the common needs of the community. The program is offered not only to alcoholics but also to those affected by cross-addiction and drug abuse.

White Deer Run offers, in addition, a Training Week Program for professionals, paraprofessionals and counselors who are likely to have alcohol or drug abusers among their clients. Arrangements for transportation and overnight lodging will be made if desired.

Koala centers and White Deer centers are specialized facilities devoted to the treatment of alcoholism and drug abuse. Until recently these two respected names in the health care field were separate entities. Now Koala and White Deer have joined forces, enabling them to provide a wider range of services over a broader geographic area. Together, White Deer and Koala are committed to a common goal of continued progress in the development of successful substance abuse treatment programs. In addition to inpatient programs for adults and adolescents, outpatient services are also available.

HORSHAM CLINIC SUBSTANCE ABUSE PROGRAM

Welsh Road and Butler Pike
Ambler, Pennsylvania 19002

(215) 643-7800

Director: Ivan Cohen, M.D.

Average Patient Census: 19
Minimum Duration of Treatment: 28 days
Cost: Covered by most major medical plans. Insurance eligible.
Detoxification Offered: Yes
Accreditation: JCAH

Designed specifically for the effective treatment of alcoholism and other chemical dependencies, the Horsham Clinic's Substance Abuse Program is a separate therapeutic unit within a restful setting on 53 acres of countryside near Philadelphia.

In addition to regular AA, NA and Al-Anon groups held on facility grounds, the recovery program includes complete physical and psychiatric evaluation, daily group psychotherapy to reinforce and extend the lecture program and individual psychotherapy sessions for each patient a minimum of 3 times per week. The emphasis is on personal awareness as well as family involvement to facilitate rehabilitation.

The needs of the alcoholic and drug-dependent woman are recognized and respected. Individualized treatment and aftercare programs are developed that are responsive to her special concerns. For additional support, an exclusively women's therapy group is conducted to address her unmet needs.

Other modalities of treatment are psychodrama, art therapy, leisure counseling, recreational therapy and relaxation and stress management techniques.

Horsham Clinic offers a comprehensive Family Education and Patient Aftercare Program. This includes Family Focus, an educational series; Family Problem-Solving Workshop; Family Group Sessions; and a Saturday morning Children of Alcoholics and Substance Abusers Group that runs concurrently with Family Group Sessions. Also available is a Family Follow-up Group, open to family members of patients who have been discharged amd maintained sobriety for at least 6 months.

LIVENGRIN FOUNDATION, INC.

4833 Hulmeville Road
Bensalem, Bucks County, Pennsylvania
19020-3099

(215) 639-2300

Director: Carl W. Illenberger
Average Patient Census: 65

Minimum Duration of Treatment: 21-day minimum; extensions when necessary
Cost: Intermediate Care, $138 per day; Primary Care, $161 per day. Insurance eligible.
Detoxification Offered: Yes
Accreditation: JCAH

A patient's stay at Livengrin usually begins with a period of detoxification in the Primary Care Unit, which is a complete medical detoxification center under the care of the medical director. The patient is then ready to proceed to the Intermediate Care Unit.

The basic treatment design of Livengrin's 21-day program is appropriate for all patients; however, each patient is treated with a plan designed to meet the needs indicated by the psychosocial history of the individual.

The underlying philosophy of the entire program is based on AA. The didactic segment of treatment includes 46 lectures by staff members, films, tapes and AA readings.

Peer group therapy sessions are held daily for a minimum of 2 hours and are led by a counselor; free time sessions by patients are encouraged. One-to-one counseling sessions are held regularly, and whenever possible concerned persons close to the patient are included with counselor and patient. There are, as well, sessions of group therapy for couples, held once a week. Psychodrama, work therapy, occupational therapy and recreational therapy are all modalities of the treatment program.

Aftercare services are designed in the final week of treatment when an assessment of needs is made by patient and primary counselor, and an aftercare plan is developed that utilizes services provided by Livengrin and/or services of outside providers.

Family therapy groups are also offered, as well as an Outpatient Clinic; a diagnostic and evaluation service is offered to industry. Complete medical, therapy and nursing staffs make up the multidisciplinary team at Livengrin.

Treatment at Livengrin is offered to cross-addicted alcoholics.

ENDLESS MOUNTAINS TREATMENT CENTER

520 Ruah Street
Blossburg, Pennsylvania 16912

(717) 638-2948

Director: Victoria Ayers
Average Patient Census: 16

Minimum Duration of Treatment: Minimum of 28 days, which can include days spent in detox
Cost: $125 per day. Insurance eligible.
Detoxification Offered: Yes
Accreditation: JCAH

Endless Mountains offers a nonhospital detoxification of 5 to 7 days and a treatment and rehabilitation program of 28 to 90 days. Extensions are possible, especially for polydrug users.

The program includes a thorough physical examination, group and individual therapy, psychodrama, one-to-one counseling, work therapy, education in addiction (lectures, films, tapes, talk sessions with former patients), activities program and AA meetings.

Admission is open to any person who abuses alcohol or other drugs. All patients must be physically and mentally capable of participating in an active, intense program and must not be maintained on any mind- or mood-altering drug.

The treatment goal is to redirect an addicted person into a responsible life free of chemical dependency. Addiction is emphasized as the primary problem for the alcholic/drug addict. Patients are guided through a separation—separation of their addiction from their living problems—and assured that if they cope first with the addiciton, they will be better able to cope with other problems. Endless Mountains promotes self-awareness of body, mind and spirit and relies heavily on a therapeutic community, enabling patients to share a group recovery experience. Families are counseled, and the continuity of care includes treatment and aftercare.

ARC/THE TERRACES

1170 South State Street
Ephrata, Pennsylvania 17522

(717) 627-0790
1-800-242-3907 in Pennsylvania
1-800-441-7345 in New England

Director: Pierre Zimmerman

Average Patient Census: 90 beds
Minimum Duration of Treatment: Adult, 29 days; adolescent, 50 days
Cost: Adult, $185 per day; adolescent, $265 per day. Insurance eligible.
Detoxification Offered: Yes
Accreditation: JCAH

ARC/The Terraces treats both adolescents (13–18) and adults (18+) who are alcohol/drug dependent or cocaine dependent, as well as affected family members. The Adolescent Program exists as a separate program within the general facility.

The Adolescent Program begins with the primary care phase: full physical examination and detoxification when indicated. Intermediate care is composed of individual therapy involving a minimum of 2 individual counseling sessions per week; group therapy, a minimum of five 1½-hour sessions per week; and various other group activities including AA meetings and special interest groups. One or more educational lectures on the nature of the disease, family dynamics and other topics each day, an educational/tutorial program for those enrolled in school prior to admission, and G.E.D. preparation and/or vocational counseling for those not enrolled, are also part of the program. Each patient also attends AA/NA meetings and weekly Step meetings. Fitness sessions supervised by the fitness specialist are scheduled on a daily basis.

The adolescent family program is an essential element, with a goal of recovery for each family member. Aftercare for both patient and family is composed of 2 years of follow-up services and additional assessment interventions and referral as needed, and provides a recovery network that includes AA, NA, Al-Anon, Alateen, other support groups and outpatient counseling.

ARC/The Terraces program for adults follows the same treatment plan. Special-issues groups meet twice a week, and patients may join after discussion with their case manager. These groups meeting regularly include: women's group, men's group, assertiveness training group and stress management group. Groups formed on the basis of patient population needs are: grief group, Children of Alcoholics group, Vietnam veterans group and gay/lesbian-issues group.

ARC/The Terraces also offers Family Forum, a weekly lecture and discussion series that focuses on "survivor roles" that family members adopt to cope with addiction, as well as a Residential Family Treatment Program.

BOWLING GREEN INN—BRANDYWINE

495 Newark Road
Kennett Square, Pennsylvania 19348

(215) 268-3588

Director: Jeffrey J. Kegley

Average Patient Census: 30
Minimum Duration of Treatment: 28 days
Cost: Approximately $5,200. Insurance eligible.
Detoxification Offered: Yes (subacute)
Accreditation: JCAH

Bowling Green Inn—Brandywine is one of a network of treatment centers owned and operated by Manor HealthCare of Silver Springs, Maryland. The Inn offers a basic 28-day, intensive, residential treatment program for men and women of any age who have an alcohol or drug problem. The program is keyed to AA philosophy, with individual treatment goals established for every resident. Techniques used in treatment include individual counseling, group therapy and psychodrama. Didactic groups utilize audiovisual media and materials developed by AA. Additional literature is furnished to residents and includes publications from AA, Hazelden and Johnson Institute.

Rather than treating the array of symptoms presented by the disease, a holistic approach is utilized. Treatment is geared toward improvements in interpersonal relationships, family life, employment, health and spiritual life, as well as general life-style improvements. All treatment methods are applied in a caring way in order to enable residents to learn that people are bridges to satisfied living. Admissions are voluntary, and individuals must be physically able to participate actively in and understand treatment approaches.

An aftercare program is offered based on assessment and is planned to include services at BGI when possible and alternatives when necessary.

In summary, Bowling Green Inn offers a 28-day residential program, a planned extended residential program for some adolescents or those dependent on drugs other than alcohol, subacute detoxification supervised by the medical director on site, an aftercare program keyed to specific needs, family-oriented treatment programs both inpatient and outpatient and 24-hour medical coverage.

CLEAR BROOK, INC.

R.D. 10, E. Northampton Street
Laurel Run, Pennsylvania 18702

(717) 823-1171

Director: Dave Lombard, President
Average Patient Census: 80

Minimum Duration of Treatment: Cross-addiction or drug addiction, 42 days; alcoholism only, 28 days
Cost: $125 per day. Insurance eligible.
Detoxification Offered: Available at Mercy Hospital
Accreditation: JCAH

Clear Brook, Inc., operates three facilities within the greater Wilkes-Barre, Pennsylvania, area. The Lodge, located in Shickshinny, is an adolescent facility; the Reagan House, also located in Shickshinny, is a family facility; the Manor, located in Wilkes-Barre, is an adult facility. Each facility offers a residential treatment program for men and women who are either alcohol or drug addicted.

Elements of the Clear Brook program include alcohol and drug education, individual counseling, group therapy, role play, AA/NA meetings both in-house and in the outer community and recreation activities.

An individualized aftercare plan is developed by the client and his or her counselor. Social life, job and home situations are dealt with. Employment guidance is available.

MALVERN

940 King Road
Malvern, Pennsylvania 19355

(215) 647-0330

Director: Joseph J. Driscoll
Average Patient Census: 20
Minimum Duration of Treatment: Detox, 10 days; rehab 28 days

Cost: $280 per day, additional charges for physician's fees, laboratory, etc. Insurance eligible.
Detoxification Offered: Yes
Accreditation: JCAH

The drug-free rehabilitation program at Malvern includes a variety of treatment modalities: individual therapy, group therapy, individual and family counseling, lectures and films on alcohol and drugs, and adjunctive therapy. These components are all carefully regulated so that each patient is presented with the total program in a logical sequence, regardless of admission date.

AA is a part of the program; patients hear talks on the Twelve Steps and attend AA meetings, held 4 times a week on the premises.

Malvern's medical staff includes physicians in the practice of general medicine or psychiatry. All patients receive a complete physical examination, including blood and urine analysis, and other tests when required. Treatment of ailments disclosed by this examination are incorporated into the individual's overall treatment plan.

Each patient is assigned to a Certified Addictions Counselor, who is primarily responsible for the overall case management. Registered nurses are on duty around the clock, and a psychological consultant is available for psychological testing. A schedule of meaningful recreational activities is supervised by a recreational activity therapist and incorporated into the program.

Members of the patient's family, especially the spouse, are encouraged to participate in family therapy at Malvern. Prior to discharge, each patient receives an individual discharge plan that is developed jointly by the patient and the treatment team and designed to meet the patient's particular needs for aftercare.

TODAY, INC.

P.O. Box 98
Newtown, Pennsylvania 18940

(215) 968-4713

Director: James J. Dougherty
Average Patient Census: 29

Minimum Duration of Treatment: 3 months, minimum; 6 months, maximum
Cost: $63 per day. Insurance eligible.
Detoxification Offered: No
Accreditation: JCAH

Today, Inc., is a residential treatment facility for substance abuse, for youths age 14 through 22 years, offering comprehensive care through group, individual and family therapy, work therapy and recreational activities, as well as an accredited educational program. The center is located on 25 acres of wooded farmland. Patients must be ambulatory and without a history of psychotic behavior. Referrals are accepted from all sources: self, other programs, government agencies, court systems, etc. Contact the intake coordinator at the number given above during normal business hours, Monday through Friday.

Today, Inc., is a nonprofit, private, nonmedical treatment program with a capacity of 32 beds. The modality is of a self-help/peer-help nature. The full-time medical staff does not dispense drugs. Within the program, an individualized treatment plan is tailored for each patient, and reentry and aftercare planning assure the newly recovered resident that a community support system will be available after completion of treatment.

Outpatient services, available to individuals of all ages, are located at the Summit Center, 602 West Street Road, Feasterville, Pennsylvania 10947.

ADDICTION TREATMENT SERVICES
THE FAIRMOUNT INSTITUTE

561 Fairthorne Avenue
Philadelphia, Pennsylvania 19128

(215) 487-4140

Director: Frank Walls, C.A.C.
Average Patient Census: 42 beds

Minimum Duration of Treatment: 28-day program
Cost: Available on request. Insurance eligible.
Detoxification Offered: Yes, by special arrangement
Accreditation: JCAH

The Addiction Treatment Service at the Fairmount Institute is designed for men and women suffering from alcohol and/or drug addiction in addition to psychiatric disorders. The goal of the service is to help patients achieve abstinence through constructive recovery while also treating the patient's psychiatric problems. This is accomplished through a coordinated program of inpatient services, support services to the family and employer and aftercare services.

The program of care is highly individualized and incorporates a variety of techniques based on the special needs of each patient. Upon admission each patient undergoes extensive assessment to determine his or her unique psychosocial, medical, family and occupational needs from which the individualized treatment plan is developed.

The principles of AA serve as the basic foundation for treatment. Each patient is introduced to the concepts of AA, attends regularly scheduled AA and NA meetings at the hospital and is encouraged to attend meetings as a support to his or her aftercare. Patient, family and employer education, family therapy, back-to-work conferences and aftercare groups are incorporated into the treatment plan. The treatment team includes recovering counselors, psychiatrists, psychologists, physicians, nursing staff, activities therapists and social workers.

Persons eligible for the Fairmount Institute's program must be at least 18 years of age, ambulatory and sufficiently oriented to benefit from the program and activities. Detoxification arrangements can be made.

MARWORTH
(A Geisinger Affiliate)

Waverly, Pennsylvania 18471

(717) 563-1112

Director: Nicholas F. Colangelo, Ph.D.
Average Patient Census: 68

Minimum Duration of Treatment: 28 days
Cost: $5,500, all-inclusive. Insurance eligible.
Detoxification Offered: Yes
Accreditation: JCAH

Marworth, located on the former family estate of Governor William Scranton, 10 miles north of the city of Scranton, is a dedicated community of recovering and caring professionals with demonstrated commitment toward alcoholics and chemically dependent individuals and their families.

After detoxification, when required, the recovery program is designed to permit participants to learn the seriousness of the disease of alcoholism and chemical dependency and how it has affected their life and that of those around them, how interaction with others provides positive reinforcement and that attendance at AA meetings is critical for long-term recovery.

The Marworth staff is especially sensitive to the needs of the referral source, be it employer, family or interested other, and lays particular stress on the importance of recognizing the need for continuing communications. Their experience has demonstrated that individual success in treatment is greatly enhanced where a working relationship exists between family member or employer and the clinical staff. Staff will report on patient's progress on a regular basis and will work to accommodate any special needs the referral source may have, including a back-to-work conference between patient, counselor and other appropriate individuals.

Emphasizing the importance of family involvement in treatment, Marworth offers educational programs on the facts and realities of alcoholism, as well as group discussions to help the family become aware of others who share common concerns and fears. Individual family counseling is also offered.

For the family member suffering from the effects of living with the alcoholic or chemically dependent person, Marworth offers a 5-day residential Family Program, for which the fee is $500, inclusive of all charges. This fee is a sliding scale based on ability to pay. A unique feature of this program is that the family does not have to have a patient in treatment before they may participate, in the belief that the family is entitled to recover even if the chemically dependent person is not willing to accept treatment.

A 2-year aftercare program, including reports to referring EAP personnel, is maintained for every patient in order to assure continued success in recovery.

CARON HOSPITAL/CHIT CHAT FARMS/CHIT CHAT WEST

Galen Hall Road
Box 277
Wernersville, Pennsylvania 19565

(215) 678-2332

Director: Richard W. Esterly
Average Patient Census: Caron Hospital, 20; Chit Chat Farms, 63; Chit Chat West, 40

Minimum Duration of Treatment: Hospital, 5 days; Farms, 28 days; West, 28 days
Cost: Hospital, $230 per day; Farms and West, $160 per day, $4,480 for 28 days. Insurance eligible.
Detoxification Offered: Yes
Accreditation: JCAH

Chit Chat Foundation provides a total comprehensive program for the treatment of alcoholics, other addicts and their families.

Caron Hospital is a specialized hospital providing detoxification, medical management and motivation through education and counseling. The program involves the most limited and prudent use of mood-altering medications.

Chit Chat Farms and Chit Chat West are two specialized treatment centers for rehabilitation. Alcoholism is treated as a family illness, and a full scope of treatment for the alcoholic and family members is provided, including inpatient programs for spouses, children and adult children of alcoholics.

The Twelve Steps of AA and Al-Anon are the philosophical basis for treatment. A multidisciplined, intensive, 4-week program directs the family to rebuilding a life free of chemical dependence. The therapeutic community is highly developed and promoted in every aspect of treatment.

Individual aftercare plans, including AA, the employer-counseling program (where appropriate), Chit Chat aftercare groups and other community programs, are a vitally important part of each patient's treatment.

Chit Chat Foundation programs utilize an interdisciplinary-team approach, in which no one professional viewpoint dominates. The therapy staff is, therefore, better able to structure a treatment approach tailored to the patient, rather than one tied to the established methods of any single discipline.

Located 10 miles west of Reading, Pennsylvania, transportation is provided, where necessary, to and from bus, railroad and airport terminals.

Rhode Island

EDGEHILL NEWPORT, INC.

200 Harrison Avenue
Newport, Rhode Island 02840

(401) 849-5700

Director: Frank Fanella

Average Patient Census: 160
Minimum Duration of Treatment: 28 days
Cost: Approximately $215 per day. Insurance eligible.
Detoxification Offered: Yes
Accreditation: JCAH

Edgehill Newport, Inc., is a comprehensive 160-bed residential alcoholism treatment facility for men and women. The modern brick buildings supplement the manor house and other buildings on the 65 acres of a former Ocean Drive estate. The 4-week program is centered around the conviction that alcoholism must be addressed as a primary illness if lasting recovery is to be obtained. Once the problem is identified, the patient shares responsibility with family, employer and the treatment staff in dealing with it realistically, as with any other disease. Treatment is offered to alcoholics only.

On admission, alcohol withdrawal will be closely supervised in a separate 20-bed unit. Initial physical and mental assessment will be done, with special attention to complications of any drug use. The patient then moves to a residential unit, where a multidisciplinary team is available for individual planning and monitoring the process of treatment. Staff includes psychologists, clergy, social workers, medical professionals and alcoholism counselors. Many are themselves recovering alcoholics.

Elements of treatment include group therapy, individual counseling, physical therapy, vocational and family counseling and an introduction to the philosophy and techniques of AA, as well as a comprehensive lecture series.

A detailed aftercare program gives attention to family, social and community networks. Discharge planning, beginning almost at admission, includes services for family, employer and significant other persons.

Transportation within 500 miles can be arranged.

HIGH POINT

1950 Tower Hill Road
North Kingstown, Rhode Island 02852

(401) 295-2511

Director: Dr. Edward T. Lees
Average Patient Census: 48 beds

Minimum Duration of Treatment: Detox, 2 days; rehab, 26 days
Cost: Detox, $262 per day; rehab, $215 per day. Insurance eligible
Detoxification Offered: Yes
Accreditation: JCAH

High Point offers a program for the treatment of alcoholism/polydrug abuse based on a process for recovery called Integrated Change Therapy. The focus of ICT as a recovery model is in helping alcoholics understand, in a coherent and systematic manner, the ICT principles: (a) that alcoholism itself is the primary problem; (b) that powerlessness over alcohol and other realities of life is real, and its antithesis, alcoholic pride, is a deadly illusion; (c) that alcoholics have dignity, goodness and purpose as worthwhile human beings—that this is their spiritual essence—and that they must learn to use this essence to deal with their alcoholism; and (d) that human relationships are difficult for everyone, but that alcoholics, in particular, must come to a new and more complementary understanding of them.

Assessment and evaluation procedures include medical histories and physical examinations, chemical abuse histories and psychological evaluations, and treatment planning is done on an individualized basis. Group therapy, individual counseling, lectures and AA meetings are augmented by specific services that may be required, such as vocational and speech therapy and others that are provided by consultants on a contractual basis. Patients under 18 years of age may be admitted on a selected basis.

The blueprint for recovery at High Point is built into the environment. Sea gulls from the nearby Atlantic Ocean wheel above the five-building complex, which is secluded in a quiet wooded area just off Route 1 South.

BUTLER HOSPITAL
Problem Drinkers' Project

345 Blackstone Boulevard
Providence, Rhode Island 02906

(401) 456-3725, Unit
(401) 456-3710, Admissions

Director: Edward B. Fink, M.D.

Average Patient Census: 16
Minimum Duration of Treatment: None Average stay after detox is 3 weeks.
Cost: $170 per day. Insurance eligible.
Detoxification Offered: Yes
Accreditation: JCAH

Butler Hospital, a private psychiatric facility, offers a rehabilitation program for alcohol abusers called the Problem Drinkers' Project.

Following detoxification, if appropriate, on an inpatient basis at Butler Hospital, patients participate in the specialized 3-week Problem Drinkers' Project at the Day Hospital.

Treatment is group-oriented, using a behavioral learning approach, and includes movies, medical education and attendence at AA meetings as a part of the treatment. Spouses and other family members are integrally involved in the program.

Patients must be 13 years of age or older and must demonstrate ability to pay for treatment.

South Carolina

FENWICK HALL

P.O. Box 688
Johns Island, South Carolina 29455

(803) 559-2461

Director: John H. Magill
Average Patient Census: 32

Minimum Duration of Treatment: 30-day average
Cost: Available on request. Insurance eligible.
Detoxification Offered: Yes
Accreditation: JCAH

The treatment program at Fenwick Hall usually requires from 30 to 45 days and incorporates innovative therapeutic techniques with a relaxed treatment environment in order to aid the recovering person physically, emotionally and spiritually.

The program begins for all persons with a series of medical, neurological and biochemical examinations to help ensure effective treatment of any hidden complications.

Therapy groups, peer evaluation and individual counseling all add to the openness necessary in an effective rehabilitation. The resources of the recovering community of AA are interwoven with other aspects of treatment, including family therapy. Active AA participation is evident in on-campus activities, as well as in community opportunities. Nutrition, recreation and physical restoration are stressed.

Family involvement begins at the time of admission, continues with an intensive 3-day residential family program during treatment and is extended through participation in aftercare. The aftercare program extends contact with each patient for at least 2 years by means of phone calls, assistance with qualified counseling help in area of residence, encouragement in continued involvement with AA, a newsletter, a 10- to 14-day "relapse prevention and management program" and alumni weekends for patients and family members.

The facilities at Fenwick Hall are a significant part of the treatment environment, with six buildings on the grounds of an historic Georgian plantation fully restored and tastefully appointed. Johns Island is 10 minutes from Charleston, and patients can be met there if requested.

ALCOHOLISM TREATMENT PROGRAM
NORTH GREENVILLE HOSPITAL

807 North Main Street
Travelers Rest, South Carolina 29609

(803) 834-7278

Director: Ray Moss
Average Patient Census: 25

Minimum Duration of Treatment: 28–42 days
Cost: 28 days, $5,000; 42 days, $7,000. Insurance eligible.
Detoxification Offered: Yes
Accreditation: JCAH

At North Greenville Hospital the alcoholism and drug dependency program is based on the belief that chemical dependency is a disease like any other, and that patients are therefore entitled to excellent medical attention to help them toward full recovery. The hospital is located in a quiet, tranquil spot in the foothills of the Blue Ridge Mountains.

The structured 4- to 6-week program is under the guidance of a well-trained, caring staff composed of physicians, nurses, addiction counselors, community consultants and other health care professionals, who focus on individual patient requirements for medical attention, education and an understanding of their disease. It is a total health concept, including the physical, intellectual, social, emotional and spiritual aspects of the patient.

Family involvement is an important part of therapy, with a suitable educational program stressing understanding of the disease and participation in treatment. A continuing-care program of 4 to 6 weeks of weekly sessions for patient and family is offered, as well as an Alumni Group and community self-help groups: AA, NA, Al-Anon and Alateen. Intervention education is also available.

The program for recovery at North Greenville emphasizes personal identity, acceptance of the problem, alternative behavioral and attitudinal patterns, setting of priorities, methods of maintaining sobriety and new patterns of problem solving.

Admissions can be arranged by telephone, and meeting and transportation from Greenville airports is also offered.

CHARTER RIVERS HOSPITAL

P.O. Box 4116
2900 Sunset Boulevard
West Columbia, South Carolina 29171

(803) 796-9911

Director: Bob Catlin

Average Patient Census: 57 beds
Minimum Duration of Treatment: 28 days
Cost: Varies; available on request. Insurance eligible.
Detoxification Offered: Yes
Accreditation: JCAH

The program at Charter Rivers Hospital offers medically supervised detoxification, if necessary, and individual, group and family counseling as part of the holistic (multidisciplinary) approach toward effectively treating the disease of addiction. All patients are also encouraged to participate in activities therapy and didactic lectures. These programs are AA/NA based philosophically. The hospital offers a program only for adults.

Patient and family aftercare services are available at all Charter Medical Addictive Disease units, emphasizing that recovery from this relentless disease is a continuing process affecting both the patient and his or her family.

Vermont

BRATTLEBORO RETREAT
ADOLESCENT ALCOHOL AND DRUG TREATMENT PROGRAM

75 Linden Street
Brattleboro, Vermont 05301

1 (800) 345-5550
1 (800) 351-4203
1 (800) 622-4492 (Vermont only)

Chief Executive Officer: William B. Beach, Jr., M.D.

Program Director: Stuart Copans, M.D.
Average Patient Census: 14
Minimum Duration of Treatment: Individualized length of stay, 2–3 months
Cost: $357 per day. Insurance eligible.
Detoxification Offered: Yes
Accreditation: JCAH

The Adolescent Alcohol and Drug Treatment Program on Osgood III is a 14-bed, coed program for the treatment of adolescents with severe drug and alcohol problems. Osgood III is designed to provide a safe, drug-free environment where adolescents, through education and treatment, begin to understand more about the nature of chemical dependency.

An interdisciplinary team of experienced professionals help the adolescent and family identify a workable approach that may include many forms of intervention, education and treatment, depending on each individual's need. The plan, based on an in-depth diagnostic evaluation, may include family, individual, group, behavioral, recreational, occupational and expressive therapies.

Teachers work with the youth, family and home school system to ensure the continuance of an uninterrupted academic program that includes a comprehensive educational assessment and individualized educational program.

The family is kept involved through family weekends and regular sessions. This reflects the program's emphasis on the importance of family dynamics and communication in effective treatment.

Discharge from the program concludes the first active phase of treatment. Reentry into family, social life and school can be a delicate transition. An intense aftercare program is developed with each adolescent to establish strong community supports that help reinforce a less problematic life-style.

BRATTLEBORO RETREAT
Adult Alcohol and Substance Abuse Program

75 Linden Street
Brattleboro, Vermont 05301

1 (800) 345-5550
1 (800) 351-4203
1 (800) 622-4492 (Vermont only)

Chief Executive Officer: William B. Beach, Jr., M.D.

Program Director: Valery Yandow, M.D.
Average Patient Census: 26 beds
Minimum Duration of Treatment: 28 days. Program length of stay is open-ended, depending on clinical needs.
Cost: $315 per day. Insurance eligible.
Detoxification Offered: Yes
Accreditation: JCAH

The Adult Alcohol and Substance Abuse Program at the Brattleboro Retreat takes a biopsychological approach to the treatment of substance abuse. Treatment planning and implementation is through a multidisciplinary team effort and is tailored to the individual's needs.

The target population is the complicated substance abuser. This population might include those with serious medical problems, the cross-addicted individual and those suffering from concomitant psychiatric disorders.

The program is highly structured and includes educational sessions, therapeutic recreation, peer support groups and treatment planning sessions. Individual psychotherapy is scheduled as indicated. Aftercare planning begins upon admission and is viewed as an extremely important part of treatment and the key to long-term recovery. Involvement in AA and NA is strongly encouraged while in treatment and is recommended upon discharge.

Direct, medically supervised detoxification is available, as well as a variety of health care and psychological services offered by the Retreat.

The program encourages family involvement in treatment. Family therapy is available. In addition, a Family Education Weekend is offered twice a month at no additional cost.

BRATTLEBORO RETREAT
Ripley Alcohol Rehabilitation Center

75 Linden Street
Brattleboro, Vermont 05301

1 (800) 345-5550
1 (800) 351-4203
1 (800) 622-4492 (Vermont only)

Chief Executive Officer: William B. Beach, Jr., M.D.

Program Director: Jane Hendrickson, R.N., M.Ed., C.A.C.
Average Patient Census: 20
Minimum Duration of Treatment: 28 days
Cost: $195 per day. Insurance eligible.
Detoxification Offered: Yes
Accreditation: JCAH

The Ripley Alcohol Rehabilitation Center is a comprehensive treatment program for alcoholic individuals who are not experiencing significant psychiatric complications, but have been unable to maintain sobriety on an outpatient basis. Treatment at Ripley is offered to alcoholics only.

Ripley Center provides an intensive, highly structured, 28-day treatment program. An individual plan for recovery developed with each person includes identification of the problems to be addressed, setting personal treatment goals and specific steps to achieve each goal. Treatment involves individual and small-group therapy, didactic groups, AA meetings and groups exploring AA's Twelve Steps and Traditions, participatory groups on topics such as family dynamics, love and sexual relationships, resistance, and denial and relapse prevention. Special emphasis is placed on discharge planning, family weekends (a no-cost educational program) and special needs counseling for women, impaired health care professionals and people whose high-stress jobs, marital status or choice of life-style affect their alcoholism.

Ripley Center's accommodations include private rooms and spacious living and meeting areas. Aftercare and follow-up activities for patients and families continue over a 2-year period.

RECOVERY HOUSE, INC.
SERENITY HOUSE

12 Church Street
P.O. Box 207
Wallingford, Vermont 05773

(802) 446-2640

Director: Rita Allaire
Average Patient Census: 20

Minimum Duration of Treatment: 28-day residential program
Cost: $65 per day. Sliding scale when appropriate. Insurance eligible.
Detoxification Offered: Yes, nonmedical
Accreditation: Licensed by State of Vermont

Serenity House is a residential alcohol treatment program whose basic treatment philosophy is oriented toward AA in the belief that AA provides the best and most successful long-term treatment for most people who have a problem with alcohol.

The term of residence varies with individual needs, but people are encouraged to stay in residential treatment for a minimum of 3 weeks in order to provide a base for a sober life. The program at Serenity House includes 9 group therapy sessions per week, including a men's group, a women's group, a problem-solving group, an educational group, and a house duty problem group, as well as attendance at a minimum of 9 AA meetings per week, either in-house or in Rutland. Each client has a minimum of 1 hour per week of one-on-one counseling.

Recovery House, Inc., includes, as well, a sister halfway house called Grace House at 35 Washington Street, Rutland, which is an extension of the program at Serenity House. The halfway-house setting introduces the now-alcohol-free client to a more mainstream setting, in which each resident is expected to become employed and responsible for his or her own support. Although the client at Grace House will continue to have individual and group counseling, he or she is expected to take a more active role in implementing his or her continuing recovery program, while continuing to receive counselor and peer support.

Recovery House offers treatment only to alcoholics.

Virginia

ALCOHOLISM RECOVERY SERVICE
Circle Terrace Hospital

904 Circle Terrace Drive
Alexandria, Virginia 22302

(703) 836-7740

Director: Evelyn Joy, M.S.W., C.A.C.
Average Patient Census: 13

Minimum Duration of Treatment: 28 days
Cost: Detox, $260 per day; $233 per day thereafter. Insurance eligible.
Detoxification Offered: Yes, if treatment follows
Accreditation: JCAH

Circle Terrace Hospital Alcoholism Recovery Service believes that alcoholism is a chronic, progressive, relapsing, and potentially fatal disease, that deserves complete and comprehensive treatment for both the alcoholic and the family. Individually designed treatment consists of education, individual and group counseling, plus total immersion in AA. Treatment is designed to achieve four specific goals: (a) learning that alcoholism is a disease; (b) self-diagnosing as having alcoholism; (c) accepting abstinence as the answer; and (d) using AA effectively as a support group to avoid relapse.

In addition to the 28-day Inpatient Program, Circle Terrace offers a Day Outpatient Program, which provides 28 days of intensive alcoholism treatment after detoxification for those who only need partial hospitalization but require the structure and intensity of an inpatient program. Cost for day outpatient is $50 per day post detox. Evening outpatients are treated in a 12-week, 36-session program, which consists of education, individual and group counseling. In addition, regular AA attendance and daily Antabuse are mandatory. Cost for evening outpatient is $30 per 2-hour session. Upon completion of these programs, all patients enter the Aftercare Program, which meets twice per week for 18 weeks. Follow-up and monitoring continue for 1 year.

Family members are expected to participate in an 8-week Concerned Persons Program that is open to all who are closely involved with the patient and focuses on education about alcoholism, its effect on the family and the establishment of a continued recovery program through Al-Anon. In addition to meeting 3 times per week for education, individual and group counseling, the primary concerned persons attend 6 aftercare groups that focus specifically on family reintegration, communications and problem solving.

Circle Terrace Hospital enjoys a strong alumni association, in-house AA and Al-Anon meetings and an active volunteer program of former patients. Located within the Washington, D.C., metropolitan area, the easily accessible residential neighborhood provides privacy and peaceful surroundings.

Treatment is offered for drugs other than alcohol if concurrent with a diagnosis of alcoholism.

ALCOHOLISM TREATMENT PROGRAM
THE ARLINGTON HOSPITAL

1701 North George Mason Drive
Arlington, Virginia 22205

(703) 558-6536

Director: Ron Rogers

Average Patient Census: 40 beds
Minimum Duration of Treatment: 28 days
Cost: Detox and inpatient, $6,000; aftercare, $680. Insurance eligible.
Detoxification Offered: Yes
Accreditation: JCAH

The Arlington Hospital Alcoholism Treatment Program offers a wide range of services for alcohol/drug-dependent people from the age of 13. These services include detoxification, inpatient, outpatient, aftercare and follow-up. The philosophy of Arlington's ATP is based on the belief that alcoholism is a chronic, progressive disease. The model of treatment is innovative in that it is a "chronic disease" model designed to meet certain goals that are believed to be essential in arresting any chronic disease. These goals include teaching the patient about the nature of the illness, helping the patient to achieve self-diagnosis, teaching the patient how to use self-help groups available in the community such as AA, Al-Anon, NA, etc., and helping the patient to assume personal responsibility for recovery.

These goals are met by use of educational presentations, individual counseling, independent study and experimental learning. A concerned-persons program is offered for friends and family. The program is staffed with professionals from a variety of disciplines, including physicians, educators, counselors, nurses, social workers and psychologists, who use a multidisciplinary-team approach in the treatment of each patient.

Referrals are made to other services when appropriate, and an extensive aftercare experience is designed for each patient, with a minimum 1-year follow-up. The same components comprise the 7-week outpatient program.

Arlington Hospital ATP, using this approach over the last 7 years, has shown that alcohol and chemical dependencies are not only treatable, but treatable with success.

MOUNTAIN WOOD LTD.

500 Old Lynchburg Road
P.O. Box 5546
Charlottesville, Virginia 22905

(804) 971-8245

Director: William C. Barbee, Jr.

Average Patient Census: 90% occupancy, 80 beds
Minimum Duration of Treatment: 28 days
Cost: $215 per day, average. Insurance eligible.
Detoxification Offered: Yes
Accreditation: JCAH

Mountain Wood, situated in the natural beauty and peacefulness of the Blue Ridge Mountains, is a private, nonprofit center for the treatment of alcoholism and drug abuse. It is also a community of professionals, staff and guests working to achieve a mutual goal: an alcohol- and drug-free life for each individual seeking treatment.

The fundamental and central principle of treatment at Mountain Wood is based on the dignity of the individual. Each guest entering Mountain Wood works with the staff in the development of a comprehensive individualized treatment plan. All guests participate in individual, group and family counseling, a physical well-being (Wellness) program and AA or NA meetings.

Some of the special features of Mountain Wood are initial consultation for patient and/or family members at no charge, 24-hour admissions, and specialized services for adolescents, women, families, cocaine and other drug dependencies.

The multidisciplinary staff of physicians, nurses, clinical psychologists, licensed counselors, social workers and counselors certified in alcoholism and drug abuse shares a common commitment and has had extensive experience in treating alcoholism and various drug addictions, including cocaine, synthetic opiates, barbiturates and tranquilizers.

These addictions are treated in special groups as a supplement to the total program. Although the primary basis for referral should be alcoholism or drug addiction, the senior treatment staff is experienced in treating psychiatric difficulties. Specialized groups and educational/tutorial services are provided for adolescents. Persons from 14 to 70 have been treated.

NEW BEGINNINGS/SERENITY LODGE

2097 South Military Highway
Chesapeake, Virginia 23320

(804) 543-6888

Director: Kay Hardin
Average Patient Census: 60-bed capacity

Minimum Duration of Treatment: Adult Unit, 30 days; Adolescent Unit, 45 days
Cost: Available on request. Insurance eligible.
Detoxification Offered: Yes
Accreditation: JCAH

Serenity Lodge is located on its own 7-acre campus and emphasizes a warm, comfortable atmosphere conducive to beginning a program of recovery.

Services include medically supervised, uncomplicated detoxification, psychosocial evaluation, individualized treatment in the context of a therapeutic community, a 12-week program of aftercare and a 2-year follow-up system.

The recovery program is staffed by chemical dependency professionals, including a medical director, an admissions intake coordinator, an activities therapist and an aftercare coordinator. This team employs treatment principles that have proven effective in confronting, understanding and arresting chemical dependency and its associated problems. An educational program consisting of films, lectures and other pertinent presentations is designed to help patients and families understand the nature of the illness and to use the tools of recovery. Each patient is assigned a counselor who coordinates the treatment team, conducts daily groups and is available to the patient for support during treatment. Program participants attend AA and NA meetings daily.

Family members are encouraged to accompany the patient to Serenity Lodge when seeking admission. At this time, or when convenient, a family program coordinator will meet with them to assess the families at no charge. There is also a family education week on chemical dependency, free of charge, where the family can learn and understand the dynamics of chemical dependency. This same service is offered to the community at large whether or not the chemically dependent family member is in residence at Serenity Lodge. Al-Anon participation is an aspect of the family program.

Aftercare planning begins soon after admission to determine which community resources may be used. A weekly 12-week aftercare group meets at Serenity Lodge to share and discuss mutual concerns of recovery. A follow-up system is initiated to encourage persons to join the alumni association for support during early phases of recovery. Serenity also has a crisis intervention group that meets once a week. The participants are trained in the techniques used to confront and deal with crisis concerning chemical dependency.

The Adolescent Program at Serenity Lodge offers a structured inpatient substance abuse treatment and rehabilitation format for the young chemically dependent patient and meets requirements for their continuing education.

THE LIFE CENTER OF GALAX

112 Painter Street, P.O. Box 27
Galax, Virginia 24333

(703) 236-2994
1-800-542-8708 (Virginia only)

Director: William W. Perkins, C.A.C.

Average Patient Census: 16
Minimum Duration of Treatment: 28 days
Cost: $4,500 minimum. Insurance eligible.
Detoxification Offered: Yes
Accreditation: JCAH

The Life Center of Galax, formerly the Waddell Center, is dedicated to a no-nonsense approach to substance abuse treatment, and the problem is treated like the chronic disease that it is. The staff includes experienced physicians and nurses trained in substance abuse, and with certified addiction counselors and other trained professionals, the ratio of patients to counselors is less than 9 to 1.

In the complete program for problem drinkers and other chemically dependent persons and their families and friends, the principles of AA and NA are heavily utilized.

Detoxification, if needed, is accomplished under medical supervision; physical examinations, laboratory tests and evaluations are done without the use of mood-altering chemicals unless an additional emotional disorder is diagnosed after withdrawal symptoms subside.

Other modalities of treatment are education through lectures, films and tapes, required attendance at AA and NA meetings, and counseling and therapy in group and individual sessions. Family services and aftercare for 6 months following discharge, as well as referral to AA, NA, Al-Anon and Alateen, are also services of the Center.

ADULT CHEMICAL DEPENDENCY TREATMENT PROGRAM
PENINSULA HOSPITAL

2244 Executive Drive
Hampton, Virginia 23666

(804) 827-1001

Director: William E. McAllister
Average Patient Census: 30

Minimum Duration of Treatment: Usually 28 days
Cost: Available on request. Insurance eligible.
Detoxification Offered: Yes
Accreditation: JCAH

The Adult Chemical Dependency Treatment Program at Peninsula Hospital employs a nonpsychiatric approach to treat chemically dependent individuals. Psychiatric evaluation is available for individuals who may require additional treatment. The program takes place in a 45-bed wing of the hospital overlooking a scenic wooded landscape. Facilities include comfortably furnished semiprivate rooms and bath, lounges, meeting rooms and indoor and outdoor areas for recreational and physical pursuits. A gymnasium and basketball court, indoor swimming pool, tennis court, campsites, fitness trail and ropes and initiatives course are available.

Peninsula Hospital places heavy emphasis on treating the chemically dependent individual without the use of other mood-altering medications. After a complete clinical assessment of all the needs of the individual, and detoxification if necessary, a clinical team develops an individual treatment plan. The plan is developed within 1 week of admission and is reviewed every 2 weeks of the hospital stay. Group therapy, leading to an understanding of the effects of dependency and supportive in developing positive attitudes, plays an important role in the program, as does family involvement. A 4-hour Orientation Session is offered every Sunday afternoon for family members and other concerned persons. In addition, an intensive 3-day Family Program is scheduled every other week, and Concerned Persons groups meet weekly in 2-hour sessions for 12 weeks. Participation in all of these programs is strongly encouraged. The philosophies of AA and NA are also of vital importance to the program.

Aftercare is an important part of discharge planning, including appropriate community resources and the hospital's aftercare program of separate and combined therapy sessions held weekly for 3 months in the Peninsula, Tidewater and Richmond areas.

Peninsula provides separate programs for adult and adolescent psychiatric treatment, as well as adolescent chemical dependency, each located in a self-contained area of the hospital, and has been approved for voluntary and involuntary admissions. Hospital staff members will meet patients, when necessary, at train or bus stations or at airports some distance from the hospital.

SHENANDOAH TREATMENT CENTER

Route 3, Box 52
Harrisonburg, Virginia 22801

(703) 434-7396

Program Administrator: Jim Hearn

Average Patient Census: 20
Minimum Duration of Treatment: 28 days
Cost: $165 per day, plus additional medical charges. Insurance eligible.
Detoxification Offered: Yes
Accreditation: JCAH

Shenandoah Treatment Center offers personal counseling, group counseling and a full family program. Education about alcoholism as a disease is offered through a series of didactic lectures.

Qualifications for admission are only that the patient be ambulatory and have a significant prehistory of alcohol or drug dependency. In addition, the patient must be willing to accept admission voluntarily and be 18 years of age or older.

Cost of the program may be covered by insurance or by individual financial arrangements.

SPRINGWOOD PSYCHIATRIC INSTITUTE

Route 4, Box 50
Leesburg, Virginia 22075

(703) 777-0800

Director: C. Gibson Dunn, M.D.

Average Patient Census: 34
Minimum Duration of Treatment: 28 days
Cost: $395–$525 per day, depending on program. Insurance eligible.
Detoxification Offered: Yes
Accreditation: JCAH

Springwood has the special capability to treat adults and adolescents with dual diagnosis, i.e., chemical dependency and a major psychiatric disorder.

Separate, intensive Adult and Adolescent Chemical Dependency Treatment programs are provided by a multidisciplinary team composed of psychiatrists, certified alcoholism counselors (all of whom are recovering), family therapists, psychiatric nurses and social workers, occupational and recreational specialists and certified special education teachers.

Both the adult and the adolescent programs include daily AA/NA, individual counseling, group and family therapy, intensive education about chemical dependency, experimental groups, socialization skills, occupational and recreational therapy and year-long aftercare. The adolescent program also includes a full schedule of academic classes in the Springwood School, a fully accredited school of special education, grades 7 through 12.

Additionally, the Springwood staff recognizes that family involvement in the treatment process is extremely important. Family members attend the Family Treatment Program, an intensive 4-day educational and experimental program, as well as family and multifamily therapy, Al-Anon attendance and a year-long aftercare program.

THE ALCOHOL AND DRUG PROGRAM OF POPLAR SPRINGS HOSPITAL

350 Wagner Road
Petersburg, Virginia 23805

(804) 733-6874

Director: W. Kenneth Helton
Average Patient Census: 30 beds

Minimum Duration of Treatment: 28–30 days
Cost: Determined by needs of the patient. Insurance eligible.
Detoxification Offered: Yes
Accreditation: JCAH

Poplar Springs Hospital is a 100-bed private psychiatric hospital located on a 16-acre wooded campus, which is convenient to the Richmond metropolitan area and Southside, Virginia. Facilities include semiprivate rooms, large community areas, a library, a learning center, gymnasium, activity therapy center and dining room.

Voluntary admissions are accepted upon referral from physicians, community agencies, family members or, in the case of adults, by patients themselves. All treatment plans are based on comprehensive assessments that include mental examination and psychosocial, psychological, nutritional, vocational and activity evaluations.

The goal of the Alcohol and Drug Treatment Program is to help individuals build lives characterized by freedom, self-direction and sobriety. Physical and medical services include specific training programs geared to wellness and health maintenance, diet and exercise. Cognitive learning in daily education groups focusing on recovery, self-awareness and interpersonal skills in group activities, family treatment, personal support through AA and related groups, skill development and occupational and recreational therapy and supportive counseling, in which a specific counselor works with the patient through detoxification, rehabilitation and aftercare—these are all integral services in treatment.

Poplar Springs, in an effort to hold costs down, makes a particular guarantee to persons who complete the program: free treatment for relapse, consisting of preventive consultation, inpatient detox and rehabilitation, as indicated by the needs of the patient, for any relapse incidents that occur within 1 year of the original discharge. Free family care, a 3- to 4-day program during patient's treatment for spouses and older children and free aftercare counseling groups at Popular Springs Hospital for 13 weeks are also part of the guarantee.

CHARTER WESTBROOK HOSPITAL

P.O. Box 9127
1500 Westbrook Avenue
Richmond, Virginia 23227

(804) 266-9671

Director: James Corcoran, M.D., Adult Unit; Martin N. Buxton, M.D., Adolescent Unit

Average Patient Census: Adults, 20 beds; adolescents, 24 beds
Minimum Duration of Treatment: 28 days
Cost: Varies; available on request. Insurance eligible.
Detoxification Offered: Yes
Accreditation: JCAH

The program at Charter Westbrook Hospital offers medically supervised detoxification, if necessary, and individual, group and family counseling as part of the holistic (multidisciplinary) approach toward effectively treating the disease of addiction. All patients are also encouraged to participate in activities therapy and didactic lectures. These programs are AA/NA based philosophically. The hospital offers programs for both adults and adolescents.

Patient and family aftercare services are available at all Charter Medical Addictive Disease units, emphasizing that recovery from this relentless disease is a continuing process affecting both the patient and his or her family.

SAINT JOHN'S HOSPITAL, INC.

Route 2, Box 389
Richmond, Virginia 23233

(804) 784-3501

Director: Mark Hierholzer
Average Patient Census: 70 beds

Minimum Duration of Treatment: 28–30 days
Cost: $295 per day. Insurance eligible.
Detoxification Offered: Provision through area detoxification hospital
Accreditation: JCAH

Saint John's Hospital operates on the following assumptions: (a) since there is no single confirmed cause of chemical dependency, the treatment program will encompass a holistic approach to the individual; (b) since alcoholism is a chronic illness for which there is no known cure, the hospital's approach will be compassionate care, not cure, seeking to arrest the disease and improve the client's life-style, which includes total abstinence from all chemicals; (c) since chemical dependency is a family disease, family members and concerned others are treated, either with or without the alcoholic in treatment; (d) since rehabilitation is the beginning of recovery, aftercare services are an integral part of the patient's treatment plan.

The staff at the hospital is multidisciplinary and functions in areas of individual treatment planning, medical management, individual, group and family counseling and many other treatment modalities.

Qualifications for admission are that the patient be 18 years of age or older, have no severe medical complications and be ambulatory. The hospital will provide transportation to and from the facility, which is 8 miles from metropolitan Richmond. No patient is arbitrarily refused admission because he has been a former patient; each is reevaluated as to appropriateness of rehabilitation at Saint John's.

SOUTHWEST VIRGINIA TREATMENT CENTER, INC.

405 Kimball Avenue
Salem, Virginia 24153

(703) 389-4761, 389-9588

Director: Theodore A. Petrocci, M.S., L.P.C.

Average Patient Census: 18
Minimum Duration of Treatment: 21 days
Cost: $5,000–6,000. Insurance eligible.
Detoxification Offered: Yes
Accreditation: State-licensed and State-certified

The program at Southwest Virginia Treatment Center is multidisciplinary, combining a modified medical model detoxification process and the state of the art, AA intensive, psychosocial treatment approach. Group therapy, lectures and films are used to maximize the psychoeducational dynamics essential to recovery. There is a Family/Concerned-Persons Program as well as AA and Al-Anon on the premises. There is also a 15-week aftercare program.

The SWTC, Inc., also offers outpatient services at the main facility and at two satellite locations, one in Blacksburg, Virginia, and the other in the Covington area.

At these facilities alcoholism and other chemical dependencies are all treated as the primary disease.

Intervention counseling, employee counseling and industrial consultation and training are available through the outpatient/EAP services.

All admissions are screened for appropriateness. Males and females must be 18 years of age or older.

West Virginia

PRESTON MEMORIAL HOSPITAL

300 South Price Street
Kingwood, West Virginia 26537

(304) 329-1400

Director: Robert Weaver

Average Patient Census: 17
Minimum Duration of Treatment: 28 days
Cost: $5,300. Insurance eligible.
Detoxification Offered: Yes
Accreditation: JCAH

Preston Alcoholism Treatment Service believes that alcoholism and drug addiction can be arrested only through total sobriety and abstinence from all forms of alcohol and drugs and that the first step in recovery is clear—to "stop using." This concept of recovery, based on the AA and NA philosophy, is implemented during the 28-day inpatient program.

Following detoxification, when appropriate, patients begin attending group therapy sessions, lectures and workshops, where coping skills are developed, and the motivation to begin commitment to lifetime abstinence and treatment is enhanced.

Individual counseling permits sharing with a counselor in one-to-one communication, and the patient is subsequently encouraged to share with the group later in group therapy. It is in the group that each chemically dependent person finds others who have experienced the same pain and struggle with the disease.

The Aftercare Program conducts weekly sessions available free to all former patients who desire to maintain an ongoing relationship with one another and the staff. The Family Program, supported by PATS' belief that recovery is a family affair, offers educational lectures, group sharing, individual family counseling, introduction to Al-Anon and recognition of the special needs of children in alcoholism-affected family groups.

Patients come to PATS to get well. Freedom from the ravages of alcohol and drugs is the goal. It is not easy but, once accomplished, is never regretted.

KOALA CENTER AT SOUTH CHARLESTON COMMUNITY HOSPITAL

30 MacCorkle Avenue
South Charleston, West Virginia 25303

(304) 744-7550

Director: Walter Shain
Average Patient Census: 8

Minimum Duration of Treatment: Adults, 30 days
Cost: Available on request. Insurance eligible.
Detoxification Offered: Yes
Accreditation: American Osteopathic Association

Koala derives its name from the custom among the Aboriginals of Australia of passing the drinking vessel around a circle. Anyone who did not wish to drink said, *"Koala,"* meaning "no drink." Later, the name was given to the little animal, native to Australia, that seldom, if ever, drinks.

Koala is a treatment hospital for alcoholism and drug abuse for both adults and adolescents and believes that alcoholism is a disease that must be treated with the same compassion, dedication and expertise as all other diseases. This facility offers, therefore, a comprehensive, multidisciplinary, individualized treatment plan in a nonjudgmental, stigma-free environment.

The program includes group therapy, family counseling, individual therapy, an introduction to AA and NA, psychological testing, psychiatric evaluation, nutrition awareness, leisure counseling and employer involvement.

CENTRAL/SOUTHERN TREATMENT CENTERS

Alabama

NEW LIFE CENTER
HILL CREST HOSPITAL

6869 Fifth Avenue South
Birmingham, Alabama 35212

(205) 833-9000

Director: Gary Lang
Average Patient Census: 16

Minimum Duration of Treatment: 20–30 days
Cost: Available on request. Insurance eligible.
Detoxification Offered: Yes
Accreditation: JCAH

The New Life Center at Hill Crest Hospital is dedicated to relieving the suffering caused by an addiction to alcohol and/or other drugs. The staff believes that each human being is unique and worthy of dignity and respect regardless of his or her addiction.

The treatment program addresses the mental, spiritual, emotional, physical and social aspects of daily living. There is a strong orientation and emphasis on the programs of AA and Al-Anon. Patients are encouraged to become involved in these programs as a way of life. The family unit and its treatment are also stressed.

There are no restrictions for admission regarding age, sex, race or creed.

CHARTER RETREAT'S RECOVERY CENTER

2205 Beltline Road
P.O. Box 1230
Decatur, Alabama 35602

(205) 350-1450

Director: Lynne Farmer, C.A.C.

Average Patient Census: 40 beds
Minimum Duration of Treatment: 28 days
Cost: Varies; available on request. Insurance eligible.
Detoxification Offered: Yes
Accreditation: JCAH

The program at Charter Retreat's Recovery Center offers medically supervised detoxification, if necessary, and individual, group and family counseling as part of the holistic (multidisciplinary) approach toward effectively treating the disease of addiction. All patients are also encouraged to participate in activities therapy and didactic lectures. These programs are AA/NA based philosophically. The Recovery Center offers both adult and young adult programs.

Patient and family aftercare services are available at all Charter Medical Addictive Disease units, emphasizing that recovery from this relentless disease is a continuing process affecting both the patient and his or her family.

CHARTER WOODS HOSPITAL

P.O. Box 1586
700 Cottonwood Road
Dothan, Alabama 36302

(205) 793-6660

Director: Aubrey White, C.A.C.

Average Patient Census: 25 beds
Minimum Duration of Treatment: 28 days
Cost: Varies; available on request. Insurance eligible.
Detoxification Offered: Yes
Accreditation: JCAH

The program at Charter Woods Hospital offers medically supervised detoxification, if necessary, and individual, group and family counseling as part of the holistic (multidisciplinary) approach toward effectively treating the disease of addiction. All patients are also encouraged to participate in activities therapy and didactic lectures. These programs are AA/NA based philosophically. The Hospital offers a program only for adults.

Patient and family aftercare services are available at all Charter Medical Addictive Disease units, emphasizing that recovery from this relentless disease is a continuing process affecting both the patient and his or her family.

MOUNTAIN VIEW RECOVERY CENTER

3001 Scenic Drive
Gadsden, Alabama 35901

(205) 547-1300, 546-9265

Director: James V. Laney
Average Patient Census: 16

Minimum Duration of Treatment: 28-day program
Cost: Verified insurance or cash deposit. Insurance eligible.
Detoxification Offered: Yes
Accreditation: JCAH

Mountain View Recovery Center is a medically supervised treatment program located within a hospital. The program is dedicated to treating the disease of alcoholism and providing medical care, psychological counseling and educational programs for the patient and his or her immediate family. The program is not an isolation ward, locked away from the rest of the hospital, nor is it a custodial program where people are left to sort out their lives on their own terms.

Mountain View is staffed by specially trained personnel who understand the disease of alcoholism and have a genuine concern for the patient's recovery.

GULF SHORES RETREAT CENTERS, INC.

P.O. Box 833
Gulf Shores, Alabama 36542

(205) 540-7320

Director: Jacob H. Clemens

Average Patient Census: 12
Minimum Duration of Treatment: 5 days
Cost: $75–165 per day
Detoxification Offered: Not applicable
Accreditation: Not applicable

Gulf Shores Retreat Centers, Pine Lodge, is a private, nonprofit facility designed to offer special services to members of the helping professions and people in recovery from the disease of addiction and their adult family members. Individual retreats are offered, designed to provide persons with a period of "time out" in order to reevaluate their life direction and career or to review their program of recovery and the Twelve Steps. The suggested minimum of stay for individual retreats is 5 days.

Guests are guided by professionals using a holistic approach to teaching better life-styles and concentrating on health, nutrition, exercise, meditation techniques, relaxation and review of spirituality. Pine Lodge is designed with serenity and peace in mind, and is located on Mobile Bay, with acres of lawn and woods and numerous outdoor activities involving nature. There are miles of beaches and a pier and boat house for fishing, swimming and boating.

Professional retreats are also offered, dealing with the problems of fatigue and frustration that lead to or result from burnout/stress, along with retreats that specialize in dealing with problems that lead to chemical abuse or problems from unresolved grief. Additionally provided are Staff Developments for alcohol/drug and mental health centers, plus bi-monthly seminars on topics relating to recovery, addiction and spirituality, with a monthly 4-day seminar on burnout for members of the helping professions. There are, as well, holiday retreats from December 21 through January 1 for professionals and recovering persons.

Gulf Shores is not a primary treatment center and does not provide detoxification, diagnostic or medical services. However, arrangements can be made for physical/psychological services with local professionals. This facility is designed for people in recovery and those coming out of inpatient residential programs who need more time and guidance in gaining stability prior to returning to their life-styles.

BROOKWOOD RECOVERY CENTER—MOBILE

Newman Road
P.O. Box 91174
Mobile, Alabama 36691

(205) 633-0900, Crisis Line
(205) 633-0906, Business Line

Director: Jerry Crowder

Average Patient Census: 40 beds
Minimum Duration of Treatment: alcoholism, 28 days; chemical dependency, 42 days
Cost: Approximately $6,600 for 28 days. Insurance eligible.
Detoxification Offered: Yes
Accreditation: JCAH

The treatment program at Brookwood Recovery Center—Mobile is designed to treat the total person and to restore him to comfortable sobriety in which he is able to choose not to drink or use mood-altering chemicals and is able to resume a healthy, productive way of life. The patient is assisted in arresting the condition and helped to develop a motivation based primarily on reason. In all cases, the goal is the achievement and maintenance of total abstinence from alcohol and other chemicals.

A therapeutic community approach is used in which every employee, from the groundskeeper to the counselors, plays a part in the physical, mental, emotional, spiritual and social rehabilitation of the patient. All aspects of the program are supervised by experienced professionals certified in the treatment of alcoholism and chemical dependency.

Brookwood—Mobile recognizes the effectiveness of AA, especially in the patient's spiritual growth. Meetings are hosted at the center, and patients are strongly encouraged to become members.

A family treatment program is also offered, with individual as well as conjoint counseling, to ensure that all those involved fully comprehend the task that lies ahead. Family members live at the center for 1 week of therapy and education while the patient is a resident.

As a part of Brookwood—Mobile's never-ending commitment to the patient, a 2-year Continuing-Care Program is provided to assist in the successful return to home, community and job.

CHARTER SOUTHLAND HOSPITAL

P.O. Box 7897
251 Cox Street
Mobile, Alabama 36690

(205) 432-8811

Director: Art Dumont, M.D.

Average Patient Census: 24 beds
Minimum Duration of Treatment: 30 days
Cost: Varies; available on request. Insurance eligible.
Detoxification Offered: Yes
Accreditation: JCAH

The program at Charter Southland Hospital offers medically supervised detoxification, if necessary, and individual, group and family counseling as part of the holistic (multidisciplinary) approach toward effectively treating the disease of addiction. All patients are also encouraged to participate in activities therapy and didactic lectures. These programs are AA/NA based philosophically. The Hospital offers a program only for adults.

Patient and family aftercare services are available at all Charter Medical Addictive Disease units, emphasizing that recovery from this relentless disease is a continuing process affecting both the patient and his or her family.

BROOKWOOD RECOVERY CENTER—BIRMINGHAM

Albritton Road
P.O. Box 128
Warrior, Alabama 35180

(205) 877-1740, Crisis Line
(205) 647-1945, Business Line

Director: Morris B. Hamilton, Jr.
Average Patient Census: 82 beds (detox, 8; residential, 74)

Minimum Duration of Treatment: alcoholism, 28 days; chemical dependency, 42 days
Cost: Approximately $7,000 for 30 days. Insurance eligible.
Detoxification Offered: Yes
Accreditation: JCAH

The Brookwood Recovery Center treatment program is designed to treat the total person and restore him or her to a comfortable sobriety in which there is a choice not to drink, as well as the ability to resume a healthy, productive way of life. The goal is to help the patient achieve and maintain total abstinence from alcohol and all other mood-altering chemicals.

Detoxification is provided under the direct supervision of the medical director. There is professional 24-hour coverage 365 days each year by registered nurses. Routine detoxification occurs at the center; acute-care detoxification is done at Brookwood Medical Center.

After detoxification the patient is transferred into a minimum 28-day inpatient, residential, alcoholism rehabilitation program that includes the following services on a daily basis: group therapy, individual therapy, family therapy, AA study groups, AA meetings, didactic groups utilizing films, lectures, videotapes, audiotapes, special lectures, study halls and recreation activities. Patients are allowed to have visitors on Sunday afternoons by prearrangement with the staff. Evaluations of patients' progress are done by the professional staff each week. When clinically indicated, patients are provided with a complete psychological evaluation by a licensed psychologist. Referrals are made to appropriate agencies and professionals as indicated. One week of the average 4-week stay is devoted to Family Week, wherein family members or significant others are invited to come to the center and participate in an intense program of group, individual, conjoint and didactic therapy and alcoholism education.

Upon completion of residential care, the patient is transferred to the Continuing-Care Program. Patients are urged to avail themselves of the full 2 years of supportive aftercare services, including regular group therapy, individual therapy, conjoint therapy and other services as they are determined needed by their Continuing-Care counselor and the patients themselves. Recharge Weekends are offered to patients at intervals throughout the 2-year program.

Brookwood Recovery Center is recognized nationally by business and industry for its impressive record in the treatment of alcoholism in the workplace.

Arkansas

CHARTER VISTA HOSPITAL

P.O. Box 1906
4253 Crossover Road
Fayetteville, Arkansas 72701

(501) 521-5731

Director: John Ezell

Average Patient Census: 20 beds
Minimum Duration of Treatment: 21 days
Cost: Varies; available on request. Insurance eligible.
Detoxification Offered: Yes
Accreditation: JCAH

The program at Charter Vista Hospital offers medically supervised detoxification, if necessary, and individual, group and family counseling as part of the holistic (multidisciplinary) approach toward effectively treating the disease of addiction. All patients are also encouraged to participate in activities therapy and didactic lectures. These programs are AA/NA based philosophically. The hospital offers a program only for adults.

Patient and family aftercare services are available at all Charter Medical Addictive Disease units, emphasizing that recovery from this relentless disease is a continuing process affecting both the patient and his or her family.

OZARK MOUNTAIN ALCOHOL RESIDENTIAL TREATMENT CENTER

508 North Vine
Harrison, Arkansas 72601

(501) 741-1212

Director: Chuck Clark
Average Patient Census: 10

Minimum Duration of Treatment: 28 days
Cost: Based on ability to pay. Insurance eligible.
Detoxification Offered: Yes
Accreditation: Arkansas Office of Alcohol and Drug Abuse Prevention

The Center, located in the town of Harrison in the beautiful mountain country of northwest Arkansas, is open to anyone who has a problem with drinking and who wants to live without alcohol.

Admission requirements are that the individual is without psychosis, has a primary diagnosis of alcoholism, is 18 years or older and comes voluntarily for treatment.

The 28-day program includes group and individual therapy, group and individual counseling, recreational activities, job preparation and introduction to AA groups and their recovery program.

The fee is established by each individual's circumstances on a sliding scale; private and group health insurance as well as Medicaid and Medicare may be utilized, and no one will be refused admission because of race, creed, color, sex or economic status.

The Center is a nonprofit organization supported by donations and government funding.

DECISION POINT

902 Caudle Avenue
P.O. Box 1174
Springdale, Arkansas 72764

(501) 756-1060

Director: Russell Guirl
Average Patient Census: Maximum 25 clients, residential

Minimum Duration of Treatment: 31 days to 6 months
Cost: Based on ability to pay; no one denied admission due to inability to pay. Not insurance eligible.
Detoxification Offered: Yes
Accreditation: Certified by the State of Arkansas

Decision Point is a private, nonprofit corporation engaged in the delivery of Intermediate Care Alcoholism Rehabilitation Treatment services to male problem drinkers/alcoholics and outpatient drug-treatment drug abusers. It is governed by a board of directors who are representative of the area served.

These services are provided by carefully selected staff members who have been certified by the Arkansas Certification Board for Alcoholism Counselors as competent in the alcoholism field. Individual treatment plans are utilized for each client's recovery program, and while any number of the various psychosocial treatment modalities may be incorporated into this plan, the principles and philosophies of the AA program are adhered to in the overall treatment efforts.

Other necessary services not directly provided by Decision Point's staff (medical, psychiatric, legal, etc.) are readily available at other nearby human service agencies through affiliate or referral service agreements. Antabuse (disulfiram) maintenance is available at the client's request, provided there has been a proper evaluation of the client prior to the initiation of such chemotherapy.

Although the maximum period allowed for the residential portion of treatment is 6 months, optimum effectiveness has been found to be attained at 45 to 60 days, followed by extended care (nonresidential) for 3 to 6 months. All fees are based on ability to pay, with the client's individual circumstances taken into account; however, no one is denied admission and/or services because of inability to pay.

A staff member or a designated, qualified volunteer is on duty at each unit 24 hours a day.

Illinois

LIGHTHOUSE/McLEAN COUNTY ALCOHOL AND DRUG ASSISTANCE UNIT, INC.

702 West Chestnut Street
Bloomington, Illinois 61701

(309) 827-6026

Director: Russell J. Hagen

Average Patient Census: 14
Minimum Duration of Treatment: 28 days
Cost: $71 per day. Insurance eligible.
Detoxification Offered: Nonmedical
Accreditation: JCAH

Lighthouse is a comprehensive alcohol and drug treatment facility offering social-setting detoxification, residential rehabilitation and outpatient and aftercare services. A private, nonprofit organization, Lighthouse provides programs that are operated in a nonhospital, freestanding facility, with services available to males and females 14 years of age and older.

All clients receive a thorough screening and diagnostic interview prior to admission. The Social Setting Detoxification Program (4 beds) provides a supervised residential setting for individuals who are experiencing only early-stage withdrawal. The Residential Program (16 beds) provides a structured therapeutic environment.

Outpatient services include individual, group and family services. Aftercare groups for individuals completing the outpatient or residential program are also provided. All services are provided by staff members, who have appropriate academic background and/or are certified by the Illinois Alcoholism Counselor Certification Board.

PARKSIDE LODGE OF CHAMPAIGN-URBANA

809 A West Church Street
Champaign, Illinois 61820

(217) 398-8616

Director: Ann Fry, M.S.W.
Average Patient Census: 20 beds

Minimum Duration of Treatment:
Average 4 weeks plus detox
Cost: Detox, $193 per day; treatment, $150 per day. Insurance eligible.
Detoxification Offered: Yes
Accreditation: JCAH

Parkside Lodge of Champaign-Urbana offers residential treatment for the adult alcoholic and/or substance abuser. A specially trained staff provides confidential preadmission screening and extensive evaluation on admission to ensure that patients and families receive the most efficient and cost-effective level of care. Therefore, the length and specific makeup of treatment depend on individual and family needs.

Multiple treatment modalities include medical/psychiatric evaluation and treatment; psychological testing; individual, group, family and employer counseling; educational lectures; films and discussion and a comprehensive family program. During treatment, patients as well as family members and friends are encouraged to participate in AA, Al-Anon, Alateen and other self-help groups in order that recovery may continue after discharge through active involvement in these groups.

Additionally, after discharge, patients and family are involved in an Aftercare Program, usually in the form of a weekly support group that meets for a minimum of 12 weeks.

Parkside Lodge also offers outpatient sevices, such as evaluations of alcohol and drug use and specialized individual and group counseling.

PRAIRIE CENTER FOR SUBSTANCE ABUSE

122 West Hill Street
P.O. Box 1501, Champaign, Illinois 61820

(217) 356-7562

Director: Larry L. Wilms

Minimum Duration of Treatment: 28 to 44 days
Cost: $75 per day. Insurance eligible.
Detoxification Offered: Yes
Accreditation: Licensed by the State of Illinois

The Prairie Center for Substance Abuse is a nonprofit organization that utilizes programs of planned intervention to aid those individuals affected by alcoholism, including families, employers and other significant persons.

The residential treatment program has a variety of treatment approaches to interrupt the destructive life-style of the alcoholic. The person is assisted in establishing a healthy approach to living through counseling, therapy, education and emotional support in a homelike environment. The program relies heavily upon the involvement of the resident in AA during the treatment period and recommends long-term maintenance in AA. Family involvement, including participation in Al-Anon, is recommended in this and all other phases of treatment.

A nonmedical social-setting detoxification unit is maintained to assist intoxicated persons in the physical withdrawal from alcohol. Outpatient care as well as a Youth Outreach Program are offered by this facility. Aftercare involves continuing support of individuals who have utilized the services of this center, and periodic contacts are made for 1 year after treatment.

CHICAGO LAKESHORE HOSPITAL
ALCOHOL AND DRUG ABUSE TREATMENT PROGRAM

4840 North Marine Drive
Chicago, Illinois 60640

(312) 878-9700

Director: Monte Meldman, M.D.
Average Patient Census: 14

Minimum Duration of Treatment: 10–28 days
Cost: Fee established by hospital. Insurance eligible.
Detoxification Offered: Yes
Accreditation: JCAH

The Alcohol and Drug Abuse Treatment Program at Chicago Lakeshore Hospital includes medical detoxification and inpatient rehabilitation programs of 10 days with a 6-month aftercare program, and 28 days with 3 months of aftercare.

Admission is available on a 24-hour basis, and alcohol- and drug-dependent adults, as well as adolescents and children, are accepted for assessment and treatment.

The inpatient program provides the following therapeutic elements within each patient's weekly schedule: individual and group counseling, employer interviews, family sessions, feelings group, relaxation training, exercise program, music therapy, Spouse and Souse group, Saturday family program, family communication exercises, movies and seminars and AA, NA, CA and Al-Anon meetings.

The hospital's accredited school provides classrooms for adolescents, and the lakefront setting accommodates outdoor picnics and sports.

Outpatient services are available, with individual, group and family counseling. Staff is available to provide evaluation and referral services at no charge.

GRANT HOSPITAL ALCOHOLISM PROGRAM

550 West Webster Avenue
Chicago, Illinois 60614

(312) 883-3925

Director: Ron Del Ciello
Average Patient Census: 18

Minimum Duration of Treatment: Variable length of stay; average of 21 days
Cost: Current hospital rates. Insurance eligible.
Detoxification Offered: Yes
Accreditation: JCAH

The Grant Hospital Alcoholism Program offers comprehensive levels of care tailored to the individual needs of each patient. Treatment includes close involvement with AA.

The inpatient unit is a 21-bed hospital program that mobilizes medical, nutritional, psychological and spiritual resources to help alcoholics implement a plan to manage the problems that will complicate recovery from the disease of alcoholism. Because of a one-to-one staff-to-patient ratio, individualized attention is assured. Services include detoxification, individual and group counseling, patient education, an introduction to AA provided by recovering volunteers and a family recovery program.

The outpatient program provides counseling for persons in the initial and advanced stages of recovery. Evaluations are provided for persons seeking assistance for alcohol-related problems and for referrals from court for DUI. An intensive 4-week outpatient rehabilitation program is designed for alcoholics not requiring hospitalization. Basic and advanced counseling groups help alcoholics further develop skills for maintaining quality sobriety.

An intervention program assists family members in their own recovery as well as motivating the alcoholic to treatment. Other family services include individual, couples, family and group counseling. Family members of patients involved in the inpatient or intensive outpatient programs participate in the family recovery program held from 9:00 A.M. to 3:00 P.M. on 3 consecutive Saturdays.

Assistance is available for designing and implementing employee assistance programs. The services include consultation, training and assessment/referral services.

The Clinical Training Program for Alcoholism Counselors is a certificate program comprised of lectures, clinical supervision groups and practicum experience. Educational and training services are available for professionals.

MERCY HOSPITAL AND MEDICAL CENTER ALCOHOLISM TREATMENT PROGRAM

Stevenson Expressway at King Drive
Chicago, Illinois 60616

(312) 567-2487

Director: Fr. Robert Shannon

Average Patient Census: 12
Minimum Duration of Treatment: 20–28 days
Cost: $329 per day. Insurance eligible.
Detoxification Offered: Yes
Accreditation: JCAH

The Mercy program is a comprehensive multidisciplinary treatment program based on the most advanced medical and therapeutic dynamics for recovery from alcoholism and drug abuse, directed toward meeting the total needs of an individual in a manner that recognizes the uniqueness, worth and dignity of each person.

The restoration of improved physiological functioning is the aim of the detoxification phase, including medical evaluation, and lasts from 3 to 5 days. This is followed by the rehabilitation phase, which focuses on helping the substance abuser (a) come to terms with problems stemming directly from the dependency and (b) to take steps to deal with these and formulate a plan of action for sustained recovery after treatment. This program encompasses a broad spectrum of treatment modalities, including communication workshops, individual counseling, activities therapy, lectures, yoga, group therapy, AA meetings and feedback group with videotape equipment.

Families, a vital part of the patient's recovery, are included in lectures, interviews, communication exercises and Al-Anon and Alateen. An outpatient program, which the patient enters after rehabilitation, is extensive and designed to complement the patient's AA program but not substitute for it. Continued contact after treatment assures continuity of care.

NEW DAY CENTERS INC.
HYDE PARK COMMUNITY HOSPITAL

5800 South Stoney Island
Chicago, Illinois 60637

(312) 643-9200, ext. 275

Director: Margo Deane
Average Patient Census: 19

Minimum Duration of Treatment: 21–28 days
Cost: $8,000 for 28 days. Insurance eligible.
Detoxification Offered: Yes
Accreditation: JCAH

Following admission into Hyde Park Community Hospital's Alcoholism Service, patients are watched closely to avoid medical complications as they withdraw from alcohol. In addition to their medical care, patients participate in individual, family and group counseling. They also attend planned exercise sessions at the YMCA, community activities, AA meetings and psychodrama sessions.

Improvement of communication skills is an important part of treatment as patients learn to get in touch with their feelings and express them appropriately. The unit also supplies training in relaxation skills.

Recovery from alcoholism begins with this 28 days, but the staff of the center feels that the final withdrawal phase may last from 6 months to 2 years. During this time the outpatient program helps the patient focus on sobriety objectives and emotional growth, the therapy considered as an outgrowth of the inpatient program. Outpatient support leads into an aftercare program wherein each patient makes a 6-month contract, stipulating their plans for staying sober with the help of a therapist, who makes contact once a month to discuss progress or problems along the path to complete adjustment to sober living.

SHERIDAN ROAD HOSPITAL
RUSH–PRESBYTERIAN–SAINT LUKE'S MEDICAL CENTER

6130 North Sheridan Road
Chicago, Illinois 60660

(312) 743-2600, ext. 172

Director: Lewis A. Lippner
Average Patient Census: 16

Minimum Duration of Treatment: 21 days, variable
Cost: $400 per day, excluding physician. Insurance eligible.
Detoxification Offered: Yes
Accreditation: JCAH within Department of Psychiatry

The Alcohol and Substance Abuse Program at Rush–Presbyterian–Saint Luke's Medical Center emphasizes warm, supportive nurturing, and the style of care is personal, with each patient assigned a physician, primary nurse and care counselor, as well as specialized care for alcoholics with psychiatric problems.

Families are included in the program plan, learning about alcoholism, receiving emotional support and discovering ways to achieve emotional health for the whole family. Employers are also invited to participate.

The treatment team begins with a consultation to explore the individual's needs. Inpatient care in a community setting encourages a feeling of belonging. Group, family and individual therapy; films; lectures and recreation are included, along with the critically important meetings of AA and Al-Anon.

Aftercare involves continual personal and phone contact. This facility also offers community seminars on alcoholism and related topics, as well as periodic workshops for professional groups.

ALEXIAN BROTHERS ALCOHOLISM TREATMENT CENTER

800 West Biesterfield Road
Elk Grove Village, Illinois 60007

(312) 981-3524

Director: Nancy Peterson, Coordinator

Average Patient Census: 20
Minimum Duration of Treatment: Medical detox, 2–5 days; rehab 3-weeks
Cost: $270 per day. Insurance eligible.
Detoxification Offered: Yes
Accreditation: JCAH

The emphasis of the program at Alexian Brothers Alcoholism Treatment Center lies in education and group interaction. Lectures, topic discussions and group processes are offered daily in a structured program. Forms of treatment include psychodrama, relaxation techniques, movies and recreational therapy and the development of crafts and hobbies. Patients are introduced to AA, Al-Anon and Alateen through meetings held at the Center, enabling the patient and family members to become familiar with this vital recovery support before discharge.

Each patient in the unit has his own physician, either a staff psychiatrist or his general physician in consultation with a staff psychiatrist. In addition, each patient has his own counselor, who is responsible for taking histories, helping with problem solving, setting treatment goals and counseling with the patient and his family. The unit is staffed at all times by registered nurses whose specialty is alcoholic rehabilitation, and an activity therapist schedules recreational activities on and off the grounds. Spiritual care is offered by a member of the Pastoral Care staff in group-discussion form, as well as on an individual basis when requested.

Every patient has a phone, as well as visiting and mail privileges, and passes to leave the hospital grounds may be granted on the second and third Sundays of the patient's stay. Plans for discharge reflect the strong commitment of the staff to make referrals that best ensure continuous recovery, and aftercare treatment is considered an essential part of the program. A 6-week primary outpatient treatment program is also available.

Programs for spouses including intervention training are available.

RIVEREDGE HOSPITAL ALCOHOLISM TREATMENT UNIT

8311 West Roosevelt Road
Forest Park, Illinois 60130

(312) 771-7000
(312) 771-6278, Crisis Line

Director: Thomas F. Martin

Average Patient Census: 9
Minimum Duration of Treatment: 28 days, with 15 weeks aftercare
Cost: $300 per day. Insurance eligible.
Detoxification Offered: Yes
Accreditation: JCAH

Riveredge Hospital evaluates persons wishing to enter the alcoholism treatment and rehabilitation program on their sincerity and willingness to cooperate and benefit from the program. The patient does not necessarily have to admit to being an alcoholic, but must recognize that there is a drinking problem affecting his or her life in some way.

The program includes counseling, alcoholism education, family groups and activities, and AA programs. Program goals are stated as: interruption of the drinking habit, achievement and maintenance of sobriety, complete medical management of illness-related symptoms, the education about and acceptance of alcoholism as a disease, the learning of constructive alternatives for coping with problems, and an aftercare and follow-up treatment following discharge that will aid the alcohol abuser in maintaining sobriety and reintegration into the community.

SOJOURN HOUSE, INC.

565 North Turner Avenue
Freeport, Illinois 61032

(815) 232-5121

Director: David L. Laney, A.C.S.W.
Average Patient Census: 22

Minimum Duration of Treatment: Detox unit, 2–4 days; residential program, 4 weeks
Cost: Detox, $110 per day; residential, $168 per day. Insurance eligible.
Detoxification Offered: Yes
Accreditation: JCAH

Sojourn House has developed a variety of strategies and activities to move toward the goal of eradicating the effects of alcoholism on the alcoholic, the family of the alcoholic and other victims, such as employers.

The detoxification program offers medical care and alcohol education and counseling to prepare the individual for treatment entry. This is followed by a residential treatment program of intensive 4-week education and counseling, providing a structured setting for persons unable to maintain sobriety in their usual environment. A family treatment program is offered in conjunction with this program as well as with the outpatient program.

Sojourn offers a structured outpatient counseling program that provides primary treatment day care and evening service, as well as aftercare counseling services. The structured outpatient program is of 4 weeks' duration.

Sojourn offers a Halfway House with a long-term program of education and counseling with a vocational focus. The average stay is 14 weeks in a structured therapeutic environment designed for the chronic alcoholic who requires long-term treatment.

Sojourn House strives to operate in the most cost-efficient and effective manner, and no one is refused services solely on the basis of inability to pay. Programs are organized so as to be eligible for a variety of reimbursement systems, such as state and federal grants, purchase of care contracts and private insurance.

ALCOHOLISM TREATMENT CENTER
Ingalls Memorial Hospital

One Ingalls Drive
Harvey, Illinois 60426

1-800-543-6543

Director: Robert L. Burns
Average Patient Census: Intermediate care, 32; adolescent program, 16

Minimum Duration of Treatment: Detox, 3–7 days
Cost: Detox, $275 per day; ICS and ACDP, $300 per day; varying fees for other ATC programs. Insurance eligible.
Detoxification Offered: Yes
Accreditation: JCAH

The Alcoholism Treatment Center of Ingalls Memorial Hospital is a comprehensive service based upon the most recent technology of alcoholism treatment. The center is composed of a 24-hour Screening and Diagnostic Service, an 18-bed Special Care Service (detoxification), a 32-bed Intermediate Care Service and a 16-bed Adolescent Chemical Dependency Service operating on a graduated length of stay. Also offered are intensive outpatient programs for adults and adolescents, as well as other outpatient services that offer a variety of programs to recovering alcoholics and chemically dependent adolescents and their families.

The center also includes a Diagnostic and Research Service Center that does neuropsychological and psychological testing of patients and provides the latest methods of biofeedback training.

The Ingalls ATC is based on a new technology of alcoholism and chemical dependency treatment that has evolved from special applied-research programs within the center, and this system allows for greater accountability and higher levels of quality control.

The Ingalls ATC specializes in industrial referrals, school and court referrals and referrals from physicians of patients who suffer specific medical complications related to alcoholism.

The Adolescent Chemical Dependency programs at Ingalls provide intervention treatment and aftercare services for both outpatients and those adolescents who require an inpatient program to begin the recovery process, and are designed to meet the special needs of young people age 12 to 21. In treatment, families are encouraged to participate in various counseling, educational and support groups. A diagnostic screening can be arranged by calling (312) 596-HELP.

ARC-CHICAGO

1776 Moon Lake Boulevard
Hoffman Estates, Illinois 60194

(312) 882-0070

Director: Frank J. Hall
Average Patient Census: 85 beds

Minimum Duration of Treatment: Adults, 28 days; adolescent residential evaluation, 10–14 days; adolescent treatment, 28–42 days
Cost: Available on request. Insurance eligible.
Accreditation: JCAH

ARC-Chicago is one of seven ARC facilities nationwide devoted exclusively to the treatment of alcoholism and other chemical dependencies in adults, adolescents and their families. The program begins with an evaluation to establish appropriateness for admission. Further evaluation is conducted after admission on both a psychological and a physical level, after which a personalized treatment plan is jointly developed by staff and client.

Education about the nature of chemical dependency, an in-depth study of AA and the Twelve Steps, as well as individual and group therapy help the patient understand the realities of the illness and take responsibility for his or her own recovery.

The adolescent program contains the same components but begins with a 2-week evaluation period and involves family, friends, school personnel and others. ARC-Chicago also employs a teacher who coordinates academic studies with work being missed at school. Length of treatment averages 4 weeks; however, like the adult program, it is determined by the patient's progress.

It is ARC's philosophy that chemical dependency is a family illness, so for their own recovery, family members join in the program for 1 week of the patient's stay, learning opportunities in the dynamics of recovery, as well as in Al-Anon and Alateen as modalities of family growth and recovery, the setting of meaningful goals and the beginning of the process of reconciliation.

An aftercare program is provided for those who successfully complete treatment and includes the family. This, in addition to AA and/or Al-Anon, provides the basis for post-treatment growth and support.

CAREUNIT
Skokie Valley Community Hospital

9600 Gross Point Road
Skokie, Illinois 60076

(312) 677-3910

Director: Sheryl Smith
Average Patient Census: 22

Minimum Duration of Treatment: Detox, 3–5 days; additional program, 21 days
Cost: Detox, $269 per day; program, $254 per day. Insurance eligible.
Detoxification Offered: Yes
Accreditation: HSA, JCAH

The intensive rehabilitation program at the CareUnit, Skokie Valley Community Hospital, begins when the patient is medically stable following detoxification. Patients attend formal rehabilitation sessions for approximately 6½ hours daily. Didactic lecture sessions, followed by discussion periods, are the educational core of the program.

Rehabilitation sessions emphasize identity, admission of problem, alternate behavior and attitudinal patterns, setting priorities, methods of continuing sobriety and new patterns of problem solving. A clinical psychologist or psychological assistant conducts group sessions for the alcoholic and the family, and the alcoholism therapist conducts a series of therapy groups for expression of feelings and goals. A weekly family session is held for family and significant others.

Patients are introduced to AA through models, such as Step Study, Panel, and Participation Meeting. Recreational-occupational therapy techniques are also part of the program.

Outpatient follow-up continues for 2 to 6 months, and family members return once a week for outpatient counseling sessions.

RYERSON CENTER

737 South Fifth Street
Springfield, Illinois 62703

(217) 544-3396

Director: Art Ritter

Average Patient Census: 12
Minimum Duration of Treatment: 28 days
Cost: Sliding scale. Insurance eligible.
Detoxification Offered: Yes
Accreditation: JCAH

The Ryerson Center believes that people abuse alcohol for a variety of reasons and that they also seek treatment for a variety of reasons. They offer a program, therefore, that utilizes many different modalities to educate, and counsel the patient, to improve general health and to give emotional support, with each individual receiving a program tailored to fit individual needs.

The Center works extensively with AA, with transportation provided to the variety of meetings available in Springfield. In addition, the health component of the treatment includes relaxation and activity therapy, lectures, group discussions and individual counseling. Assertiveness workshops are one of the educational tools employed to improve communication skills and to encourage the sharing of experiences and the giving of mutual support. Residents of the Ryerson Program help each other to gain a better self-image and open the door for self-motivation, an essential ingredient for successful recovery.

In addition to the inpatient program, should the individual require further inpatient support as he or she seeks to reenter the work force, a 28-bed Ryerson Center Halfway House is available for aftercare. There are also three separate outpatient programs including: Options, which offers recovering alcoholics individual, family and group counseling; McCambridge House Women's Center, which offers counseling to the female alcoholic; and Phoenix 7 Drug Abuse Program, which provides individual and group counseling for the individual who has problems with drugs other than alcohol.

LAKE COUNTY ALCOHOLISM TREATMENT CENTER
LAKE COUNTY HEALTH DEPARTMENT
MENTAL HEALTH DIVISION

2400 Belvedere Road
Waukegan, Illinois 60085

(312) 689-6540, 689-6541

Director: Edward S. Ravine, M.A., C.C.D.C.
Average Patient Census: 18 (detox, 9; rehab, 9)

Minimum Duration of Treatment: Detox, 4 days (patient must be discharged on fifth hospital day); rehab, 14 days
Cost: Detox, $150 per day; rehab, $100 per day. Insurance eligible.
Detoxification Offered: Yes
Accreditation: Licensed by the State of Illinois

Upon arrival of a prospective patient at Lake County, his or her medical and physical condition is evaluated by the nurse on duty, and the patient is seen as soon as possible by the physician, who determines necessary laboratory tests. Detoxification is closely monitored; withdrawal symptoms are treated with medication, though tranquilizing drugs are used minimally and discontinued as early as possible.

Patients are seen in group therapy as soon as they are physically stable and encouraged to talk out their fears and anxieties with staff and peers. In addition, they receive education on the disease of alcoholism and the mandatory therapy attempts to stimulate motivation toward sobriety. Educational lectures and movies are held in the evening, and individual counseling is available as necessary. Antabuse is encouraged for those individuals for whom it is deemed appropriate.

The 14-day Rehabilitation Program is available for selected patients following detoxification and includes education, counseling and AA meetings. Family involvement is strongly encouraged at this time.

Referrals include rehabilitation in another facility, outpatient counseling at Lake County, psychological and psychiatric treatment where indicated and participation in Lake County's Aftercare Program for follow-up in those cases where no further referral is made.

Indiana

CHEMICAL DEPENDENCY TREATMENT PROGRAM
Saint John's Medical Center

2015 Jackson Street
Anderson, Indiana 46014

(317) 646-8383

Director: George Horaitis, M.A., C.A.C., C.D.C.

Average Patient Census: 14
Minimum Duration of Treatment: 21–28 days
Cost: $135 per day, plus physician's ancillary charge. Insurance eligible.
Detoxification Offered: Yes
Accreditation: JCAH

Saint John's Medical Center Chemical Dependency Treatment Program provides a comprehensive inpatient rehabilitation program designed to meet the needs of chemically dependent persons and their families. The program is highly individualized to meet the needs of each patient.

One aspect of this program is the specialized intervention service element, which is designed to help families help the alcoholic who does not want help. During rehabilitation, other modalities include individual, group and family counseling, lectures, seminars, recreational therapy and pastoral/spiritual therapy. Also included are Step groups, both AA and NA, relapse-prevention planning and ongoing medical management.

In March 1985 the program moved into a $4-million freestanding facility that features atriums with multilevel gardens, an aerobic exercise area, day rooms with fireplaces and dining and family areas. The facility was designed to promote patient dignity and self-respect and to improve confidentiality.

A special week-long program is provided for families, as well as a special service for children. If clinically indicated, the entire family can be admitted for intensive family treatment. "The Chemical Dependency Program—where recovery begins with love" is this facility's watchword.

CAMERON TREATMENT CENTER

416 East Maumee Street
Angola, Indiana 46703

(219) 665-2141

Director: Wes Eral

Average Patient Census: 10
Minimum Duration of Treatment: 28 days
Cost: $135 per day. Insurance eligible.
Detoxification Offered: Yes
Accreditation: State-accredited

The medical management phase of treatment at Cameron Treatment Center involves admission, evaluation and development of treatment plans. Routine admission procedures include a complete medical examination and, if required, close observation by medical and nursing staffs to ensure complete and safe withdrawal from alcohol or drugs. Psychological and sociological assessments are conducted to determine the patient's appropriateness for dependency treatment.

There are 3 daily lectures, many given by recovering persons, on the nature of the illness, and each patient is assigned to a therapy group that meets daily with their counselor. Through a supportive-confrontive process, patients are encouraged to relate to themselves and others as feeling persons and to identify destructive behavior. The intensity of these sessions helps patients to learn healthy ways to recognize and deal with feelings. Peer-group pressure teaches behavior modification, growth in self-insight and self-acceptance. Counselors assist patients in building trust in the therapy process and develop individual treatment plans. Chaplains help patients with the impairment of their spiritual relationships.

Family therapy is held to be essential, and the family is encouraged to spend a week during treatment sharing in all aspects of the program. Through extensive education and intensive group therapy, families learn that they are not alone with their problems and understand their roles in the patient's past behavior, present progress and future growth. An individualized aftercare program is developed with each patient and family.

SERENITY HALL
MARGARET MARY COMMUNITY HOSPITAL

321 Mitchell Road
Batesville, Indiana 47006

(812) 934-6630

Director: Carolyn Bruder, A.C.S.W.

Average Patient Census: 25
Minimum Duration of Treatment: 28 days
Cost: $3,800. Insurance eligible.
Detoxification Offered: Yes
Accreditation: JCAH

The program at Serenity Hall, Margaret Mary Community Hospital, is a 28-day treatment that includes detoxification. Basically, the program seeks to orient the patient to a new way of life without alcohol. The general educational and training sessions, led or supervised by counselors, consist of films; lectures; and individual, family and group therapy. The program is strongly AA-oriented. AA meetings are held nightly.

Serenity Hall also provides an aftercare program. Patients are encouraged to follow up with this program after treatment.

The only qualifications for admission are that patients have an alcohol/drug-dependency problem and can afford the treatment.

ALCOHOLIC TREATMENT PROGRAM
SAINT MARY'S MEDICAL CENTER

Warrick Hospital
1116 Millis Avenue
Boonville, Indiana 47601

(812) 897-0110

Director: Matthew Maguire
Average Patient Census: 24, age 16 and over

Minimum Duration of Treatment: 3–4 weeks
Cost: Hospital daily rate. Insurance eligible.
Detoxification Offered: Yes, admitted through Emergency Room, Warrick Hospital
Accreditation: JCAH

The Saint Mary's Medical Center Alcoholic Treatment Program is designed to meet the specific needs, problems and circumstances of the individual.

There are three essentially different dimensions to the program—medical detoxification, inpatient rehabilitation and outpatient treatment. Components of the program include medical diagnosis and treatment, individual counseling, group counseling, educational lectures, films, nutrition, family therapy, family education, employer education, community outreach and self-help therapy. Structured social activities are scheduled. AA meetings are held on the unit, and transportation to AA meetings off the unit is provided.

Outpatient services are offered both at Warrick Hospital and on the Saint Mary's Medical Center campus in Evansville.

In addition to the medical director and his assistants, the unit is staffed by registered nurses, certified alcoholism counselors and ancillary personnel. Psychiatric and psychological evaluations and consultations are available.

KOALA CENTER

2223 Poshard Drive
P.O. Box 1549
Columbus, Indiana 47202

(812) 376-1711

Director: John Solomon

Average Patient Census: 30
Minimum Duration of Treatment: Adults, 30 days
Cost: Available on request. Insurance eligible.
Detoxification Offered: Yes
Accreditation: JCAH

Koala derives its name from the custom among the Aboriginals of Australia of passing the drinking vessel around a circle. Anyone who did not wish to drink said, *"Koala,"* meaning "no drink." Later, that name was given to the little animal, native to Australia, that seldom, if ever, drinks.

Koala is a treatment hospital for alcoholism and drug abuse for both adults and adolescents and believes that alcoholism is a disease that must be treated with the same compassion, dedication and expertise as all other diseases. This facility offers, therefore, a comprehensive, multidisciplinary, individualized treatment plan in a nonjudgmental, stigma-free environment.

The program includes group therapy, family counseling, individual therapy, introduction to AA and NA, psychological testing, psychiatric evaluation, nutrition awareness, leisure counseling and employer involvement.

A 5-day family program is also available to help the family establish its own recovery plan. A 1-year aftercare program is offered that is also available to the community at large, and includes counseling for those needing to make changes in their personal lives and offers marital and family counseling as well.

One of the most frustrating problems in treating alcoholism or drug abuse is dealing with the relapsed individual. This person has already undergone treatment, but for one reason or another has started using drugs or alcohol again. Continued traditional treatment may seem hopeless to the person's family or employer and may prove costly and ineffective as well. Koala Centers developed the Critical Care Rehabilitation Program to reduce the human and financial cost of relapse.

The program for critical-care patients includes participation in special group discussions, lectures, and individual therapy sessions that concentrate on the prevention of future relapse. This program also encourages the involvement of the family and employer in order to improve the potential for a positive outcome.

A special outpatient follow-up program is developed before discharge that will include contact with AA and NA. The patient stays in the CCR program from 3 to 6 weeks, depending on his or her condition and the extent of the relapse. Criteria for admission are determined on an individual basis. The patient does not have to be a previous patient of Koala or White Deer.

RENAISSANCE CENTER FOR ADDICTIONS TREATMENT

600 East Boulevard
Elkhart, Indiana 46514

(219) 522-5522

Director: Robert Eppelein
Average Patient Census: Adults, 28; adolescents, 12

Minimum Duration of Treatment: 28 days
Cost: Detox, $162.50 per day; rehab, $142.50 per day. Insurance eligible.
Detoxification Offered: Yes
Accreditation: JCAH

Renaissance, Center for Addictions Treatment, is a comprehensive addictions-treatment facility offering both inpatient and outpatient care to adults and adolescents. For appropriate patients, a combination of inpatient and outpatient treatment is developed. The program is a Hazelden model and uses a multidisciplinary team. Medical detoxification and aftercare are also offered, as well as necessary medical and psychological testing. Renaissance also has an outpatient Family Program. The average length of stay for the inpatient program is 28 days, and for the outpatient it is 6 weeks.

COUNTERPOINT CENTER OF VALLE VISTA HOSPITAL

898 East Main Street
P.O. Box 304
Greenwood, Indiana 46142

(317) 887-1922

Director: Ed Pannell

Average Patient Census: 40 beds
Minimum Duration of Treatment: 28-day program
Cost: Available on request. Insurance eligible.
Detoxification Offered: Yes
Accreditation: JCAH

CounterPoint Center is a Chemical Dependency Program for adults and adolescents. The center is part of an international network of chemical dependency treatment centers located throughout the United States and Europe.

Chemical dependency is recognized as a primary disorder: chronic, progressive and potentially fatal, and prone to relapse if not properly treated. The disease factor is basic to treatment, which is provided by a multidisciplinary team of skilled professionals, many themselves recovering. All areas of a person's life are affected by chemical dependency. Therefore, the physical, emotional, social and spiritual needs of patients are all addressed through the treatment program.

Detoxification is the first phase of treatment. Following stabilization of acute medical problems, patients begin an intensive program of rehabilitation. The Twelve Steps of AA and NA are emphasized, and patients are expected to have selected an AA or NA group and a temporary sponsor by the time they are to begin the aftercare program. An individualized plan for aftercare is formulated with patient and family during the last week of treatment. Weekly group therapy is provided at no extra cost for 1 year, with a 2-year advisement period.

Family and significant others are included in treatment from the time of admission, with family assessment and couples and family therapy several times each week. Crisis intervention is also available.

For employers, the staff maintains open communications with EAP counselors and supervisors. Employers are included in the treatment process from the beginning, through discharge and into follow-up care.

FAIRBANKS HOSPITAL, INC.

8102 Clearvista Parkway
Indianapolis, Indiana 46256

(317) 849-8222

Director: R. H. Wagener
Average Patient Census: 94 (adolescents, 28; adults, 66)

Minimum Duration of Treatment: 4 weeks plus detox period
Cost: Detox unit, $157 per day; adolescent unit, $159 per day; adult rehab unit, $140 per day; plus ancillary charges. Insurance eligible.
Detoxification Offered: Yes
Accreditation: JCAH

The stated purpose of Fairbanks Hospital is to provide the best possible care for persons with alcohol and other drug problems through an individualized and comprehensive treatment program.

The total treatment concept is implemented by an interdisciplinary team of professionals made up of physicians, psychiatrists, counselors, nurses and a psychologist, all of whom have been specifically trained in the treatment of alcoholism.

After arranging for admission, family members should accompany the patient to Fairbanks, where they will be introduced to the treatment program. Medical evaluation and detoxification, depending on the patient's needs, follows. The recovery program can then begin, and this consists of education; counseling on group, family and individual levels; an introduction to AA; and counseling with the patient's employer if deemed necessary. At the end of this phase, usually 3 weeks, patient and counselor work together on an aftercare plan.

The Fairbanks Outpatient Center is important both to the discharged patient and for those who need supportive care but need not be hospitalized. In recognition of the specialized problems of female alcoholics, Fairbanks has developed a specific Women's Program as an adjunct to the general program.

Fairbanks' 28-bed adolescent unit is the first of its kind in the State of Indiana. The program is 35 days in length.

KOALA ADOLESCENT CENTER

1404 South State Avenue
Indianapolis, Indiana 46203

(317) 783-4084 in Indiana
1-800-622-4711

Director: Sheldon Whinstein

Average Patient Census: 60 beds
Minimum Duration of Treatment: 42 days
Cost: Available on request. Insurance eligible.
Detoxification Offered: Yes
Accreditation: JCAH

Koala derives its name from the custom among the Aboriginals of Australia of passing the drinking vessel around a circle. Anyone who did not wish to drink said, *"Koala,"* meaning "no drink." Later, the name was given to the little animal, native to Australia, that seldom, if ever, drinks.

Millions of adolescents today have a serious problem with alcohol and other drugs, and the Koala Adolescent Center believes that these young people require specialized programs and facilities separate from the adult treatment program. When an entire facility, program and staff are committed to meeting the special needs of the adolescent patient and their family, the incidence and frequency of relapse is greatly diminished. The Center's concentrated programs for adolescents provide therapeutic rehabilitation in a positive environment designed to help develop alternative life-styles and behavior. A new facility is presently under construction and renovation. Built in 1867, it served as a home for Civil War orphans. The battle lines are different now, but the tradition of this facility in helping youth will go on.

This facility opened early in March 1985 and will greatly enhance the care available for adolescents in the United States, and in Indiana in particular.

SOUTHERN INDIANA MENTAL HEALTH CENTER

207 West Thirteenth Street
Jeffersonville, Indiana 47130

(812) 283-4491

Director: Joe B. Brill, M.D.
Average Patient Census: 47 beds for alcohol/drug and psychiatric disorders

Minimum Duration of Treatment:
Inpatient, usually 2 weeks
Cost: $91–103 per day; doctor's fees, $40 per day. Insurance eligible.
Detoxification Offered: Yes
Accreditation: JCAH

Southern Indiana Mental Health Center provides alcoholism treatment services to persons admitted to the program, as well as appropriate services and/or referrals for families.

Specific services include screening for admission; inpatient treatment services; medical detoxification; physical examination; group and individual therapy; AA, Al-Anon and Alateen services; Antabuse therapy; women's group and 5-day partial-hospitalization program. The center also does evaluation for referral to other treatment services within and outside the center and outpatient follow-up.

The center is open for referrals 24 hours a day, although preferred screening times are 9:00 A.M. to 8:30 P.M. on weekdays and 8:30 A.M. to 12:00 noon on Saturdays. Patients can be seen on a walk-in basis, but it is preferable to call for an appointment. Persons in physical distress should be cleared first by the emergency room staff.

KOALA CENTER

1711 Lafayette Avenue
Lebanon, Indiana 46052

(317) 482-3711

Director: Bob Edwards
Average Patient Census: 62

Minimum Duration of Treatment: Adults, 30 days
Cost: Available on request. Insurance eligible.
Detoxification Offered: Yes
Accreditation: JCAH

Koala derives its name from the custom among the Aboriginals of Australia of passing the drinking vessel around a circle. Anyone who did not wish to drink said, *"Koala,"* meaning "no drink." Later, that name was given to the little animal, native to Australia, that seldom, if ever, drinks.

Koala is a treatment hospital for alcoholism and drug abuse for both adults and adolescents and believes that alcoholism is a disease that must be treated with the same compassion, dedication and expertise as all other diseases. This facility offers, therefore, a comprehensive, multidisciplinary, individualized treatment plan in a nonjudgmental, stigma-free environment.

The program includes group therapy, family counseling, individual therapy, introduction to AA and NA, psychological testing, psychiatric evaluation, nutrition awareness, leisure counseling and employer involvement.

A 5-day family program is also available in order to help the family establish its own recovery plan. A 1-year aftercare program is offered that is also available to the community at large and includes counseling for those needing to make changes in their personal lives as well as marital and family counseling.

One of the most frustrating problems in treating alcoholism or drug abuse is dealing with the relapsed individual. This person has already undergone treatment, but for one reason or another has started using drugs or alcohol again. Continued traditional treatment may seem hopeless to the person's family or employer and may prove costly and ineffective as well. Koala Centers developed the Critical Care Rehabilitation Program to reduce the human and financial cost of relapse.

The program for critical-care patients includes participation in special group discussions, lectures and individual therapy sessions that concentrate on the prevention of future relapse. This program also encourages the involvement of the family and employer to improve the potential for a positive outcome.

A special outpatient follow-up program is developed before discharge that will include contact with AA and NA. The patient stays in the CCR program from 3 to 6 weeks depending on his or her condition and the extent of the relapse. Criteria for admission are determined on an individual basis. The patient does not have to be a previous patient of Koala.

Iowa

LINCOLN CENTER

1340 Mount Pleasant Street
Burlington, Iowa 52601

(319) 753-0138

Director: Philip L. Shirely
Average Patient Census: 18

Minimum Duration of Treatment: 3 months
Cost: Sliding fee scale. Not insurance eligible.
Detoxification Offered: No
Accreditation: Iowa Department of Substance Abuse

The residential program at Lincoln Center provides a substance-free therapeutic community for the treatment of men and women having life problems with substance abuse. Treatment is individualized, in a family-like setting.

Residents actively participate in their own treatment and progress through a series of therapeutic levels. Promotion to each level results in increased responsibility and challenges. The intention of the program is to assist persons to obtain independent, substance-free and responsible ways of living.

Families and the person's significant others are strongly encouraged to become part of the individual's treatment.

Lincoln Center is one of a variety of substance abuse programs offered by the Southwest Iowa Council on Alcohol and Drug Dependency Service through whose administration offices, located at Lincoln Center, additional information on their education, consultation and outpatient services may be obtained. Their services include evaluation and assessment, individual and family counseling, information, referral, prevention and emergency services. All services are completely confidential.

SEDLACEK TREATMENT CENTER
MERCY HOSPITAL

701 Tenth Street, S.E.
Cedar Rapids, Iowa 52403

(319) 398-6226

Director: William P. Marsh
Average Patient Census: 55

Minimum Duration of Treatment: No minimum; each patient individually assessed
Cost: Hospital per diem for double room, $181 per day. Insurance eligible.
Detoxification Offered: Yes
Accreditation: JCAH

The Sedlacek Treatment Center's stated objective is to create a setting in which patients and significant others have the opportunity to reestablish self-esteem and raise levels of awareness in order to live satisfying and meaningful lives without the use of mind-altering drugs. The program is composed of five separate, yet highly integrated, components: medical detoxification, comprehensive rehabilitative inpatient treatment, outpatient treatment, aftercare and the family program.

If needed, detoxification, as well as treatment for other extenuating physical problems, is initiated in an atmosphere of acceptance and caring, and under continuous medical supervision. Treatment begins as patients come to recognize that because of chemical abuse their lives have become less than manageable. The therapeutic needs of patients are assessed, and each is assigned to appropriate components of a "Needs Wheel," which includes, in part, the following: self-esteem-development sessions, group therapy, educational audiovisuals and lectures, physical fitness and relaxation training, individual counseling, effective communication training and the AA philosophy and Twelve Steps.

The Outpatient Treatment Program is patterned after the comprehensive inpatient treatment program and includes five 3-hour sessions per week for approximately 12 weeks.

The Family Program is based on recognition that chemical dependency is a family illness that destroys not only the individual but the quality of family life as well. The core of the Family Program is group sessions, and the foundation, as with the inpatient program, is the presentation and discussion of methods for building self-esteem.

Aftercare consists of weekly group therapy sessions in which former patients and their families meet to share feelings and experiences as well as fears, problems and joys.

POWELL III ALCOHOLISM TREATMENT UNIT
Iowa Methodist Medical Center

1200 Pleasant Street
Des Moines, Iowa 50308

(512) 283-6431, 283-6454

Director: Stan M. Haugland, M.D., Medical Director; Dick McCarthy, Program Director

Average Patient Census: 40
Minimum Duration of Treatment: 28 days
Cost: Inpatient, $200 per day. Insurance eligible.
Detoxification Offered: Yes
Accreditation: JCAH

The treatment program at the Powell III ATU is AA oriented, based on the disease concept of alcoholism, with a strong reality-therapy direction and heavy emphasis on group work, on dealing with feelings and on the family program.

The interdisciplinary staff includes medical personnel, nursing staff, alcoholism counselors, social workers, chaplains and a full-time psychologist. Admission requirements are a diagnosis of alcohol or other drug dependence and mental and physical ability to participate in the program. The handicapped are accepted, and psychiatric diagnoses are referred to the psychiatric unit.

The family program consists of Tuesday night lectures and groups, with a pretreatment group and intervention planning. Wednesday is Concerned Person's Day for inpatient, with a full 1-week family program at about week 3 of inpatient stay, as well as a Children's Feelings Group for age 4 to 11.

A full outpatient program is available, with families required to go through treatment with the patient, at a cost of $1,050 per family, which some insurance companies will cover. A new adolescent program is also available with a capacity for eight patients with parents. All patients must have a physician's statement or medical examination to certify appropriateness for outpatient programs.

Referrals come from AA, NA, families, EAPs, courts (commitments accepted), physicians, attorneys, clergy and self.

Powell III has an average outpatient census of thirty couples for a 5-week program of 100 hours at a cost of $20 per hour per couple.

FOREST CITY TREATMENT CENTER

Forest City, Iowa 50436

(515) 582-3113

Average Patient Census: 28

Minimum Duration of Treatment: 35 days
Cost: $4,500. Insurance eligible.
Detoxification Offered: Yes
Accreditation: JCAH

Forest City Treatment Center adheres to the illness concept of chemical dependency and recognizes that chemical dependency interferes with the individual's life in every aspect, thus inhibiting his or her freedom to function. Forest City endeavors to enable the chemically dependent persons and their families to achieve a new life that is chemical-free.

Through physical, emotional and spiritual help, as well as through establishing new guidelines for family relationships and social behavior, the Center offers clients and their families a treatment concept that enables the entire family to overcome the ravages of addiction.

The Center feels that helping the families of chemically dependent persons is imperative. The family is encouraged to spend a week at the Center sharing in all aspects of the program. Through extensive education about alcoholism and its effects on the patient and the family unit, plus intensive group therapy with the patient, the families learn that they are not alone in dealing with their problems and begin to realize their role in the patient's past behavior, present progress and future growth.

ZION TREATMENT CENTER

Rural Route 1
Box 200
Orient, Iowa 50858

(515) 337-5385

Director: George Ratashak

Average Patient Census: 16
Minimum Duration of Treatment: 4–5 weeks
Cost: $300–1,200; sliding scale. Insurance eligible.
Detoxification Offered: No
Accreditation: Iowa State licensure

The Zion treatment program is based on AA's Twelve Step Rehabilitation Program, with concentration on the first through fifth Steps.

The day is divided into morning group assignment sessions, and afternoon group problem sessions, which include lectures and reading from the AA book. Movies are usually shown in the evenings. Zion also offers family counseling.

Since there is no detoxification unit, Zion requires clients to be in a sound state of mind and health before admission.

GORDON CHEMICAL DEPENDENCY CENTER FOR ADOLESCENTS

St. Luke's Medical Center, 2 East
2700 Pierce Street
Sioux City, Iowa 51104

(712) 258-4578

Director: Kermit Dahlen

Average Patient Census: Adolescents (13–19 years of age only), 26
Minimum Duration of Treatment: 45–90 days
Cost: $150 per day. Insurance eligible.
Detoxification Offered: Yes
Accreditation: JCAH

The Gordon Chemical Dependency Center is a comprehensive inpatient facility specifically for adolescents. The program, utilizing the Twelve Steps of AA, as well as standard therapies, is tailored to individual needs.

The treatment center, located within Saint Luke's Medical Center, has an affiliation agreement with the hospital that provides 24-hour medical coverage, including dentists, ophthalmologists, neurologists and other specialists. The Gordon program also has an accredited on-site school program that is mandatory for all residents.

The inpatient therapy program addresses the cognitive, affective and spiritual aspects of each individual. Within the structure are written expectations and rules with established consequences, to assist the individual in the learning of creative problem solving, good judgment and other life-coping skills. The program includes lectures on topics such as chemical dependency, relationships, sexuality, nutrition, personal hygiene and others. Group and individual therapy are provided to each client daily.

Family therapy is an important component, and each patient's entire family will be involved, receiving on the average, six 2-hour sessions while their son or daughter is in treatment. For families living at a distance, arrangements will be made for residence at the facility in order to ensure the necessary family support and therapy.

The Gordon program provides a complete continuing-care program for all clients after discharge.

MARIAN HEALTH CENTER CHEMICAL DEPENDENCY UNIT

2101 Court Street
Sioux City, Iowa 51104

(712) 279-2180

Director: Joanna Riegel

Average Patient Census: 30–35
Minimum Duration of Treatment: 28 days
Cost: $125 per day. Insurance eligible.
Detoxification Offered: Yes
Accreditation: JCAH

Criteria for admission to the Chemical Dependency Unit at Marian Health Care Center include evidence of chemical dependency in individual behavior, a reasonable assurance that the individual can function well enough, after detoxification, to meet the mental and physical demands of the treatment program and personal commitment to the completion of the 30-day program.

The multidisciplinary staff includes physicians who conduct physical examinations and nursing personnel who proceed with detoxification, if required, and with continued evaluation of the patient. Intensive rehabilitation is accomplished through cooperation of a dedicated staff of counselors on alcoholism, psychologists, clergymen, medical personnel and members of AA.

Treatment is based on the philosophy of AA and utilizes psychological testing, formal and informal group therapy, lectures and films, as well as individual interviews and counseling sessions with alcoholism counselors, psychologists and clergymen. Treatment is determined by individual needs.

Patients are admitted by the attending physician or the unit medical director.

Families of patients are encouraged to take part in the treatment program; a week-long family program of group therapy, lectures and counseling sessions is offered, as well as an additional 3-week outpatient program based on Al-Anon philosophy. Aftercare involves a return to the unit for at least twelve weekly group sessions for patient and spouse. If distance is a factor, follow-up is referred to the patient's local agencies.

Kansas

VALLEY HOPE ALCOHOLISM TREATMENT CENTER

Box 312
1816 North 2nd Street
Atchison, Kansas 66002

(913) 367-1618

Director: David Ketter, M.A.
Average Patient Census: 65

Minimum Duration of Treatment: 30 days or longer if needed
Cost: Approximately $3,000 for 30-day treatment; $89 per day for spouse treatment in conjunction with alcoholic. Insurance eligible.
Detoxification Offered: Yes
Accreditation: JCAH

The treatment program at Valley Hope consists of a well-planned, proven-successful, individually tailored series of medical, psychological, social, spiritual, vocational and recreational therapies.

The facility has a highly trained professional staff covering all areas of the treatment program, including 24-hour nursing care. The program is designed for 30 days, but longer stays are geared to the needs of the individual. Patients are given a thorough orientation in the AA and Al-Anon way of life.

Valley Hope is a private, nonprofit, nonsectarian organization with treatment centers in Norton, Kansas; Cushing, Oklahoma; O'Neill, Nebraska; and Booneville, Missouri. Outpatient counseling centers are located in Greater Kansas City and Wichita, Kansas; and in Lincoln, Nebraska.

CHEMICAL DEPENDENCY PROGRAM
Bethany Medical Center

51 North Twelfth Street
Kansas City, Kansas 66102

(913) 281-8951

Director: C. L. Engebritson

Average Patient Census: 21–25
Minimum Duration of Treatment: 28 days
Cost: $6,500. Insurance eligible.
Detoxification Offered: Yes
Accreditation: JCAH

The Chemical Dependency Program at Bethany Medical Center is a reality-oriented unit, staffed by a professional team that includes physicians, psychologists, alcohol and drug counselors and recreational therapists. The main thrust of the program is family oriented, with emphasis on a multidisciplinary program of individual and group therapy, exercise and recreational therapy.

Phase one of the program begins with medical detoxification, lasting 4 to 5 days, and is followed by approximately 21 days of intensive individual counseling, group work and activity therapy. A primary counselor and nurse are assigned to each patient on admission and follow the patient through inpatient care into the continuing-recovery program of 11 months. AA and Al-Anon are an integral part of Bethany's program.

An Alumni Association, open to any patient and family who complete the inpatient portion of the program, helps with volunteer work in the unit and holds social events, such as the parties at the unit and other community activities.

Bethany also has a primary out-treatment at 7840 Washington Boulevard, (913) 334-6300, at a cost of $1,600. The intensive 4-week out-treatment program has a treatment philosophy consistent with the inpatient program.

A 1-year aftercare program is provided to all patients completing the treatment programs.

NORTON VALLEY HOPE ALCOHOLISM TREATMENT CENTER

Box 510
Norton, Kansas 67654

(913) 877-5101

Director: Kenneth C. Gregoire, Ph.D.
Average Patient Census: 66

Minimum Duration of Treatment: 30 days; individual need determines length of stay
Cost: Patient, $97 per day; spouse, $87 per day. Insurance eligible.
Detoxification Offered: Yes
Accreditation: JCAH

Valley Hope is a private, nonprofit, nonsectarian organization dedicated to doing something about the destructive forces of alcoholism and drug abuse. The staff believes that alcoholics and drug addicts are unique human beings who deserve to be treated as individuals.

The treatment program has three principal components: medical, psychological and spiritual, with other areas such as legal, vocational, recreational and financial receiving consideration as well. All these programs are marked by a genuine concern for the patient.

The counseling team is composed of clinical psychologists, counselors specially trained in alcoholism and related addictions and staff chaplains. There is a strong emphasis on orientation into the AA and Al-Anon way of life, and patients are urged to become involved in these programs after treatment. The family unit and its treatment is also stressed.

Valley Hope offers training sessions for clergy and others in the field of alcoholism, as well as a 1-year alcoholism counselor training course.

There are Valley Hope treatment centers in Atchison, Kansas; Cushing, Oklahoma; and O'Neill, Nebraska. These are listed by state in this directory. Valley Hope outpatient counseling centers are located in Greater Kansas City and Wichita, Kansas; and in Lincoln, Nebraska.

ALCOHOL AND DRUG ABUSE RECOVERY PROGRAM
Menninger Clinic

P.O. Box 829
Topeka, Kansas 66601

(913) 273-7500

Director: Robert W. Conroy, M.D.
Average Patient Census: 12

Minimum Duration of Treatment: Open-ended; usually 4 weeks
Cost: Approximately $350 per day. Insurance eligible.
Detoxification Offered: Yes
Accreditation: JCAH

The Alcohol and Drug Abuse Recovery Program of the C. F. Menninger Memorial Hospital carries on the Menninger tradition of over 60 years; highly trained professional staff members use knowledge in a caring way to help people achieve greater personal fulfillment and satisfaction. The unique aspects of the Menninger program include the following five features: (1) a medically oriented and supervised treatment program that includes comprehensive diagnosis and an individualized treatment plan, with emphasis on mental and physical health; (2) a high treatment staff-to-patient ratio of two-to-one; (3) consideration for the family of the patient, with the active involvement of the family in the patient's total treatment program, including participation in a family workshop; (4) an intensive follow-up program without additional cost to the patient or family; and (5) treatment designed not simply for abstinence but for improved functioning in all areas of life. The program stresses active involvement in AA, NA, Al-Anon and Nar-Anon, and emphasizes the disease concept.

The ratio of staff members to patients is more than two to one, and the staff believes that even the most complicated and difficult-to-treat alcohol- and drug-abuse problems can be treated on the unit. An active follow-up program is encouraged.

The interdisciplinary team includes alcoholism counselors, social workers, nursing personnel, clinical psychologist, recreational therapist, chaplains and psychiatrists.

The unit accepts only voluntary admissions and operates with an open-door policy.

ALCOHOLISM TREATMENT UNIT
Saint Joseph Medical Center

3600 East Harry
Wichita, Kansas 67218

(316) 689-4850

Director: Joseph Heeb

Average Patient Census: 58
Minimum Duration of Treatment: Approximately 30 days
Cost: $186 per day. Insurance eligible.
Detoxification Offered: Yes
Accreditation: JCAH

The ATU at Saint Joseph's provides a multidisciplinary-team approach to alcoholism and to soft drug addiction, in a medical-center setting, for adults and adolescents.

On admission, each patient receives a physical examination as well as laboratory and X-ray evaluation, with supervised medical detoxification as needed. The many diagnostic and therapeutic facilities of Saint Joseph Medical Center offer an extension of services not readily available in most alcoholism programs. Following assessment and detoxification, the approach of the program is a team effort as each patient's physical, psychological and social complications are assessed by a psychologist, nurses, physicians and certified counselors. These observations are shared in daily staff meetings.

The patient is assigned to a counselor who serves as case manager throughout treatment, where various modalities are used, including lectures, counseling, literature, group therapy, family counseling, couples therapy, films, tapes, and AA, NA and Al-Anon meetings. Families, at no charge, have to be involved in the family program.

Each patient is seen by the aftercare counselor before discharge in order to establish an individual aftercare plan. Aftercare groups meet weekly for 2 years and include family members. There is no charge for the aftercare program.

Efforts are geared toward ease of admission, and advanced reservations are encouraged. Adolescents, age 13 to 18, are also accepted when special admission criteria are met and are admitted to the adolescent treatment component.

PARALLAX PROGRAM, INC.

532 North Broadway
Wichita, Kansas 67214

(316) 267-3395

Director: Milton F. Fowler

Average Patient Census: 20
Minimum Duration of Treatment: 6 months maximum
Cost: $65 per day. Insurance eligible.
Detoxification Offered: No
Accreditation: State of Kansas

Parallax Program, Inc., services residents of Kansas, age 16 and upward, for alcohol and drug dependency. Referrals are evaluated in a series of interviews based on admission criteria of need and motivation.

Upon admission, clients receive a complete physical by staff physician; laboratory testing; psychological evaluation; compilation of social, legal and drug histories; counseling for treatment-plan formation and orientation to the program. During the 7- to 10-day admission period, the appropriateness of the referral is evaluated, and inappropriate clients are referred elsewhere for treatment.

Clients in residential treatment are served by a treatment team consisting of their primary counselor, administrative and nursing staff, clinical psychologist and secondary team counselors. Treatment plans are updated every 30 days, in cooperation with client input, and are reviewed by the consultant clinical psychologist and treatment team.

The curriculum includes, but is not limited to, the following: recreational, occupational and nutritional therapy; vocational/educational guidance and placement; spirituality; volunteer service to the community; alcohol and drug education; social-survival skills; communication and family therapy; NA and AA groups and milieu therapy.

Follow-up is achieved by the Aftercare Specialist with weekly meetings, random drug screenings and counseling services, and continues for a minimum of 1 year.

Kentucky

CHARTERTON HOSPITAL

P.O. Box 400
507 Yager Avenue
LaGrange, Kentucky 40031

(502) 222-7148

Director: Carole Woods

Average Patient Census: 66 beds
Minimum Duration of Treatment: 30 days
Cost: Varies; available on request. Insurance eligible.
Detoxification Offered: Yes
Accreditation: JCAH

The program at Charterton Hospital offers medically supervised detoxification, if necessary, as well as individual, group and family counseling as part of the holistic (multidisciplinary) approach toward effectively treating the disease of addiction. All patients are also encouraged to participate in activities therapy and didactic lectures. These programs are AA/NA based philosophically. The hospital offers both adult and adolescent programs.

Patient and family aftercare services are available at all Charter Medical Addictive Disease units, emphasizing that recovery from this relentless disease is a continuing process affecting both the patient and his or her family.

CHARTER RIDGE HOSPITAL

3050 Rio Dosa Drive
Lexington, Kentucky 40509

(606) 269-2325

Director: Ted Godlaski

Average Patient Census: 22 beds
Minimum Duration of Treatment: 21 days
Cost: Varies; available on request. Insurance eligible.
Detoxification Offered: Yes
Accreditation: JCAH

The program at Charter Ridge Hospital offers medically supervised detoxification, if necessary, as well as individual, group and family counseling as part of the holistic (multidisciplinary) approach toward effectively treating the disease of addiction. All patients are also encouraged to participate in activities therapy and didactic lectures. These programs are AA/NA based philosophically. The hospital offers programs only for adults.

Patient and family aftercare services are available at all Charter Medical Addictive Disease units, emphasizing that recovery from this relentless disease is a continuing process affecting both the patient and his or her family.

CHEMICAL DEPENDENCY UNIT
MCDOWELL APPALACHIAN REGIONAL HOSPITAL

Box 247
McDowell, Kentucky 41647

(606) 377-2411

Director: Glenda Lawson
Average Patient Census: 5

Minimum Duration of Treatment: 5, 7, 14, and 28 days
Cost: Available on request. Insurance eligible.
Detoxification Offered: Yes
Accreditation: JCAH

McDowell ARH Chemical Dependency Unit is located in a rural, 60-bed hospital in the foothills of southeastern Kentucky, in a small, secluded community that is, however, easily accessible.

Admission is open to men and women at least 16 years of age, with a verified need for residential treatment for alcohol/drug problems and a willingness to participate in the program, with family or concerned person involvement if possible.

The CDU at McDowell offers 7-, 14-, and 28-day programs, all based on the philosophy of AA and the self-help techniques of rational-emotive therapy. Treatment is divided into three phases in order to provide appropriate programs for all individuals. Phase I includes detoxification, assessment and a careful look at the illness of chemical dependency. Steps 1, 2 and 3 of AA are explored in an effort to initiate a strong recovery program. Phase II is geared to individual needs regarding feelings, communication and more in-depth rational-emotive therapy and involves lectures, AVs, individual assignments, and group and individual counseling.

Phase III is geared to aftercare, suggested continued involvement in AA and Al-Anon, post-treatment plans and recommended outpatient counseling.

GOODMAN HILL HOSPITAL

656 Berger Road
P.O. Box 7609
Paducah, Kentucky 42001

(502) 444-0444

Director: Susan A. Yates
Average Patient Census: 20

Minimum Duration of Treatment: None
Cost: Adult detox, $267 per day; adult rehab, $222 per day; adolescent detox, $280 per day; adolescent rehab, $235 per day. Insurance eligible.
Detoxification Offered: Yes
Accreditation: JCAH application accepted

Goodman Hill is an 80-bed facility located on 26 acres of wooded hillside. Its primary mission is the professional, humanitarian and specialized treatment of chemically dependent persons and their families. The comprehensive, interdisciplinary program is designed to enable patients to return to healthy, productive and chemical-free lives.

The majority of patients at Goodman Hill are adults, but the facility includes a 20-bed adolescent unit for patients between 13 and 18 years of age.

Underlying the treatment of alcoholism, sedativism and chemical dependency is the conviction that these diseases affect physical, emotional and spiritual well-being, and the staff is dedicated to the treatment of the "whole person."

Patients are provided with full medical and clinical advantages available in a hospital environment, as well as proven treatment methods, including intensive individual and group psychotherapy, complete substance detoxification and creative physical and recreational therapy. Involvement with such groups as AA is strongly encouraged.

Intensive inpatient care of 28 days is followed by an aftercare program that is tailored to the needs of the individual and, if warranted, his or her family.

Louisiana

BATON ROUGE CHEMICAL DEPENDENCY UNIT

4040 North Boulevard
P.O. Box 4109
Baton Rouge, Louisiana 70806

(504) 387-7900

Director: Ed Wishart
Average Patient Census: 51

Minimum Duration of Treatment: Adolescents (age 13 and up), approximately 5-week program; adults, approximately 4-week program
Cost: Adolescents, approximately $8,500; adults, approximately $6,050. Insurance eligible.
Detoxification Offered: Yes
Accreditation: JCAH

This facility is a 4- to 5-week chemical dependency inpatient treatment center that meets the need of chemically dependent patients, with adolescent and adult programs that operate conjointly. Adolescents of 13 years and older are accepted for treatment. The philosophy is aligned with the National Association of Alcoholism Treatment Programs' concept with a strong orientation to AA.

Following admission procedures, medical and psychological evaluation and intake group, the patient is assigned to a primary counselor. There is a full week of intense family treatment toward the end of the treatment program. A 2-year aftercare program follows, and adolescent halfway-house facilities are available.

LA MAISON, EQUILIBRIA

2300 Government Street
3621 Government Street
Baton Rouge, Louisiana 70806

Telephone: See below for individual numbers

Director: Victor Hoard

Average Patient Census: 10 and 24, respectively
Minimum Duration of Treatment: 3- to 6-month program
Cost: $1,075 per month. Insurance eligible.
Detoxification Offered: No
Accreditation: Louisiana Department of Health and Human Resources

Two specific programs are offered at La Maison and Equilibria for particular groups of those affected by chemical dependency.

La Maison offers inpatient treatment to women over the age of 15. Individual treatment plans for patients are based on their specific needs in the following areas: chemical dependency, physical and mental needs, psychological and emotional needs, social and family, vocational and educational, spiritual ethico/religious, sexual, financial and legal. Information and admission: (504) 383-8541.

Equilibria offers the same individualized treatment planning and program for men 18 years and older. Admission and information: (504) 389-9836.

Both units emphasize the importance of recognizing the differing needs of the patient involved and strive to meet a broad range of these needs that involve aspects of chemical dependency, as well as the resulting inbalance in other areas of the patient's life.

A private outpatient counseling service is available: Recovery Resources, (504) 383-0678. The average length of primary treatment is 3 months, with an additional 3 months of aftercare.

SILKWORTH CENTER

2414 Bunker Hill Drive
Baton Rouge, Louisiana 70808

(504) 928-6633

Director: Barry R. Mangham, C.S.A.C.
Average Patient Census: Detox, 12 beds; rehab, 18 beds

Minimum Duration of Treatment: Detox, 5–7 days; rehab, 21 days
Cost: Detox, $337 per day; rehab, $180 per day. Insurance eligible.
Detoxification Offered: Yes
Accreditation: JCAH

Silkworth Treatment Center is composed of two individual specialized programs for the evaluation and treatment of chemical dependency.

The Detoxification, Evaluation, Assessment and Referral Unit (DEAR) offers a 4- to 7-day inpatient treatment of medical detoxification from alcohol or other mood-altering drugs, as well as a complete medical, mental and emotional evaluation of the patient, and a thorough assessment of the family system. At the conclusion of this period, the interdisciplinary team makes recommendation and referral to either recognized community outpatient resources, such as private or group counseling and AA, or to the more structured support of their own, or another, inpatient program.

The inpatient program at Silkworth, acknowledging that chemical dependency erodes every part of the individual's psychic powers, which include social, spiritual, emotional, volitional and physical capabilities, bases the rehabilitative process on a variety of services. The process is accomplished through individual and group therapy, and through a series of lectures, films, and oral and written assignments. Silkworth emphasizes the AA/Al-Anon Twelve Step philosophy, and meetings are held while in treatment.

The Family and/or Significant-Other Program is offered, and involvement is strongly encouraged. At the successful completion of the inpatient rehabilitation program, the patient and family may enter the Continued Care Program for weekly lectures and group therapy. Silkworth recommends up to 2 years of continued care. AA and Al-Anon involvement are integral parts of this program.

CHEMICAL DEPENDENCY UNIT OF ACADIANA

2520 North University Avenue
P.O. Box 91526
Lafayette, Louisiana 70509

(318) 234-5614

Director: Ron Weller
Average Patient Census: 60

Minimum Duration of Treatment: Adolescents, approximately 5 weeks; adults, approximately 4 weeks
Cost: Adolescents, approximately $9,500; adults, approximately $6,850. Insurance eligible.
Detoxification Offered: Yes
Accreditation: JCAH

This facility is a 4- to 5-week chemical dependency inpatient treatment center that meets the need of chemically dependent patients, with adolescent and adult programs that operate conjointly. Adolescents of 13 years and older are accepted for treatment. The philosophy is aligned with the National Association of Alcoholism Treatment Programs' concept, with a strong orientation to AA.

Following admission procedures, medical and psychological evaluation and intake group, the patient is assigned to a primary counselor. There is a full week of intense family treatment toward the end of the treatment program. A 2-year aftercare program follows, and adolescent halfway-house facilities are available.

CHEMICAL DEPENDENCY TREATMENT CENTER
SAINT PATRICK HOSPITAL

524 South Ryan Street
Lake Charles, Louisiana 70601

(318) 436-2511

Director: Patricia J. Roy, R.N.

Average Patient Census: 17
Minimum Duration of Treatment: Approximately, 28 days
Cost: Approximately $4,800. Insurance eligible.
Detoxification Offered: Yes
Accreditation: JCAH

The Chemical Dependency Treatment Center at Saint Patrick Hospital bases its treatment approach on the belief that alcoholism and/or drug dependency is a primary, progressive and fatal disease, and that without treatment it will get worse, never better. The program was developed in consultation with Hazelden Foundation and is based on the Twelve Steps of AA. Patients attend AA while in treatment and are expected to work toward their fifth step before completing the program.

Treatment begins with medical examination, in cooperation, when possible, with the family physician, and continues with a full daily program involving informational films and lectures, individual and group therapy, nutrition and fitness programs and constant medical evaluation. When patients begin to understand that their dependency is a disease, that they have been sick, not "morally bad," then medical expertise backed by unconditional love begins to work wonders toward recovery.

Particular attention is paid to family involvement. A 40-hour outpatient family program is offered. This is free to families of inpatients and costs $40 per session to the general public. There is, as well, a Special People Program for children, age 6 through 12, who are living in a chemically dependent environment; there is no charge for this program.

Aftercare consists of a 6-month to 1-year program for patients, families and children, for which there is no charge if patients have completed the 28-day core program and are attending AA, NA or Al-Anon.

BOWLING GREEN INN OF SAINT TAMMANY

P.O. Box 417
701 Florida Avenue
Mandeville, Louisiana 70448

(504) 626-5661 or 1-800-432-0877

Director: George R. Rozelle, Ph.D.
Average Patient Census: 26

Minimum Duration of Treatment: alcoholism, 28 days; drug abuse, 56 days
Cost: Detox and evaluation (first 7 days), $220 per day; $190 per day thereafter. Insurance eligible.
Detoxification Offered: Yes (subacute)
Accreditation: JCAH

Bowling Green Inn offers a short-term, intensive, residential treatment program for men and women of any age who have an alcohol or drug problem, either psychologically or physically dependent. Persons aged 14 to 80 are eligible.

Individual treatment goals are established for each resident, and techniques utilized in reaching them include: individual counseling, group therapy, didactic groups utilizing audiovisual materials, recreational and social activities and thorough exposure to AA. Many different approaches may be used, such as Transactional Analysis, Gestalt, reality therapy, behavior modification, movement therapy and supportive confrontation within a therapeutic-community context.

A particular program for the spouse is offered, including 1 or 2 weeks conjointly with the mate in treatment. In addition, for the recovering alcoholic who has achieved physical sobriety but who desires greater self-awareness and understanding, they offer a 28-day residential program.

Emphasis is placed on discharge planning for aftercare. A 2-year, community-based aftercare program is provided. Bowling Green Inn is licensed by the state of Louisiana, Department of Health and Human Resources, as a specialty hospital.

Bowling Green Inn of Saint Tammany is located in a quiet, wooded area on the north shore of Lake Ponchartrain, providing privacy and seclusion from outside distractions, as well as easy access from all directions.

The Institute for Better Living BGI-ST's outpatient-services program, offers services in the area of individual, marital, family and group therapy for chemically dependent persons and for individuals and families who may be experiencing problems not related to drugs or alcohol.

COUNTERPOINT CENTER OF NEW ORLEANS (CPC)

1421 General Taylor Street
New Orleans, Louisiana 70115

(504) 895-8605

Director: Nancy Heatherington

Average Patient Census: 28 beds
Minimum Duration of Treatment: 28 days
Cost: Available on request. Insurance eligible.
Detoxification Offered: Yes
Accreditation: JCAH

CounterPoint Center is a Chemical Dependency Program for adults and adolescents. The Center is part of an international network of chemical dependency treatment centers located throughout the United States and Europe.

Chemical dependency is recognized as a primary disorder: chronic, progressive and potentially fatal, and prone to relapse if not properly treated. The disease factor is basic to treatment, which is provided by a multidisciplinary team of skilled professionals, many themselves recovering. All areas of a person's life are affected by chemical dependency. Therefore, the physical, emotional, social and spiritual needs of patients are all addressed through the treatment program.

Detoxification is the first phase of treatment. Following stabilization of acute medical problems, patients begin an intensive program of rehabilitation. The Twelve Steps of AA and NA are emphasized, and patients are expected to have selected an AA or NA group and a temporary sponsor by the time they are to begin the aftercare program. An individualized plan for aftercare is formulated with patient and family during the last week of treatment. Weekly group therapy is provided at no extra cost for 1 year, with a 2-year advisement period.

Family and significant others are included in treatment from the time of admission, with family assessment and couples and family therapy several times each week. Crisis intervention is also available.

For employers, the staff maintains open communications with EAP counselors and supervisors. Employers are included in the treatment process from the beginning, through discharge and into follow-up care.

NEW LIFE CENTER
DePaul Hospital

1040 Calhoun Street
New Orleans, Louisiana 70118

(504) 899-8282

Director: Peter Egan

Average Patient Census: 44-bed capacity
Minimum Duration of Treatment: Detox, 4–7 days; rehab, 21–28 days
Cost: Available on request. Insurance eligible.
Detoxification Offered: Yes
Accreditation: JCAH

The recovery program at New Life Center, DePaul Hospital, consists of a three-phase process: 2- to 7-day assessment/detoxification, a 28-day residential therapeutic community, and outpatient aftercare focusing on family treatment of the disease of addiction/alcoholism.

Other services include free Family Intervention Training in a 6-session program aimed at getting the alcoholic/addict to accept treatment.

KOALA CENTER AT OPELOUSAS GENERAL HOSPITAL

520 Prudhomme Lane
Opelousas, Louisiana 70570

(318) 948-8070

Director: Fred Hill
Average Patient Census: 15

Minimum Duration of Treatment: Inpatient, 30 days
Cost: Available on request. Insurance eligible.
Detoxification Offered: Yes
Accreditation: JCAH

Koala derives its name from the custom among the Aboriginals of Australia of passing the drinking vessel around a circle. Anyone who did not wish to drink said, *"Koala,"* meaning "no drink." Later, the name was given to the little animal, native to Australia, that seldom, if ever, drinks.

Koala is a treatment hospital for alcoholism and drug abuse for both adults and adolescents; they believe that alcoholism is a disease that must be treated with the same compassion, dedication and expertise as all other diseases. This facility offers, therefore, a comprehensive, multidisciplinary, individualized treatment plan in a nonjudgmental, stigma-free environment.

The program includes group therapy, family counseling, individual therapy, an introduction to AA and NA, psychological testing, psychiatric evaluation, nutrition awareness, leisure counseling and employer involvement.

ALCOHOLISM RECOVERY UNIT
Schumpert Medical Center

800 Main Building
915 Margaret Place
P.O. Box 21976
Shreveport, Louisiana 71120

(318) 227-4288

Director: Dick Hogan, C.S.A.C.
Average Patient Census: 15
Minimum Duration of Treatment: 28 days
Cost: $175 per day plus physician's charges. Insurance eligible.
Detoxification Offered: Yes
Accreditation: JCAH

Schumpert Medical Center, owned and operated by the Sisters of Charity of the Incarnate Word, opened an alcoholic treatment unit in 1957. The present facilities were expanded and remodeled in 1979. The ARU offers a 28-day treatment program for alcoholics and other addicted persons in a general hospital setting.

Patients attend daily educational lectures, group therapy, open discussions and daily films on alcoholism and recovery, as well as AA meetings both in and out of the hospital.

Family members are directly involved in treatment during the patient's treatment program, including a 2-day Family Marathon, and all continue to attend weekly group therapy sessions for a minimum of 6 weeks following discharge. Spiritual counseling and an ongoing involvement with AA receive strong emphasis throughout treatment. An aftercare program for patients and family members is included in the cost of treatment for a minimum of 6 weeks after hospital discharge.

Schumpert Medical Center is part of Shreveport's extensive hospital complex, serving the people of north Louisiana, southwestern Arkansas and east Texas, locally referred to as the Ark-La-Tex.

CHARTER FOREST HOSPITAL

9320 Linwood Avenue
Shreveport, Louisiana 71106

(318) 688-3930

Director: Michael Womack, C.A.C.

Average Patient Census: 49 beds
Minimum Duration of Treatment: 30 days
Cost: Varies; available on request
Detoxification Offered: Yes
Accreditation: JCAH pending

The program at Charter Forest Hospital offers medically supervised detoxification, if necessary, and individual, group and family counseling as part of the holistic (multidisciplinary) approach toward effectively treating the disease of addiction. All patients are also encouraged to participate in activities therapy and didactic lectures. The hospital offers both adult and adolescent programs.

Patient and family aftercare services are available at all Charter Medical Addictive Disease units, emphasizing that recovery from this relentless disease is a continuing process affecting both the patient and his or her family.

Michigan

ALCOHOLISM INFORMATION AND REFERRAL CENTER
Emma L. Bixby Hospital

818 Riverside Avenue
Adrian, Michigan 49221

(517) 263-0711, ext. 411

Director: Edward M. Skinner, M.A., C.S.W.
Average Patient Census: 10

Minimum Duration of Treatment: Presently a 21-day program
Cost: Averages $2,700–3,000, including physician services, lab, alcoholism and occupational therapy. Insurance eligible.
Detoxification Offered: Yes
Accreditation: JCAH

AIRC is a comprehensive hospital-based alcoholism program providing a full range of clinical services, including detoxification, residential treatment, outpatient therapy, aftercare services and AA availability.

Other program services of this facility include Crisis Services, the Family Program, Spouse Education Program, an Alcohol Highway Safety Program and Employee Assistance Programming involving consultation, diagnosis and referral. Youth Services, Agency Consultation and Training, and Community Education are also available.

The AIRC is eligible to receive third-party reimbursement. AIRC provides routine follow-up to referring agencies. Admission should be prearranged through the AIRC program.

THE LIFE CENTER OF AUBURN HILLS

1360 Doris Road
Auburn Hills, Michigan 48057

(313) 373-2660

Director: Donald R. Pipes

Average Patient Census: 24 beds
Minimum Duration of Treatment: 21 days
Cost: $250 per day. Insurance eligible.
Detoxification Offered: No
Accreditation: Pending

The Life Center of Auburn Hills is designed to provide specialized state-of-the-art treatment to adults afflicted by severe alcoholism, drug abuse and multichemical dependency.

Comprehensive treatment by a dedicated, highly skilled, professional staff is focused on one specific goal—individual recovery. Individual, group and family therapy address the medical, psychological and spiritual needs of patients. Family involvement is strongly encouraged to provide support to the chemically dependent person for a new life-style of abstinence from chemicals. Special emphasis is placed on the Twelve Step program of AA.

The Family Intervention Program, a free community service, can assist families in dealing with the chemically dependent family member, with the goal of motivating the addicted person to seek treatment.

NEW DAY CENTER OF BATTLE CREEK ADVENTIST HOSPITAL

165 North Washington Avenue
Battle Creek, Michigan 49016

(616) 964-7121, ext. 535

Director: Daniel L. Richardson
Average Patient Census: Adult, 25; adolescent, 20

Minimum Duration of Treatment: Adult, 28 days; adolescent, 45 days
Cost: Adult, $5,000–5,500; adolescent, $10,000–12,000. Insurance eligible.
Detoxification Offered: Yes
Accreditation: JCAH

New Day Center believes in and offers specialized treatment for special populations, such as the treatment program for women. The adult counseling staff is composed of both male and female therapists with related expertise in the treatment of the individual adult male and female.

New Day's treatment philosophy is based on the disease concept of alcoholism and chemical dependency, as well as on the belief that only total abstinence can halt the progress of the disease; but since this disease is one of denial, the recovery process must often begin with a forced intervention by others into the person's life in order to break into the individual's systematic, defensive denial barriers.

The treatment program combines AA's Twelve Steps with medical, educational and psychological efforts, and the holistic approach also implements other treatment modalities, such as exercise and recreation.

Communication with the referring agent is stressed at New Day, whether that agent be an employee assistance program, a human service agency, school, law or independent health professional. Precare services and communications include case screening, consultation, psychosocial evaluation, confrontation and intervention to ensure appropriate treatment. During residential treatment, communications begin with notice of the client's arrival and initial reports that assess attitudes, progress and personality changes. Referring agents are invited to a midterm review for evaluation and assessment of each client and projection from the residential phase into aftercare, during which reports are provided on the patient's involvement, attitudes and progress.

New Day also offers a complete outpatient treatment program for those patients who can best be treated on this basis. The costs of this program are covered by most insurance providers; where there is no coverage, charges may be assessed on a sliding fee scale.

BRIGHTON HOSPITAL

12851 East Grand River Avenue
Brighton, Michigan 48116

(313) 227-1211 (Inpatient Services)
(313) 227-6143 (Outpatient Services)

Director: Ivan C. Harner, Executive Director; Russell F. Smith, M.D., Medical Director

Average Patient Census: 63 beds
Minimum Duration of Treatment: Determined individually for each patient
Cost: Approximately $174 per day. Insurance eligible.
Detoxification Offered: Yes
Accreditation: JCAH

Founded in 1950, Brighton is committed exclusively to total treatment of a total illness—physical, mental, social and spiritual. The Brighton program is based on the certainty that detoxification, while crucial, is only the smallest first step toward true and sustained recovery. Brighton Hospital offers much more than just physical recovery, with an intensive and practical education in the form of lectures, one-to-one counseling, group therapy, AA meetings, relaxation therapy and an excellent family program. The facility is situated on 69 beautiful acres, 35 miles northwest of Detroit, and emphasizes a relaxed, noninstitutional character. Recreational facilities include a nine-hole golf course, a private lake for fishing, tennis court and volleyball and horseshoe courts.

The keystone of the program is the recovery philosophy of AA. Brighton Hospital's ultimate goal is the restoration of the individual to a reasonably serene, happy and productive life.

INSIGHT AT COLOMBIERE

Box 39
9075 Big Lake Road
Clarkston, Michigan 48016

(313) 625-0400 (Clarkston Line)
(313) 767-3021 (Flint Line)

Director: James E. Stone, C.D.A.C., C.A.C.

Average Patient Census: 47
Minimum Duration of Treatment: 28-day program
Cost: Approximately $170 per day. Insurance eligible.
Detoxification Offered: Arrangements made at nearby hospitals
Accreditation: JCAH

Insight's residential program specializes in short-term, intensive treatment through structured therapy and aftercare programs aimed at the primary goal of educating people to understand and deal effectively with their alcoholism.

Upon admission, each client undergoes a complete medical, psychological, and needs assessment upon which a comprehensive 4-week treatment plan is formulated. A qualified therapist works one to one with each client, addressing individual needs, and the relationship between client and therapist is a powerful component of the recovery program. Each therapist handles an average of six clients. Frequent sessions determine and support the direction of treatment and its necessary modifications.

Insight's program welcomes input from the entire therapeutic community: client groups, families, employers, nursing staff, physicians, and support staff. Lectures and therapy sessions, AA meetings and an Al-Anon meeting are held in the same building.

Each client has a private room. The facility is located on 400 acres in a rural setting.

An aftercare plan including local support systems assists clients in adjustments to job and family situations, and clients are strongly encouraged to return to Insight for "booster" sessions.

PHOENIX ALCOHOLISM THERAPY SERVICES
Garden City Osteopathic Hospital
(Other locations listed below)

6245 North Inkster Road
Garden City, Michigan 48135

(313) 421-3374

Director: Philip O'Dwyer, M.A., C.S.W., C.A.C.

Average Patient Census: 30
Minimum Duration of Treatment: Average stay, 7–14 days
Cost: Available on request. Insurance eligible.
Detoxification Offered: Yes
Accreditation: JCAH

The Core-Shell Treatment System that is in place in all Phoenix locations focuses on matching the patient to the type of treatment that will meet his or her specific needs and was developed in the belief that individuals with alcohol problems are more different than they are alike.

The Primary Care Module is the entry point. When the individual seeks assistance for problems related to alcohol use, his or her initial contact, the Primary Care Worker, attends to the immediate needs of the patient, develops a case history and prepares the patient for the assessment process.

The Assessment Module provides comprehensive evaluation designed to identify unique problems and needs and explores medical, physiological, pharmacological, social and psychological areas. When the assessment is completed, Primary Care and Assessment workers meet with patient and family for treatment planning when, from the arena of available resources, that intervention which best matches the patient's unique need is selected.

There are four Phoenix locations providing treatment for individuals with substance abuse problems: Garden City, as listed above, provides both inpatient and outpatient therapy. Phoenix ATS at Saint Mary Hospital, 36475 Five Mile Road, Livonia, Michigan 48152, also provides inpatient and outpatient therapy. Phoenix at Eleven Oaks, 26393 Dequindre, Madison Heights, Michigan 48071, provides outpatient therapy to individuals with substance abuse and/or emotional problems. Baywood Clinic, 15645 Farmington Road, Livonia, Michigan 48154, provides a variety of outpatient interventions designed to assist with substance abuse and/or emotional problems. Patients are referred to this location after completing the primary-care and assessment phases at one of the other Phoenix locations.

HENRY FORD HOSPITAL MAPLEGROVE

6773 West Maple Road
West Bloomfield, Michigan 48033

(313) 661-6100

Director: Thomas T. Groth

Average Patient Census: Maplegrove, residential, 50; Detroit Center, IPD, 16; intensive outpatient, 40
Minimum Duration of Treatment: 21 days residential
Cost: $7,500. Insurance eligible.
Detoxification Offered: Yes
Accreditation: JCAH

Henry Ford Hospital's Department of Chemical Dependency is among the pioneers in the Midwest for the development of full family treatment programs. The department offers a wide range of services for both adults and adolescents in a holistic family model, with an AA philosophy, available both on a residential and an outpatient basis.

Patients to be admitted to the various programs are evaluated during initial assessment interviews. Patients must also be accompanied by family and/or significant other throughout the program's duration.

Various program services at these facilities include residential treatment at Maplegrove and Detroit Center, as well as intensive outpatient programs at Troy and Dearborn Center. Follow-up treatment is available at all centers. Intervention services, nutritional education, an Impaired Physician's Program, Cocaine Specialty Services and an extensive Community Education Program are also offered.

Minnesota

HAZELDEN FOUNDATION

Box 11
Center City, Minnesota 55012

(612) 257-4010

Director: Harold A. Swift, Administrator

Average Patient Census: 173
Minimum Duration of Treatment: 30 days average
Cost: $98 per day. Insurance eligible.
Detoxification Offered: Yes
Accreditation: JCAH

    Hazelden combines the services of a specialized rehabilitation center with an atmosphere designed to be especially helpful to the 2,500 men and women who participate annually in residential care. The facilities include 128 beds in single and semiprivate rooms located in six primary rehabilitation units, as well as a 22-bed medical services and detoxification unit, a 23-bed extended-care unit and 18 beds for family treatment.

    Physical, mental, social and spiritual factors are taken into consideration in the rehabilitation program. Professionals and experts in all these fields, a total staff of 500 persons plus trainees, consultants and volunteers, function as a coordinated team. The multidisciplinary program that has been developed at Hazelden has become internationally recognized as a model in treating chemical dependency. This therapy and the suggested aftercare therapy emphasize the self-disciplinary measures practiced by AA, the concept of reality therapy with a goal of total abstinence. Mutual assistance and self-help are important factors in the program. Group therapy, the closeness of unit living and the fact that all residents have the same illness combine to produce a therapeutic environment in which residents help themselves by helping each other.

    Hazelden also offers an extended rehabilitation program, an outpatient program for women, a Family Center Residential Program, residential aftercare, Fellowship Club halfway-house services and a Renewal

Center program to support ongoing recovery in the years following treatment.

In addition to these rehabilitation programs, Hazelden offers an accredited counselor-training program, ongoing continuing-education workshops and seminars, clergy training, Prevention Center services, employee assistance services, research and evaluation services and a large selection of educational materials.

PARKVIEW WEST YOUTH AND FAMILY CENTER

14400 Martin Drive
Eden Prairie, Minnesota 55344

(612) 934-7555

Director: John Hagen
Average Patient Census: 20

Minimum Duration of Treatment: 5–7 weeks
Cost: Available on request. Insurance eligible.
Detoxification Offered: No
Accreditation: JCAH

Parkview West Youth and Family Center believes that dependence on mood-altering chemicals hinders or disrupts the growth process necessary for an adolescent to develop into a mature, decision-making adult, and offers an environment of guidance and support to help young people and their families continue in their developmental process.

Staff assessment of the young person's problems and needs helps the family determine the most effective course of action; parents are interviewed with their child, and then the adolescent is given a chance to talk with the intake counselor alone. If a chemical dependency problem is identified, a full inpatient evaluation period is recommended. This requires 7 to 14 days' residence that includes psychological testing, medical examination and monitoring, consultations with referral and family sources and one-to-one counseling, leading to a plan of treatment or other recommendations to appropriate community resources.

Inpatient treatment, if required, includes group and individual therapy, lectures, recreation, tutoring and work with the chaplain on spiritual enrichment. In academic studies, course credits are earned that will transfer to school when the client returns. A Family Week of 5 full days of lectures, counseling and parenting-skills classes is held during the second or third week of treatment.

A full 15-week aftercare program is required for clients living in the area, with family participation, including involvement in AA, Al-Anon,

Alateen and Families Anonymous. For out-of-state clients, an outside referral network is utilized wherever possible.

GOLDEN VALLEY HEALTH CENTER

4101 Golden Valley Road
Golden Valley, Minnesota 55422

(612) 588-2771

Director: Steve Kamber
Average Patient Census: 42 beds
  (adolescents, 36)

Minimum Duration of Treatment: Adults, 21–28 days; adolescents, 45–60 days
Cost: Approximately $300 per day. Insurance eligible.
Detoxification Offered: Yes
Accreditation: JCAH

The Golden Valley Health Center is a 251-bed hospital that has two CareUnits specializing in the family treatment of alcohol and other drug dependencies for adults and adolescents. Patients undergo a complete physiological and psychological examination and detoxification under the supervision of the medical director of the facility. The treatment program is personalized to fit individual needs and consists of individual and group therapy, participation in specific activities, lectures and films designed to increase the patient's understanding of his or her disease and appropriate ways to enjoy life free from chemical dependency. Families are invited to join in the treatment program, which is designed to free family members from the effects of the disease in areas such as behavior, attitudes and life-styles.

Recovery continues following the patient's discharge. Patients return to the CareUnit for aftercare 2 evenings a week for a specified period following discharge. Family units participate once weekly in the aftercare program. Patients and their families are encouraged to explore other resources, such as AA, Al-Anon, Alateen, NA and others, to which they were introduced during their inpatient stay. Aftercare is free to all patients—for a lifetime, if desired.

BRIDGEWAY CENTER

22 Twenty-seventh Avenue, S.E.
Minneapolis, Minnesota 55414

(612) 332-4262

Director: Phillip Kelly
Average Patient Census: 44

Minimum Duration of Treatment: 60–180 days
Cost: $75 per day. Insurance eligible.
Detoxification Offered: No
Accreditation: Minnesota Department of Health, Minnesota Department of Human Services

Bridgeway Center provides long-term care for the elderly chemically dependent patient based on the premise that all persons are unique and valuable. Chemically dependent residents are helped to become responsible for participating in their own recovery. The goal of the program is teaching residents to recognize their own strengths and to work toward developing their full potential.

Elderly men and women addicted to alcohol or other chemicals have special needs, and effective treatment requires attention to general health problems, issues of aging, such as grief and depression from loss of friends or spouse, as well as specific treatment of chemical dependency. At Bridgeway, this treatment, based on the philosophy of AA, also includes consideration for the unique health and psychosocial problems of the aged.

The program offers individualized chemical-dependency services, and necessary nursing care, under physician supervision. Also included are individualized treatment planning, psychosocial testing and one-to-one counseling, group therapy, grief and women's groups, recreational and relaxation therapy, health teaching, medication misuse/abuse education, intergenerational family services and aftercare.

Each resident is assigned a chemical dependency counselor who oversees case management and discharge planning, which includes support services and living arrangements coordinated with community social service agencies.

PARKVIEW TREATMENT CENTER

3705 Park Center Boulevard
Minneapolis, Minnesota 55416

(612) 929-5531

Director: Jack Erickson

Average Patient Census: 25
Minimum Duration of Treatment: Open-ended
Cost: $164 per day. Insurance eligible.
Detoxification Offered: No
Accreditation: JCAH

Parkview believes (a) that a chemical-dependency problem affects the whole person; (b) that an important aspect of recovery is internal and spiritual in nature and, further, (c) that active involvement in the self-help principles of AA, Al-Anon and NA make a significant difference in a personal program of growth and recovery.

The residential program is designed for individuals who require a closed, protective environment. Following admission, evaluation procedures are conducted, including physical exams and psychological testing. After data are thoroughly assessed, patient and staff together work out a personalized treatment plan. This program involves group and individual therapy, exercise, recreation and proper nutrition. All program elements are mandatory. Patients are expected to do the fourth and fifth Step of AA with the chaplain while in treatment. Other special services offered are yoga therapy, meditation therapy, aerobic therapy, back-to-work conferences and special-issues groups. Families of inpatients spend 1 full week at the Center, and close relatives and friends are intensely involved throughout the program.

The specialized aftercare program involves groups of patients and family, which meet weekly for 1 year led by specially trained aftercare group leaders. This program, in addition to AA and/or Al-Anon, provides the basis for post-treatment growth and support. Parkview also provides ongoing exchanges of patient information to all referrants.

SAINT MARY'S CHEMICAL DEPENDENCY SERVICES
SAINT MARY'S REHABILITATION CENTER

2512 South Seventh Street
Minneapolis, Minnesota 55454

(612) 338-2234 local
1-800-231-2234 outside Minnesota
1-800-338-2234 in Minnesota

Director: Jay L. Hauge

Average Patient Census: 85–90
Minimum Duration of Treatment: 21–28 days
Cost: Inpatient, $160 per day; outpatient, $65 per day. Insurance eligible.
Detoxification Offered: Yes
Accreditation: JCAH

In 1968, Saint Mary's recognized the need for the treatment of chemical dependency. Now, well into its second decade of treating alcoholism and drug addiction, the pioneering spirit of Saint Mary's, through diligence, perseverance and dedication, has attained national recognition. Experience, research and innovation have made Saint Mary's the standard by which other treatment facilities are judged. Flexible and adaptive, Saint Mary's continues to lead and to evolve, always striving to improve and adapt its program to the most contemporary methods.

Saint Mary's realizes that chemical dependency, although chronic and progressive, is not unconquerable. Patients can and do recover. Because chemical dependency affects all aspects of a person, physical, psychological and spiritual, the treatment program involves all of these areas. The team approach uses the expertise of a physician, nursing staff, chemical dependency counselors and spiritual care counselors, all working in harmony, to make the patient's goal of recovery attainable. Patients must abstain from all mood-altering chemicals unless prescribed by a physician, and there is access to complete medical facilities at Saint Mary's Hospital.

The effects of chemical dependency are not limited to the patient alone. Family members frequently share the burden with the patient, and therefore all involved parties are encouraged to share in the recovery process, with both daytime and evening programs available to them.

Saint Mary's opened one of the first adolescent programs in the Midwest in 1972, a complete 50-bed facility available to those between the ages of 13 and 17.

The aftercare program of 2 years' duration provides the time and continuing support essential to recovery. Weekly group sessions for patients, families and close friends provide this element, and alumni groups in many different cities help newly discharged patients realize they are not alone in the continuing work of recovery.

PINE MANORS, INC. #1

Route 2, Box 190
Pine City, Minnesota 55063

(612) 629-6769

Director: James R. Anderson, C.C.D.P.

Average Patient Census: Primary program, 26; detox, 8
Minimum Duration of Treatment: 28 days
Cost: $77 per day. Insurance eligible.
Detoxification Offered: Yes
Accreditation: States of Minnesota and Wisconsin

Pine Manors, Inc. #1, admits those persons, male or female, 15 years of age or older, who are ambulatory.

Patients with chemical dependency are examined through educational, medical and psychological/psychiatric testing and diagnosis. Chemical dependency screening and primary treatment are followed by educational training and restitution through community services. This facility also provides aftercare and follow-up, as well as Public Information and Awareness, and the Employee Relationship Program.

It is the stated philosophy at Pine Manor to encourage a contented and responsible life-style, free of mood-altering chemicals, through positive attitudes, self-acceptance, forgiveness and sense of purpose, using the full Twelve Steps of AA.

Located on picturesque Pokegama Lake, Pine Manor is centrally situated between Minneapolis, Duluth and Saint Cloud.

HAZELDEN PIONEER HOUSE

11505 36th Avenue North
Plymouth, Minnesota 55441

(612) 559-2022

Director: Jim Heaslip
Average Patient Census: 56

Minimum Duration of Treatment: 4–6 weeks average
Cost: Admission fee, $430; $98 per day thereafter. Insurance eligible.
Detoxification Offered: Yes
Accreditation: JCAH

Hazelden Pioneer House is a private, nonprofit, chemical-dependency unit on the north shore of Medicine Lake in Plymouth, Minnesota. The program offers primary inpatient treatment for chemically dependent persons age 14 to 30, male and female, prescreened for program appropriateness.

The individualized program includes group therapy, one-to-one counseling, psychological testing, family conferences, family groups, aftercare planning and groups and an overall education program. There is a structured school program in cooperation with the local school district.

Spouses and significant others are included in the treatment process, and therapy is made available to them in the form of Couples Group, Family Therapy and Family Conferences. Hazelden Pioneer offers a flexible program geared to individual needs, with assessment interview and individualized treatment planning.

THE GABLES

604 Fifth Street Southwest
Rochester, Minnesota 55902

(507) 282-2500

Director: Mary Keyes
Average Patient Census: 30-bed capacity

Minimum Duration of Treatment: Open-ended; patient is asked for at least a 3-month commitment
Cost: $100 per day, subject to change; ancillary medical charges additional. Insurance eligible.
Detoxification Offered: No. Use community hospital.
Accreditation: JCAH (in process 1984)

The Gables provides a full-day curriculum of care, in a residential setting, for women age 18 and over. The philosophy of treatment is based on the Twelve Step program of AA, the disease concept of alcoholism and the recognition of chemical dependency as a whole-person and family illness.

The professional staff at The Gables is committed to several concepts of wellness. Issues addressed in the program are: spirituality, sexuality, eating disorders, communications, family issues/concerns, codependency and issues pertinent to children of alcoholics. Psychological and medical problems are addressed and treated by appropriate professional and medical staff.

The general goal of the entire program is to help women take responsibility for their behavior and to learn more appropriate ways to handle their particular life situations. Therapy in one-on-one and group sessions, exercise, nutrition, education and family therapy will alter those parts of a woman's life in which she reacts to the family and to the social-interactive processes that have supported the dependency and fostered its progression. Suppressed feelings are allowed to surface in a safe environment and can be recognized and dealt with in a supportive and therapeutic manner. Insight, knowledge, assertiveness training and behavior modification all play an important part in the restructuring of a life free from chemical use.

The staff works cooperatively to develop individual treatment plans for each client and to present intensive daily therapy sessions and individual daily counseling during the week. Weekends are structured for leisure planning, therapy assignments and women's activities.

The Gables is an extended treatment facility, particularly helpful with those women who have already experienced primary treatment and are again having difficulty. It is housed in a completely renovated and elegantly decorated mansion in a quiet, residential neighborhood.

MAYO CLINIC ALCOHOL AND DRUG DEPENDENCY UNIT
Mayo Clinic and Rochester Methodist Hospital

Mayo Clinic
Rochester, Minnesota 55901

(507) 286-7593

Director: Bill Walker, C.C.D.P.

Average Patient Census: 33
Minimum Duration of Treatment: 4 weeks
Cost: Available on request. Insurance eligible.
Detoxification Offered: Yes
Accreditation: JCAH

The overall objective of the treatment program of the Alcoholism and Drug Dependency Unit is to arrest the pathological use of alcohol or other drugs and to begin the basic life changes necessary to eliminate dependence on these agents.

Therapy employed in the program includes medical, psychological, social and spiritual measures. Provided in the general treatment program are daily information sessions composed of lectures, discussions and films for both patients and interested relatives, which educate them about alcohol dependency. Small group-therapy meetings are held twice daily for patients in order to permit honest examination of themselves and their problems. Daily physical exercise in the hospital gymnasium is part of the program. There are also scheduled evening activities, such as films, discussions, crafts, recreation, family and spouse programs and AA meetings. Other aspects of therapy include individual counseling, medical or psychiatric treatment, library reading and visiting with relatives.

Family participation is encouraged for the benefit of themselves as well as that of the patient. The spouse is encouraged to attend morning informational meetings, scheduled evening Al-Anon meetings and a weekly program of education and group therapy.

NEW CONNECTION PROGRAMS, INC.

73 Leech Street
St. Paul, Minnesota 55102

(612) 224-4384

Director: Patrick Stevens

Average Patient Census: 40
Minimum Duration of Treatment: 28 days
Cost: Available on request. Insurance eligible.
Detoxification Offered: No
Accreditation: JCAH

New Connection Programs, Inc., is a private, nonprofit agency designed to meet the needs of chemically dependent and chemically abusive adolescents. Established in 1970, NCP provides several treatment, community and consultation services regarding adolescent chemical use.

New Connection believes recovery from adolescent chemical use is secure only when the adolescent is treated respectfully. Familial systems and relationships are explored in depth, and families are motivated to achieve recovery together. This time-proven process has enabled thousands of adolescents and their families to return to or begin healthy lifestyles.

In 1984, NCP obtained its second outpatient site in Cottage Grove, Minnesota, to complement the previous existing full range of services: primary inpatient and extended residential programs, and day and evening outpatient. The New Connection Program assessment is available through these programs. A copyrighted workbook is used to provide the individual with insights into their chemical problem. Family assessment is followed by an intensive parent education program during the adolescent treatment phase.

Treatment at New Connection nurtures adolescents back to health with a caring approach. Group, individual and family therapy form the base of the comprehensive program working with individual needs.

ALCOHOL AND CHEMICAL DEPENDENCY UNIT
SAINT CLOUD HOSPITAL

1406 Sixth Avenue North
Saint Cloud, Minnesota 56301

(612) 255-5612

Director: James L. Forsting

Average Patient Census: 50
Minimum Duration of Treatment: Adults, 18–35 days; adolescents, 30–60 days
Cost: Costs vary. Insurance eligible.
Detoxification Offered: Yes
Accreditation: JCAH

Saint Cloud Alcohol and Chemical Dependency Unit is multidisciplinary in nature, serving men and women age 12 and older on both an inpatient and an outpatient basis. The facility has 35 adult-bed and 15 adolescent-bed programs, plus an intensive outpatient program for 15 patients in a structured 16-week program.

Treatment consists of lectures, films, family and individual education, occupational therapy and recreational therapy. Participation in AA is strongly emphasized, and the Twelve Steps are integrated into the treatment process. Overall objectives include the attainment of abstinence and continuous participation in AA as a means of improving the quality of life in the areas of family functioning, physical health, social adjustment, spiritual development and emotional and vocational well-being.

MOUNDS PARK HOSPITAL

200 Earl Street
St. Paul, Minnesota 55109

(612) 774-5901, ext. 278

Director: Duane Bertelsen
Average Patient Census: 20

Minimum Duration of Treatment: 10–28 days, or detox and outpatient
Cost: $162 per day, which includes doctor, family and aftercare charges. Insurance eligible.
Detoxification Offered: Yes
Accreditation: JCAH

On admission to the program at Mounds Park, any urgent health need, such as detoxification, is first attended to, along with a physical examination, interviews and tests to assess the patient's present physical health.

During the residential stay, the patient hears lectures, sees films and has other educational experiences to provide knowledge of the effects of chemical abuse, and other physical, social and mental aspects of the disease.

Patients are introduced to the principles of AA through lectures, readings, talks by AA members and attendance of AA meetings in the community at least once in the course of treatment.

Individual consultations with counselors are held regularly to determine progress and find solutions to problems. Consultations are also held with the patient and his or her family and with the patient and employer. A family program is offered to the family.

A warm, accepting atmosphere underlies the themes of "Tough Love" and individual responsibility. The Aftercare Group is a transition program meeting once a week for 8 weeks, and attendance at these meetings is expected of all patients in order to get the full benefit of the program.

SAINT JOHN'S CHEMICAL DEPENDENCY TREATMENT CENTER

Saint John's Hospital
403 Maria Avenue
Saint Paul, Minnesota 55106

(612) 228-3471

Director: Joan Whitmer

Average Patient Census: 64
Minimum Duration of Treatment: 10–30 days
Cost: $145 plus doctor's fee. Insurance eligible.
Detoxification Offered: Yes
Accreditation: JCAH

When treatment begins at Saint John's inpatient program, withdrawal from mood-altering chemicals is done under the supervision of medical personnel.

At the start of the chemical dependency treatment, each patient is assigned a focal therapist to tailor the program to the individual's needs and to meet regularly with him or her for counseling sessions.

The philosophy of treatment at Saint John's CDTC is based on the principles of AA and includes lectures, films and personal and group counseling. Psychologists and psychiatrists are available on a consulting basis, as well as clergy or other spiritual advisors. Though time is tightly scheduled, there is free time allotted for reading, reflection, exercise and visits to outside AA meetings.

Saint John's also offers Adult and Adolescent Outpatient Treatment. The adolescent-program services closely parallel those provided to adult patients, with the addition of classroom education.

The Family Program is an integral part of treatment for all ages and is designed as a special Family Week Program, involving family members and significant others, in order that they may learn more about the disease concept of chemical dependency and participate in the individual group sessions, both with and without the patient.

An aftercare program is provided for all residents, inpatient or outpatient, and each is assigned to an aftercare group that meets once a week for 8 weeks in order to keep the principles learned in treatment alive and functioning.

JAMESTOWN ADOLESCENT TREATMENT PROGRAM

11550 Jasmine Trail North
Stillwater, Minnesota 55082

(612) 429-5307

Director: Jack T. Vigen, M.S.S.W.
Average Patient Census: 24

Minimum Duration of Treatment:
 Individualized, average 4–6 months
Cost: $147 per day. Insurance eligible.
Detoxification Offered: No
Accreditation: JCAH

Jamestown is a primary, long-term, residential treatment program for twenty-four adolescents, age 14 to 18, who have demonstrated chemical abuse concomitant with some number of mixed emotional, behavioral, legal, family, academic/learning, medical, victimization, psychiatric and/or developmental difficulties. Jamestown provides a multidisciplinary treatment program with the milieu of a treatment community. Treatment planning is individualized.

Jamestown has a dual licensure from the state of Minnesota for the treatment of chemical abuse and the treatment of emotional disturbance in adolescents and has JCAH accreditation as a chemical-abuse and psychiatric residential treatment program.

The program is most appropriate for the adolescent who might be termed dual-disability or multiproblemed, the young person who ordinarily poses a placement problem either due to lack of clarity in the chemical dependency diagnosis or because he or she seems unamenable to or inappropriate for traditional treatment. These individuals are strongly considered for admission.

Located on a 10-acre site in a rural suburb of the Twin Cities, Jamestown ordinarily advises a preplacement interview to determine the young person's appropriateness for admission. Referrals are welcome from other treatment programs, state/county court or social services agencies, EAPs, school systems, parents, and community-based mental/chemical health professionals.

Mississippi

THE PINES ALCOHOL REHABILITATION CENTER

2026 College Avenue
Columbus, Mississippi 39701

(601) 327-7916

Director: Florian Donatelli

Average Patient Census: 16 (men only)
Minimum Duration of Treatment: 6 weeks
Cost: None
Detoxification Offered: Yes
Accreditation: Certified by Mississippi Division of Alcohol and Drug Abuse and State Department of Mental Health

It is the purpose of The Pines Alcohol Rehabilitation Center to restore men affected by a drinking problem to a productive place in society.

The staff at The Pines consider alcoholism as a threefold and treatable illness. "We believe it is a physical, an emotional and a spiritual illness, which, though it can never be cured, can be arrested. In short, we believe a man truly affected with alcoholism can never safely drink again, but we also believe that we can motivate him to change to the point where he sees drinking as a detriment to a better life."

The basic philosophy of their treatment is the Twelve Steps of AA. Their basic books for study are the Big Book of AA, the Twelve Steps and the Twelve Traditions. The staff at The Pines will, however, use any methods necessary to prepare and motivate residents in order to bring about the necessary personality change. They therefore utilize encounter groups, group and individual therapy and counseling, movies, literature and tapes. They believe that peer-group therapy is the ultimate key to effecting successful change and ultimate recovery, not from drinking alcohol but from the disease of alcoholism.

DENTON CENTER
Region VI Alcoholism Rehabilitation Center

P.O. Box 1505
Greenwood, Mississippi 38930

(601) 453-6211

Director: Kinloch Gill, Jr., Ph.D.
Average Patient Census: 18 males

Minimum Duration of Treatment: Minimum, 30 days; maximum, 6 months.
Cost: None
Detoxification Offered: Yes
Accreditation: Certified by Mississippi Division of Alcohol and Drug Abuse, State Department of Mental Health

Denton Center offers a structured and comprehensive residential treatment program designed to help the individual male alcoholic arrest his drinking problem and develop necessary coping skills for functioning independently. Denton Center offers a homelike setting, encouraging residents to share their experiences and their search for alternatives in dealing with their problems.

Admission criteria are: (a) all admissions must be voluntary and based on a genuine desire to stop drinking; (b) the primary problem must be alcohol dependency; (c) the Center serves only males 18 years and older; and (d) participants must be residents of one of the following Mississippi counties: Attaba, Carroll, Grenada, Holmes, Humphreys, Leflore, Montgomery or Sunflower.

Denton Center is staffed with qualified professionals who understand the problem of alcoholism. All contacts and treatment remain confidential.

COUNTERPOINT CENTER OF SAND HILL HOSPITAL

12222 Highway 49 North
Gulfport, Mississippi 39505

(601) 831-1700

Director: Charles LeCluyse, Adolescent Program

Average Patient Census: 20 beds
Minimum Duration of Treatment: 28-day program
Cost: Available on request. Insurance eligible.
Detoxification Offered: Yes
Accreditation: JCAH

CounterPoint Center is a chemical dependency program for adolescents. The center is part of an international network of chemical dependency treatment centers located throughout the United States and Europe.

Chemical dependency is recognized as a primary disorder: chronic, progressive and potentially fatal, and prone to relapse if not properly treated. The disease factor is basic to treatment, which is provided by a multidisciplinary team of skilled professionals, many themselves recovering. All areas of a person's life are affected by chemical dependency. Therefore, the physical, emotional, social and spiritual needs of patients are all addressed through the treatment program.

Detoxification is the first phase of treatment. Following stabilization of acute medical problems, patients begin an intensive program of rehabilitation. The Twelve Steps of AA and NA are emphasized, and patients are expected to have selected an AA or NA group and a temporary sponsor by the time they are to begin the aftercare program. An individualized plan for aftercare is formulated with patient and family during the last week of treatment. Weekly group therapy is provided at no extra cost for 1 year, with a 2-year advisement period.

Family and significant others are included in treatment from the time of admission, with family assessment and couples and family therapy several times each week. Crisis intervention is also available.

For employers, the staff maintains open communications with EAP counselors and supervisors. Employers are included in the treatment process from the beginning, through discharge and into follow-up care.

BROOKWOOD RECOVERY CENTER—JACKSON

5354 I-55 South Frontage Road
Jackson, Mississippi 39212

(601) 372-9788

Director: Paul A. Brown, C.A.D.C.
Average Patient Census: 40 beds

Minimum Duration of Treatment:
  Alcoholism, 28 days; chemical dependency, 42 days
Cost: Approximately $7,000 for 28 days. Insurance eligible.
Detoxification Offered: Yes
Accreditation: JCAH

The treatment program at Brookwood Recovery Center—Jackson, both inpatient and outpatient, follows the disease model and is based on the fundamental concepts of AA, NA, Al-Anon and Alateen. The family program is 5 days residential.

After medical detoxification and psychological testing, the patient transfers to primary treatment, consisting of films, lectures, group and individual therapy, reading and written assignments, and going through the fourth and fifth steps of AA/NA. After completion of this 4- to 6-week intensive therapy, the patient is transferred to continuing care for a period of 2 years. During this aftercare period of treatment the patient will attend therapy sessions on an outpatient basis as his or her needs dictate, from once a week or less. The aftercare treatment reinforces and strengthens involvement of the whole family in AA, NA, Al-Anon and Alateen in order to increase the chances of a long-term sobriety.

Brookwood Recovery Center—Jackson assists business and industry in starting and maintaining effective EAPs, and assists families, friends, churches, etc., with intervention training and counseling. In addition, staff is available for community education for schools, churches, civic groups, etc.

CHEMICAL DEPENDENCY CENTER
MISSISSIPPI BAPTIST MEDICAL CENTER

1225 North State Street
Jackson, Mississippi 39201

(601) 968-1102

Director: Mary B. Ross

Average Patient Census: Maximum 80
Minimum Duration of Treatment: None
Cost: $115 per day, excluding lab, drugs, X ray. Insurance eligible.
Detoxification Offered: Yes
Accreditation: JCAH

The program at the Chemical Dependency Center is based on the philosophy of AA. Patients progress through the first five Steps of the AA program while in treatment and continue their recovery in an aftercare program.

Medical and nursing care is provided for detoxification and, if required, throughout the course of treatment.

To be eligible for admission, patients must be chemically dependent and capable of total self-care after detoxification.

The Chemical Dependency Center also offers the following programs: Adolescent Program, Family Program, Outpatient Program and Employee Rehabilitation Program.

SERENITY HOUSE

711 Royal Street
Laurel, Mississippi 39440

(601) 428-7241

Director: Chuck Bagley, M.A., C.A.D.C.
Average Patient Census: 12–13 males

Minimum Duration of Treatment: 6 weeks
Cost: Fees are assessed by the Department of Public Welfare based upon participant's income.
Detoxification Offered: Yes
Accreditation: Licensed by the State of Mississippi

Serenity House is a 13-bed facility for male alcoholics, with a staff of nine recovering chemically addicted and professionally trained counselors who have particular empathy for the problems of the alcoholic.

Opened in 1979 with an open-door policy welcoming any man who sought help in coping with the problems created by his drinking, the facility now offers medical and social detoxification. This program is funded by the Mississippi State Department of Public Welfare, the Mississippi Department of Mental Health, Division of Alcohol and Drug Abuse and the Region XII Commission on Mental Health and Retardation and offers a complete and caring rehabilitative program to participants. Particular efforts are made to adapt aspects of the program, as well as the duration of stay, to the particular needs of the individual. The program is designed to assess individual strengths and needs and to assist individuals in the area of psychological, physiological, sociological and spiritual deficits. The program is strongly AA-oriented.

HARMONY HOUSE

2806 Seventh Street
Meridian, Mississippi 39301

(601) 693-1001

Director: Gene May

Average Patient Census: Females, 4; males, 12
Minimum Duration of Treatment: 30 days
Cost: None
Detoxification Offered: Social
Accreditation: Licensed by the State of Mississippi

Harmony House is a state-funded halfway-house program offering, in a home atmosphere, a rehabilitation program designed to help the resident face the two basic realities of his or her situation: first, that he or she is sick and needs help, and second, that his or her illness can be arrested.

Services include social detoxification in a nonmedical setting, educational experiences aimed toward the illness of alcoholism, an introduction to the philosophy of AA, recreational activities, in-house work therapy, reality orientation, assertiveness training, instruction in communication skills, prevocational training and referral and aftercare follow-up.

The facility is designed primarily to serve residents of Clarke, Jasper, Kemper, Lauderdale, Leake, Neshoba, Newton, Scott and Smith counties who desire help with a drinking problem.

HAVEN HOUSE

Route 4, Box 32
Oxford, Mississippi 38655

(601) 234-7237

Director: Billy Smith
Average Patient Census: 13

Minimum Duration of Treatment: 30–90 days
Cost: Title XX eligible, no cost; others, $18 per day. Insurance eligible.
Detoxification Offered: Yes
Accreditation: State Department of Mental Health and State Department of Public Welfare

Haven House offers a comprehensive approach in dealing with alcohol dependence, encompassing physical, social, spiritual, educational and psychological needs of the alcoholic.

Services include general activities, such as individual and group counseling, family counseling, communication skills, self-awareness training, prevocational and vocational training and transportation for the client, as necessary, for these or other needed services.

Medical and remedial services include Antabuse therapy, as an adjunct to other therapies, and medication checks provided by qualified professionals.

Title XX eligibility will be determined by the appropriate County Department of Public Welfare, but there is potential to serve three non-eligible residents.

Criteria for admission include a willingness to participate in the program and live by program policies. Residents must be 18 years of age or older, or have written consent from their parents or legal guardian.

Haven House will offer a new beginning, endeavoring to serve as a meaningful transition from addiction to adequacy in coping without dependence on alcohol.

Missouri

RALEIGH HILLS HOSPITAL
Saint Louis County

1033 Manchester Road
Ellisville, Missouri 63011

(314) 227-4400

Director: Paul W. Rexroat, Ph.D.
Average Patient Census: 25–35

Minimum Duration of Treatment: Inpatient, 3 weeks; aftercare, full year
Cost: Available on request. Insurance eligible.
Detoxification Offered: Yes
Accreditation: JCAH

Raleigh Hills Hospital offers a comprehensive program for the treatment of adults who are dependent on alcohol or drugs. A team approach is used in treating each individual. Under the supervision of the medical director, highly qualified staff provide educational and treatment experiences that lead to recovery. These professionals are from the disciplines of psychology, nursing, social work, counseling and recreational therapy. The 3-week structured program includes individual therapy, group and family counseling, educational lectures and films, stress management, biofeedback, recreational and occupational therapies and aversion therapy, as appropriate. The program strongly supports the role of AA, NA and other groups in helping individuals regain their place within the community. During hospitalization, patients attend meetings held both at the hospital and in the community.

The family is encouraged to participate in specific treatment activities, such as Al-Anon and Alateen meetings, lectures and family groups. Through therapy the family is educated about the disease process and problems affecting the addicted person.

Discharge planning begins at the time of admission and becomes increasingly focused toward the end of hospitalization. Aftercare includes continued consultation with the physician, attendance of group meetings with former Raleigh Hills patients and support meetings such as AA, appropriate to various schedules and locations. Patients who have received aversion therapy during hospitalization may return for additional treatments throughout the year. Charges for additional treatments will be incurred on a per-visit basis.

Raleigh Hills has recently been completely renovated, and the semi-private rooms are colorful and cheerful; the comfortable surroundings are conducive to treatment and recovery. The hospital is located on 5 spacious acres in west Saint Louis County.

HEALTHQUEST
TRINITY LUTHERAN HOSPITAL

3030 Baltimore Street
Kansas City, Missouri 64108

(816) 753-4600

Director: L. C. Smith, M.S.W.

Average Patient Census: 10
Minimum Duration of Treatment: 28 days
Cost: $205 per day. Insurance eligible.
Detoxification Offered: Yes
Accreditation: JCAH

Healthquest offers a culturally specific substance abuse treatment program geared exclusively to the black troubled employee and dependents who are experiencing difficulties due to alcohol and other chemical addiction.

The program is drug-free, except during detoxification, which is medically managed. The center is staffed by a multidisciplinary team of professionals experienced in working with Afro-Americans who are chemically dependent. The program features daily individual and group therapy sessions, a family component, and aftercare for 2 years following treatment.

Healthquest emphasizes a unique blend of the principles of AA and Rational Behavior Therapy and cites this culturally specific treatment's 73% success rate, measured 1 year after treatment. It notes that the program is geared particularly to referrals from industry and labor groups.

KOALA CENTER
(FORMERLY WHITE DEER RUN TREATMENT CENTER)

P.O. Box 90
Lonedell, Missouri 63060

(314) 629-5100

Director: Jerry Martin
Average Patient Census: 18

Minimum Duration of Treatment: Adults, 30 days
Cost: Available on request. Insurance eligible.
Detoxification Offered: Yes
Accreditation: JCAH

Koala Centers and White Deer centers are specialized facilities devoted to the treatment of alcoholism and drug abuse. Until recently these two respected names in the health care field were separate entities. Now Koala and White Deer have joined forces, enabling them to provide a wider range of services over a broader geographic area. Together, White Deer and Koala are committed to a common goal of continued progress in the development of successful substance abuse treatment programs.

These centers use a multidisciplinary approach to treatment designed to obtain the most positive results. They offer individualized programs that include 4- to 6-week inpatient care for adults and adolescents, outpatient services and an intensive family program. The centers work closely with employers and unions, physicians, school systems, parent groups, court officials and clergy, as well as with other groups who become involved in the problems of alcohol or drug abuse.

COUNTERPOINT CENTER OF WELDON SPRING HOSPITAL

5931 Highway 94 South
St. Charles, Missouri 63301

(314) 441-7300

Director: Sterling Brown
Average Patient Census: 32 beds

Minimum Duration of Treatment: 28-day program
Cost: Available on request. Insurance eligible.
Detoxification Offered: Yes
Accreditation: JCAH

CounterPoint Center is a chemical dependency program for adolescents. The center is part of an international network of chemical dependency treatment centers located throughout the United States and Europe.

Chemical dependency is recognized as a primary disorder: chronic, progressive and potentially fatal, and prone to relapse if not properly treated. The disease factor is basic to treatment, which is provided by a multidisciplinary team of skilled professionals, many themselves recovering. All areas of a person's life are affected by chemical dependency. Therefore, the physical, emotional, social and spiritual needs of patients are all addressed through the treatment program.

Detoxification is the first phase of treatment. Following stabilization of acute medical problems, patients begin an intensive program of rehabilitation. The Twelve Steps of AA and NA are emphasized, and patients are expected to have selected an AA or NA group and a temporary sponsor by the time they are to begin the aftercare program. An individualized plan for aftercare is formulated with patient and family during the last week of treatment. Weekly group therapy is provided at no extra cost for 1 year, with a 2-year advisement period.

Family and significant others are included in treatment from the time of admission, with family assessment and couples and family therapy several times each week. Crisis intervention is also available.

For employers, the staff maintains open communications with EAP counselors and supervisors. Employers are included in the treatment process from the beginning, through discharge and into follow-up care.

CAREUNIT HOSPITAL OF SAINT LOUIS

1755 South Grand Boulevard
Saint Louis, Missouri 63104

(314) 771-0500

Director: Vince Sullivan
Average Patient Census: Adults, 38; adolescents, 38

Minimum Duration of Treatment: Adults, 21–28 days; adolescents, 45–60 days
Cost: Approximately $300 per day. Insurance eligible.
Detoxification Offered: Yes
Accreditation: JCAH

CareUnit Hospital is a facility specializing in the family treatment of alcohol and other drug dependencies for adults and adolescents. Patients undergo a complete physiological and psychological examination and detoxification under the supervision of the medical director of the facility. The treatment program is personalized to fit individual needs and consists of individual and group therapy, participation in specific activities, lectures and films designed to increase the patient's understanding of his or her disease, and appropriate ways to enjoy life free from chemical dependency. Families are invited to join in the treatment program, which is designed to free family members from the effects of the disease in areas such as behavior, attitudes and life-styles.

The recovery continues following the patient's discharge from the hospital. Patients return to the CareUnit for aftercare 2 evenings a week for a specified period following discharge. Family units participate once weekly in the aftercare program. Patients and their families are encouraged to explore other resources, such as AA, Al-Anon, Alateen, NA and others, to which they were introduced during their inpatient stay. Aftercare is free to all patients—for a lifetime, if desired.

CareUnit Hospital of Saint Louis also offers outpatient and day care treatment and has an 18-bed Eating Disorders Unit, a 21-bed Stress Center and a 20-bed Adolescent Stress Center.

THE EDGEWOOD PROGRAM
SAINT JOHN'S MERCY MEDICAL CENTER

615 South New Ballas Road
Saint Louis, Missouri 63141

(314) 569-6500

Director: Lyle Cameron
Average Patient Census: 52 beds

Minimum Duration of Treatment: Approximately 30 days
Cost: Acute care, $205 per day for 2–3 days; comprehensive care, $190 per day. Insurance eligible.
Detoxification Offered: Yes
Accreditation: JCAH

The Edgewood Program is the Chemical Dependency Department of Saint John's Mercy Medical Center. The staff includes recovery-trained counselors, physicians, registered nurses, psychologists, psychiatrists, social workers, dieticians, pharmacologists and clergy.

Treatment includes the physical aspects of the illness, psychological assistance, sociological help for healthy integration back into society and spiritual guidance to nurture or revive the patient's spiritual awareness. The counselors, many of whom are recovering from the illness, assist the patient in understanding the steps toward recovery by offering appropriate and sensitive attention to the individual's needs. Aftercare is available, at no additional charge to the patient, upon successful completion of the inpatient program.

TURNING POINT
PARK CENTRAL HOSPITAL

440 South Market Street
Springfield, Missouri 65806

(417) 865-5581

Director: Svenn A. Sollid, M.S., C.A.C.
Average Patient Census: 20

Minimum Duration of Treatment: 28 days; detox only, 3–7 days
Cost: Detox, $350 per day; primary program, $275 per day. Insurance eligible.
Detoxification Offered: Yes
Accreditation: JCAH

Turning Point, a hospital-based alcoholism and drug abuse treatment program, believes that effective treatment requires long-term contact to achieve continued success.

The program includes evaluations, intervention, detoxification, treatment of related health problems, counseling for individual, family and employer, group therapy, educational seminars, concurrent family treatment and introduction to community resources such as AA.

The program is kept flexible in recognition of individual needs and special circumstances, and respect for the dignity and privacy of each individual is a major goal for staff and patient alike.

Turning Point's facilities are contained within a special section of the full-service hospital, ensuring privacy and confidentiality. Patients normally share a room with one other person selected for compatibility, which provides the reinforcement that comes from sharing the experience with someone of similar needs.

Aftercare includes weekly group sessions and individual counseling if necessary, as well as 2-years' follow-up.

Nebraska

INDEPENDENCE CENTER

2440 Saint Mary's Avenue
Lincoln, Nebraska 68502

1-800-472-7845; Adults: (402) 473-5268, Youth: (402) 473-5394, Evaluation: (402) 473-5912

Director: Ron Namuth

Average Patient Census: 110 in all primary programs
Minimum Duration of Treatment: 30 days
Cost: Adult inpatient, $3,900; youth inpatient, $4,800; partial care, $1,700. Aftercare and family programs are included. Insurance eligible.
Detoxification Offered: Yes
Accreditation: JCAH

Independence Center's treatment programs are based on the disease theory of chemical dependency and strongly oriented to the philosophies of AA, NA and Al-Anon. The Center offers distinctive residential programs for youth, men and women. All of them include detoxification, 24-hour nursing coverage supervised by physicians and psychological and psychiatric services as needed. The adult treatment cycle is 30 days, and the youth cycle is 45 days.

All programs offer lectures, readings, individual counseling, recreational therapy, nutritional counseling, pastoral care, AA meetings and focus groups on self-esteem, peer relations, grief and relaxation.

Outpatient programs include a 6-week Partial-Care Program meeting days or evenings for adults and a Special-Services Program with weekly meetings. Youth are offered a 2-week educational program for prevention and a 4-week Partial-Care Program for abuse/dependency.

Aftercare support groups meet on a weekly basis, and former patients contribute hundreds of hours a month as volunteers and members of the Alumni Association.

Families are served by information calls, which is a free service offered 24 hours a day. Monthly information meetings and Family Intervention classes help people respond to a chemical dependency. Families are encouraged to attend their own partial-care treatment program for 1 week of days or 2 weeks of evenings.

The Center offers professionals and employers evaluations, consultations and medical interventions by an R.N. as free services. A variety of training programs are given to employers and human service professionals.

EPPLEY CHEMICAL DEPENDENCY SERVICES
Nebraska Methodist Hospital

3612 Cuming Street
Omaha, Nebraska 68131

(402) 397-3150, ext. 521

Director: William Crooks

Average Patient Census: 110
Minimum Duration of Treatment: Approximately 35 days
Cost: $132 per day. Insurance eligible.
Detoxification Offered: Yes
Accreditation: JCAH

Eppley Chemical Dependency Services at Methodist Midtown Hospital is designed to treat chemically dependent adults and adolescents, as well as family members and significant others who have been affected by the disease of chemical dependency.

Treatment programs are based on the disease concept, total abstinence and the philosophy of AA, and utilize a multidisciplinary approach whose goal is to help the patient confront the illness realistically, to build a new system of values and to live as a responsible, functioning human being. The treatment team consists of physicians, nurses, medical specialists, psychologists, counselors and a pastoral care staff. Program components are detoxification, individual counseling, group therapy, special-needs groups, education, pastoral guidance and aftercare. In addition, the adolescent program incorporates school tutoring and recreational therapy.

Because the entire family suffers from the consequences of having a chemically dependent member in its midst, Eppley sees the entire family becoming the focus of treatment. Both day and evening outpatient programs are available to assist those individuals in the understanding of the disease and the steps that can be taken toward their own recovery through an Al-Anon–based philosophy and involvement. A 9-week adult outpatient program is also offered.

Eppley's 13-month accredited counselor training program is nationally recognized. There is, in addition, a 7-month counselor-training program for degreed individuals with experience in the helping professions.

ALCOHOLISM TREATMENT CENTER
IMMANUEL MEDICAL CENTER

6901 North Seventy-second Street
Omaha, Nebraska 68122

(402) 572-2016

Director: Jim Mays
Average Patient Census: Inpatient, 29; family, 15

Minimum Duration of Treatment: Inpatient, 28 days; partial care, 6 weeks; family, 2 weeks; outpatient, 3 weeks
Cost: Variable with program. Insurance eligible.
Detoxification Offered: Yes
Accreditation: JCAH

Treatment at Immanuel Alcoholism Treatment Center is a combination of determination on the part of the patient, plus the development, through staff and programs, of the heightening awareness of how behavior and relationships have affected and will continue to affect his life. The Center itself is a valuable therapy "tool," in that it provides a setting conducive to relaxation and openness between patient and family, patient and patient, and patient and staff.

A complete physical examination, followed by 2-day detoxification, if necessary, are completed on admission. Medical care is an integral part of each patient's program throughout the course of treatment.

The 28-day rehabilitation program includes psychologically oriented lectures by staff and interested outside personnel; AA orientation; a lecture series to acquaint patients with the workings of AA; daily recreation with both indoor and outdoor activities; group and couples counseling emphasizing communication and concern between patients, families and staff; and special activities of films and guest lectures.

The Family Program is a comprehensive service that involves participants in group and individual counseling, psychological tests, medical treatment, and an introduction to Al-Anon.

NEBRASKA PSYCHIATRIC INSTITUTE

602 South Forty-fifth Street
Omaha, Nebraska 68106

(402) 559-5000

Director: Merrill T. Eaton, M.D.
Average Patient Census: 95 beds total

Minimum Duration of Treatment: As indicated by symptoms
Cost: Approximately $260 per day, plus physician charges. Insurance eligible.
Detoxification Offered: Yes
Accreditation: JCAH

Nebraska Psychiatric Institute is the Department of Psychiatry at the University of Nebraska Medical Center. As such, teaching and research are among its primary objectives. A full range of health services is available by a treatment team composed of psychiatrists, psychiatric residents, medical students, social workers, vocational rehabilitation specialists, recreational and occupational specialists, clinical and experimental psychologists, volunteer counselors and human services technicians.

NPI does not have an alcoholism treatment program per se; in that there is no specified alcoholism unit or defined length of treatment. Patients at various stages of their alcohol problem are treated, however, and services include detoxification, inpatient hospitalization, and day and outpatient treatment. An individualized treatment program is established for each patient, and the treatment team meets regularly to evaluate the patient's progress.

There is no special admission requirement other than space; as a teaching facility, NPI sets a limit on the number of patients admitted under one particular diagnosis, that is, alcoholism or any other diagnosis.

VALLEY HOPE ALCOHOLISM TREATMENT CENTER

Box 918, North Tenth Street
O'Neill, Nebraska 68763

(402) 336-3747

Director: Keith Willis, Ph.D.

Average Patient Census: 50
Minimum Duration of Treatment: 30 days; 6-week maximum
Cost: $97 per day. Insurance eligible.
Detoxification Offered: Yes
Accreditation: JCAH

Valley Hope is a private, nonprofit, nonsectarian organization, with a treatment program that consists of a well-planned, proven-successful, individually tailored series of medical, psychological, social, spiritual, vocational and recreational therapies.

Each person who comes to Valley Hope for guidance is treated as a unique individual, and treatment recommendations are based on individual requirements made by trained counselors and with the aid of psychological testing. Patients are given a thorough orientation into the AA and Al-Anon way of life.

There are Valley Hope Treatment Centers in Norton and Atchison, Kansas; Cushing, Oklahoma; and Booneville, Missouri. These are listed by state in this directory. Valley Hope outpatient counseling centers are located in Greater Kansas City and Wichita, Kansas; and in Lincoln, Nebraska.

WEST NEBRASKA EPPLEY CHEMICAL DEPENDENCY SERVICES

4021 Avenue B
Scottsbluff, Nebraska 69361

(308) 632-0282

Director: Harry A. Waltemath

Average Patient Census: 12
Minimum Duration of Treatment: 30 days
Cost: $145 per day. Insurance eligible.
Detoxification Offered: Yes
Accreditation: JCAH

Inpatient care at the Chemical Dependency Unit at West Nebraska General Hospital is divided into three phases: detoxification, inpatient therapy and aftercare.

Detoxification is a medically supervised withdrawal regimen provided for those needing medical care during this potentially life-threatening process. Inpatient therapy is designed to help the chemically dependent person understand and accept his or her treatable illness. Educational lectures and films, group therapy, individual counseling and peer therapy, as well as an introduction to AA are provided, as the patient, along with his or her counselor, establishes an individualized treatment plan, setting the personal goals and objectives to be completed in this inpatient phase. The third phase, aftercare, is a 10-week program, with the individual returning to the unit once a week for group therapy sessions.

In addition, in recognition that alcoholism and/or drug dependency is a family illness, the CDU offers to families a 2-week day care program (or a 3-week evening care program) that includes lectures, films, group therapy, individual counseling and discussions designed to help family members understand their roles in the disease process and to help them get rid of the guilt, shame and anger usually associated with the illness. A 10-week aftercare program is provided for participants, as well as an introduction to Al-Anon.

North Dakota

CROSSROADS CENTER OF SAINT JOHN'S HOSPITAL

510 South 4th Street
Fargo, North Dakota 58103

(701) 232-3331, ext. 414 or 419

Director: John J. Allen
Average Patient Census: 30

Minimum Duration of Treatment: 5–6 weeks
Cost: Daily fees in addition to fees for other services. Insurance eligible.
Detoxification Offered: Yes
Accreditation: JCAH

Crossroads Center of Saint John's Hospital provides both inpatient and outpatient treatment, diagnostic services and aftercare for the chemically dependent person and their family members.

Both inpatient and outpatient services are of 5-weeks' duration and include the following: informational and educational lectures, group therapy, individual and family counseling, educational programs for family, spiritual counseling and psychiatric consultation as necessary. AA and NA participation and appropriate referrals to community services are also part of the program, and aftercare group counseling involves one session weekly for 10 weeks.

Any individual between the age of 21 and 65 may be admitted. Patients under 21 or over 65 are required to have preadmission interviews. All persons must be able to participate actively in the program.

UNITED RECOVERY CENTER

Medical Park
Box 6002
Grand Fork, North Dakota 58206

(701) 780-5900

Director: Bill Payne

Minimum Duration of Treatment: Adults, 28 days; adolescents, 42 days
Cost: Detox, $190 per day; adults, $115 per day; adolescents, $150 per day. Insurance eligible.
Detoxification Offered: Yes
Accreditation: JCAH

United Recovery Center bases its program on the conviction that every aspect of the patient, including physical, mental, emotional, spiritual and social, is affected by addiction and that every area needs attention in the recovery process.

The treatment program is flexible in order to adapt to the individual needs of each patient, but generally includes the following steps: Evaluation consists of professional analysis of the client's condition to determine whether an alcohol or drug dependency exists. This is followed by detoxification under medical supervision. Inpatient treatment after detox offers a primary therapeutic program; a structured living experience focuses on the development of skills that will enable patients to manage their lives more effectively. Also offered is a longer program designed especially for adolescents who are experiencing chemical- and life-management problems.

Aftercare includes weekly group support and counseling for both patients and family members as they learn to adjust to daily living without the use of alcohol and other drugs.

The Center also offers community outreach programs, intervention assistance and consulting services for business, industry and educational and health care institutions.

HEARTVIEW FOUNDATION

1406 Second Street, N.W.
Mandan, North Dakota 58554

(701) 663-2321

Director: Will O. Wells, Ph.D.
Average Patient Census: Adults, 64; adolescents, 27

Minimum Duration of Treatment: Adults, 28 days; adolescents, 35 days
Cost: Adults, average cost $3,800; adolescents, average cost $5,600. Insurance eligible.
Detoxification Offered: Yes
Accreditation: JCAH

Heartview operates on the basic premise that alcoholism and other addictions are treatable illnesses. Using a variety of therapeutic methods, the addiction counselors, medical doctors, psychiatrist, trained nurses and clergymen work cooperatively to help the patient and his or her family understand and deal effectively with each facet of the addiction problem. Treatment occurs through many disciplines: physical, psychological, emotional, spiritual, social and educational.

Counselors provide individual, group and family therapy, as well as a strong informational and educational lecture series to assist the addicted individual and his or her family understand the addiction process. Families are urged to take an active part in treatment and attend a Family Week for a 5-day program of lectures, group therapy and private counseling. Accommodations for nine families are available on the Heartview campus.

Heartview is firmly committed to the philosophy of AA, and participation is encouraged in AA/NA both during and after treatment.

Heartview has an adolescent unit designed specifically to meet the needs of chemically dependent adolescents. Programming is for adolescents age 18 and under. Programming takes place 7 days a week, including programming for parents on weekends.

CHEMICAL DEPENDENCY UNIT
SAINT JOSEPH'S HOSPITAL

Third Street, S.E., and Burdick Expressway
Minot, North Dakota 58701

(701) 857-2480

Average Patient Census: 20
Minimum Duration of Treatment: 28 days
Cost: $5,000. Insurance eligible.
Detoxification Offered: Yes
Accreditation: JCAH

Director: Allen Gillette, M.S., M.A.C.

The Chemical Dependency Unit of Saint Joseph's Hospital is a private, nonprofit organization designed to treat those individuals and their families who suffer from alcoholism and other drug dependencies.

The mode of treatment is group therapy, conducted by two certified addiction counselors assigned to each group. A week-long family week, mandatory for every patient's treatment, occurs during the third week of treatment.

A strong chaplaincy program is available to each patient. This is designed to guide the patient through the fourth and fifth Steps of AA, and all AA principles are strongly emphasized throughout the program.

Two in-house AA meetings are held each week. Recreational therapy is mandatory for 1½ hours a day, along with many milieu activities.

The treatment team at Saint Joseph's CDU is composed of a medical director, clinical director, four inpatient counselors, two outpatient/aftercare counselors, a chaplain, consulting psychologist and psychiatrist and eight registered nurses.

Outreach services are also available at Bottineau and Rolla Hospitals.

Ohio

BETHESDA ALCOHOL AND DRUG TREATMENT PROGRAM

7N 619 Oak Street
Cincinnati, Ohio 45206

(513) 569-6014

Director: Mark Davis

Average Patient Census: 24 plus detox accommodations
Minimum Duration of Treatment: 4 weeks; longer if needed
Cost: $173 per day. Insurance eligible.
Detoxification Offered: Yes
Accreditation: JCAH

The Bethesda Alcohol and Drug Treatment Program bases its philosophy on the premise that alcoholism is a treatable disease and offers a therapeutic program for persons and their families who suffer from this disease. Bethesda believes that a very similar pattern exists with many other mood-altering drugs, and that the myth that alcoholism and certain other dependencies are in any way mutually exclusive is erroneous. Similarities far outweigh differences, and similar treatment can be effectively utilized for both.

The inpatient program offers medical examination, detox if necessary, and individual counseling. A variety of group counseling and therapy sessions serve as the primary means of treatment. AA-related activities are integrated into the program, and additional activities in the form of required reading, selected films, recreation, therapeutic passes for realistic testing of the patient's treatment plan, and referrals to other community resources are provided.

Stress is also laid upon the importance of the Family Program, as well as the Aftercare Program for both inpatient and Family Program graduates. Aftercare is a part of the total treatment program, a 1-year continuing effort toward promotion of comfortable transition into a new and satisfying life-style.

CAREUNIT HOSPITAL OF CINCINNATI

3156 Glenmore Avenue
Cincinnati, Ohio 45211

(513) 481-8822

Director: Conrad Foss
Average Patient Census: Adults, 48; adolescents, 36

Minimum Duration of Treatment: Adults, 21–28 days; adolescents, 45–60 days
Cost: Approximately $300 per day. Insurance eligible.
Detoxification Offered: Yes
Accreditation: JCAH

CareUnit Hospital is a facility specializing in the family treatment of alcohol and other drug dependencies for adults and adolescents. Patients undergo a complete physiological and psychological examination and detoxification under the supervision of the medical director of the facility. The treatment program is personalized to fit individual needs and consists of individual and group therapy, participation in specific activities, and lectures and films designed to increase the patient's understanding of his or her disease and appropriate ways to enjoy life free from chemical dependency. Families are invited to join in the treatment program, which is designed to free family members from the effects of the disease in areas such as behavior, attitudes and life-styles.

The recovery continues following the patient's discharge from the hospital. Patients return to the CareUnit for aftercare two evenings a week for a specified period following discharge. Family units participate once weekly in the aftercare program. Patients and their families are encouraged to explore other resources, such as AA, Al-Anon, Alateen, NA and others, to which they were introduced during their inpatient stay. Aftercare is free to all patients—for a lifetime, if desired.

CareUnit of Cincinnati also offers an outpatient treatment program.

ALCOHOL REHABILITATION CENTER
CLEVELAND METROPOLITAN GENERAL HOSPITAL

3395 Scranton Road
Cleveland, Ohio 44109

(216) 459-5677

Director: Robert L. Smith, Ph.D.
Average Patient Census: 10–15

Minimum Duration of Treatment: 2 weeks
Cost: Inpatient, $375 per day; day care, $90 per day. Insurance eligible.
Detoxification Offered: Yes, in conjunction with rehab.
Accreditation: Ohio Department of Health

The Alcohol Rehabilitation Center offers inpatient detoxification, rehabilitation, day care treatment and aftercare to those experiencing problems with alcohol abuse and alcoholism, as well as to those who are dually addicted.

Inpatient and day care patients are treated together in group sessions. The program consists of educational lectures, group therapy sessions, family therapy sessions, individual counseling and involvement with AA or NA. The group and educational sessions deal with such subjects as diagnosis, medical aspects of the illness, cross-addictions, dietary aspects, attitudes, social skills, sexuality, community resources available to the patient and the AA philosophy toward rehabilitation.

Patients completing either the inpatient or the day care program are encouraged to attend a 12-week aftercare program in addition to participation in AA/NA as a support system. Discharged patients are followed for 2 years by clinical secretaries, who telephone on a regular basis.

ADOLESCENT ALCOHOLISM TREATMENT PROGRAM— TALBOT HALL
Saint Anthony Hospital

1450 Hawthorne Avenue
Columbus, Ohio 43203

(614) 251-3760

Director: Richard R. Schnurr, M.A., C.A.C.

Average Patient Census: 26
Minimum Duration of Treatment: Average 4 weeks
Cost: Available on request; hospital per diem. Insurance eligible.
Detoxification Offered: Yes
Accreditation: JCAH

The Adolescent Alcoholism Treatment Program at Talbot Hall, Saint Anthony Hospital, treats alcoholism as a disease and provides a total inpatient treatment regimen that includes medical, psychological and spiritual elements. The goal of the program is total abstinence and contented sobriety. Emphasis is placed on teaching patients to feel good about themselves without the use of alcohol or other drugs. The Twelve Steps of AA are basic to the program.

After detoxification-evaluation, patients are tested psychologically, and the first 7 days involve motivation assessment as well. Upon acceptance into a treatment group, individual and group therapy begin, with other parts of the program including physical, recreational and occupational therapy, psychodrama, lectures and AA meetings. "Quiet times" each day are used for self-assessment.

Family involvement is required in both individual and group counseling. The Aftercare Program is extensive and includes weekly meetings for patients and families for 12 weeks. AA, Al-Anon or FA activity is also required for families.

There is also a treatment program for adults at Talbot Hall, with a 28-day time frame and a similar treatment approach.

BROOKWOOD RECOVERY CENTER—COLUMBUS

349 Ridenour Road
Columbus, Ohio 43230

(614) 471-1601, Crisis Line
(614) 471-2552, Business Line

Director: Chris Gerber
Average Patient Census: 50 beds

Minimum Duration of Treatment: Alcoholism, 28 days; chemical dependency, 42 days
Cost: Approximately $6,400 for 28 days. Insurance eligible.
Detoxification Offered: Yes
Accreditation: JCAH

The treatment program at Brookwood Recovery Center is designed to treat the total person and to restore him to comfortable sobriety in which he is able to choose not to drink or use other mood-altering chemicals and is able to resume a healthy, productive way of life. The patient is assisted in arresting the condition and helped to develop a motivation based primarily on reason. In all cases, the goal is the achievement and maintenance of total abstinence from alcohol and other chemicals.

A therapeutic-community approach is used in which every employee, from the groundskeeper to the counselors, plays a part in the physical, mental, emotional, spiritual and economic rehabilitation of the patient. All aspects of the program are supervised by experienced professionals certified in the treatment of alcoholism and chemical dependency.

Brookwood recognizes the effectiveness of AA, especially in the patient's spiritual growth. Meetings are hosted at the center, and patients are strongly encouraged to become members.

A family treatment program is also offered, with individual as well as conjoint counseling, to ensure that all those involved fully comprehend the task that lies ahead. Family members live at the center for 1 week of therapy and education while the patient is a resident.

As part of Brookwood's never-ending commitment to the patient, a Continuing-Care Program is maintained to assist in the successful return to home, community and job.

LAKELAND INSTITUTE

3500 Kolbe Road
Lorain, Ohio 44053

(216) 282-7106

Director: Seth F. Nieding, A.C.S.W., C.A.C.
Average Patient Census: 60

Minimum Duration of Treatment: Individualized lengths of stay
Cost: Outpatient, $20 per day; partial hospitalization, $80 per day; Residential, $225 per day; hospital, $263 per day. Insurance eligible.
Detoxification Offered: Yes
Accreditation: JCAH

Treatment at the Lakeland Institute is based on the philosophy that chemical dependency is a highly treatable, but complex, progressive illness that negatively affects not only the individual but the family and significant others. Four small living communities of twelve persons each are the basic grouping in the Lorain Community Hospital's award-winning freestanding chemical dependency treatment center. Staff members have found that living groups of twelve are ideal for the group portions of the residential program.

Detoxification, medical examination and psychosocial assessment are parts of the first phase of treatment, with families taking part in the assessment proceedings. During the 28-day Phase Two, individuals receive a combination of educational instruction and group therapy as a basis for understanding and personal growth. Supplementing these activities are individual, marital and family therapy. One day per week is Family Day. All family members and significant others are required to attend and participate in treatment with the resident.

The philosophy of AA plays a significant role in treatment. AA, Al-Anon and Alateen meetings are held at the institute. Other treatment methods include recreational therapy, spirituality group, relaxation-response instruction and emotional identification.

Admission to Lakeland Institute, which may be arranged by individual, family member or referral, is open to males and females, age 13 and over.

Lakeland Institute also offers primary outpatient, partial hospitalization and intensive aftercare services.

ALCOHOLISM TREATMENT CENTER
The Toledo Hospital

2142 North Cove Boulevard
Toledo, Ohio 43606

(419) 241-3662

Director: William J. Shanahan, Ph.D.
Average Patient Census: Adults, 32; adolescents, 26

Minimum Duration of Treatment: Adults, 28 days; adolescents, 35 days
Cost: Adults, $192.99 per day; adolescents, $225.99 per day; additional cost for detox. Insurance eligible.
Detoxification Offered: Yes
Accreditation: JCAH

The traditional adult program at the Toledo Hospital requires an average 4-week stay. During this period the patient is provided with care by a treatment team that includes various counselors, nurses and medical consultants. Other specialists are called upon as needed.

Patients entering adolescent treatment can expect to spend the first 7 days in the detoxification/evaluation stage. Following this assessment, the patient will become involved in the regular treatment program.

It is mandatory for the immediate family of both adult and adolescent patients to be involved in the program. The center provides weekly family counseling and a 4-session family education program on chemical dependency. Attendance at family support group meetings, such as Al-Anon and Tough Love, is also required. Admission to the program may be denied or a discharge may be imposed if these conditions cannot or are not being met.

Participation in aftercare completes the patient's treatment process. Aftercare participation is done in conjunction with the patient's referral source. The aftercare group meets once a week, with the length of time depending upon the adjustment in the community.

In conjunction with traditional therapeutic approaches, the Toledo Hospital Alcoholism Treatment Center places heavy emphasis on AA and similar self-help programs.

THE CAMPUS

905 South Sunbury Road
Westerville, Ohio 43081

(614) 895-1000

Director: Bart Flaherty
Average Patient Census: 20

Minimum Duration of Treatment: Assessment, 5–7 days; treatment, 3–4 weeks
Cost: $175 per diem. Insurance eligible.
Detoxification Offered: Yes, by contract with hospital
Accreditation: Ohio Department of Health

The Campus is a primary residential treatment facility serving adolescents age 12 to 18 who are experiencing problems with alcohol and other mood-altering chemicals. Chemical dependency is viewed as a problem that initially affects the adolescent emotionally, socially and developmentally, and as one that distresses each family member. Throughout the treatment process, The Campus strives to serve the needs of the adolescent while providing a system of support to guide the family in developing a program for recovery. The primary goal is to help the adolescent develop the skills and the desire to cope with the stresses of adolescence in a responsible, chemically free manner.

Since The Campus treats only adolescents, all of the staff's energy goes into meeting their very special needs. The residents have few distractions from treatment. Three hours each day are set aside for school in a special class with a teacher and tutors. Ten hours each day are devoted to treatment. The therapeutic power of positive peer-group pressure is an underlying element of treatment. Group therapy and individual therapy are combined with a loving but firm and structured approach that clearly defines each individual's limits and needs. The steps of AA and NA programs are the yardstick for treatment and recovery. Beyond this, The Campus is totally committed to the idea that families suffer along with their dependent adolescent and that they, too, have a right to recover.

The family program offered at The Campus goes far beyond education. The ultimate goal is to provide each family member with the skills necessary for long-term recovery and wellness. This is accomplished within a framework of weekly family sessions plus 1 full Family Week, when family members join the dependent adolescent in the treatment process.

The Campus emphasizes that recovery involves body, mind, emotion and spirit. This holistic approach, combined with the love and understanding so necessary in successful treatment, has allowed this facility to help adolescents even when they don't want help.

ALCOHOLISM TREATMENT UNIT—SERENITY HALL
Saint John's and West Shore Hospital

29000 Center Ridge Road
Westlake, Ohio 44145

(216) 835-6059

Director: John Harnish

Average Patient Census: 24
Minimum Duration of Treatment: 5 days, maximum not limited
Cost: $3,000–4,000 for 2 weeks. Insurance eligible.
Detoxification Offered: Yes
Accreditation: JCAH, A.O.A.

Serenity Hall inpatient treatment is in a general hospital, and both detoxification and rehabilitation services are offered. Detoxification consists of a complete examination by the physician plus a discontinuation, over a 4-day period, of all chemicals, including alcohol.

The rehabilitation usually lasts for 2 weeks and consists of group therapy daily, AA speakers, a physical exercise program and personal counseling.

A 2-week outpatient program is available to each patient, plus 8 weeks of aftercare, with 2-year follow-up.

GREENE HALL

1141 North Monroe Drive
Xenia, Ohio 45385

(513) 372-8011

Director: John C. Yeager
Average Patient Census: Detox, 10; rehab, 38

Minimum Duration of Treatment: Variable
Cost: Detox, $221 per day; rehab, $143.50 per day. Insurance eligible.
Detoxification Offered: Yes
Accreditation: JCAH

Greene Hall, a department of Greene Memorial Hospital, is a private, not-for-profit corporation dedicated to the treatment of men and women who have become harmfully involved with alcohol and other mood-altering chemicals.

New residents are initially assigned to the medical detoxification section of Greene Hall for evaluation of their physical needs and for the duration and specifics of their particular detoxification program. Thereafter, transition to rehabilitation begins, consisting initially of a treatment-planning week. Out of that treatment-planning process will come a program individually designed to enable that individual to learn how to live fully and productively without chemicals. The modalities used to such an end are lectures, films, group therapy, family therapy and heavy attendance in AA and NA meetings. Mutual assistance and self-help are vital aspects in the rehabilitation process. The group sessions, the closeness of living and the fact that all residents can identify with the same illness, combine to produce a therapeutic milieu.

In addition, there are other complementary programs, including a family program lasting an entire week, an outpatient program that offers an opportunity to solidify initial therapeutic gains made, and aftercare groups that bring together graduates in various stages of recovery who have much to offer each other in regard to strengths found in their new way of life.

Greene Hall also offers a Family Intervention Service whereby the chemically dependent person's family can learn confronting techniques that can bring their chemically dependent family member nearer to treatment and rehabilitation.

ALCOHOLISM TREATMENT PROGRAM

Good Samaritan Medical Center

800 Forest Avenue
Zanesville, Ohio 43701

(614) 454-5928

Director: Gerald E. Linn
Average Patient Census: 15 beds

Minimum Duration of Treatment: 21–28 days
Cost: Available on request. Insurance eligible.
Detoxification Offered: Yes
Accreditation: JCAH

Good Samaritan's ATP is committed to the disease concept, and their aim is to provide the continuity of care necessary to deal with alcohol and other mood-altering drug dependencies as a primary, progressive, chronic and fatal illness, as well as to offer comprehensive treatment and aftercare services.

Referrals are accepted from both professional agencies and families and friends. A preadmission interview is desirable with the applicant and family and/or close friends. Motivation toward active participation in the full program is considered high priority for admission.

After detoxification, and when the medical director deems it advisable, the patient is admitted to the therapy phase of the program. This consists of group and family therapy sessions, individual counseling, educational lectures and involvement in AA and other self-help groups.

The Family Awareness Program is a 3-week, revolving series of educational sessions open to the public, held every Saturday from 9:00 A.M. to 12 noon, based on the belief that it is important for those closest to the alcoholic to learn to recognize the early signs of the disease and to make the decision to help themselves regardless of whether the alcoholic chooses to stop drinking.

Oklahoma

VALLEY HOPE ALCOHOLISM TREATMENT CENTER

P.O. Box 47
Cushing, Oklahoma 74023

(918) 225-1736
1-800-722-5940

Director: Al Roberts

Average Patient Census: 65
Minimum Duration of Treatment: 30 days
Cost: $97 per day. Insurance eligible.
Detoxification Offered: Yes
Accreditation: JCAH

Cushing Valley Hope is a freestanding alcoholism treatment center offering a comprehensive in-residence program of approximately 30-days' duration.

Valley Hope treats men and women 15 years of age and older and approaches alcoholism from its medical, social, emotional and spiritual aspects.

THE OAKS REHABILITATIVE SERVICES CENTER

628 East Creek Street
McAlester, Oklahoma 74501

(918) 423-6030 and 423-6350

Director: Paul Hackler
Average Patient Census: 45

Minimum Duration of Treatment: 6 weeks and up to 1 year
Cost: Sliding scale. Insurance eligible.
Detoxification Offered: Yes, nonmedical
Accreditation: State of Oklahoma Mental Health, Alcohol and Drug Division

The Oaks Rehabilitative Services Center is a comprehensive chemical dependency treatment program that offers nonmedical detoxification, residential care, outpatient counseling, day treatment and aftercare services. The program has been certified for 75 treatment beds for men, women and youth.

There are two separate programs for the chemically dependent: the alcohol recovery program and the drug abuse treatment program. Both offer the chemically dependent a wide range of learning experiences for learning to live without dependency on alcohol and drugs. The programs offer group counseling and individual counseling services that are structured to provide the client with a useful package of coping skills and an improved capacity for being more responsible for their lives.

Treatment modalities include AA and NA, rational self-counseling, stress management, social skills, assertiveness training, reality therapy, relaxation training, biofeedback and Gestalt awareness experiences.

Clients admitted must be ambulatory, have a primary problem of chemical dependency and have no major psychotic symptoms.

RALEIGH HILLS HOSPITAL

130 A Street, S.W.
Miami, Oklahoma 74354

(918) 542-1836

Director: Edward Malewski
Average Patient Census: 25

Minimum Duration of Treatment: 21 days after detox.
Cost: Available on request. Insurance eligible.
Detoxification Offered: Yes
Accreditation: JCAH

The adult and adolescent substance abuse programs at Raleigh Hills Hospital provide a comprehensive and multidisciplinary approach to the treatment of alcoholism and drug abuse. The adult 21-day and the adolescent 6- to 8-week individualized treatment programs assist individuals to overcome their dependency upon alcohol and other drugs and develop solutions to their dependency-related problems.

The treatment plan for both programs includes group and individual therapy, stress management, substance-abuse education, nutritional counseling, pastoral counseling, marriage counseling, vitamin therapy, social services, employer's advocacy and aftercare services.

The program strongly supports the role of AA and NA in helping individuals regain their places within the community.

BROOKWOOD RECOVERY CENTER—TULSA

201 South Garnett
Tulsa, Oklahoma 74128

(918) 438-4257

Director: Robert A. Alario

Average Patient Census: 40 beds
Minimum Duration of Treatment: 28 days
Cost: Available on request. Insurance eligible.
Detoxification Offered: Yes
Accreditation: JCAH

The Lifemark program at Brookwood Recovery Center follows the disease model of alcoholism and is based on the fundamental concepts of AA, Al-Anon and Alateen. The core of the treatment philosophy is that the power to stay sober resides in a group rather than in an individual. The addicted individual cannot rely on willpower alone; rehabilitation, to be successful, must provide a totally new life-style.

After medical detoxification, medical examination and psychological testing, the basic program provides for a minimum of 35 hours per week of formalized individual, group and family counseling, and this is supplemented by vocational, employment and social services as needed, as well as regular AA and/or NA meetings.

The period of intensive therapy and controlled environment is insufficient to obtain permanent, lasting results without further reinforcement. Therefore the aftercare program maintains contact and strengthens participation in the principles of therapy and AA and affords the patient and family the opportunity to work through any problems arising after discharge.

Brookwood—Tulsa also offers industrial consultation with a special industry Hotline Service, intervention counseling, community educational services and adolescent assessment and referral.

South Dakota

KEYSTONE TREATMENT CENTER

425 North Lawler
P.O. Box 159
Canton, South Dakota 57013

(605) 987-2751

Director: Wallace W. Feller

Average Patient Census: 26
Minimum Duration of Treatment: 30 days, longer if needed
Cost: $3,900 for 30 days. Insurance eligible.
Detoxification Offered: Yes
Accreditation: JCAH

Treatment at Keystone is based on the philosophy of the AA Twelve Steps to a new life. Included in the treatment program are one-to-one counseling with experienced alcohol and drug counselors, 80 half-hour lectures, group discussion therapy, group reading of AA literature, films, spiritual counseling on request, establishment of home AA contact, family counseling and aftercare counseling.

Complete detoxification for both alcoholics and drug addicts is provided. Routine laboratory work is done on admission. If patients require hospitalization, they are admitted to Canton-Inwood Hospital and admitted to Keystone when their condition is no longer acute. Registered nurses are on duty 24 hours a day, and full medical services are available from Keystone's two staff physicians.

Sober former patients and other members of AA may return to Keystone on a VIP (visiting-inpatient) program. At special reduced rates, they may take advantage of all facilities and programs for as many days as they wish.

A Family Program has been instituted that includes lectures, group therapy and an introduction to Al-Anon. Keystone is located on 33 acres in a rural community.

RIVER PARK OF SOUTH DAKOTA

Box 1216
801 East Dakota
Pierre, South Dakota 57501

(605) 224-6177

Director: Glenn L. Jorgenson, President;
Joseph Cruse, M.D., Medical Director

Average Patient Census: Pierre, 30; Rapid City, 18; Sioux Falls, 20
Minimum Duration of Treatment: 30 days
Cost: $160 per day. Insurance eligible.
Detoxification Offered: Yes
Accreditation: JCAH and licensed by the State of South Dakota

River Park is a private, nonprofit alcoholism and drug resource center with inpatient treatment facilities located in Pierre, Rapid City and Sioux Falls, and branch offices located in Aberdeen, Brookings, Deadwood, Mitchell and Watertown.

Clients are admitted by referral and in an alcohol-free condition. Detoxification can be accomplished at home or, if desired, the client can be admitted to Saint Mary's Hospital in Pierre immediately prior to admission to River Park.

Treatment is based on intensive use of the Twelve Steps of AA, as well as lectures, films, tapes and both group and individual counseling.

River Park also offers consultation services, educational services, intervention, aftercare and follow-up, and outpatient services. Five-day intensive therapy programs for family members are offered at the Pierre, Sioux Falls and Rapid City facilities.

Complete consultation services, with follow-up monitoring and evaluation, are available for employee assistance programs.

GATEWAY ALCOHOLISM TREATMENT CENTER

P.O. Box 76
Yankton, South Dakota 57078

(605) 665-3671

Director: William L. Schroeder

Average Patient Census: 35
Minimum Duration of Treatment: 28 days
Cost: Depends on ability to pay.
Insurance eligible
Detoxification Offered: No
Accreditation: State of South Dakota

At Gateway Alcoholism Treatment Center, treatment follows the Minnesota model, using AA principles and peer therapy as the basis of the program.

Other specific areas of the program include recreational planning and therapy, vocational testing and training, relaxation training, spiritual counseling and psychological testing and counseling.

Tennessee

PARKVIEW TENNESSEE

8614 Harrison Bay Road
Harrison, Tennessee 37341

(615) 344-3437

Director: Gerald D. Shulman
Average Patient Census: Adolescents, 35; adults, 36; family, 21

Minimum Duration of Treatment: Approximately 4 weeks
Cost: Available on request. Insurance eligible.
Detoxification Offered: No
Accreditation: JCAH

Parkview offers primary treatment for the disease of alcoholism or other chemical dependency to both adults and adolescents. The program begins with evaluation, establishing the appropriateness for admission. Further evaluation is conducted after admission on both a psychological and a physical level, after which a personalized treatment program is jointly developed by staff and client.

Education about the nature of chemical dependency, an in-depth study of AA and the Twelve Steps, and individual and group therapy help the patient to understand the realities of the illness and take responsibility for his or her own recovery.

The adolescent program contains the same components but begins with a 2-week evaluation period and involves family, friends, school personnel and others. Parkview also employs a teacher who coordinates academic studies with work being missed at school. Length of treatment averages 4 weeks; however, like the adult program, it is open-ended and determined by the patient's progress.

It is Parkview's philosophy that chemical dependency is a family illness, so for their own recovery, family members join in the program for 1 week of the patient's stay, for learning opportunities in the dynamics of recovery as well as in Al-Anon and Alateen as modalities of family growth and recovery, the setting of meaningful goals and the beginning of the process of reconciliation.

A 1-year aftercare program is provided for those who successfully complete treatment, and includes the family. The cost of this program, which meets once a week for 2 hours, is included in the cost of treatment. This, in addition to AA and/or Al-Anon, provides the basis for post-treatment growth and support.

ALCOHOLISM TREATMENT UNIT
Saint Mary's Medical Center

Oak Hill Avenue
Knoxville, Tennessee 37917

(615) 971-6761

Director: Worley Fain, Ed.D.

Average Patient Census: 30
Minimum Duration of Treatment: About 28 days
Cost: $6,000–7,500. Insurance eligible.
Detoxification Offered: Yes
Accreditation: JCAH

The Alcoholism Treatment Unit of Saint Mary's Medical Center uses a comprehensive approach in treating alcoholism and focuses on the following areas: (a) medical management during the detoxification and treatment phase; (b) an educational process aimed at symptom identification and management of the disease; (c) an organizational process aimed at life management; (d) a psychological process aimed at realizing one's ultimate potential; and (e) a 10-week aftercare program consisting of 2 groups per week: one for the recovering patients, and one for the patient and the spouse.

The primary objective is to develop conditions of safety and permissiveness. An examination of issues related to alcoholism gives patients an opportunity to see the congruity or incongruity between their principles and those issues.

Since Saint Mary's believes alcoholism to be a family illness, with the family, in many cases, as sick as or sicker than the alcoholic, they offer an Intervention Class for family members to teach them how to confront the alcoholic. Once treatment has been initiated, the family is encouraged and expected to participate in the family classes each week.

KOALA CENTER AT UNIVERSITY MEDICAL CENTER

1411 Baddour Parkway
Lebanon, Tennessee 37087

(615) 444-8165

Director: Fay Bradford
Average Patient Census: 11

Minimum Duration of Treatment: 30-day inpatient, adults and adolescents
Cost: Available on request. Insurance eligible.
Detoxification Offered: Yes
Accreditation: JCAH

Koala derives its name from the custom among the Aboriginals of Australia of passing the drinking vessel around a circle. Anyone who did not wish to drink said, *"Koala,"* meaning "no drink." Later, the name was given to the little animal, native to Australia, that seldom, if ever, drinks.

Koala is a treatment hospital for alcoholism and drug abuse for both adults and adolescents and believes that alcoholism is a disease that must be treated with the same compassion, dedication and expertise as all other diseases. This facility offers, therefore, a comprehensive, multidisciplinary, individualized treatment plan in a nonjudgmental, stigma-free environment.

The program includes group therapy, family counseling, individual therapy, an introduction to AA and NA, psychological testing, psychiatric evaluation, nutrition awareness, leisure counseling and employer involvement.

CARE UNIT
MADISON HOSPITAL

500 Hospital Drive
Madison, Tennessee 37115

(615) 868-7010

Director: Walt Edgell, III

Average Patient Census: 22
Minimum Duration of Treatment: 28 days
Cost: Approximately $225 per day. Insurance eligible.
Detoxification Offered: Yes
Accreditation: JCAH

Madison Hospital Care Unit offers its program in a physical setting that includes a lake in a park made up of rolling green acres, providing a serene setting for rehabilitation.

The program includes films, lectures, family seminars and AA/Al-Anon meetings, as well as therapeutic activities that include a physical fitness program and recreational activities for all patients, families and alumni.

Staffing includes 24-hour crisis response, a professional team of nurses, a social worker, counselor, psychologist, physician and program director. Services of the facility are available to anyone over the age of 18.

CHARTER LAKESIDE HOSPITAL

P.O. Box 341308
2911 Brunswick Road
Memphis, Tennessee 38134

(901) 377-4700

Director: Jim Hays, C.A.C.

Average Patient Census: 52 beds
Minimum Duration of Treatment: 28 days
Cost: Varies; available on request. Insurance eligible.
Detoxification Offered: Yes
Accreditation: JCAH

The program at Charter Lakeside Hospital offers medically supervised detoxification, if necessary, and individual, group and family counseling as part of the holistic (multidisciplinary) approach toward effectively treating the disease of addiction. All patients are also encouraged to participate in activities therapy and didactic lectures. These programs are AA/NA based philosophically. The hospital offers programs for both adults and adolescents.

Patient and family aftercare services are available at all Charter Medical Addictive Disease Units, emphasizing that recovery from this relentless disease is a continuing process affecting both the patient and his or her family.

CUMBERLAND HEIGHTS

Route 2, River Road
Nashville, Tennessee 37209

(615) 352-1757

Director: John W. North

Average Patient Census: 50 (37 men, 13 women)
Minimum Duration of Treatment: 30 days
Cost: $3,500. Insurance eligible.
Detoxification Offered: Yes
Accreditation: JCAH

Cumberland Heights, situated on 177 acres beside the Cumberland River, is a private, nonprofit organization that strives to provide the best in quality care at the lowest possible cost. The treatment philosophy of this freestanding treatment center is strongly oriented to AA and drug-free living. Admission is open to men and women 18 years of age and older who agree to stay for the tenure of treatment recommended by the staff, and great emphasis is placed on the patient's commitment to complete the program.

After treatment, the patient is encouraged to stay involved for 1 evening a week until a year of continuous sobriety has been achieved.

Cumberland Heights has an inpatient capacity for thirty-one men and sixteen women, and special attention is given to the unique needs of women patients. There are also 8 infirmary beds and 4 motel units usually reserved for visiting members of patients' families.

Patients are encouraged to use the Twelve Steps of AA during the 28-day program of lectures, group therapy, and individual work with a counselor who assists the patient in the development of a treatment plan. Cumberland Heights also works to help the patient's family, business associates and friends to understand and participate in the recovery program.

VANDERBILT INSTITUTE FOR TREATMENT OF ADDICTIONS (VITA)

Zerfoss Building, 4th Floor
Vanderbilt University MCN
Nashville, Tennessee 37232

(615) 322-6158

Director: Jane Zibelin, R.N., C.S.A.C.

Average Patient Census: 12
Minimum Duration of Treatment: 21 days
Cost: $4,500 for 21-day rehab. Insurance eligible.
Detoxification Offered: Yes
Accreditation: JCAH

The Vanderbilt Institute for Treatment of Alcoholism (VITA) provides a comprehensive treatment program that stresses personal, individualized care. The multidisciplinary staff includes physicians, nurses, counselors, social worker, spiritual care counselor, family therapist and nutritional and recreational experts.

Designed for individuals 18 years of age and older, VITA provides the essential first step toward a new life of sobriety. Upon admission, each patient is given a thorough medical evaluation on which an appropriate medical treatment regimen is based. A systematic analysis of the patient's social patterns is also conducted and the results used to design an individually tailored program to provide adaptive social behaviors and skills necessary to create a life-style free from alcohol/drugs. A complete family program is included.

The VITA program is based on the principles of abstinence and the philosophy of AA. Aftercare is also provided for both patients and their families.

KOALA CENTER AT HARTON REGIONAL MEDICAL CENTER

P.O. Box 460
Tullahoma, Tennessee 37388

(615) 455-0601

Director: Tom Anderson
Average Patient Census: 9

Minimum Duration of Treatment: 30-day inpatient
Cost: Available on request. Insurance eligible.
Detoxification Offered: Yes
Accreditation: JCAH

Koala derives its name from the custom among the Aboriginals of Australia of passing the drinking vessel around a circle. Anyone who did not wish to drink said, *"Koala,"* meaning "no drink." Later, the name was given to the little animal, native to Australia, that seldom, if ever, drinks.

Koala is a treatment hospital for alcoholism and drug abuse for both adults and adolescents and believes that alcoholism is a disease that must be treated with the same compassion, dedication and expertise as all other diseases. This facility offers, therefore, a comprehensive, multidisciplinary, individualized treatment plan in a nonjudgmental, stigma-free environment.

The program includes group therapy, family counseling, individual therapy, an introduction to AA and NA, psychological testing, psychiatric evaluation, nutrition awareness, leisure counseling and employer involvement.

Texas

BROOKWOOD RECOVERY CENTER—ALVIN

Alvin Community Hospital
301 Medic Lane
Alvin, Texas 77511

(713) 331-4184, Crisis Line
(713) 331-6141, ext. 285/286, Business Line

Director: Donald Gloistein
Average Patient Census: 20
Minimum Duration of Treatment: 28–42 days
Cost: $7,000–10,000. Insurance eligible.
Detoxification Offered: Yes
Accreditation: JCAH

Brookwood Recovery Center—Alvin is a hospital-based facility especially designed to create an environment that supports the commitment of their program to recovery. The program is based on the belief that alcoholism and chemical dependency are primary diseases and that the effects of these diseases can best be overcome through comprehensive treatment of the whole family.

Following the principles of AA and Al-Anon, the program provides a peer group therapy process that puts these principles into practice. It includes, under a multidisciplinary professional staff, intense, honest, confrontative and supportive peer-group therapy, individual and family counseling, individual treatment plans, Step meetings, didactic sessions and AA meetings.

The family program, more than 40 hours of structured involvement, thoroughly explores the codependent nature of the family illness and provides workable tools for family recovery. The Continuing-Care Program begins upon discharge and involves the family and patient for 2 years.

Brookwood—Alvin also offers industrial consultation, intervention counseling, community educational services and adolescent assessment and referral.

COUNTERPOINT CENTER OF SUNRISE HOSPITAL

701 West Randol Mill Road
Arlington, Texas 76012

(817) 261-3121

Director: Larry Machen
Average Patient Census: 40 beds

Minimum Duration of Treatment: 28-day program
Cost: Available on request. Insurance eligible.
Detoxification Offered: Yes
Accreditation: JCAH

CounterPoint Center is a Chemical Dependency Program for adults and adolescents. The center is part of an international network of chemical dependency treatment centers located throughout the United States and Europe.

Chemical dependency is recognized as a primary disorder: chronic, progressive and potentially fatal, and prone to relapse if not properly treated. The disease factor is basic to treatment, which is provided by a multidisciplinary team of skilled professionals, many themselves recovering. All areas of a person's life are affected by chemical dependency. Therefore, the physical, emotional, social and spiritual needs of patients are all addressed through the treatment program.

Detoxification is the first phase of treatment. Following stabilization of acute medical problems, patients begin an intensive program of rehabilitation. The Twelve Steps of AA and NA are emphasized, and patients are expected to have selected an AA or NA group and a temporary sponsor by the time they are to begin the aftercare program. An individualized plan for aftercare is formulated with patient and family during the last week of treatment. Weekly group therapy is provided at no extra cost for 1 year, with a 2-year advisement period.

Family and significant others are included in treatment from the time of admission, with family assessment and couples and family therapy several times each week. Crisis intervention is also available.

For employers, the staff maintains open communications with EAP counselors and supervisors. Employers are included in the treatment process from the beginning, through discharge and into follow-up care.

THE FAULKNER CENTER

1900 Rio Grande
Austin, Texas 78705

(512) 482-0075

Director: John Waterbury
Average Patient Census: 70 beds

Minimum Duration of Treatment: 4 weeks
Cost: Available on request. Insurance eligible.
Detoxification Offered: Yes
Accreditation: Texas Commission on Alcoholism

The Faulkner Center offers an integrated program of services focusing on family recovery in a therapeutic treatment setting. These services include an inpatient program, intervention, aftercare and a Family Week experience.

Treatment consists of detoxification and initial assessment followed by the 4-week therapeutic program of individualized treatment. Family Week, involving family members in a 7-day treatment experience with some mixed group therapy, occurs during approximately the third week of inpatient stay.

Elements of the treatment program are education about alcoholism and chemical dependency, group therapy and a strong emphasis on the Twelve Steps of AA as a way to build a sober life. In addition, Faulkner also provides a codependent program, with 4 weeks of intensive treatment.

An education, coaching and counseling program is available for families and others interested in intervention. Aftercare is also provided to dependent and codependents to enable them to continue their recovery.

The Faulkner approach is that alcoholism and other forms of chemical dependency are illnesses that affect the family and others who have been close to the addicted person, and therefore focuses its program on family illness.

STARLIGHT VILLAGE HOSPITAL

Elm Bass Road
P.O. Box 317
Center Point, Texas 78010

(512) 634-2212

Director: Annabel Lindner

Average Patient Census: 31
Minimum Duration of Treatment: 28 days
Cost: $1,800 per week, average. Insurance eligible.
Detoxification Offered: Yes
Accreditation: JCAH

Starlight Village Hospital offers complete medical detoxification, as well as alcohol and drug abuse education. The program has an AA orientation.

Voluntary and involuntary admissions are accepted, as well as court commitments, with 24-hour contact and admission.

The professional staff includes physicians, a clinical psychologist, registered nurses, licensed vocational nurses, certified substance-abuse counselors, and other support staff.

Physician's fees, lab, X ray, drugs, group and individual therapy, psychological testing, as well as room and board, are all included in the average cost per week.

BROOKWOOD ADOLESCENT CENTER—WESTGATE

Westgate Medical Center
4405 North I-35
Denton, Texas 76201

(817) 566-4040

Director: Kevin Cedergren

Average Patient Census: 24 beds
Minimum Duration of Treatment: 38–43 days
Cost: $12,000. Insurance eligible.
Detoxification Offered: Yes, subacute
Accreditation: JCAH

Brookwood Adolescent Center—Westgate provides comprehensive chemical dependency recovery services for young people age 12 to 17. The program is based on a philosophy of AA and Al-Anon, with specific emphasis on the needs, life-styles and relationships of adolescents and their families and on the belief that chemical dependency is a treatable disease. Abstinence and a return to healthful living are attainable goals at Brookwood Adolescent.

There are three phases of care in the program. Phase I offers a safe, secure environment for evaluation, intervention and referral of young people experiencing problems with chemical use. For those adolescents in need of treatment, the Phase II inpatient program provides the opportunity to change those things in their life that are harmful, while learning the tools of recovery. Phase III Aftercare is a 2-year program provided on an outpatient basis. The adolescent begins aftercare with daily attendance and completes the program with involvement as an alumnus.

Throughout the Brookwood Adolescent Program, the young person is treated in a less and less restrictive form of care, continually giving him more and more responsibility for his own recovery.

The codependent nature of this illness is recognized and treated. Family involvement is integral throughout the inpatient and aftercare programs. Parents and siblings receive specialized care and support as the concerned persons of the adolescent.

Brookwood Adolescent Center—Westgate recognizes the need for continuing education and awareness within the community and is committed to assist in that effort.

BROOKWOOD RECOVERY CENTER—WESTGATE

4601 North I-35
Denton, Texas 76201

(817) 565-8100
Metro 434-3540 or 434-3549

Director: John S. Saylor

Average Patient Census: 40 (capacity 64)
Minimum Duration of Treatment: 28 days
Cost: $7,200–10,600. Insurance eligible.
Detoxification Offered: Yes, for patients continuing in rehabilitation
Accreditation: TCA, JCAH

Brookwood Recovery Center—Westgate is a freestanding facility especially designed to create an environment that supports the commitment of the program to recovery. The program is based on the belief that alcoholism and chemical dependency are primary diseases and that the effects of these diseases can best be overcome through comprehensive treatment of the whole family.

Following the principles of AA and Al-Anon, the program provides a peer-group therapy process that puts these principles into practice. It includes, under a multidisciplinary professional staff, intense, honest, confrontative and supportive peer-group therapy, individual and family counseling, individual treatment plans, Step meetings, didactic sessions and AA meetings. Patients are medically detoxified under the care of a full-time medical director and around-the-clock nursing care. Patients with coexisting psychiatric problems receive psychiatric evaluation and treatment.

A family treatment program is also offered, with individual as well as conjoint counseling, to ensure that all those involved fully comprehend the task that lies ahead. Family members live at the center for 1 week of therapy and education while the patient is a resident.

The Continuing-Care Program begins upon discharge and involves the family and patient for 2 years. Recognizing the special needs of business and industry, back-to-work sessions with the employer, regular counselor contact for the EAP and confidential release of records, where appropriate, are provided.

CAREUNIT HOSPITAL OF DALLAS—FORT WORTH

1066 West Magnolia
Fort Worth, Texas 76104

(817) 336-2828

Director: Dorothy Grasty
Average Patient Census: adults, 43; adolescents, 26

Minimum Duration of Treatment: Adults, 21–28 days; adolescents, 45–60 days
Cost: Approximately $300 per day. Insurance eligible.
Detoxification Offered: Yes
Accreditation: JCAH

CareUnit Hospital is a facility specializing in the family treatment of alcohol and other drug dependencies for adults and adolescents. Patients undergo a complete physiological and psychological examination and detoxification under the supervision of the medical director of the facility. The treatment program is personalized to fit individual needs and consists of individual and group therapy, participation in specific activities, lectures and films designed to increase the patient's understanding of his or her disease and appropriate ways to learn to enjoy life free from chemical dependency. Families are invited to join in the treatment program, which is designed to free family members from the effects of the disease in areas such as behavior, attitudes and life-styles.

The recovery continues following the patient's discharge from the hospital. Patients return to the CareUnit for aftercare 2 evenings a week for a specified period following discharge. Family units participate once weekly in the aftercare program. Patients and their families are encouraged to explore other resources, such as AA, Al-Anon, Alateen, NA and others. Aftercare is free to all patients—for a lifetime, if desired.

CareUnit of Dallas—Fort Worth also has a 13-bed Eating Disorders Unit.

SCHICK SHADEL HOSPITAL

4101 Frawley Drive
Fort Worth, Texas 76118

(817) 284-9217

Director: William T. McClintock, M.B.A., F.A.C.H.A.
Average Patient Census: 22

Minimum Duration of Treatment: 10 days, plus two 2-day reinforcement stays, plus detox when needed
Cost: $9,475 plus detox fees. Insurance eligible.
Detoxification Offered: Yes
Accreditation: JCAH

The program at Schick Shadel is an intensive 14-day (after detox) inpatient medical treatment of the grave, progressive medical disease, alcohol addiction. As the first "daughter" hospital of the original Shadel Clinic of Seattle, the facility uses the specialized medical techniques developed and perfected there over the last 50 years.

These techniques include every-other-day medical aversion treatments that create an active distaste for various forms of alcohol. On alternate days, each patient receives specialized narcotherapy given by a specially trained and certified nurse anesthetist. Pentothal interviews are a part of the narcotherapy sessions.

Schick Shadel provides full medical detoxification. Counseling emphasizes education about every aspect of the disease and includes two group sessions and one-on-one counseling sessions each day during the initial 10 days of treatment after detox.

For an average census of twenty-two patients, the facility has a staff of over eighty people, about half of whom are highly trained professionals, including nurses, psychologists and alcoholism counselors.

At discharge, the patient is scheduled to return to the hospital for two reinforcement admissions, each of 2 days' duration, at 1 and 3 months after discharge. There is, as well, a highly organized 2-year aftercare and follow-up program at no charge.

ALCOHOLIC REHABILITATION THERAPY PROGRAM
Saint Joseph Hospital

1919 LaBranch Street
Houston, Texas 77002

(713) 757-7507

Director: Sr. Mary Amelia Shannon

Average Patient Census: 32
Minimum Duration of Treatment: Average of 21–28 days
Cost: Fee for services. Insurance eligible.
Detoxification Offered: Yes
Accreditation: JCAH

Since 1966, the Alcoholic Rehabilitation Therapy Program at Saint Joseph Hospital has been an integral part of the Department of Psychiatry. Created to provide a complete rehabilitation program for alcoholics, the plan includes intensive care for the acute stages, continuing through rehabilitation, partial hospitalization and family counseling.

The program makes facilities available for AA, Alateen and Al-Anon meetings. To provide intensive discussion of problems, two groups meet daily for inpatients, with separate meetings for outpatients. Patients and their families are offered specialized orientation discussion meetings, allowing a more complete understanding of the illness.

Under the guidance of the director of Clinical Service, who is a psychiatrist, a coordinator/counselor is assisted by male and female counselors from family-oriented groups and by pastoral-care counselors in a one-to-one relationship. This is in addition to various therapy groups as prescribed for patients and families. Throughout the rehabilitation program, the patient's own psychiatrist supervises each step. A medical prescription for therapy in keeping with the patient's needs is part of a well-rounded program.

Short-term and long-term outpatient services are also available, in addition to a short-term inpatient program (Thursday to Sunday). Aftercare groups are available to discharged patients at no charge.

LA HACIENDA TREATMENT CENTER

P.O. Box 1
Hunt, Texas 78024

(512) 238-4222

Director: James H. Walker
Average Patient Census: 30

Minimum Duration of Treatment: Dependent on physician's diagnosis and recommendations
Cost: Fee for services. Insurance eligible.
Detoxification Offered: Yes
Accreditation: JCAH

The intensive, individualized care at La Hacienda, which typically lasts from 4 to 6 weeks, is designed to accomplish four things: (1) recognition by the patient that the problem exists; (2) the beginning of treatment of the physical and psychological problems brought on by alcohol or drugs; (3) the motivation of the patient toward continuing treatment; and (4) the education of patients and their families about avenues of treatment open to them.

Patients receive a combination of treatment methods designed to meet their unique physical, mental and spiritual needs: counseling, family therapy, recreational therapy and corrective physical fitness.

The aftercare program eases patients back into their home environment and gives them tools they can use in their lifelong struggle for sobriety. Aftercare may include referrals to self-help groups; individual, marital, family or group therapy on an outpatient basis; and the preparation of a home exercise program.

BROOKWOOD RECOVERY CENTER—KATY

5638 Medical Center Drive
Katy, Texas 77450

(713) 392-3456

Director: Manley Jones

Average Patient Census: 64 (adults, 52; adolescents, 12)
Minimum Duration of Treatment: 28–42 days
Cost: $8,500–15,400. Insurance eligible.
Detoxification Offered: Yes
Accreditation: JCAH

Brookwood Recovery Center—Katy is a freestanding facility especially designed to create an environment that supports the commitment of their program to recovery. The program is based on the belief that alcoholism and chemical dependency are primary diseases and that the effects of these diseases can best be overcome through comprehensive treatment of the whole family.

Following the principles of AA and Al-Anon, the program provides a peer-group therapy process that puts these principles into practice. It includes, under a multidisciplinary professional staff, intense, honest, confrontative and supportive peer-group therapy; individual and family counseling; individual treatment plans; Step meetings; didactic sessions; and AA meetings.

The family program, more than 40 hours of structured involvement, thoroughly explores the codependent nature of the family illness and provides workable tools for family recovery. The Continuing-Care Program begins upon discharge and involves the family and patient for 2 years. Recognizing the special needs of business and industry, the center's stated purpose is to return the employee to full productivity in the shortest possible time and to stabilize the process of reentry.

Brookwood—Katy also offers a comprehensive adolescent program of 35 days for youths age 12 to 17.

CHARTER RIO GRANDE HOSPITAL

6020 Springfield Avenue
Laredo, Texas 78041

(512) 722-0900

Director: Daniel Ramirez

Average Patient Census: 16 beds
Minimum Duration of Treatment: 28 days
Cost: Varies; available on request.
Insurance eligible.
Detoxification Offered: Yes
Accreditation: JCAH pending

The program at Charter Rio Grande Hospital offers medically supervised detoxification, if necessary, and individual, group and family counseling as part of the holistic (multidisciplinary) approach toward effectively treating the disease of addiction. All patients are also encouraged to participate in activities therapy and didactic lectures. These programs are AA/NA based philosophically. The hospital offers programs only for adults.

Patient and family aftercare services are available at all Charter Medical Addictive Disease units, emphasizing that recovery from this relentless disease is a continuing process affecting both the patient and his or her family.

BROOKWOOD RECOVERY CENTER—CHOCOLATE BAYOU

638 Harbor Road
Liverpool, Texas 77577

(713) 439-1202, Crisis Line
(713) 331-7823, Business Line

Director: Don L. Devens

Average Patient Census: 48
Minimum Duration of Treatment: 28–42 days
Cost: $13,000–15,000. Insurance eligible.
Detoxification Offered: Yes
Accreditation: JCAH

Brookwood Recovery Center—Chocolate Bayou is a freestanding facility exclusively suited to meet the needs of adolescents age 12 to 18. The program is based on the theory and practice that chemical dependency is a primary disease that responds best to the comprehensive treatment of the whole family. The program follows the principles of AA and Al-Anon.

Treatment is divided into three distinct phases. Phase I is Inpatient Evaluation. This includes a complete physical, psychological, emotional, spiritual and interpersonal exploration of the adolescent's relationship to mood-altering chemicals and their harmful consequences on his or her life. This phase lasts 7 to 14 days.

Phase II is Inpatient Treatment. This includes individual and group therapy, Step work, family-systems assignments and recreational and educational programs conducted by certified instructors and teachers. This phase lasts 28 days.

Phase III is Outpatient Aftercare. This includes transition from evaluation and treatment back to home, school and community, moving through three parts: from intense daily activities for 6 weeks, to weeknight groups for 12 weeks and finally to weekly sessions for up to a year.

The unique family program establishes a parallel track of treatment for the codependent family members in order to reunite and reorganize the family without the chemically dependent relationships.

CHARTER PLAINS HOSPITAL

P.O. Box 98490
801 North Quaker Avenue
Lubbock, Texas 79499

(806) 744-5505

Director: Jerome Tilles, M.D.

Average Patient Census: 16 beds
Minimum Duration of Treatment: 28 days
Cost: Varies; available on request. Insurance eligible.
Detoxification Offered: Yes
Accreditation: JCAH pending

The program at Charter Plains Hospital offers medically supervised detoxification, if necessary, and individual, group and family counseling as part of the holistic (multidisciplinary) approach toward effectively treating the disease of addiction. All patients are also encouraged to participate in activities therapy and didactic lectures. These programs are AA/NA based philosophically. The hospital offers programs only for adults.

Patient and family aftercare services are available at all Charter Medical Addictive Disease units, emphasizing that recovery from this relentless disease is a continuing process affecting both the patient and his or her family.

CHARTER PALMS HOSPITAL

P.O. Box 5239
1421 East Jackson Avenue
McAllen, Texas 78501

(512) 631-5421

Director: Paul Pineda

Average Patient Census: 20 beds
Minimum Duration of Treatment: 21 days
Cost: Varies; available on request. Insurance eligible.
Detoxification Offered: Yes
Accreditation: JCAH pending

The program at Charter Palms Hospital offers medically supervised detoxification, if necessary, and individual, group and family counseling as part of the holistic (multidisciplinary) approach toward effectively treating the disease of addiction. All patients are also encouraged to participate in activities therapy and didactic lectures. These programs are AA/NA based philosophically. The hospital offers programs only for adults.

Patient and family aftercare services are available at all Charter Medical Addictive Disease units, emphasizing that recovery from this relentless disease is a continuing process affecting both the patient and his or her family.

BROOKWOOD RECOVERY CENTER—PARK PLACE

Park Place Hospital
3050 Thirty-ninth Street
Port Arthur, Texas 77642

(409) 983-2064

Director: Jack R. Martin

Average Patient Census: 18 beds
Minimum Duration of Treatment: 28–42 days
Cost: $7,200–10,700. Insurance eligible.
Detoxification Offered: Yes
Accreditation: JCAH

Brookwood Recovery Center—Park Place is a hospital-based unit in a general acute hospital. It is designed to create an environment that supports the commitment of the program to recovery. The program is based on the belief that alcoholism and chemical dependency are primary diseases and that the effects of these diseases can best be overcome through comprehensive treatment of the whole family.

Following the principles of AA and Al-Anon, the program provides a peer-group therapy process that puts these principles into practice. It includes, under a multidisciplinary professional staff, intense, honest, confrontative and supportive peer-group therapy, individual and family counseling; individual treatment plans; Step meetings; didactic sessions; and AA meetings.

The family program, more than 40 hours of structured involvement, thoroughly explores the codependent nature of the family illness and provides workable tools for family recovery. The Continuing-Care Program begins upon discharge and involves the family and patient for 2 years.

The staff recognizes the employer's need to return the employee to full productivity in the shortest possible time and to stabilize the process of reentry into the work environment.

The Center also offers industrial/business alcohol in-service programs, assessment/interventions and community educational programs.

BROOKWOOD RECOVERY CENTER—VILLA DE TEJAS

14747 Jones Maltsberger
San Antonio, Texas 78247

(512) 494-4477, Crisis Line
(512) 494-1237, Business Line

Director: Harold Dutcher, Jr.
Average Patient Census: 72 beds

Minimum Duration of Treatment: Alcoholism, 30 days; chemical dependency, 45 days
Cost: Approximately $10,000 for 30 days; $15,000 for 45 days. Insurance eligible.
Detoxification Offered: Yes
Accreditation: In process

The Brookwood—Tejas staff combines 174 years of sobriety and 223 years of experience in treating the problems of alcoholism, addiction and stress, and is totally staffed by people who are dedicated to an improvement in the quality of life for those who seek help. From this considerable pool of experience comes a commitment to the idea that each person has worth, value and dignity and will prove trustworthy if treated with understanding and respect.

The intensive inpatient treatment program employs a here-and-now orientation to first discover, then understand, the physical, psychological and spiritual problems that accompany substance addiction. The dedicated professional staff utilizes a multifaceted approach leading to the client's growth and healthful lasting sobriety. The staff provides detoxification, psychiatric/psychological testing, alcoholism counseling, family treatment inclusion, group therapy, individual therapy, personal-growth group, physical therapy, relaxation therapy, aftercare in fourteen Texas cities and a solid understanding of the fundamental spiritual and action principles of AA, Al-Anon and Alateen.

WHITE RIVER RETREAT

Star Route 2
Box 123
Spur, Texas 79370

(806) 263-4334 and (806) 263-4211

Director: Judy A. Smith, C.A.D.A.C.

Average Patient Census: 15
Minimum Duration of Treatment: 30–65 days
Cost: $1,870, first week; $1,795 per week thereafter. Insurance eligible.
Detoxification Offered: Yes
Accreditation: Texas Commission on Alcoholism

White River Retreat is a privately owned center for the treatment of alcoholism and other drug dependencies. Patients are accepted for 4 to 8 weeks of residential therapy that includes in-depth study of the disease of alcoholism and the use of the program of AA for drug-free living. Aftercare services are included in the program.

All meetings and discussion groups are open to family members, close friends and selected other visitors. It is strongly recommended that family and friends visit the patient at the retreat, only after the first week's residence and permission has been secured from the director or other designated staff member. Knowledge of the nature and principles of the therapeutic program involved is necessary, and participation of close family members in the recovery process is considered most important.

Located on White River Lake between Crosbyton and Spur, the retreat is housed in three separate buildings. The central section faces west, and its spacious dining and meeting area is glass-enclosed to heighten the beauty of west Texas sunsets over the lake.

Affiliated with the Crosbyton Clinic Hospital, a 50-bed general hospital, White River Retreat has three psychologists on the staff, qualified nursing around the clock and five certified alcohol and drug-abuse counselors. Mario Pena, Jr., M.D., is the medical director.

Wisconsin

ALCOHOLIC TREATMENT UNIT
Bellin Memorial Hospital

P.O. Box 1700
744 South Webster Avenue
Green Bay, Wisconsin 54305

(414) 433-3629

Director: Robert W. Fry
Average Patient Census: 17
Minimum Duration of Treatment: 28 days
Cost: Insurance eligible.
Detoxification Offered: Yes
Accreditation: JCAH

Bellin Memorial Hospital's Alcoholic Treatment Unit offers rehabilitative programs for alcoholics referred and admitted to the program by a physician.

The 28-day inpatient program is based upon the principles and practices of AA, offering the support and education concerning alcohol dependency that can come from practice of AA precepts.

In addition, it offers a Family Program and a 4-month aftercare program to bring additional support to the recovering alcoholic and his or her family.

The unit also provides an intensive outpatient program for adults and adolescents with alcohol and/or drug problems.

ROCK COUNTY HEALTH CARE CENTER

P.O. Box 351
Janesville, Wisconsin 53547

(608) 755-2500

Director: Dennis Kirchoff
Average Patient Census: 12 Rock County residents only

Minimum Duration of Treatment: Detox, 3–5 days maximum; Active Treatment Program, 25–45 days
Cost: Sliding scale. Insurance eligible.
Detoxification Offered: Yes
Accreditation: JCAH

Rock County understands that, with drugs and alcohol so readily available, we all make choices for ourselves about their use. For those for whom continued use results in chemical dependency, it offers a treatment program designed to reverse the alteration of mind and body that such dependency causes. Rock County Health Care Center believes further that, as with any disease or illness, the earlier this treatment begins, the more successful recovery is likely to be.

The treatment is based on assessment of individual needs and may include one or several of the types of treatment they offer. These include: Medical Services, if needed; a residential program available for those who need an intensive treatment experience in a structured environment; Day Treatment Services for daily individual and group counseling; Outpatient Services, where trained counselors are available to assist those who wish to examine their alcohol and drug use; Aftercare Services for those who have completed treatment, offering a program to support the recovery process; and Family Services for counseling and referral services, available to anyone concerned about chemical abuse by someone they know.

Rock County residents only are eligible for this program.

SAINT CATHERINE'S ALCOHOLISM/CHEMICAL DEPENDENCY PROGRAM
Saint Catherine's Hospital

3556 Seventh Avenue
Kenosha, Wisconsin 53140

(414) 396-4360

Director: Jeanne Stark, R.N.
Average Patient Census: 16

Minimum Duration of Treatment: Assessed on individual need, up to 28 days
Cost: Varies with level of care. Insurance eligible.
Detoxification Offered: Yes
Accreditation: JCAH

Saint Catherine's Alcoholism/Chemical Dependency Program provides care and understanding for the total person, recognizing each person's uniqueness and individuality. Treatment encompasses the physical, emotional and spiritual needs of each patient.

The length and extent of services are based on assessment and identification of specific needs. Services include detoxification for individuals requiring medical and nursing intervention and counseling support to assure stabilization. Rehabilitation is offered in a confidential, retreatlike setting for those requiring structured and intensive treatment. A Family Program of services to family or significant others affected by alcoholism or chemical dependency is available, whether or not the chemically dependent person is in treatment. The Aftercare Program offers ongoing support of treatment gains through formal and informal activities after treatment, including 2-year follow-up appointments to support recovery and affirm treatment outcome. Day Service is also available for those who reside in a supportive environment but require daily intensive treatment, as are outpatient services that include individual or group counseling for the continued needs and issues associated with recovery.

Treatment programs utilize the principles of AA, and patients are introduced to and involved in AA and other support groups throughout the treatment experience. Admission is not based on ability to pay and may be arranged 24 hours a day by phone.

The address of the retreat center is Saint Catherine's Benet Lake Center, 12603 Two hundred twenty-fourth Avenue, Benet Lake, Wisconsin 53102.

CHEMICAL DEPENDENCY REHABILITATION PROGRAM
Saint Francis Medical Center

700 West Avenue South
La Crosse, Wisconsin 54601

(608) 785-0940, ext. 2556

Director: Conan Nelson
Average Patient Census: 18

Minimum Duration of Treatment: 21–28 days
Cost: Regular hospital rate. Insurance eligible.
Detoxification Offered: Yes
Accreditation: JCAH

Saint Francis uses the "Team" concept in its Chemical Dependency Program, utilizing counselors, doctors, nurses, clergy and social workers to work individually and in groups with each patient.

The program includes lectures to educate patients on the nature of chemical dependence, group therapy to identify and communicate to others the problems involved in alcoholism, an introduction to AA and Al-Anon and recreational therapy both on and off the hospital grounds. In addition, there is a structured reading program, individual counseling and involvement in the Family Program, with counseling for the patient and his or her family unit.

The Aftercare Plan is constructed prior to the completion of the inpatient program, and its purpose is to provide each patient with the best possible chance for recovery.

APEC—Alcoholism Program and Education Center
Madison General Hospital

202 South Park Street
Madison, Wisconsin 53715

(608) 267-6291

Director: Brian M. Boegel, A.C.S.W.
Average Patient Census: 20–24

Minimum Duration of Treatment: Detox, 2–5 days; inpatient rehab, 21–28 days
Cost: Depends on individual care. Insurance eligible.
Detoxification Offered: Yes
Accreditation: JCAH

The comprehensive program at the APEC Unit of Madison General Hospital includes intervention, assessment, education, counselor training, family services, alternatives therapy, outpatient treatment, aftercare and a 2-year follow-up program.

The qualifications for admission include a screening by the staff on the APEC unit and a willingness to participate in all program activities.

The primary goal of the program is to facilitate health in chemically dependent persons and family members in all areas of being: physical, psychological, social and spiritual.

DE PAUL REHABILITATION HOSPITAL

4143 South Thirteenth Street
Milwaukee, Wisconsin 53221

(414) 281-4400

Director: A. Bela Maroti, President

Average Patient Census: 99
Minimum Duration of Treatment: 26–30 days
Cost: Varies. Insurance eligible.
Detoxification Offered: Yes
Accreditation: JCAH

De Paul Rehabilitation Hospital offers a comprehensive program for treatment of individuals suffering from alcohol or drug abuse. The inpatient program usually lasts for 1 month and, at completion, some individuals go on to outpatient services. For those severely impaired by chemical dependency, an Extended-Care Program, lasting up to 200 days, is available when support of this kind is indicated.

A number of other specialized services are offered by De Paul. These include a day hospital program, adolescent treatment, family intervention, family and children's recovery programs, impaired professionals program, seniors program, dual-disabilities service, crisis line, community education and occupational programming. The hospital also provides research and evaluation consultation, program design and implementation and contract management services. For more information about De Paul, contact the Public Relations Department at (414) 281-4400, extension 405.

DEWEY CENTER

1220 Dewey Avenue
Milwaukee, Wisconsin 53213

(414) 258-4094

Director: Susan O'Connell, M.S.W.

Average Patient Census: 30
Minimum Duration of Treatment: 2–4 weeks
Cost: $203 per day. Insurance eligible.
Detoxification Offered: Yes
Accreditation: JCAH

The program at Dewey Center is initiated, when necessary, by detoxification under medical direction. Assessment by the multidisciplinary staff leads to the individualized treatment plan developed in conjunction with the patient.

The rehabilitation phase is AA oriented, and each patient participates in daily group therapy, individual counseling, educational lectures and seminars, activities and art therapy, leisure-time counseling, family education and counseling and guidance with the fourth and fifth Steps of AA. The program functions within the context of a therapeutic treatment community that facilitates trusting relationships, mutual confrontation and support.

Each patient and family develops an aftercare plan that includes self-help groups and appropriate counseling.

KETTLE MORAINE HOSPITAL

P.O. Box C
4839 North Hewitts Point Road
Oconomowoc, Wisconsin 53066

(414) 567-0201

Director: Scott Martin
Average Patient Census: 58

Minimum Duration of Treatment: Adults, 30 days average; adolescents, 42 days average, including 10-day evaluation period
Cost: $200 per diem, including physician's services. Insurance eligible.
Detoxification Offered: Yes
Accreditation: JCAH

The goals of treatment at Kettle Moraine Hospital are to assist persons in establishing a recovery program and life-coping and relationship skills that will enable them to function without alcohol and other drugs. The treatment program is designed to meet the needs of men and women, adolescents and adults.

The program's philosophy is based around the first five Steps of the AA program and includes group therapy, individual counseling, educational lectures, occupational therapy, specialty groups, spiritual counseling, orientation to AA and attendance at outside AA meetings, adolescent study groups, relaxation and physical exercise groups. Treatment planning, therapeutic approach and aftercare planning are tailored to individual needs.

Family involvement is an essential component of the inpatient program, as well as varied outpatient programs being offered for all family members and significant others with varying needs.

GEMINI HOUSE
WINNEBAGO MENTAL HEALTH INSTITUTE

Box 9
Winnebago, Wisconsin 54985

(414) 235-4910

Director: Tom Jadin

Average Patient Census: 20
Minimum Duration of Treatment: Average stay is 3 months
Cost: $118 per day. Insurance eligible.
Detoxification Offered: No
Accreditation: JCAH

Gemini House is designed specifically for treatment of individuals diagnosed as both mentally ill and chemically dependent, based on their philosophy that both are treatable diseases that are compounded by the dysfunctions they create.

Treatment begins with extensive diagnostic and evaluative processes, and in the second phase moves on to specific individually designed therapies, including individual and group counseling, assertiveness training, leisure-skills development, family counseling, work therapy and AA groups.

The third phase of treatment may include work outside of the program area for 15 hours each week, as well as participation in community/family activities. Prior to discharge, referrals are made to home agencies, and plans for the return of the individual to the community are discussed, based on the mutual goal of assisting in the reintegration of the individual into community life.

R.O.A.D.
WINNEBAGO MENTAL HEALTH INSTITUTE

Box H
Winnebago, Wisconsin 54985

(414) 235-4910

Director: Dan Malesevich

Average Patient Census: 10 (14- to 18-year-olds)
Minimum Duration of Treatment: Usual stay is 90 days. Can be extended
Cost: $137 per day. Insurance eligible.
Detoxification Offered: No
Accreditation: JCAH

R.O.A.D. (Reflections of a Dream) residents enter treatment for the purpose of changing their life-styles in general, and for stopping the intake of chemicals in particular.

The first 3 to 4 weeks of treatment involve educating the individual residents with chemical dependency information. It is a time for residents to begin to learn about chemical dependency and how this information applies to their lives. Chemical dependency implies that people have lost their ability to use drugs in a socially acceptable manner, and as a result their life-style has become unmanageable. Most R.O.A.D. residents fit this description, and once they have intellectually begun to understand their problem, some emotional growth and general values clarification needs to take place.

The program is open to young people from throughout the state of Wisconsin. Selection is made on a case-by-case basis, and all residents must be seen at a preplacement appointment prior to admission.

The program offers the opportunity to become involved in a variety of activities, including karate, tennis, golf, sailing and, after appropriate training, a Wilderness Experience on a 4-day survival trip. Group therapy in a number of specific areas, including values clarification, sex education, nutrition, confrontation and others are offered, with emphasis throughout the program on peer involvement and parent involvement in a counseling program. School courses are taught, depending on each individual's academic needs.

Each resident must be approved for admission by his or her county unified board.

WESTERN TREATMENT CENTERS

Alaska

CHARTER NORTH HOSPITAL

2530 DeBarr Road
Anchorage, Alaska 99504

(907) 338-7575

Director: Frank Moran, C.A.C.

Average Patient Census: 40 beds
Minimum Duration of Treatment: 28 days
Cost: Varies; available on request. Insurance eligible.
Detoxification Offered: Yes
Accreditation: JCAH

The program at Charter North Hospital offers medically supervised detoxification, if necessary, and individual, group and family counseling as a part of the holistic (multidisciplinary) approach toward effectively treating the disease of addiction. All patients are also encouraged to participate in activities therapy and didactic lectures. These programs are AA/NA based philosophically. The hospital offers both adult and adolescent programs.

Patient and family aftercare services are available at all Charter Medical Addictive Disease units, emphasizing that recovery from this relentless disease is a continuing process affecting both the patient and his or her family.

NORTHPOINT, INC.

2401 East Forty-second Street
Anchorage, Alaska 99504

(907) 338-7686

Director: Obed Nelson

Average Patient Census: 40
Minimum Duration of Treatment:
  Outpatient, 12 weeks
Cost: $2,900. Insurance eligible.
Detoxification Offered: No
Accreditation: State-approved

Northpoint is Alaska's first private, intensive outpatient treatment clinic for alcohol and drug abuse. Services are limited to adults and their families.

The program, which is abstinence-oriented and supports the philosophy of AA/NA, is designed to help Alaskans in whose lives alcohol, cocaine and other drugs are playing an ever-increasing role. It allows such persons to remain with their work and family responsibilities while attending either day or evening programs.

The programs are staffed by trained professionals and conducted in strict confidence. All clients are involved in structured educational groups that support positive life-style changes, as well as individual, group and family counseling.

Approximately 35% of Northpoint clients report drugs other than alcohol as primary problems. In addition to direct treatment of chemical dependency, Northpoint offers intervention training and therapy for adult children of alcoholics. The multidisciplinary staff includes physicians, nurses, psychologists, pharmacists and counselors.

Northpoint charges on a fee-for-service basis, and most clients secure reimbursement by third-party payers. The staff will assist persons in seeking reimbursement. Offering workshops, lectures and seminars on various aspects of alcohol and drug problems, the staff will also provide consultation services to meet the needs of groups, organizations and business.

NUGEN'S RANCH

P.O. Box 871545
Wasilla, Alaska 99687

(907) 376-4534

Director: Henrietta Nugen

Average Patient Census: 38
Minimum Duration of Treatment: 6 months minimum, 2 years maximum
Cost: $48 per day. Not insurance eligible.
Detoxification Offered: No
Accreditation: State Office of Alcoholism

The program at Nugen's Ranch is specifically designed for chronic alcoholics in Alaska who have been through short-term programs without success and who have been screened and referred by their locally designated alcoholism treatment center.

Each individual accepted at Nugen's Ranch is seen as a person with special needs, and past actions are not judged. The objectives of the program include the following: (a) to provide a therapeutic environment for each resident; (b) to facilitate constructive interaction between resident, peers and staff; (c) to create a realization of the resident's intrinsic worth and dignity as an individual; (d) to help growth to maturity and acceptance of responsibility for one's own actions; (e) to help set realistic goals for each individual; and (f) to help the individual bring about his or her own recovery so that he or she becomes a useful member of the community.

Stringent admission requirements include: that clients be sober for 72 hours before arrival, that clients have received detoxification treatment three or more times within the 6-month period preceding referral, and that clients accept voluntary treatment, admitting that they are alcoholics who need help to arrest their condition.

Arizona

ALCOHOL AND DRUG ABUSE CENTER
Phoenix General Hospital

1950 West Indian School Road
P.O. Box 21331
Phoenix, Arizona 85015

(602) 279-4411, ext. 5224

Director: Joyce Faith

Average Patient Census: 15–20 women
Minimum Duration of Treatment: 3–4 weeks, 21-day program
Cost: $6,500–7,500. Insurance eligible.
Detoxification Offered: Yes
Accreditation: AOA

Phoenix General Hospital's Alcohol and Drug Abuse Center has for the past 5 years been a leader in the treatment of the chemically dependent woman and her family.

The female detoxification and 21-day rehabilitation program includes medical management, individual and group counseling, education about the disease, introduction to AA and the Twelve Steps of Recovery, and 6 months to 1 year of aftercare.

Other services include a female daytime Outpatient Program, evening coed Outpatient Program, male inpatient detoxification, intervention and pretreatment program, and a Family and Children's Program.

Other special services include methadone-free heroin detoxification, building up to drinking-period admission (for the recovering man or woman who feels vulnerable to relapse), free confidential consultations, and educational programs designed for public education as well as business and industry.

EBONY HOUSE INC.

6222 South Thirteenth Street
Phoenix, Arizona 85040

(602) 276-4288

Director: C. N. Hall
Average Patient Census: 12

Minimum Duration of Treatment: 30–60 days
Cost: Sliding scale. Not insurance eligible.
Detoxification Offered: No
Accreditation: Arizona Department of Health Services

Ebony House offers a program that is designed to meet the specific needs of blacks, minorities and other ethnic groups that seek to overcome alcoholism and other alcohol-related problems.

Treatment is offered in four phases: (1) recognition, as clients recognize that they have a problem with alcohol and related character defects; (2) acceptance, as clients accept the fact that alcoholism is an illness and can only be arrested through therapeutic treatments; (3) willingness to work toward recovery from that illness; and (4) commitment to continue to work toward recovery after leaving the program.

Staff members provide individually designed programs to fit each individual's specific needs through individual and group counseling, family counseling, and educational and rehabilitative programs and activities.

Upon discharge, clients are encouraged to attend AA in-house meetings twice weekly. Ebony House encourages all clients to resume normal activities as soon as their condition allows, and they are encouraged to pay their own way as soon as they resume work.

Located in southeast Phoenix, in a neighborhood that consists of blacks and other minorities, Ebony House policy is to turn no one away for lack of funds, or because of color, race and/or creed. Treatment is offered for alcoholism only.

O'RIELLY CARE CENTER
Saint Joseph's Hospital

350 North Wilmot Road
P.O. Box 12069
Tucson, Arizona 85732

(602) 296-3211, ext. 2528
1-800-THE-HOPE (Arizona Watts line)
Director: Bill Winton
Average Patient Census: 18
Minimum Duration of Treatment: 2–4 weeks
Cost: Varies. Insurance eligible.
Detoxification Offered: Yes
Accreditation: JCAH

The Frank C. O'Reilly Care Center is a separate building adjacent to Saint Joseph's Hospital, providing privacy, warmth and comfort, as well as a walled patio inviting outdoor leisure. Admission may be by the request of the client, the family, the physician or a concerned other; each client will need a statement from his or her own doctor or a Center physician before admission. Detoxification, when needed, is available at Saint Joseph's or any other local hospital.

The intensive 3- to 4-week inpatient treatment program involves lectures, group and individual therapy, family groups, leisure planning, physical activity and recreation, movies and tapes. The principles of AA, Al-Anon and Alateen are employed throughout, and meeting attendance at these groups is seen as a vital part of the overall support system.

Family involvement in such ways as counseling, family focus week, movies, lectures and interaction with other families is an important part of treatment, as is the 2-year aftercare for clients and families for reinforcement, encouragement and personal growth. The Center is also designed to help employers salvage a valuable asset to their business—their employees.

The O'Reilly Care Center also offers an outpatient day and outpatient evening program, as well as a highly successful intervention program.

WESTCENTER

3838 North Campbell Avenue
Tucson, Arizona 85719

(602) 795-0952

Director: Jacquelyn St. Germaine
Average Patient Census: 28

Minimum Duration of Treatment: 21 days after detox; extended stays available if therapeutically necessary
Cost: $244 per day; doctor's fees additional. Insurance eligible.
Detoxification Offered: Yes
Accreditation: AOA

Westcenter offers admission to any person with an alcoholism, cocaine or other drug problem who is seeking rehabilitation. A 21-day rehabilitation program provides a healthy, hospital-supported, non-threatening environment to meet the needs of the alcoholic. These needs —physical, social, psychological, emotional and spiritual—are met through the use of personal and group counseling, lectures, stress management and a multitude of related activities. A week-long family counseling program is offered to all families.

Westcenter also provides outpatient treatment for patients and their families at a cost of $48 per session, meeting 3 to 5 nights a week for 4 to 6 weeks, depending on need. Family members are included at no additional cost.

A 24-hour crisis line is also available: (602) 327-5431.

WESTCENTER ADOLESCENT PROGRAM

3838 North Campbell Avenue
Tucson, Arizona 85719

(602) 795-2556

Director: Jacquelyn St. Germaine
Average Patient Census: 12

Minimum Duration of Treatment: 30 days after detox; 45 days recommended
Cost: Available on request. Insurance eligible.
Detoxification Offered: Yes
Accreditation: AOA

Westcenter Adolescent Program provides inpatient and outpatient care for adolescents age 12 to 18 who have alcohol, cocaine or other drug problems. An intensive family program is offered to all families. The inpatient program normally runs 30 to 45 days, and patients receive individual, group and family counseling, lectures and recreational therapy, as well as continue their schoolwork for credit.

Westcenter Adolescent Program also provides outpatient treatment to adolescents and families for $30 per 2-hour session. The sessions are held 3 nights a week for 6 weeks. There is no charge for family members.

A 24-hour crisis line is available: (602) 795-2556. Assessments and referrals are provided free of charge.

THE MEADOWS

P.O. Box 97
Wickenburg, Arizona 85358

(602) 684-2815
1-800-621-4062 outside Arizona

Director: James P. Mellody
Average Patient Census: 50

Minimum Duration of Treatment: 5½ weeks average. Longer stays when appropriate.
Cost: $238 per day, plus $95 per day for definitive observation. Additional costs for psychological testing, physical examination and treatment, etc. Insurance eligible.
Detoxification Offered: Yes
Accreditation: JCAH

The program at The Meadows is oriented toward group therapy and generally proceeds through three phases: (1) awareness, a period in which the patient becomes aware of the disease of chemical dependency and its impact upon the lives of dependent people and their families; (2) acceptance, a period in which the patient accepts the reality of the illness, as well as responsibility for his or her own recovery; and (3) action, a period in which the patient develops the courage to make decisions, adopts new behaviors and attitudes, and commits himself or herself to a new way of life. Throughout treatment the patient is exposed to in-depth study of AA and the Twelve Steps. Lectures and group psychotherapy sessions are held daily. Individual counseling is scheduled as appropriate, and psychological and spiritual counseling are an integral part of the treatment program.

The staff at The Meadows believes that the family is integral to treatment and asks that as much of the family as possible spend a week of therapy for themselves; this period is normally scheduled in the third or fourth week of the patient's treatment.

The facility is located on 13 acres of high desert landscape and offers a relaxed and informal setting, providing both seclusion for meditation and areas for group interpersonal communications. The therapy staff utilizes an interdisciplinary-team approach to recovery and structures a treatment program tailored to the individual patient's needs. The program offers individual and group counseling; psychological evaluation; and marriage, family, social and financial counseling; as well as 24-hour medical and nursing supervision.

California

ACTON REHABILITATION CENTER

30500 North Arrastre Canyon Road
Acton, California 93510

(805) 947-4191

Director: Roger Welch

Average Patient Census: 300
Minimum Duration of Treatment: 90 days
Cost: $20 per day. Insurance eligible.
Detoxification Offered: No
Accreditation: State of California

The Acton Rehabilitation Center, set in the high desert 55 miles north of Los Angeles, offers comfortable cabin- and dormitory-style accommodations and provides nonintensive medical and rehabilitative services to 265 men and 40 women residents.

Admission criteria include: desire for admission to the program; age limits of 18 to 64, but those over 64 may be admitted depending on physical condition; clients must be ambulatory; clients must be substance-free for at least 3 days, preferably 5; and no hard drug users or clients with violent behavior are eligible. All residents of Los Angeles County are eligible.

Psychosocial services in the treatment program include individual treatment and discharge planning, individual and group therapy, occupational and recreational therapy, religious services, residential community councils, vocational education and training, work therapy and referrals.

A sister center, Warm Springs Rehabilitation Center, serves 200 residents (males only) with a like program, at 38200 Lake Hughes Road, Castaic, California 91310, (805) 257-2342. Both centers offer, besides residential care, 24-hour ambulatory medical care and participation in AA, as well as the Alcoholic Olympics.

ALTA VISTA

3600 San Dimas
Bakersfield, California 93301

(805) 327-7621

Director: James Nielson, M.S.W.
Average Patient Census: 20 beds

Minimum Duration of Treatment: 1 year, including aftercare
Cost: Total inpatient-outpatient, $7,800; outpatient only, $1,700–2,000. Insurance eligible.
Detoxification Offered: Yes
Accreditation: JCAH

Alta Vista is a 20-bed, freestanding facility, located on 3 semisecluded acres exclusively for the treatment of chemical dependency. The program is designed to end a person's dependence on alcohol or other drugs and to assist in the building of a new life for that person.

Patients spend 1 to 3 days under close medical supervision during their physical withdrawal from alcohol or drugs. Each patient then participates in one, or a combination of, the following programs: 3-week inpatient, 3-week day treatment, or 20-week outpatient plans. Family members participate simultaneously in a family treatment program.

Treatment modalities consist of individual, group and family therapy in combination with films, assigned readings, exercise and leisure counseling, all of which help patients and their families to improve relationships, learn new coping skills and maintain sobriety.

Aftercare services provided result in a year-long treatment program from time of admission.

CAREUNIT
Alta Bates Hospital

3001 Colby at Ashby
Berkeley, California 94705

(415) 549-3080

Director: Daniel J. Graney, M.A.
Average Patient Census: 15

Minimum Duration of Treatment: Based on individual patient's needs
Cost: Available on request. Insurance eligible.
Detoxification Offered: Yes
Accreditation: JCAH

The Alta Bates CareUnit is a 3- to 5-week inpatient program, staffed by an interdisciplinary team that includes an alcoholism therapist, social worker, psychologist, medical doctor and a staff of specially trained nurses.

The program includes medical detoxification, psychotherapy, structured and unstructured groups, educational sessions, individual and family counseling and an aftercare program that is strongly oriented toward AA. Attendance at AA meetings is an integral part of the program. Medically rather than psychiatrically oriented, Alta Bates CareUnit utilizes outside consultants for patients with emotional or psychiatric problems requiring ongoing therapy. The primary modality is the peer group, but each patient is approached as an individual, with a treatment plan developed by the entire team.

Alta Bates CareUnit strongly encourages family, friends and significant others to become involved as much as possible. Family sessions and weekend workshops are an important part of the program. After discharge, aftercare support groups are offered, as well as crisis counseling for the patient and family.

Intervention, a process used to instill motivation to seek help in the addicted, may be arranged with a phone call. For information call the CareUnit.

Staff members are available for crisis counseling for family members, and for in-service seminars, workshops or speaking engagements, as well as advice on the establishment of alcoholism programs in industry and community.

BRIGHTSIDE ACT CENTER

24945 Valley Way
Carmel, California 93923

(408) 624-4995

Director: George Staub
Average Patient Census: 15

Minimum Duration of Treatment: 30-day inpatient; 2-year aftercare
Cost: $6,900. Insurance eligible.
Detoxification Offered: Yes
Accreditation: Licensed by the State of California as a Chemical Dependency Recovery Hospital

Brightside ACT Center—Carmel is a 22-bed, freestanding Chemical Dependency Recovery Hospital (CDRH), licensed as such by the State of California on January 12, 1984. This is a fairly new licensing category established in 1982, and Brightside ACT Center is the fifth such facility in the state to receive the new license. A freestanding CDRH is a specialty hospital designed and staffed exclusively for the treatment of addictive diseases. Brightside ACT Center is licensed to treat adults only.

The philosophy of Brightside ACT Center is consistent with the philosophy of Saint Benedict's ACT and Saint Benedict's Health System—to give glory to God through service to man. Specifically, in terms of alcoholism and chemical-dependency treatment, this means providing a full range of interdisciplinary services in a caring community for the treatment of dependency through a united effort of Sisters, trustees, physicians, personnel, students and volunteers, including members of the fellowship of AA, Al-Anon and Alateen.

Treatment at Brightside ACT Center follows a medical model and is supervised by a highly skilled staff of physicians, nurses, counselors, therapists and other allied professionals. Guided by the recognition that the disease of addiction affects the whole person, treatment focuses on the four major facets of the illness: physiological, psychological, social and spiritual. Treatment begins with a minimum of 24 hours of close observation (detoxification), which includes a complete physical examination, medication when warranted and a comprehensive drinking/drug history taken by a skilled counselor.

Following close observation, when the medical staff determines that the patient has reached a stable state physically, definitive treatment begins. Each patient is involved in a carefully structured program of education, individual counseling and intensive group therapy. The families of patients and/or their significant others are involved in the treatment process. An aftercare program is structured for each patient and maintained for two years.

Brightside is staffed by experienced professionals with specialized training in the treatment of addictive diseases. All treatment staff are licensed or certified, and major disciplines are represented throughout the duration of treatment. Skilled staff provide 24-hour-a-day medical and nursing care. Bilingual services in English and Spanish are available.

AMETHYST WOMEN'S RECOVERY PROGRAM
COLLEGE HOSPITAL

10802 College Place
Cerritos, California 90701

(213) 924-9581

Director: Jean Fromm, Ph.D.

Average Patient Census: 8–10
Minimum Duration of Treatment: 21–28 days
Cost: $380 per day. Insurance eligible.
Detoxification Offered: Yes
Accreditation: JCAH

The Amethyst Program is limited to women in the belief that such programs are needed for a number of complex but definite reasons.

First, treatment programs are traditionally geared toward the male.

The recognition that alcoholism and drug dependency are equal-opportunity diseases has come only in recent years, and women are the minority in hospital treatment programs, some estimates showing that one in seven patients are women.

Further, women have different needs than do males, and this program addresses those needs: parenting skills, training for independence, working through anger, guilt over children, increasing self-esteem and vocational and survival skills.

Women's programs, such as Amethyst, also respond to research that has shown women less active in mixed therapy groups than in all-female groups, and to the belief that when the need for approval from men can be put aside, therapy proceeds much faster. The all-female program also speaks to the greater stigma directed at the woman who is either alcoholic or drug dependent, which unfortunately prevails even in mixed therapy groups.

College Hospital also provides a Help Line: 1-800-352-3381.

NEW BEGINNINGS PROGRAM
DOMINGUEZ VALLEY HOSPITAL

3100 South Susana Road
Compton, California 90221

(213) 639-2664

Director: JoAnn Hahn
Average Patient Census: 19

Minimum Duration of Treatment: 28 days, plus detox for normal program
Cost: $280 per day approximately. Insurance eligible.
Detoxification Offered: Yes
Accreditation: JCAH

New Beginnings' comprehensive treatment program is interdisciplinary, combining medical, educational and counseling services with a strong emphasis on family involvement. The treatment team recognizes alcoholism/chemical dependency as a primary illness. The length of treatment is flexible, and an individual response is made to each patient's needs. The variety of treatment methods all emphasize the need for the continuing support of AA or NA.

The program has three phases. Phase One is detoxification, 3 to 6 days, with medical management of acute withdrawal and treatment of medical complications. Phase Two is the rehabilitation treatment and education program and includes continued medical treatment and observation, individual counseling, group therapy, lectures and discussions, audiovisual training sessions, family therapy and peer-group interaction.

Phase Three is aftercare, including weekly visits for 1 year and specific individualized support for each patient and family to help in making a sober adjustment to personal relationships and a successful reentry into the workplace. New Beginnings also offers a Family Program that recognizes the family's need for education, therapy and support.

The stated goal of the complete program is to provide treatment specifically designed for the individual needs of each patient in a warm atmosphere that blends concern, love and trust with high professional standards. In this climate, the seed of sobriety is nurtured, and most patients completing the program leave with a new sense of responsibility and self-worth.

Persons of both sexes with problems related to alcohol or other addictive drugs may be admitted. If the patient does not have a personal physician, the program medical director will provide all necessary physician services. All admissions are voluntary, and services are confidential, protecting the rights of the patient, family and referral source.

ALCOHOLISM AND DRUG RECOVERY UNIT
CORONADO HOSPITAL

250 Prospect Place
Coronado, California 92118

(619) 238-3736

Director: Ron Arble
Average Patient Census: 8–10

Minimum Duration of Treatment: Detox, 3–7 days; rehab, 28 days
Cost: Varies, depending on services needed. Insurance eligible.
Detoxification Offered: Yes
Accreditation: JCAH. Affiliated with Naval Reserve Association.

The philosophy of the Coronado Hospital Alcoholism and Drug Recovery Unit is that alcoholism and addiction to other drugs is a disease that affects not only the identified person but the whole family, and that total abstinence from all mood-altering drugs, including alcohol, is necessary for continued recovery.

The program includes detoxification, medical treatment for any other physical problems, group and individual counseling, recreational activities, nutritional counseling, pastoral counseling, need assessments, discharge planning and field trips.

Any referring physician may apply for temporary staff privileges if he or she wishes to act as attending physician, or may, again on request, be consulted and informed throughout the patient's treatment.

Participation of family and friends in the family program is strongly encouraged and consists of evening and day education, counseling and group therapy.

The aftercare phase of the ADRU program consists of Relapse Prevention Groups, Alcoholic Groups, Coalcoholic Groups and Couples Groups.

The patients and families are introduced to AA, NA, Al-Anon, Alateen and ACA. The patients attend 5 AA meetings each week, both in-house and in the community. Pastoral counseling is available for the fifth Step of AA.

Outpatient Day Care services, Intervention Training, Intervention Assessments and referrals are available.

An intensive outpatient program designed for the chemically dependent and the family, meets 4 nights a week and is available to the family even if the addicted person refuses to attend. The program consists of educational sessions, individual counseling and group therapy for the chemically dependent, the spouse, the children, couples and the family.

STARTING POINT OF ORANGE COUNTY

350 West Bay Street
Costa Mesa, California 92627

(714) 642-3505

Director: Don Beld
Average Patient Census: 59 beds

Minimum Duration of Treatment: 28 days plus detox
Cost: Approximately $5,500. Insurance eligible.
Detoxification Offered: Yes
Accreditation: JCAH

Starting Point is a facility specializing in the family treatment of alcohol and other drug dependencies. The 28-day inpatient program focuses on the medical, psychological and spiritual aspects of the diseases of alcoholism and drug dependency, utilizing a multidisciplinary-team approach by a physician, a psychologist, substance abuse counselors, therapists and a clergy counselor. Strong family involvement, consisting of 1 full day a week of group therapy and educational programs for each family member, is emphasized.

Starting Point also features a strong aftercare program, which stresses participation in self-help groups such as AA, Al-Anon, Alateen, NA and others. Starting Point is a wholly owned subsidiary of Comprehensive Care Corporation.

CAPISTRANO BY THE SEA HOSPITAL AND CLINIC

33915 Del Obispo
Dana Point, California 92629

(714) 496-5702

Director: Hal Day
Average Patient Census: 15

Minimum Duration of Treatment: 3 weeks minimum, 6 weeks maximum
Cost: Average $310 per day includes medical care, group therapy and physical activities. Insurance eligible.
Detoxification Offered: Yes
Accreditation: JCAH

Capistrano by the Sea Hospital Alcohol and Drug Program provides detoxification and rehabilitation services to those addicted persons who wish to restructure their daily habits and change their emotional responses to events in their daily lives. These changes are accomplished with the assistance of trained staff and the patient's support system. Patients attend individual and group therapy sessions, educational groups, AA, NA, CA, community recreation events, arts and crafts classes and weekly meetings, where they discuss their progress with the staff. Family therapy is required.

Patients can be self-referred, and all receive aftercare and follow-up services. Psychologists are permitted to admit and treat patients in the hospital under the supervision of the medical director or staff psychiatrist.

The serene setting of the hospital on a bluff overlooking the Pacific Ocean is utilized through outdoor group-therapy sessions, picnics, jogging through eucalyptus groves and swimming at the beach.

A discharge-planning group is conducted weekly by the treatment-team social worker, utilizing information from other members to formulate a plan for each patient's future after he or she leaves the hospital. If the patient no longer requires hospitalization but is not yet prepared to return to the stresses of daily living, the social worker will assist the family in planning for discharge and placement outside the home. Capistrano by the Sea also stresses the importance of referral of patients back to their personal physician for follow-up care at the time of discharge.

RANCHO PARK HOSPITAL

109 East Chase Avenue
El Cajon, California 92020

(619) 579-1666

Director: Patricia Mulcahy, R.N., C.A.C.
Average Patient Census: 30-bed inpatient program

Minimum Duration of Treatment: Approximately 6–8 weeks
Cost: Available on request. Insurance eligible.
Detoxification Offered: Yes
Accreditation: Pending

Rancho Park Hospital provides a comprehensive substance-abuse treatment program specifically developed to deal with the unique needs of the chemically dependent population.

The program is designed to help people overcome their problems and to return to a productive drug-free life-style. The highly structured therapeutic environment offers a drug-free approach that utilizes various treatment modalities. These include both individual and group therapy, physical, recreational and expressive therapies, leisure-skills counseling and self-help counseling.

Family participation is essential in all phases of the treatment through involvement in family therapies, specialized meetings and aftercare groups.

ALCOHOLISM RECOVERY PROGRAM
Saint Rose Hospital

27200 Calaroga Avenue
Hayward, California 94545

(415) 783-6544

Director: K. Jane Benson
Average Patient Census: 13

Minimum Duration of Treatment: Rehab, 8 weeks (includes 2 weeks inpatient and 6 weeks outpatient)
Cost: Inpatient, $5,390. Insurance eligible.
Detoxification Offered: Yes
Accreditation: JCAH

The stated purpose of the Alcoholism Recovery Program at Saint Rose Hospital is to provide comprehensive services for chemically dependent adults and their families that will enable them to become chemically free, self-sufficient, independent and responsible for their own well-being.

The program consists of medically supervised detoxification, if necessary, followed by an innovative 8-week rehabilitation program—a 2-

week inpatient stay combined with 6 weeks of outpatient treatment. During this time, patients and their families participate in educational lectures and group and individual counseling. Patients and families are also introduced to AA and Al-Anon. During the course of treatment other professional resources may be utilized to deal with concurrent problems the patient and his or her family may be experiencing, such as marital conflict or financial difficulty. Upon discharge from treatment, patients are enrolled in weekly aftercare sessions that are designed to support the goals made during treatment.

An intensive 6-week outpatient program is also available at a cost of $950. There is no charge for the 1 year of aftercare or for consultation and intervention for families and others concerned about a chemically dependent person. Also offered are consultation for business and industry, an alumni association and a speakers bureau.

ALCOHOLISM TREATMENT UNIT
Ross Hospital

1111 Saint Francis Drake Boulevard
Kentfield, California 94904

(415) 453-7800, ext. 333, weekdays; ext. 272, nights and weekends

Director: Christopher Eskeli, M.F.C.C.

Average Patient Census: 15
Minimum Duration of Treatment: 24 days, includes 3-day minimum medical detox
Cost: $350 per day. Insurance eligible.
Detoxification Offered: Yes
Accreditation: JCAH

The ATU at Ross General Hospital offers a 21- to 30-day alcoholism treatment program, including medical detoxification if necessary. The detoxification service is available to those patients who are willing to make a commitment to continue with the 21-day treatment program, and admission qualifications include appropriateness for group therapy.

A separate detoxification program is offered for those unable to complete the 21-day program. This detoxification program is only for those who (a) are unable to complete the 21-day program due to insurance coverage, funds, etc.; (b) are already in contact with an appropriate AA Twelve Step program before and after detoxification; and (c) are on a "one time only" basis.

The clear goal of the program is total abstinence from alcohol and drugs, and strong emphasis is placed upon long-term recovery through support offered by AA and other Twelve Step programs.

The Family Program is an integral part of the treatment program.

Involvement of family members in the therapy and educational programs is offered, as well as 2-year aftercare for the patient and family after completion of the inpatient program.

THE McDONALD CENTER
SCRIPPS MEMORIAL HOSPITAL

9888 Genesee Avenue
La Jolla, California 92037

(619) 458-4300, 1-800-382-HELP

Director: Len Baltzer
Average Patient Census: 88 beds (adults, 64; adolescents, 24)

Minimum Duration of Treatment: Adults, 4 weeks average; adolescents, 45 days
Cost: Available on request. Insurance eligible.
Detoxification Offered: Yes
Accreditation: JCAH

The McDonald Center, a freestanding facility on the Scripps Memorial Hospital campus, believes that alcoholism and/or drug addiction is a disease and needs treatment and that medical expertise, backed by unconditional love, can work wonders toward recovery.

This recovery begins with a warm, loving hug as patients enter the new treatment center. After a physical examination, days are filled with informational films and lectures, individual and group therapy, nutrition and fitness programs and constant medical evaluation.

Because alcoholism/drug addiction is a family disease, family recovery is basic to the treatment. Families are required to participate in the program, including 5 days as outpatients during Family Week.

The Adolescent Program takes place in the Steele Pavilion, which has been especially designed for adolescents. There will be a complete assessment and evaluation by a team of specialists, who set up an individual program to meet the special needs of the teenager. Peer pressure is used as a positive tool for recovery. Daily group activities, arts and crafts, sports, recreation and daily meetings of AA or NA are included. Classroom education continues in the state-licensed private school during treatment, with a specially trained teacher who designs the study program and arranges for reentry into school after treatment.

Aftercare is part of the adult, adolescent and outpatient programs. Weekly meetings offer continuing support, as does ongoing attendance at AA or NA.

The McDonald Center also offers a 6- to 8-week adult outpatient program that takes place weekday evenings.

A free information session takes place every Wednesday at 2:30 P.M., which often leads to helping even those who don't want help through the intervention process.

NEW BEGINNINGS PROGRAM—ADOLESCENT
Doctors' Hospital of Lakewood

Clark Avenue Division
5300 North Clark Avenue
Lakewood, California 90712

(213) 866-9711

Director: Anne Penhollow

Average Patient Census: 15
Minimum Duration of Treatment: 60–90 days for normal program
Cost: $310 per day approximately. Insurance eligible.
Detoxification Offered: Yes
Accreditation: JCAH

The adolescent New Beginnings' program recognizes alcohol and drug dependency as a primary illness. The stated goal of this program is to provide treatment specifically designed for the individual needs of each young person in an atmosphere that blends concern, love and trust with high professional treatment standards. New Beginnings feels that in this climate the seed of sobriety is planted and allowed to grow while patients learn to interact with others in a positive and supportive way.

The comprehensive treatment program is interdisciplinary and combines medical, educational and counseling services with a strong emphasis on family involvement and peer support. The program involves a therapeutic milieu designed to aid in the resolution of behavioral problems that adolescents may manifest, a full-time teacher so that the adolescent may return to school with little loss of class position, a recreational therapist to teach and encourage participation in active, healthy outlets for youthful energy and 1 year of aftercare for patients and family members.

The unit is open to young people age 11 to 18 who have problems related to alcohol or other addictive drugs, including those who have special medical or psychiatric needs. Admissions are voluntary, and all services to patients and family members are completely confidential.

NEW BEGINNINGS PROGRAM—ADULT
Doctors' Hospital of Lakewood

Clark Avenue Division
5300 North Clark Avenue
Lakewood, California 90712

(213) 866-9711

Director: Anne Penhollow

Average Patient Census: 17
Minimum Duration of Treatment: 28 days plus detox for normal program
Cost: $300 per day approximately. Insurance eligible.
Detoxification Offered: Yes
Accreditation: JCAH

New Beginnings' comprehensive treatment program is interdisciplinary, combining medical, educational and counseling services with a strong emphasis on family involvement. The treatment team recognizes alcoholism/chemical dependency as a primary illness. The length of treatment is flexible, and an individual response is made to each patient's needs. The variety of treatment methods all emphasize the need for the continuing support of AA or NA.

The program has three phases. Phase One is detoxification, 3 to 6 days, with medical management of acute withdrawal and treatment of medical complications. Phase Two is the rehabilitation treatment and education program and includes continued medical treatment and observation, individual counseling, group therapy, lectures and discussions, audiovisual training sessions, family therapy and peer-group interaction. Phase Three is aftercare, including weekly visits for 1 year and specific individualized support for each patient and family to help in making a sober adjustment to personal relationships and a successful reentry into the workplace. New Beginnings also offers a Family Program that recognizes the family's need for education, therapy and support.

The stated goal of the complete program is to provide treatment specifically designed for the individual needs of each patient in a warm atmosphere that blends concern, love and trust with high professional standards. In this climate, the seed of sobriety is nurtured and most patients completing the program leave with a new sense of responsibility and self-worth.

Persons of both sexes with problems related to alcohol or other addictive drugs may be admitted. If the patient does not have a personal physician, the program medical director will provide all necessary physician services. All admissions are voluntary, and services are confidential, protecting the rights of the patient, family and referral source.

CHEMICAL DEPENDENCY UNIT
Antelope Valley Hospital Medical Center

1600 West Avenue J
Lancaster, California 93534

(805) 948-0421

Director: Darlene Place, R.N., M.S.
Average Patient Census: 16-bed unit

Minimum Duration of Treatment: Minimum of 3 days only for special cases and must be prearranged. Average stay is 4 weeks.
Cost: Inpatient, approximately $8,000; day care outpatient, $1,100; evening outpatient, $360 per month. Insurance eligible.
Detoxification Offered: Yes
Accreditation: JCAH

The Chemical Dependency Unit at Antelope Valley Hospital is a medically supervised treatment center located within a hospital setting. It treats the disease of alcoholism as a family disease and provides medical care, psychological counseling and educational programs for the patient as well as his or her immediate family.

To qualify for admission, patients must show a willingness to participate in the 3- to 4-week detoxification and rehabilitation program.

The unit is staffed by specially trained personnel who understand the disease of alcoholism and who have a genuine concern for the patient's recovery. Often, one or more members of the team may be recovered alcoholics themselves, with a unique insight into the special kind of suffering their patients have endured.

A 2-year aftercare program is included in the cost, as it is in the 7-week outpatient program that is also offered, by this facility.

The staff is uniquely prepared to care for the impaired nurse. Out-of-state patients are accepted in the Impaired Nurse Program.

MEMORIAL COASTVIEW
Memorial Medical Center of Long Beach

455 Columbia
P.O. Box 1428
Long Beach, California 90801

(213) 426-6619

Director: Steve Brodie
Average Patient Census: Adults, 38; adolescents, 12

Minimum Duration of Treatment: Adults, 21 days and detox; adolescents, 45–90 days
Cost: Detox, $360 per day; adult rehab, $200 per day; adolescent rehab, $281 per day. Insurance eligible.
Detoxification Offered: Yes
Accreditation: JCAH

Memorial Coastview, a part of Memorial Medical Center, is an innovative modern facility designed to enable the professional treatment team to produce the highest quality care for patients.

In the Adult Program, close medical attention is paid during the critical detoxification period, after which the patient begins the rehabilitation phase of treatment, staying in the adult unit and undergoing intensive therapy and education to understand his or her disease and how to control it. An individual treatment plan is developed by staff and patient together, a plan that encourages self-responsibility and the development of relationships with peers and significant others. A typical patient day includes community meeting, "One Day at a Time" group, lecture, group therapy, men's and women's groups, family group therapy, study and reading time, AA group, second lecture and relaxation group. A full 12-month aftercare program, and a week-long, full-day family program are also part of Memorial Coastview's program, as well as a Day Care Program for those who do not require detox but participate in the same intensive program as inpatients.

The Adolescent Program for chemically dependent teenagers, age 11 to young adult, is housed in a separate, secure wing with attractive semiprivate rooms. A positive, caring attitude is reflected by the staff and an education program is available, designed as a process of transition to lead the adolescent back into the educational mainstream, with small classes, individualized attention and coursework geared to the particular student's level. Small group therapy sessions, individual counseling, drug education, life-skills development, student government and attendance at AA, NA, CA, Alateen and other support groups are some of the elements of the program. Family members participate throughout the course of treatment. Upon completion of the program, all patients and appropriate family members will be scheduled to attend weekly sessions of therapy and education. Attendance at self-help groups will be monitored and academic tutoring provided. Patients will be further involved with their alumni association and volunteer activities with patients in the inpatient phase of treatment.

MEN'S TWELFTH STEP HOUSE

Harbor Area
1005 East Sixth Street
Long Beach, California 90802

(213) 437-9759

Average Patient Census: 48 (men only)
Minimum Duration of Treatment: Open
Cost: $55 per week. Not insurance eligible.
Detoxification Offered: No

Director: Jim Ford

The Men's Twelfth Step House is a nonprofit, state-chartered facility designed to help the sick alcoholic into permanent sobriety. The house was started in 1953 by a group of Long Beach alcoholics who, having achieved sobriety themselves, realized the need for a recovery home available to sick and suffering alcoholics. Admission may be through referral by physician, clergyman, detox center, or may be accomplished by the alcoholic himself who is willing to accept help in his search for rehabilitation.

Payment is expected at the time of entry or, alternatively, as a moral commitment on the part of the resident to find employment and pay as soon as he is able. Efforts are made to put the resident in touch with the proper agencies in fields outside the scope of the house's function who assist men who need temporary or permanent employment.

The house provides individual help on personal problems and actively encourages residents to attend AA meetings that are held at the house several times a week. The program is based, in part, on work and holding a job. Every resident is expected to share in the household chores. Potential successful sobriety occurs when a resident has made a personal discovery of the nature of his disease, understands its progressive and chronic aspect and becomes aware of its relationship to his emotional and physical well-being.

ALCOHOLISM CENTER FOR WOMEN

1147 South Alvarado Street
Los Angeles, California 90006

(213) 381-7805

Director: Brenda L. Underhill

Average Patient Census: 15
Minimum Duration of Treatment: 4 weeks
Cost: Sliding scale. Insurance eligible.
Detoxification Offered: No
Accreditation: CAARH

The Alcoholism Center for Women is a nonprofit, community-based program, funded by Los Angeles County. The center is well into its tenth year of services, not only to women with an alcohol abuse problem but to women at high risk—adult children of alcoholics, lesbians, rape victims, and incest/battering survivors. The Center also serves family members and concerned members of the community. No one is turned away for lack of funds.

The Recovery Services Program, for both residents of the 15-bed Recovery Home and for nonresident participants, provides individual counseling, structured peer-oriented groups in alcohol education, coping and survival skills, assertiveness training and self-esteem building, vocational guidance, social services and social and recreational activities. In essence, each woman's recovery plan is designed to meet her total needs and goals, fortifying and enhancing her sober life-style.

Aftercare groups are available for up to a year for those women who have either gone through this program or who have 6 months' sobriety and have not previously been in a treatment program. Space is also provided for all-women AA and Al-Anon meetings and groups in the women's community.

Prevention and outreach components, through the Center's speakers bureau, provide the community with presentations, workshops, seminars and panels. Training and consultant services are also offered to other treatment agencies, hospitals, schools, employee assistance programs, and human services professionals. Educational material pertaining to women and alcoholism and women at high risk for alcohol abuse is developed and distributed, and ACW also answers requests for information on a local and nationwide level.

Programs are also provided, both educational and counseling, for adult daughters of alcoholics, incest/battering survivors, significant others of alcoholics, and women with compulsive-behavior problems.

CAREUNIT HOSPITAL OF LOS ANGELES

5035 Coliseum Street
Los Angeles, California 90016

(213) 295-6441

Director: Jack Gronewald
Average Patient Census: Adults, 64; adolescents, 20

Minimum Duration of Treatment: Adults, 21–28 days; adolescents, 45–60 days
Cost: Approximately $300 per day. Insurance eligible.
Detoxification Offered: Yes
Accreditation: JCAH

CareUnit Hospital is a facility specializing in the family treatment of alcohol and other drug dependencies for adults and adolescents. Patients undergo a complete physiological and psychological examination and detoxification under the supervision of the medical director of the facility. The treatment program is personalized to fit individual needs and consists of individual and group therapy, participation in specific activities, lectures and films designed to increase the patient's understanding of his or her disease and appropriate ways to enjoy life free from chemical dependency. Families are invited to join in the treatment program, which is designed to free family members from the effects of the disease in areas such as behavior, attitudes and life-styles.

The recovery continues following the patient's discharge from the hospital. Patients return to the CareUnit for aftercare 2 evenings a week for a specified period following discharge. Family units participate once weekly in the aftercare program. Patients and their families are encouraged to explore other resources, such as AA, Al-Anon, Alateen, NA and others, to which they were introduced during their inpatient stay. Aftercare is free to all patients—for a lifetime, if desired.

CareUnit Hospital of Los Angeles also has a Hispanic Unit for the treatment of Spanish-speaking patients, and a 20-bed Eating Disorders Unit. The telephone number of the Hispanic Unit is (213) 292-0195.

NEW BEGINNINGS PROGRAM
Century City Hospital

2070 Century Park East
Los Angeles, California 90067

(213) 201-6730

Director: Richard Werner, L.C.S.W.
Average Patient Census: 16

Minimum Duration of Treatment: 28 days plus detox for normal program
Cost: Detox, approximately $315 per day; rehab, approximately $275 per day. Insurance eligible.
Detoxification Offered: Yes
Accreditation: JCAH

New Beginnings' comprehensive treatment program is interdisciplinary, combining medical, educational and counseling services with a strong emphasis on family involvement. The treatment team recognizes alcoholism/chemical dependency as a primary illness. The length of treatment is flexible, and an individual response is made to each patient's needs. The variety of treatment methods all emphasize the need for the continuing support of AA or NA.

The program has three phases. Phase One is detoxification, 3 to 6 days, with medical management of acute withdrawal and treatment of medical complications. Phase Two is the rehabilitation treatment and education program and includes continued medical treatment and observation, individual counseling, group therapy, lectures and discussions, audiovisual training sessions, family therapy and peer-group interaction. Phase Three is aftercare, including weekly visits for 1 year and specific individualized support for each patient and family to help in making a sober adjustment to personal relationships and a successful reentry into the workplace. New Beginnings also offers a Family Program that recognizes the family's need for education, therapy and support.

The stated goal of the complete program is to provide treatment specifically designed for the individual needs of each patient in a warm atmosphere that blends concern, love and trust with high professional standards. In this climate, the seed of sobriety is nurtured, and most patients completing the program leave with a new sense of responsibility and self-worth.

Persons of both sexes with problems related to alcohol, cocaine or other addictive drugs may be admitted. If the patient does not have a personal physician, the program medical director will provide all necessary physician services. All admissions are voluntary, and services are confidential, protecting the rights of the patient, family and referral source.

MONTE VILLA HOSPITAL

P.O. Box 947
Morgan Hill, California 95037

(408) 226-3020

Director: Ronald M. Davis
Average Patient Census: 45

Minimum Duration of Treatment:
Approximately 28 days
Cost: $310 per day. Approximately $9,800 for full program. Insurance eligible.
Detoxification Offered: Yes
Accreditation: JCAH

Monte Villa Hospital admits patients with acute addictive disease and/or psychiatric complications. The program consists of complete medical and psychiatric workup, as well as detoxification. There is 24-hour admission available.

The full treatment program, with clinical specialties, has AA orientation. A family program and aftercare are included.

ALCOHOLISM/CHEMICAL DEPENDENCY RECOVERY UNIT
MEDICAL CENTER OF NORTH HOLLYWOOD

12629 Riverside Drive
North Hollywood, California 91607

(818) 763-6261

Director: James L. Crossen

Average Patient Census: 14
Minimum Duration of Treatment: 21 days, or detox only
Cost: $4,800. Insurance eligible.
Detoxification Offered: Yes
Accreditation: JCAH

Admission to the Alcoholism/Chemical Dependency Recovery Unit at the Medical Center of North Hollywood includes the taking of a full medical history, physical examination, a substance-abuse history and a psychosocial evaluation. The rehabilitation program begins as soon as the patient is medically stable and includes a full spectrum of services under the direction of the recovery team of medical doctors, chemical dependency therapists, R.N.'s, and other professionals as indicated. The program is AA Twelve Step–centered and works to achieve the goals of lasting sobriety and optimal health of body, mind, emotion, spirit and relationships.

A detailed action-discharge plan is developed during the inpatient phase for implementation in the outpatient follow-up period, which continues for 2 to 6 months and involves participation of the patient and family members in once-a-week outpatient counseling sessions. There is, in addition, an emphasis upon the importance of involvement with AA, Al-Anon and Alateen.

NEW BEGINNINGS PROGRAM
OJAI VALLEY COMMUNITY HOSPITAL

1306 Maricopa Highway
Ojai, California 93023

(805) 646-1401

Director: Kristine A. Kepp
Average Patient Census: 10

Minimum Duration of Treatment: 28 days plus detox for normal program
Cost: Rehab, approximately $264 per day; detox, approximately $363 per day. Insurance eligible.
Detoxification Offered: Yes
Accreditation: JCAH

New Beginnings' comprehensive treatment program is interdisciplinary, combining medical, educational and counseling services with a strong emphasis on family involvement. The treatment team recognizes alcoholism/chemical dependency as a primary illness. The length of treatment is flexible, and an individual response is made to each patient's needs. The variety of treatment methods all emphasize the need for the continuing support of AA or NA.

The program has three phases. Phase One is detoxification, 3 to 6 days, with medical management of acute withdrawal and treatment of medical complications. Phase Two is the rehabilitation treatment and education program and includes continued medical treatment and observation, individual counseling, group therapy, lectures and discussions, audiovisual training sessions, family therapy and peer-group interaction. Phase Three is aftercare, including weekly visits for 1 year and specific individualized support for each patient and family to help in making a sober adjustment to personal relationships and a successful reentry into the workplace. New Beginnings also offers a Family Program that recognizes the family's need for education, therapy and support.

The stated goal of the complete program is to provide treatment specifically designed for the individual needs of each patient in a warm atmosphere that blends concern, love and trust with high professional standards. In this climate, the seed of sobriety is nurtured, and most patients completing the program leave with a new sense of responsibility and self-worth.

Persons of both sexes with problems related to alcohol, cocaine, Valium, speed or other addictive drugs may be admitted. If the patient does not have a personal physician, the program medical director will provide all necessary physician services. All admissions are voluntary, and services are confidential, protecting the rights of the patient, family and referral source.

NEW BEGINNINGS PROGRAM
Ontario Community Hospital

550 North Monterey Avenue
Ontario, California 91764

(714) 988-3844

Director: Susan Howe
Average Patient Census: 16

Minimum Duration of Treatment: 28 days plus detox for normal program
Cost: Detox, approximately $365 per day; rehab, approximately $260 per day. Insurance eligible.
Detoxification Offered: Yes
Accreditation: JCAH

New Beginnings' comprehensive treatment program is interdisciplinary, combining medical, educational and counseling services with a strong emphasis on family involvement. The treatment team recognizes alcoholism/chemical dependency as a primary illness. The length of treatment is flexible, and an individual response is made to each patient's needs. The variety of treatment methods all emphasize the need for the continuing support of AA or NA.

The program has three phases. Phase One is detoxification, 3 to 6 days, with medical management of acute withdrawal and treatment of medical complications. Phase Two is the rehabilitation treatment and education program and includes continued medical treatment and observation, individual counseling, group therapy, lectures and discussions, audiovisual training sessions, family therapy and peer group interaction. Phase Three is aftercare, including weekly visits for 1 year and specific individualized support for each patient and family to help in making a sober adjustment to personal relationships and a successful reentry into the workplace. New Beginnings also offers a Family Program that recognizes the family's need for education, therapy and support.

The stated goal of the complete program is to provide treatment specifically designed for the individual needs of each patient in a warm atmosphere that blends concern, love and trust with high professional standards. In this climate, the seed of sobriety is nurtured, and most patients completing the program leave with a new sense of responsibility and self-worth.

Persons of both sexes with problems related to alcohol or other addictive drugs may be admitted. If the patient does not have a personal physician, the program medical director will provide all necessary physician services. All admissions are voluntary, and services are confidential, protecting the rights of the patient, family and referral source.

CAREUNIT HOSPITAL OF ORANGE

401 South Tustin Avenue
Orange, California 92666

(714) 633-9582

Director: Anne Finn
Average Patient Census: Adults, 62; adolescents, 32

Minimum Duration of Treatment: Adults, 21–28 days; adolescents, 45–60 days
Cost: Approximately $300 per day. Insurance eligible.
Detoxification Offered: Yes
Accreditation: JCAH

CareUnit Hospital is a facility specializing in the family treatment of alcohol and other drug dependencies for adults and adolescents. Patients undergo a complete physiological and psychological examination and detoxification under the supervision of the medical director of the facility. The treatment program is personalized to fit individual needs and consists of individual and group therapy, participation in specific activities, as well as lectures and films designed to increase the patient's understanding of his or her disease and appropriate ways to enjoy life free from chemical dependency. Families are invited to join in the treatment program, which is designed to free family members from the effects of the disease in areas such as behavior, attitudes and life-styles.

The recovery continues following the patient's discharge from the hospital. Patients return to the CareUnit for aftercare 2 evenings a week for a specified period following discharge. Family units participate once weekly in the aftercare program. Patients and their families are encouraged to explore other resources such as AA, Al-Anon, Alateen, NA and others, to which they were introduced during their inpatient stay. Aftercare is free to all patients—for a lifetime, if desired.

Dr. Joseph A. Pursch, noted alcoholism treatment expert, maintains an office at CareUnit Hospital of Orange and is a frequent lecturer at the facility.

RECOVERY SERVICES
Saint Joseph Hospital

1100 West Stewart Drive
Orange, California 92667

(714) 771-8080

Director: Joseph J. Zuska, M.D., Medical Director; Max A. Schneider, M.D., Associate Director

Average Patient Census: 30–36
Minimum Duration of Treatment: Detox, 2–8 days; recovery services, 21–28 days
Cost: $7,500–8,500 average for 25–28 days. Insurance eligible.
Detoxification Offered: Yes
Accreditation: JCAH

The program at Saint Joseph Hospital is open to chemically dependent persons, with a primary emphasis on alcohol and prescription abuse. Patients must be 17 years or older. The inpatient services consist of detoxification plus a recovery program, usually 21 to 28 days.

This facility also provides family counseling, outpatient services, consultation, community outreach, day care and aftercare. There are AA, PA, Al-Anon and Alateen meetings on the unit. Free intervention services are available.

An intensive family program is designed for patients and their families in order to assist and enhance the recovery process. The program consists of lectures on recovery and codependency; recovery, codependent, family and couples groups; and individual sessions.

STARTING POINT

Adult Hospital
8773 Oak Avenue
Orangevale, California 95662

(916) 988-5700

Adolescent Hospital
1001 Grand Avenue
Sacramento, California 95838

(916) 929-5383

Director: Jack Sumner

Average Patient Census: Adult, 68 beds; adolescent, 25 beds
Minimum Duration of Treatment: Adult, 28 days plus detox; adolescent, 30–60 days
Cost: Adult, approximately $5,500; adolescent, varies according to length of stay. Insurance eligible.
Detoxification Offered: Yes
Accreditation: JCAH

Starting Point is a facility specializing in the family treatment of alcohol and other drug dependencies. The 28-day inpatient program focuses on the medical, psychological and spiritual aspects of the diseases of alcoholism and drug dependency, utilizing a multidisciplinary team approach by a physician, a psychologist, substance-abuse counselors, therapists and a clergy counselor. Strong family involvement, consisting of 1 full day a week of group therapy and educational programs for each family member, is emphasized.

Starting Point also features a strong aftercare program, which stresses participation in self-help groups such as AA, Al-Anon, Alateen, NA and others. Starting Point is a wholly-owned subsidiary of Comprehensive Care Corporation.

In northern California, Starting Point also has an outpatient program in San Jose, (408) 727-0781, and contract programs at Roseville Community Hospital, (916) 782-0646, and Vesper Hospital in Hayward, (415) 537-7714.

CASA DE LAS AMIGAS

160 North El Molino
Pasadena, California 91101

(213) 792-2770

Director: Jeanette Bird
Average Patient Census: 23 (women only)

Minimum Duration of Treatment: 2 months, up to 1 year
Cost: Based on ability to pay. Insurance eligible.
Detoxification Offered: No
Accreditation: JCAH

"The House of Friends" is, as its name implies, a quiet, friendly home where women who wish to overcome their problem with drinking can find friends who will work with them to achieve a happy sobriety, permitting a return to responsible living with families and communities.

The Casa's program includes many group activities for the residents, as well as carefully guided sessions of individual counseling and therapy. Although the Casa has no official connection with AA, it does utilize the philosophy and experience of AA, and regular attendance at AA meetings in the community is a basic part of the program.

Recognizing that an integral part of recovery is regaining self-respect that comes from being self-supporting and independent, all residents are asked to pay a reasonable charge per week to help defray costs, although it is partially funded under the Los Angeles County Alcohol Budget in order to assist women who cannot pay the full charges, and no woman is refused the opportunity for recovery offered by the Casa because of inability to pay. The facility serves women who can show 24 hours of sobriety prior to admission and for whom alcohol is a primary addiction.

NEW BEGINNINGS PROGRAM
DOCTORS' HOSPITAL OF PINOLE

2151 Appian Way
Pinole, California 94564

(415) 724-1520

Director: Carol Leahy
Average Patient Census: 9

Minimum Duration of Treatment: 28 days plus detox for normal program
Cost: $330 per day approximately. Insurance eligible.
Detoxification Offered: Yes
Accreditation: JCAH

New Beginnings' comprehensive treatment program is interdisciplinary, combining medical, educational and counseling services with a strong emphasis on family involvement. The treatment team recognizes alcoholism/chemical dependency as a primary illness. The length of treatment is flexible, and an individual response is made to each patient's needs. The variety of treatment methods all emphasize the need for the continuing support of AA or NA.

The program has three phases. Phase One is detoxification, 3 to 6 days, with medical management of acute withdrawal and treatment of medical complications. Phase Two is the rehabilitation treatment and education program and includes continued medical treatment and observation, individual counseling, group therapy, lectures and discussions, audiovisual training sessions, family therapy and peer-group interaction. Phase Three is aftercare, including weekly visits for 1 year and specific individualized support for each patient and family to help in making a sober adjustment to personal relationships and a successful reentry into the workplace. New Beginnings also offers a Family Program that recognizes the family's need for education, therapy and support.

The stated goal of the complete program is to provide treatment specifically designed for the individual needs of each patient in a warm atmosphere that blends concern, love and trust with high professional standards. In this climate, the seed of sobriety is nurtured, and most patients completing the program leave with a new sense of responsibility and self-worth.

Persons of both sexes with problems related to alcohol or other addictive drugs may be admitted. If the patient does not have a personal physician, the program medical director will provide all necessary physician services. All admissions are voluntary, and services are confidential, protecting the rights of the patient, family and referral source.

ALCOHOLISM TREATMENT SERVICE
POMONA VALLEY COMMUNITY HOSPITAL

1798 North Garey Avenue
Pomona, California 91767

(714) 623-8715, ext. 1203

Director: J. Donald Scherbart, M.D.
Average Patient Census: 25–28

Minimum Duration of Treatment: 28 days with prepaid aftercare of two days per inpatient day
Cost: Approximately $350 per day. Insurance eligible.
Detoxification Offered: Yes
Accreditation: JCAH

At the Alcoholism Treatment Service of Pomona Valley Community Hospital, Phase I is medical management; a complete physical examination, including laboratory work. A physician monitors alcohol and drug detoxification symptoms and any medical complications resulting from alcohol.

Phase II includes assignment to a case manager, who is the patient's anchor and advocate in the treatment process, taking an in-depth alcohol/drug psychosocial history with patient and family and organizing a treatment plan for each member of the family.

Special forms of group therapy provide situations for exploring and discovering human relationships, trust, sharing, support, self-discovery and self-acceptance, growth and awareness. Some of these special groups are: men's groups, women's groups, significant-other-person groups, groups for teens, preteens and preschoolers, physical conditioning, recreation and leisure time, stress management, relaxation, meditation, self-hypnosis, art therapy, psychodrama, values clarification groups, recovery planning, family communication group, parenting-skills group, self-esteem group, sexuality groups, grief group and the self-help groups of AA, Step Study, Al-Anon, Alateen, Cocaine Anonymous, Pills Anonymous and Overeaters Anonymous.

Lecture series, movies, family education, activities therapies and a weekly program of spiritual alternatives are part of the program. Antabuse is recommended for all patients who the physician feels are physically able to take it.

Following inpatient stay, aftercare groups, held daily and each weekday evening for patient and family, assist in adjustment to sobriety and being in the community.

The staff is a highly experienced interdisciplinary team including registered nurses, physicians, marriage and family counselors, clinical chaplain, M.S.W.'s, alcoholism counselors, activities therapists and unit coordinators. There are staff members with special skills in working with bicultural and bilingual patients, as well as a sensitivity to the needs of patients with varying life-styles and sexual preferences.

BETTY FORD CENTER
At Eisenhower

39000 Bob Hope Drive
Rancho Mirage, California 92270

1-800-854-9211
(619) 340-0033

Director: John T. Schwarzlose

Average Patient Census: Inpatient, 60; outpatient, 15
Minimum Duration of Treatment: 28 days
Cost: Inpatient, $5,500; outpatient, $1,950. Insurance eligible.
Detoxification Offered: Yes
Accreditation: JCAH

The Betty Ford Center at Eisenhower is a 60-bed inpatient chemical dependency recovery hospital. This unique California licensing category allows rehabilitation rates at about a third of normal hospital-based programs.

The program will consider any person 18 years of age or older who is dependent on a mood-altering chemical. Minimum length of stay is 4 weeks. Family participation is mandatory, with an intensive 5-day family treatment program.

The Betty Ford Center also offers an intensive primary outpatient program. This program consists of 4 sessions a week, 4 hours per session, with normal treatment lasting for 6 weeks. The center offers aftercare for both inpatient and outpatient programs, with the normal recommended length of 1 year.

RALEIGH HILLS HOSPITAL

1600 Gordon Street
Redwood City, California 94061

(415) 368-4134

Director: Jeff Winter
Average Patient Census: 18

Minimum Duration of Treatment: 3–4 weeks
Cost: Available on request. Insurance eligible.
Detoxification Offered: Yes
Accreditation: JCAH

Raleigh Hills Hospital is a private, acute psychiatric hospital specializing in alcohol and chemical dependency programs. Located in a convenient, secluded section of Redwood City on 2 acres of lawns and gardens, it serves clients throughout the Bay Area.

A multidisciplinary team that includes physicians, psychiatrists, psychologists, nurses, social workers, counselors and support staff develops individual treatment programs to meet special client needs. A psychosocial model is the treatment modality, which includes group and family therapy, individual counseling, biofeedback, stress management, testing, education, recreation therapy and relaxation techniques—a comprehensive program aimed at helping clients to evaluate all aspects of their lifestyle and the reasons behind addiction.

A 1-year aftercare component to provide ongoing support and assistance to clients and families is an integral part of the program, and the Papillon Club, the alumni of Raleigh Hills Hospital, provides a lifetime of supportive activities and friendships.

ALCOHOLISM RECOVERY SERVICES
Sequoia Community Hospital

Whipple Avenue and Alameda
Redwood City, California 94062

(415) 367-5504

Director: Louis R. Morin, Director;
  Barry M. Rosen, Medical Director
Average Patient Census: 28

Minimum Duration of Treatment:
  Inpatient, 10–30 days; aftercare, continuous
Cost: $280 per day in hospital district; $292 per day out of hospital district. Insurance eligible.
Detoxification Offered: Yes
Accreditation: JCAH

The Alcoholism Treatment Unit at Sequoia Hospital provides a multifaceted approach to meet the individual alcoholic's problems. The program combines medical detoxification and counseling and rehabilitation services, as well as aftercare group participation sessions.

Each resident is assigned to a primary counselor who works with the patient throughout the program, and one-to-one counseling is available at request, as well as a scheduled activity. Group lectures and discussion groups are a continuing aspect of the program, as are the regular AA meetings.

The facility recognizes the primary role of the family in recovery and requires the resident to be responsible for family involvement in the regular Al-Anon and Alateen meetings.

The program is designed throughout to ensure the active participation of the alcoholic in his own recovery process. The skills and expertise of physicians, registered nurses, counselors and lay persons, including recovered alcoholics, are utilized in the total program, which is aimed at redirecting the patient's attitudes toward the need for alcohol in their lives.

Outpatient services, including intensive group therapy, didactic presentations, medical supervision and aftercare, are also available. The service consists of 3 months of 2-hour sessions on 3 evenings per week.

NEW BEGINNINGS PROGRAM
ALISAL COMMUNITY HOSPITAL

333 North Sanborn Road
Salinas, California 93905

(408) 424-5663

Director: Daniel A. Esparza
Average Patient Census: 13

Minimum Duration of Treatment: 28 days plus detox for normal program
Cost: Detox, approximately $300 per day; rehab, approximately $235 per day. Insurance eligible.
Detoxification Offered: Yes
Accreditation: JCAH

New Beginnings' comprehensive treatment program is interdisciplinary, combining medical, educational and counseling services with a strong emphasis on family involvement. The treatment team recognizes alcoholism/chemical dependency as a primary illness. The length of treatment is flexible, and an individual response is made to each patient's needs. The variety of treatment methods all emphasize the need for the continuing support of AA or NA.

The program has three phases. Phase One is detoxification, 3 to 6 days, with medical management of acute withdrawal and treatment of medical complications. Phase Two is the rehabilitation treatment and education program and includes continued medical treatment and observation, individual counseling, group therapy, lectures and discussions, audiovisual training sessions, family therapy and peer-group interaction. Phase Three is aftercare, including weekly visits for 1 year and specific individualized support for each patient and family to help in making a sober adjustment to personal relationships and a successful reentry into the workplace. New Beginnings also offers a Family Program that recognizes the family's need for education, therapy and support.

The stated goal of the complete program is to provide treatment specifically designed for the individual needs of each patient in a warm atmosphere that blends concern, love and trust with high professional standards. In this climate, the seed of sobriety is nurtured, and most patients completing the program leave with a new sense of responsibility and self-worth.

Persons of both sexes with problems related to alcohol or other addictive drugs may be admitted. If the patient does not have a personal physician, the program medical director will provide all necessary physician services. All admissions are voluntary, and services are confidential, protecting the rights of the patient, family and referral source.

ALCOHOL AND DRUG TREATMENT PROGRAM/FAMILY CENTER
Sharp-Cabrillo Hospital

3475 Kenyon Street
San Diego, California 92110

(619) 222-0411

Director: Marvin E. Prigmore

Average Patient Census: 30
Minimum Duration of Treatment: Depends upon treatment needs
Cost: Insurance eligible.
Detoxification Offered: Yes
Accreditation: JCAH

The Alcohol and Drug Treatment Program/Family Center is an intensive, continuum-of-care program that consists of inpatient care, outpatient care, family therapy, children's programs, adult children's programs and relapse-prevention programs.

Admission may be in person or through a physician, family member or significant other. The facility is open 24 hours a day for emergency admissions. Transportation from a nearby airport is provided if needed.

The program is initiated with a medical profile constructed from thorough assessment by the clinical staff. Individual programs are designed based upon that evaluation. These programs include an emphasis upon family recovery and self-assessment through education, group therapy, recreational therapy and a strong involvement in the program by family members and significant others who are a part of the patient's community life.

The Center is a 50-bed, cottage-style unit of the Sharp-Cabrillo Hospital and is located close to the waterfront. There is a sustained effort to offer a relaxed and friendly atmosphere, and it is the philosophy of the unit that recovery goes beyond simply restoring a person to helping him or her learn to function at a much higher level than before. The outpatient program stresses continuing support and encourages participation by family members in that process. The family program is a stand-alone program. The children's program is also a separate stand-alone program, dedicated to children and for children. It is not an adjunct to family care.

ALCOHOLISM/SUBSTANCE ABUSE PROGRAM
Mesa Vista Hospital

7850 Vista Hill Avenue
San Diego, California 92123

(619) 278-4110

Director: Neil P. Dubner, M.D.; Robert Dean, R.T.R., Program Director
Average Patient Census: 12

Minimum Duration of Treatment: 21–28 days
Cost: $285 per day. Physician billing is separate from hospital charges; fees do not include medication. Insurance eligible.
Detoxification Offered: Yes
Accreditation: JCAH

Mesa Vista Hospital Alcoholism/Substance Abuse Program (ASAP) is divided into three phases: detoxification, rehabilitation and aftercare.

Detoxification: The object of this phase is to provide medically safe passage through withdrawal, making a start toward long-term abstinence, and may last anywhere from 1 to 7 days, depending on individual variables.

Rehabilitation: Phase Two is devoted to providing a structured, supportive recovery period. During this "working phase," patients begin to confront their illness and the behavior patterns and defenses that serve to perpetuate their disease. ASPA's multidisciplinary approach of individual and group therapy, educational sessions, AA and NA meetings, family meetings and activity therapy, both occupational and recreational, help create an effective foundation for successful lifelong recovery.

Aftercare: This third phase begins at discharge and involves 10 weekly aftercare sessions. In addition to using other therapeutic supports, aftercare helps to ensure a successful transition to home, job and community. Weekly groups, facilitated by program recovery counselors, are designed to help problem-solve, support and reinforce progress made during hospitalization. Upon termination of aftercare, graduates are encouraged to continue with AA/NA, the Alumni Association, outpatient therapy and other resources.

The hospital atmosphere is unlike most institutional settings in that the environment is warm, comfortable and aesthetically appealing. It features semiprivate and private rooms, open patios, a Japanese garden and greenhouse, a large dining room, a chapel and gift shop. In addition to the occupational therapy workshop, there is a gymnasium, swimming pool and jogging track.

GOLDEN GATE FOR SENIORS

637 South Van Ness Avenue
San Francisco, California 94110

(415) 626-7553

Director: Donald J. Frolli
Average Patient Census: 18

Minimum Duration of Treatment: 2 months
Cost: Sliding scale to $675 per month. Insurance eligible.
Detoxification Offered: No
Accreditation: California Department Alcohol/Drug Programs

Golden Gate for Seniors is a Social Model Alcohol Recovery Home for men and women 55 years of age and older. Length of stay is 2 months to 1 year.

The program provides a peer-oriented setting that allows individuals time to begin recovery from alcoholism. During their stay, residents participate in educational groups that include information about alcoholism, sober living and problems pertinent to their age group. Assistance is provided to the individual to address health problems, as well as to eventual placement in housing conducive to maintaining sobriety.

Support is provided through AA, as well as an alumni group, for those completing the program. Intake is by appointment for screening. The applicant must be ambulatory and free from alcohol prior to screening.

Golden Gate is unique in that there is no upper age limit for residents. Treatment is offered for drugs other than alcohol if alcoholism is the primary diagnosis.

RECOVERY ALLIANCE
San Pedro Peninsula Hospital

1300 West Seventh Street
San Pedro, California 90732

(213) 832-3311, ext. 3077 or 3277

Director: David C. Schoerner
Average Patient Census: 35
Minimum Duration of Treatment:
  Average 25 days

Cost: Detox, $375 per day; rehab, $225 per day; Adults, 8-week aftercare, $1,250; children under 18 free. Insurance eligible.
Detoxification Offered: Yes
Accreditation: JCAH

Following detoxification, the program at Recovery Alliance at the San Pedro Peninsula Hospital offers a full inpatient rehabilitation program stressing education in alcoholism, individual and group therapy, and intensive individual and family therapy.

The program includes community education, consultation and evaluations, referral and placement, interventions, medical support and emergency services.

In addition, the facility is a teaching unit with the capacity to offer education to industry in industrial program development, as well as a counselor intern program and physician resident-training program.

There is a strong emphasis upon aftercare, with total family participation heavily stressed both during treatment and in the aftercare period. A structured outpatient program is available, with emphasis upon aftercare follow-up and family participation, in a program offering 105 therapy-hours for all family members.

PINECREST HOSPITAL

2415 De La Vina Street
Santa Barbara, California 93105

(805) 682-2511

Director: Beth G. Buxton
Average Patient Census: 17

Minimum Duration of Treatment: 28 days
Cost: $12,400 includes detox, inpatient and 8 weeks aftercare for patient and family. Insurance eligible.
Detoxification Offered: Yes
Accreditation: JCAH

The goals of therapy at Pinecrest are sobriety and self-integration. Sobriety, defined as total abstinence from mood-altering drugs and alcohol, or freedom from compulsive eating, is a fundamental aim for the identified patient. The program of achieving self-integration and healthy autonomy is emphasized equally for patients and family members. This process nurtures acceptance of the illness, responsibility for personal actions and nonmanipulative intimacy and support. Affiliation with long-term support groups such as AA, NA, OA and Al-Anon is strongly encouraged.

Treatment styles include the confrontation of games, alibis and ways of not taking responsibility for behavior and/or feelings; insistence that the client do at least half the therapeutic work; working on change rather than working on coping or adjusting; and, finally, support of work that is sincere, however minimal. Pinecrest invests energy in each client in differing degrees according to needs. There are some who want to deal with one overriding issue and some who choose not to explore their feelings. The latter will probably benefit from other features of the program at Pinecrest, such as education and milieu therapy.

SCHICK SHADEL HOSPITAL

45 East Alamar Avenue
Santa Barbara, California 93105

(805) 687-2411

Director: Gordon F. Baker

Average Patient Census: 20
Minimum Duration of Treatment:
   Inpatient, 10 days; aftercare, 1–2 years
Cost: $650 per day. Insurance eligible.
Detoxification Offered: Yes
Accreditation: JCAH

The primary objective of treatment is total abstinence from mood-altering substances. Treatment is based, following detoxification if necessary, on a 10-day program of counterconditioning (aversion) and Pentothal therapy, and individual and group counseling. Also included are lectures on various aspects of alcoholism—risk factors, guilt, addiction and setting priorities. There is also a complete physical examination and counseling with the medical director.

The family education program, offered each weekend, allows family members to come to the hospital for education about the disease of alcoholism and for discussion of the effects of alcohol on family relationships. Individual counseling for family members is available during the week as well.

The aftercare program, which is set up while the patient is in the hospital, emphasizes support groups that are available: family, alumni, AA and the church. At least two reinforcement treatments are scheduled as part of the aftercare program.

The hospital will supply a more detailed description of their therapeutic methods, which will explain the techniques employed.

Drugs other than alcohol will be treated if usage is secondary to alcohol.

AZURE ACRES CHEMICAL DEPENDENCY TREATMENT CENTER

2264 Green Hill
Sebastopol, California 95472

(707) 823-3385

Director: Uwe Gunnerson, M.A., C.A.C.; William T. Hopper, M.D., Medical Director
Average Patient Census: 23

Minimum Duration of Treatment: 28 days
Cost: $980 nonrefundable deposit; 4-week program, $3,920; Sober Retreat Weekends, $50 per night. Insurance eligible.
Detoxification Offered: Nonmedical detox only as part of the 28-day program.
Accreditation: State of California

At Azure Acres special emphasis is placed upon individual, group and family counseling, as well as instruction, life planning, personal growth, aftercare and the principles of AA.

The program is highly structured and intensive, involving approximately 10 hours of programming per day. This includes one educational session and one group counseling session each day, with individual counseling every 2 days and AA meetings 3 times a week.

Emphasis is upon individualized life planning and aftercare planning, and each resident is exposed to a personalized, family-oriented, goal-centered program designed to make a significant, positive, long-term impact upon his or her life.

In addition, Azure Acres offers Retreat Weekends beginning any time after 2:00 P.M. Friday and extending through the AA meetings at 3:00 P.M. on Sunday.

The facility is housed in a rustic redwood lodge surrounded by 30 acres of wooded, rolling hills, offering a quiet and private environment for rehabilitative experiences.

Transportation to and from airports in San Francisco and the general Bay Area is available on request.

GENESIS: DEPENDENCY TREATMENT PROGRAM
South Coast Medical Center

31872 Coast Highway
South Laguna, California 92677

(714) 499-1311

Director: Muriel Zink, C.A.C.
Average Patient Census: 22

Minimum Duration of Treatment: Usually a 4-week stay
Cost: Approximately $11,000. Insurance eligible.
Detoxification Offered: Yes
Accreditation: JCAH

South Coast Medical Center has been providing comprehensive, professional treatment for alcohol and drug dependencies since 1973, when the first CareUnit in the nation was opened. In 1983, South coast introduced GENESIS, a revised treatment program that focuses on lifestyle change and relapse prevention.

Admissions are accepted 24 hours a day for any adult with a harmful dependency on alcohol, prescription medications, cocaine or other drugs. Free consultations are available at any time with a member of the GENESIS team. Intervention service is also available.

A medical, psychological and interpersonal approach to recovery is the primary focus of the first 4 weeks of live-in experience, as well as of the structured weekly groups of aftercare that follow. Treatment involves individual counseling and a variety of educational and therapy specialty groups. Music therapy, meditation techniques, exercise and biofeedback modalities are also offered.

GENESIS is designed for familly and codependents to participate in educational lectures, couples and group therapy and other activities that support the recovery process. Al-Anon, Alateen and Adult Children of Alcoholics meetings are held weekly at the hospital.

GENESIS now offers comprehensive outpatient treatment in Laguna Niguel. Six months of treatment at this accessible location costs $2,000. For information call (714) 495-2999.

CHARTER PACIFIC HOSPITAL

4025 West Two Hundred Twenty-sixth Street
Torrance, California 90505

(213) 373-7733

Director: John Epson, Adult Program; Richard Gayton, Ph.D., Adolescent Program

Average Patient Census: Adults, 16; adolescents, 20
Minimum Duration of Treatment: Adults, 28 days
Cost: Varies; available on request. Insurance eligible.
Detoxification Offered: Yes
Accreditation: JCAH

The program at Charter Pacific Hospital offers medically supervised detoxification, if necessary, and individual, group and family counseling as a part of the holistic (multidisciplinary) approach toward effectively treating the disease of addiction. All patients are also encouraged to participate in activities therapy and didactic lectures. These programs are AA/NA based philosophically. The hospital offers both adult and adolescent programs.

Patient and family aftercare services are available at all Charter Medical Addictive Disease units, emphasizing that recovery from this relentless disease is a continuing process affecting both the patient and his or her family.

TUSTIN COMMUNITY HOSPITAL

14662 Newport Avenue
Tustin, California 92681

(714) 838-9600, ext. 5842

Director: Ella May Green, R.N., B.A.

Average Patient Census: 18
Minimum Duration of Treatment: 25 days
Cost: $8,500. Insurance eligible.
Detoxification Offered: Yes
Accreditation: JCAH

Tustin Community Hospital offers a special advisory service to family members, employers and others who are involved with alcohol or chemically dependent persons in order to help those who must deal with the problems learn to intervene effectively in the inevitable downward spiral that is the result of dependency. If you want to help but don't know how, information is available at this facility. There is no charge for this service.

Admission may be either by referral by physicians or by direct admission through the Emergency Room, where admission screening is offered at all times.

Treatment is in four phases: (1) primary care for detox or physical damage caused by substance abuse; (2) recovery, a comprehensive rehabilitative program lasting from 21 to 25 days; (3) the Family Program, which offers a curriculum of education, caring and sharing; and (4) the Aftercare Program, consisting of 12 once-a-week group sessions and includes other concerned members of the patient's life.

A program specifically designed for adolescents struggling with the disease of alcoholism and/or chemical dependency emphasizes three stages of treatment: (1) admitting that there is a problem; (2) changing attitudes and life-style; and (3) building communication and coping skills. An important feature of this program is involvement with the adolescent's family, as well as the continuation of education in conjunction with the local school district. Although residence is within the hospital, therapy and education sessions occur in a specially designed "home" environment.

PATHWAYS ALCOHOLISM CENTER
VALLEY PRESBYTERIAN HOSPITAL

15107 Vanowen Street
Van Nuys, California 91405

(213) 782-6600, ext. 2985
(213) 902-2985

Director: Paul Rosenberg, M.D., Medical Director; Ross McNutt, Program Coordinator

Average Patient Census: 20
Minimum Duration of Treatment: None, usual stay is 3–5 weeks
Cost: Detox, $400 per day; inpatient, $300 per day. Insurance eligible.
Detoxification Offered: Yes
Accreditation: JCAH

Pathways Alcoholism Treatment Center offers inpatient care and community output services. Staffed by specially trained nurses, therapists, counselors and physicians, Pathways has 24-hour accessibility to the Valley Presbyterian Hospital's comprehensive health services.

Treatment programs, depending on individual needs, include detoxification, individual consultation, group therapy, alcohol education, diet management, psychiatric evaluation and occupational and recreation therapy. Family participation is an important part of the Pathways program.

Acute patients undergo a short period of detoxification, usually 1 to 3 days, receiving a complete medical checkup and psychiatric evaluation as soon as possible. Thereafter, individualized treatment programs begin, with particular emphasis on group involvement. The intensive program helps the alcoholic to understand his illness and begin the process of becoming more honest with himself and others through therapy groups and activities. Family groups meet 3 evenings a week to improve communication between family members. Additional psychiatric consultations can be arranged as needed for both individual and family counseling.

Pathways encourages participation in community organizations (AA, Al-Anon, etc.), and the Pathways Volunteer Guild. Former patients may choose to participate in a wide range of volunteer activities and are offered a training program in counseling skills.

HACIENDA HELP SERVICES, INC.

1019 East Santa Clara Street
P.O. Box 1946
Ventura, California 93002

(805) 648-3157

Director: Ernie Goe
Average Patient Census: 50

Minimum Duration of Treatment: 10 months to 1 year
Cost: Sliding scale, minimum $201 per month. Not insurance eligible.
Detoxification Offered: Yes, social
Accreditation: California Department of Drug and Alcohol Programs.

Hacienda Help Services provides live-in rehabilitation with vocational training. Therapy involves one-on-one and group counseling, supported by Christian-principled living arrangements.

The stated goal of the facility is meeting the physical, mental and spiritual needs of recovery for single men and women, married couples, single parents and whole families.

Colorado

CPC: COTTONWOOD HILL, INC.

13455 West 58th Avenue
Arvada, Colorado 80001

(303) 420-1702

Director: Dr. John Mallams

Average Patient Census: 25
Minimum Duration of Treatment: 30 days
Cost: $195 per day. Insurance eligible.
Detoxification Offered: Yes
Accreditation: JCAH

Cottonwood Hill is a large, rambling, contemporary home situated on 8 acres of rolling meadow on the outskirts of Denver, offering the quiet seclusion of country living conducive to healing and tranquillity.

The Cottonwood Hill program is based on the Twelve Steps of AA, and patients, while in treatment, are expected to begin incorporating into their lives the first five Steps and are educated and directed toward the remaining seven.

The patient population is drawn essentially from employee assistance programs. The first week of stay is designed to break through patient resistance by helping in the assembling of information that will permit insight into the harm created by dependency, by evaluation and planning. As treatment progresses, the dynamics of catharsis and acceptance are augmented by education by means of books, lectures, films and specifically assigned written homework.

By the fourth week of treatment, significant others enter their own treatment program, which is separate and complete, housed away from the patient, lasts an intensive 5 days and closes with the significant others writing out their own aftercare plan for their ongoing recovery.

Graduates of Cottonwood Hill maintain contact with the treatment process through eight mandatory aftercare sessions; conferences, dinners and workshops keep graduates in touch, and there is supportive maintenance through regular phone calls, bulletins and questionnaires.

DAY AT A TIME UNIT
Boulder Psychiatric Institute

311 Mapleton Avenue
Boulder, Colorado 80302

(303) 441-0526

Director: John P. Haws, M.D.
Average Patient Census: 7

Minimum Duration of Treatment: 28–30 days, with extension if necessary
Cost: Inpatient, $8,000 for 28 days. Insurance eligible.
Detoxification Offered: Yes
Accreditation: JCAH

The inpatient program at Day At A Time Alcohol and Drug Treatment Unit is a 30-day program, and most health insurances cover the majority of the cost.

The program offers a physical examination, psychiatric examination, psychological testing, social-work assessment and adjunctive-therapy assessment. The rest of the program consists of group and individual therapy, plus educational segments on the disease of chemical dependency. A Family Program is included for family members and significant others. Aftercare is provided for both the patient and the family and is included in the total price of the program.

For persons whose treatment needs can be met in ways other than the traditional inpatient stay, there is an Adult Evening Treatment Program, running for 5 weeks, 4 evenings per week, at a cost of $1,500. Family involvement and aftercare for patient and family are included but there is an additional charge for this. Patients may be admitted for a 7- to 14-day detoxification and assessment and then become part of the Adult Evening or Day Program for the remainder of the treatment experience.

Day At A Time also offers a 6-week Family Education Program, which is open to the community at no charge, as well as free evaluation service for anyone concerned about his or her own or someone else's drug or alcohol use and will assist with formal intervention when indicated. A day program for outpatients is also offered at this facility.

ADDICTION RECOVERY UNIT
Saint Luke's Hospital

601 East Nineteenth Avenue
Denver, Colorado 80203

(303) 869-2280

Director: Gary E. Tayar
Average Patient Census: Adults, 60 beds; adolescents, 20 beds

Minimum Duration of Treatment: Adults, 21 days; adolescents, 45 days
Cost: $203 per day adult and adolescent. Insurance eligible.
Detoxification Offered: Yes
Accreditation: JCAH (licensed by Alcohol and Drug Abuse Division of Colorado Department of Health)

The Addiction Recovery Unit at Saint Luke's offers four special programs in addition to its alcoholism/drug dependency rehabilitation program.

Intervention Training guides family members and others who are close to the affected individual in finding ways to design a method by which reality can be presented to the person who is suffering from alcohol/drug dependency, in an acceptable way.

The Outpatient Program is presented as a viable alternative to individuals in the earlier stages of alcohol/drug dependency in not requiring hospitalization or loss of time from work. The program consists of 3-hour sessions, 4 nights a week, for a 5-week period. One night a week is set aside for AA/Al-Anon participation. Five family sessions on Friday nights provide an opportunity for all family members to involve themselves in the therapeutic process. The Outpatient Program also offers a Level II series including education and therapy.

The Adolescent Program acknowledges the similarities and the differences between adolescent and adult addiction. An interesting aspect of this program includes behavior modification and reality therapy and involves the 5-day Colorado wilderness experience offered by Outward Bound, offering new ways to solve problems and experience new "highs" without the use of alcohol/drugs.

The importance of aftercare is stressed and offered to adults, adolescents and family members. Saint Luke's brochure concludes, "You alone can do it . . . but you can't do it alone."

THE CENTRE, INC.
Rocky Mountain Hospital

4701 East Ninth Avenue
Denver, Colorado 80220

(303) 321-0270

Director: Larry Gibson, M.D., Medical Director; Maureen Tarrant, M.B.A., Administrative Officer
Average Patient Census: 15
Minimum Duration of Treatment: 28 days

Cost: Detox, $400 per day; rehab, $275 per day; lab and X ray, $125; physician, $25 per day plus $100 H&P; psychologist, $500 (includes complete psychological testing). Insurance eligible.
Detoxification Offered: Yes
Accreditation: JCAH (licensed by Alcohol and Drug Abuse Division of Colorado Department of Health)

The Centre therapy program is holistic in nature and includes one-on-one sessions with a primary therapist, group sessions, educational lectures and films. "Rounds," a daily therapeutic session guided by the staff, provides a structure in which patients learn to express their feelings and emotions. A full-time recreational therapist helps patients restructure their leisure time and physical health into an alcohol- and drug-free life-style. Each patient has daily yoga classes and meets with a nutritionist about diet and eating problems.

The Centre's motto is "Recovery with Dignity." The medical model of treatment for dependency disorders and disabilities involves family members as well as the primary patient. The Centre works with employers or provides guidance for career alternatives if appropriate. AA and Al-Anon meetings are an integral part of the program both inside and outside the institution. A 12-month aftercare plan is developed before discharge and monitored by the Clinical Therapy Department.

The Centre accepts referral from medical, legal and religious professionals, courts, agencies, schools and former patients. Patients come from all walks of life and from all age groups. Evaluation and intervention services are available on a consultation basis. The program is a bridge to AA.

Dr. Larry Gibson, considered a pioneer in the field of treatment for substance abuse, has treated over eight thousand individuals. The Centre, Inc., serves as a training facility for physician, psychological-substance-abuse and recreational-therapist interns. Clinical staff includes highly skilled and experienced professionals, recovering chemical-abuse persons, as well as nonaddicted persons. The nursing staff is composed of persons with long experience in the field.

MOUNT AIRY PSYCHIATRIC CENTER
ALCOHOL/DRUG ABUSE TREATMENT PROGRAM

4455 East Twelfth Avenue
Denver, Colorado 80220

(303) 322-1803

Director: Karen J. Schoenhals

Average Patient Census: 14
Minimum Duration of Treatment: None
Cost: Available on request; ($280+ per day). Insurance eligible.
Detoxification Offered: Yes
Accreditation: JCAH

Mount Airy Psychiatric Center admits patients from age 12, and diagnoses span a wide spectrum from adjustment problems to acute psychiatric disorders. Special programs include the Children's Treatment Program, the Therapeutic Community Program, the Adolescent Program and a General Psychiatric Program.

The Addictions Treatment Team services the entire hospital, offering a specialized approach to addictions treatment beginning with medically supervised detoxification. The patient is then introduced to the educational, supportive and therapeutic aspects of the program, which include individual and group counseling and places special emphasis on family and concerned others; in fact, such groups are an integral part of the program. Post-treatment support is offered in a number of ways, including referral to AA or NA, to Mount Airy Partial Hospitalization Program, to support groups or to outpatient services. Individual contact with discharged patients is maintained for 6 to 12 months to provide follow-up support. Additionally, outpatient drug-abuse treatment is offered, including the educational, supportive and therapeutic aspects of the inpatient program.

The Mount Airy Foundation administers the Mount Airy Psychiatric Center, the leading community hospital in the area for those who wish to be treated by psychiatrists of their own choice. The Center is the oldest and largest private, not-for-profit psychiatric hospital in Colorado with a primary focus on individually designed patient treatment plans. There are approximately 200 psychiatrists on the medical staff.

HARMONY FOUNDATION, INC.

P.O. Box 1989
Estes Park, Colorado 80517

(303) 586-4491

Director: W. A. Dixon

Average Patient Census: 30
Minimum Duration of Treatment: 28-day program, extension if needed
Cost: $4,620, all-inclusive. Insurance eligible.
Accreditation: JCAH

The Harmony program focuses on the needs of the individual, utilizing group therapy, one-to-one counseling, lectures, films and peer support in a 28-day experience.

Specific goals in Harmony's treatment philosophy include the development of a thorough understanding of alcohol as a drug, alcoholism as a disease and the alcoholic and/or chemically dependent person as a person who can live a beautiful, productive life chemical-free. Emphasis is placed on the development of an improved self-image, understanding of interpersonal relationships and the ability to identify, accept and share feelings. The philosophies, programs and experiences of AA are vital components of the overall presentation.

Harmony Foundation offers a 5-day residential program for family members.

ISLAND GROVE REGIONAL TREATMENT CENTER

421 North Fifteenth Avenue
Greeley, Colorado 80631

(303) 356-6664

Director: David S. Mundy
Average Patient Census: 15–30

Minimum Duration of Treatment: Detox, 5 days; halfway house, 33 days
Cost: Detox, $65 per day; halfway house, $22 per day. Insurance eligible.
Detoxification Offered: Yes
Accreditation: State of Colorado Health Department

The program at Island Grove Center has four components: a detoxification program with a 15-bed capacity, a halfway house with a 15-bed capacity, a DUI program (under state guidelines) at a cost of $12.50 per session and outpatient treatment with no limit on duration of treatment at a cost of $15 per hour. All fees, with the exception of the DUI program, are based on a sliding fee scale.

Island Grove Center deals primarily with alcohol addiction but has staff available for polydrug abuse in conjunction with alcohol.

THE ARK

10930 Hondo
P.O. Box 626
Green Mountain Falls, Colorado 80819

(303) 684-9483

Director: Howard L. McFadden

Average Patient Census: 20
Minimum Duration of Treatment: 21 days
Cost: $165 per day, all-inclusive. Insurance eligible.
Detoxification Offered: No (see description of program)
Accreditation: JCAH

The ARK, established in 1971, its counselors themselves recovering alcoholics and certified by the State of Colorado Department of Health in counseling, maintains a consulting psychiatrist and physician on call 24 hours a day. The ARK has also established transfer agreements with local hospitals for those in need of detoxification.

In the belief that understanding of the alcoholic's problems is the key to a recovery program, the ARK develops an individual treatment plan through intensive assessment and evaluation to assure that each person in treatment is directed toward a goal in recovery that is comfortable for that individual, because stopping drinking is not the problem, whereas staying stopped is. Therefore, the maintenance of sobriety is the goal for each person in an individualized way.

In the recognition that alcoholism is a true family illness, a Family Program—an intensive outpatient program of 3½ days—is provided at this facility.

PARKSIDE LODGE OF COLORADO

8801 Lipan Street
Thornton, Colorado 80221

(303) 430-0800

Director: Ron Dreier
Average Patient Census: 44

Minimum Duration of Treatment: 21 days minimum, 45 days maximum
Cost: Detox, $107 per day; residential, $195 per day. Insurance eligible.
Detoxification Offered: Yes
Accreditation: JCAH

Parkside Lodge is a community-based, nonhospital facility with a medical staff, professionally trained clinicians, psychologists, spiritual advisors and family therapists.

The program offers confidential preadmission screening and evaluation to help patients and families receive the most suitable and cost-effective level of care.

Patients are assigned to an interdisciplinary team that includes personnel from various professional backgrounds: clergy, counselors and nurses. When indicated, the program can utilize the diagnostic and medical services of the local community hospital. Multiple treatment modalities include medical/psychiatric evaluation and treatment, psychological testing, counseling for individuals, groups, families and employers, and educational programs, such as lectures, films and discussion groups.

The aftercare program involves a weekly support group that meets for 12 weeks following discharge, as well as referral to local AA and Al-Anon groups.

PERSONAL DEVELOPMENT CENTER

6275 West Thirty-eighth Avenue
Wheatridge, Colorado 80033

(303) 422-2286

Director: Susan A. Brock
Average Patient Census: Licensed for 15 beds

Minimum Duration of Treatment: 28-day norm
Cost: $175 per day base, plus physical and lab costs. Insurance eligible.
Detoxification Offered: No (see description of program)
Accreditation: JCAH

Personal Development Center is a freestanding facility located in a lovely Victorian house, providing a homelike atmosphere.

Programs include 28-day residential, day care/night care, an outpatient program and aftercare. The staff includes a family specialist who deals with dysfunctional families.

This facility follows the basic philosophy of AA and accepts patients who are ambulatory, not psychotic, age 18 and over, and are not drinking. Persons who are intoxicated are referred to Jefferson County Receiving Unit or to Saint Joseph's Hospital for detoxification.

Anyone under 18 is referred to Personal Development Center, Adolescent, Inc., with the stipulation that the entire family become involved in the treatment program.

Hawaii

SALVATION ARMY ADDICTION TREATMENT FACILITY

3264 Waokanaka Street
Honolulu, Hawaii 96817

(808) 595-6371

Director: Lawrence Williams

Average Patient Census: 86
Minimum Duration of Treatment: Varies
Cost: $45 per day approximately.
  Insurance eligible.
Detoxification Offered: Yes (alcohol only)
Accreditation: JCAH

The Salvation Army Addiction Treatment Facility offers a variety of services for the treatment of alcohol and polysubstance abuse.

- Behavioral Health Continuum of Care for Special Populations: This program is specifically addressed to the special needs of chronic alcoholics, multiethnic drug abusers, women, children, troubled employees, Pacific Islanders, etc. The approach is not only to treat the illness but to promote health and well-being.
- Residential Care Program for Alcoholics: This is a 30-day program, 90-day program, or longer if necessary. Structure includes group, individual and some family counseling. Educational and resocialization activities are provided.
- Outreach and Intake Department: This unit provides full-range initial contact services for Hawaii's residents, including crisis intervention, assessment, screening, referral and intake components for residential programs at ATF.
- Residential Care Program for Drug Abusers—Eureka House: Average stay is 1 year, with participation in group and individual psychotherapy, as well as vocational, educational and resocialization activities.
- Women's Way: This is a program for women with dependent children who cannot seek or accept treatment since they lack suitable care for

their children. A unique residential treatment service is offered to women *and* their children as a family unit and is aimed toward spouse-abused victims as well as alcohol and drug abusers and abused or addicted pregnant women. Treatment includes self-awareness training, parenting skills, health and vocational education, with day care, counseling and recreational activities for the children.

SA/ATF also offers an outpatient program and a continuing emphasis on spiritual-growth opportunities, from which residents may choose to find additional support.

SAND ISLAND HALFWAY HOUSE
Hawaii Alcoholism Foundation

P.O. Box 3045
Honolulu, Hawaii 96802

(808) 841-2319

Director: Sidney Kline
Average Patient Census: 27

Minimum Duration of Treatment: 45 days, no maximum
Cost: $25 per day. Not insurance eligible.
Detoxification Offered: No
Accreditation: State of Hawaii, Department of Health

The primary objective of the Hawaii Alcoholism Foundation, a non-profit organization, is to provide a residential treatment and recovery program for adult, male, ambulatory citizens of the state of Hawaii who are suffering from the disease of alcoholism. Admissions are effected without regard for race, creed or financial status.

The major activities of the program are centered on getting the alcoholic off the street and into treatment to the end that he may attain and maintain sobriety and return to society as a tax asset rather than a liability.

The core of the treatment process is the program of AA, and that philosophy is the base for individual, group and family counseling.

The primary area served by the Foundation is metropolitan Honolulu, but clients are accepted from any part of the state of Hawaii.

WOMEN'S ALCOHOL TREATMENT CENTER OF HAWAII
SAINT FRANCIS HOSPITAL

2230 Liliha Street
Honolulu, Hawaii 96817

(808) 547-6490

Director: Judith Doktor

Average Patient Census: 15
Minimum Duration of Treatment: 30 days
Cost: $90 per day; $8,100 for 90-day program. Insurance eligible.
Detoxification Offered: No
Accreditation: JCAH

The Women's Alcohol Treatment Center of Hawaii at Saint Francis Hospital in Honolulu is a 90-day program that is specifically for women of 18 and older and geared to their needs. The principles of AA are very much a part of the treatment, which includes individual and group therapy and special groups, such as assertiveness training, as well as outside speakers to discuss issues of special interest to women and education about alcoholism. A follow-up aftercare program continues for 6 months after treatment.

CASTLE ALCOHOLISM AND ADDICTIONS PROGRAM

640 Ulukahiki Street
Kailua, Hawaii 96734

(808) 263-4429

Director: Tina Dameron
Average Patient Census: 16

Minimum Duration of Treatment: 28-day program
Cost: $5,500 (Detox, $271 per day; recovery, $196 per day). Insurance eligible.
Detoxification Offered: Yes
Accreditation: JCAH

The Alcoholism and Addictions Program at Castle Medical Center is a social-model program in an acute hospital setting.

The concepts of the recovery program rely heavily on the philosophy of AA, and a family systems approach is also incorporated in the approach to treatment. An aftercare program is included.

Idaho

PORT OF HOPE WEST

P.O. Box 973
Anderson Hall
College of Idaho Campus
Caldwell, Idaho 83606

(209) 454-2500

Director: Mike Tardani
Average Patient Census: 18

Minimum Duration of Treatment: 4–5 weeks
Cost: Full fees: Detox, $55 per day; rehab, $68 per day. Most individual charges based on sliding fee scale. Insurance eligible.
Detoxification Offered: Yes
Accreditation: State of Idaho

Port of Hope West operates a residential facility and three outpatient centers in southwest Idaho. Programs are designed to provide effective, specialized treatment for women, men, young persons and their families who are affected by alcoholism and/or chemical dependency.

Social-model detoxification, nonmedical and residential, is accomplished without the use of mood-altering drugs, with medical treatment made available in the community if necessary. The treatment program is an intensive therapeutic and educational one of 14 to 35 days, with length of stay depending on the severity of alcoholism/chemical dependency, the client's support system in the community, and his or her progress in treatment. Residents adhere to a disciplined daily schedule of group therapy, lectures, films, recreation and individual counseling. Attendance at AA/NA meetings is also required, mail and telephone privileges are screened and visiting is limited, allowing residents to concentrate on the program. Family members and significant others are encouraged to participate in family counseling and specific educational classes.

Outpatient programs, available in Nampa, Caldwell, Emmett and Payette, generally include the treatment modalities mentioned above. A special Adolescent Outpatient Program includes the same modalities but is oriented to the special needs of persons under 18.

Port of Hope West is part of a private, nonprofit organization—Magic Valley Alcohol Recovery Centers, Inc.—which also provides services at a residential center in Twin Falls and outpatient offices in Mountain Home, Burley, Hailey and Twin Falls.

PINE CREST HOSPITAL

2301 North Ironwood Place
Coeur d'Alene, Idaho 83814

(208) 666-1441

Director: Robert L. Russell
Average Patient Census: 9

Minimum Duration of Treatment: 21–28 days
Cost: $250 per day approximately. Insurance eligible.
Detoxification Offered: Yes
Accreditation: JCAH

Pine Crest Hospital's comprehensive residential alcoholism treatment program transcends many traditional methods by addressing the totality of the problem. A full multidisciplinary staff uses a team approach that is provided in a quiet, dignified environment.

All admissions receive physical and laboratory evaluation. Detoxification, if needed, is accomplished with minimal medication under physician care.

The basic 21-day treatment program is individualized and reality-based and includes medical interviews, individual and group therapy, education and AA orientation. Family counseling is an integral part of most treatment plans, involving individual counseling and family problem-solving sessions, as well as encouragement toward involvement in Al-Anon activities. A personalized aftercare program with specific short- and long-term goals is devised, which may include recommendation for continued care on an outpatient basis, referral to other agencies and, most particularly, involvement in the fellowship and principles of AA.

Some of the special recovery services at Pine Crest include occupational and recreational therapy, Women's Group, Self-Image Group, Adolescent Program, Wrap-up groups, therapeutic assignments, stress management, grief therapy and crisis intervention. The ultimate goal of the multifaceted approach is to untangle the individual's complexity of problems while laying the groundwork for continued sobriety through the proven principles of AA.

SAINT BENEDICT'S ACT CENTER

2003 Lincoln Way
P.O. Box 711
Coeur d'Alene, Idaho 83814

(208) 667-9591

Director: Leo P. Dolan, Ph.D.

Average Patient Census: 18
Minimum Duration of Treatment: 28 days
Cost: $190 per day. Insurance eligible.
Detoxification Offered: Yes
Accreditation: JCAH

Saint Benedict's ACT Center has four treatment, intervention, prevention and information programs encompassing the entire scope of alcoholism and drug abuse care: information and referral, detoxification center, alcohol information school and inpatient treatment.

The staff of caring, concerned professionals includes a physician, nursing personnel for medical services, certified professional counselors, psychologists, vocational specialists, clergy and guest speakers. The inpatient program takes AA and Al-Anon steps and principles as its main theme in using the Hazelden modality of treatment and uses every available opportunity to reach, educate and support the families, employers and friends of residents.

The facility is located in the new Kootenai Medical Center, a district full-service hospital. Saint Benedict's ACT staff will provide professional guidance and assistance for the alcoholic, family, employer and community.

WALKER CENTER FOR ALCOHOLISM AND CHEMICAL DEPENDENCY TREATMENT

P.O. Box 541
Gooding, Idaho 83330

(208) 934-8461

Director: Tim Kelly
Average Patient Census: 16

Minimum Duration of Treatment:
   Average 28 days, with 2-year aftercare
Cost: $5,900 average. Insurance eligible.
Detoxification Offered: Yes
Accreditation: JCAH in process,
   state-licensed

The Walker Center is a hospital-based, 24-bed, inpatient alcoholism treatment facility providing detoxification and inpatient rehabilitation, with a comprehensive array of interdisciplinary treatment services, a structured family therapy program and a 2-year aftercare program.

The treatment program is approximately 30 days long and begins with detoxification for an average of 2 or 3 days. This is followed by a full program phase that includes lectures, group therapy, individual counseling, AA meetings and the first five Steps of AA.

Aftercare consists of one group therapy session per week, with individual and family counseling as needed, and lasts for 2 years.

Qualification for admission is determined by one of the treatment staff on duty, i.e., primary counselors, associate counselors or nursing staff. Arrangements may be made by phoning the facility.

MERCY CAREUNIT
Mercy Medical Center

1512 Twelfth Avenue Road
Nampa, Idaho 83651

(208) 466-4531

Director: Keri Christian
Average Patient Census: 15

Minimum Duration of Treatment: None; average stay 26 days followed by 12 weeks outpatient
Cost: $6,500. Insurance eligible.
Detoxification Offered: Yes
Accreditation: JCAH

Mercy CareUnit uses a team approach to the care and treatment of the alcoholic and chemically dependent patient and provides a therapeutic environment for both immediate and long-term care of the alcoholic, his or her understanding of the disease and maintenance of sobriety.

The purpose of the unit also includes the provision of a suitable and educational environment wherein the family of the alcoholic may learn to understand the disease and participate in the treatment program, in a 4-week outpatient service while the patient is in treatment.

The treatment team includes medical director, alcohol therapist, M.S.W. family therapist, clinical social worker, specialized nurses and the program coordinator. Through various treatment modalities, emphasis is placed on improving self-esteem, admission and acceptance of the problem, alternate behavior patterns, priority setting, new patterns of problem solving and methods of maintaining sobriety.

Twelve weeks of aftercare involves weekly sessions for patients and families as well as community self-help groups such as AA. The follow-up program of 12 months is research follow-up of sobriety and includes monthly face-to-face contact with patient and family.

Montana

RIMROCK FOUNDATION

1231 North Twenty-ninth
P.O. Box 30374
Billings, Montana 59101

(406) 248-3175
1-800-841-2874 (in Montana)

Director: David W. Cunningham

Average Patient Census: 28
Minimum Duration of Treatment: Detox, 3 days; residential, 28 days
Cost: $5,600, all-inclusive (or sliding fee scale). Insurance eligible.
Detoxification Offered: Yes
Accreditation: JCAH

Rimrock Foundation is a nonprofit organization dedicated to the rehabilitation of chemically dependent men, women and youth and their families. Rimrock's innovative family center offers an AA-oriented treatment program tailored to meet the needs of the often-neglected, concerned family members and others who suffer along with the chemically dependent person. Twenty-four-hour emergency services are available 7 days a week in the Medical Evaluation/Detoxification Unit, with medical and counseling staff to assist patients with acute medical problems relating to chemical dependency.

In the residential treatment program the chemically dependent person is assisted in confronting his or her illness, its symptoms and its manifestations. Patients receive a physical and psychological assessment from which an individualized treatment plan is developed by a clinical team, with counseling and treatment supported by consulting psychiatrists and psychologists. Treatment modalities include group therapy, which focuses on the Twelve Steps of AA, education, and individual therapy.

Other programs offered by Rimrock include family outpatient programs with teenage, children's and concerned-persons groups, individual aftercare programs, educational and consulting services and a Management Assistance Program.

HILL TOP RECOVERY CENTER

1020 Assiniboine Avenue
P.O. Box 750
Harve, Montana 59501

(406) 265-9665

Director: Otto Kvaalen
Average Patient Census: 15

Minimum Duration of Treatment: 28 days
Cost: $125 per day. Insurance eligible.
Detoxification Offered: No
Accreditation: Montana State Alcohol and Drug Division, Montana Department of Health and Environmental Sciences

Hill Top Recovery Center is a private, nonprofit corporation providing specialized chemical-dependency treatment. The 28-day residential treatment program includes individualized assessment rehabilitation and planning. Patients complete a personal-growth program involving the first five Steps of AA. Individual, group and family counseling are provided.

Outpatient services are provided in a five-county surrounding area, and an Intensive Outpatient Program is available to local residents. Patients without insurance coverage are charged an adjusted fee based on their ability to pay.

Nevada

CAREUNIT HOSPITAL OF NEVADA

5100 West Sahara
Las Vegas, Nevada 89102

(702) 362-8404

Director: David Van Moorlehem
Average Patient Census: 50 beds
   (adolescents only)

Minimum Duration of Treatment: 45–60 days
Cost: Approximately $300 per day. Insurance eligible.
Detoxification Offered: Yes
Accreditation: JCAH

CareUnit of Nevada is a facility specializing in the family treatment of alcohol and other drug dependencies for adolescents. Patients undergo a complete physiological and psychological examination, as well as detoxification under the supervision of the medical director of the facility. The treatment program is personalized to fit individual needs and consists of individual and group therapy, participation in specific activities, lectures and films designed to increase the patient's understanding of his or her disease and appropriate ways to enjoy life free from chemical dependency. Families are invited to join in the treatment program, which is designed to free family members from the effects of the disease in areas such as behavior, attitudes and life-styles.

The recovery continues following the patient's discharge. Patients return to the CareUnit for aftercare 2 evenings a week for a specified period following discharge. Family units participate once weekly in the aftercare program. Patients and their families are encouraged to explore other resources, such as AA, Al-Anon, Alateen, NA and others, to which they were introduced during their inpatient stay. Aftercare is free to all patients—for a lifetime, if desired.

TRUCKEE MEADOWS HOSPITAL

1240 East Ninth Street
Reno, Nevada 89512

(702) 323-0478

Director: Sean Moore, M.Ed., C.S.A.C.
Average Patient Census: 25

Minimum Duration of Treatment: Adult, 30 days; adolescent, 60 days
Cost: $9,000 per month. Insurance eligible.
Detoxification Offered: Yes
Accreditation: JCAH

Truckee Meadows Hospital has both adolescent and adult alcohol and drug treatment programs for individuals suffering from the effects of alcoholism and/or drug addiction.

There are three main parts to these programs: (1) detoxification and medical care: a complete medical workup; (2) intermediate care: individual and group therapy, alcohol and drug education, participation in the self-help groups, family treatment, occupational therapy and recreational therapy; and (3) aftercare: a weekly meeting in the Outpatient Center in the form of a problem-solving group that lasts for 2 years and is included in the cost of hospitalization.

Counselors are available during the working day for consultation with patients and/or family, and at night there is a staff member available to speak with the ex-patient on the phone. Patients may also attend ongoing groups as they wish.

TMH Outpatient Center is also available as a service to the community, offering outpatient counseling to those impaired individuals who, because of the level of their problem, are not candidates for inpatient treatment. The cost of the outpatient program is $40 per session.

New Mexico

CAREUNIT HOSPITAL OF ALBUQUERQUE

505 High Street N.E.
Albuquerque, New Mexico 87102

(505) 848-8088

Director: Dee Elliott
Average Patient Census: Adults, 40; adolescents, 30

Minimum Duration of Treatment: Adults, 21–28 days; adolescents, 45–60 days
Cost: Approximately $300 per day. Insurance eligible.
Detoxification Offered: Yes
Accreditation: JCAH

CareUnit Hospital is a facility specializing in the family treatment of alcohol and other drug dependencies for adults and adolescents. Patients undergo a complete physiological and psychological examination, as well as detoxification under the supervision of the medical director of the facility. The treatment program is personalized to fit individual needs and consists of individual and group therapy, participation in specific activities, lectures and films designed to increase the patient's understanding of his or her disease and appropriate ways to enjoy life free from chemical dependency. Families are invited to join in the treatment program, which is designed to free family members from the effects of the disease in areas such as behavior, attitudes and life-styles.

The recovery continues following the patient's discharge from the hospital. Patients return to the CareUnit for aftercare 2 evenings a week for a specified period of time following discharge. Family units participate once weekly in the aftercare program. Patients and their families are encouraged to explore other resources, such as AA, Al-Anon, Alateen, NA and others, to which they were introduced during their inpatient stay. Aftercare is free to all patients—for a lifetime, if desired.

DAYBREAK
Presbyterian Hospital Center

1100 Central, S.E.
Albuquerque, New Mexico 87102

(505) 841-1031

Director: Mary Townsley-Murray, M.S.
Average Patient Census: 12

Minimum Duration of Treatment: Assessed according to patient needs
Cost: Detox, normal hospital room rate; rehab, $175 per day. Insurance eligible.
Detoxification Offered: Yes
Accreditation: JCAH

Daybreak is designed for individuals and their families for whom drinking or drug use is a problem. The program is specifically designed for persons in the early or middle stages of the disease of chemical dependency when treatment has been shown to be more effective.

After detoxification, intensive inpatient services are provided under medical supervision. Personal physicians can continue treatment of other medical conditions. Treatment services include medical care, counseling, education and aftercare. Family members are involved in treatment, and there is an intensive 30-hour-week family program. Involvement in AA, NA and Al-Anon are important in the program. Strict guidelines to assure confidentiality are followed. Aftercare includes structured sessions that provide continued support for patients and families.

Daybreak also offers an intensive outpatient/partial-hospitalization program, consultations and interventions to assist family members.

VISTA SANDIA HOSPITAL

501 Almeda Boulevard, N.E.
Albuquerque, New Mexico 87113

(505) 823-2000

Director: Roland Metivier

Average Patient Census: 14
Minimum Duration of Treatment: 21 days
Cost: Available on request. Insurance eligible.
Detoxification Offered: Yes
Accreditation: JCAH

Vista Sandia Hospital, located in a tranquil setting 10 miles north of Albuquerque, offers a comprehensive drug and alcohol treatment program consisting of detoxification, treatment and aftercare. There are comfortable rooms opening to patios, providing unique indoor-outdoor freedom of environment, with the beauty and serenity of the Sandia Mountains as a backdrop.

Patients receive intensive medical care during their period of detoxification, which precedes an average treatment stay of 3 to 4 weeks. The treatment program includes comprehensive neurological and psychological testing when indicated, individual psychotherapy and group therapy, education through lectures and films, occupational and recreational therapy and vocational-counseling assistance.

Recognizing that dependency also disrupts the lives of the family members, Vista Sandia offers an outpatient family program for spouses, parents and children. This component is aimed at educating the family about chemical dependency and preparing the family to participate in the recovery process.

Aftercare treatment is planned for each individual and his or her family. Aftercare includes participation in weekly group session for patients and family members, outpatient therapy with their physician when indicated and involvement in community support groups, such as AA, NA, Al-Anon, Alateen and OA.

CAVERN LODGE

109 North Guadalupe
Carlsbad, New Mexico 88220

(505) 887-6585

Director: Thomas Tutor

Average Patient Census: 18–20
Minimum Duration of Treatment: 21 days
Cost: Based on ability to pay; $0–1,900. Insurance eligible.
Detoxification Offered: Yes

Cavern Lodge is a facility operated by the State of New Mexico Health and Environmental Department Alcoholism Bureau.

It is licensed as a special medical hospital for the treatment of alcoholism, with a bed capacity of 20. Admission requires the individual to be suffering primarily from alcoholism or alcohol abuse.

Cavern Lodge is unique in terms of being the only Lodge, in the New Mexico State system, that offers a 21-day residential treatment schedule.

DAYBREAK
SAN JUAN REGIONAL MEDICAL CENTER

801 West Maple Street
Farmington, New Mexico 87401

(505) 327-4613

Director: Scott Davy, M.S.
Average Patient Census: 12

Minimum Duration of Treatment: 28-day program; shorter or longer stays by prior arrangement
Cost: $210 per day. Insurance eligible.
Detoxification Offered: Yes
Accreditation: JCAH

Daybreak, the alcoholism treatment program at San Juan Regional Medical Center, is designed to help individuals achieve and maintain a life-style free from the use or abuse of alcohol through education, treatment and motivation. The goal is to help persons become aware of their drinking patterns and the effect on their everyday lives. Medical assistance is provided for recovery from the damaging effects of alcohol, and an alternative life-style is presented in which it is more enjoyable and rewarding to live without alcohol than with it.

Since alcohol affects all aspects of an individual, comprehensive assessment is given each person on admission, and a personalized treatment program is developed that is addressed to any medical problems or any family, marriage, job or financial concerns. The family is directly involved in the treatment program.

The Daybreak program is specifically designed for those in the early and middle stages of the disease, when treatment is more effective, and therefore early identification and prevention are a primary goal. Services include inpatient detoxification, if required, residential treatment, and an outpatient program for those who can maintain sobriety without residential care. An individualized aftercare program provides continued contact and support following treatment.

FOUR WINDS ALCOHOLISM REHABILITATION CENTER

1313 Mission Avenue
P.O. Box 736
Farmington, New Mexico 87499

(505) 327-7218

Director: Cynthia Johnson

Average Patient Census: 20
Minimum Duration of Treatment: 28 days
Cost: Sliding scale fees for New Mexico residents. Insurance eligible.
Detoxification Offered: Yes
Accreditation: Licensed by the State of New Mexico

Four Winds is a comprehensive alcoholism treatment center serving a multicultural population in San Juan County, New Mexico.

This facility offers a nonmedical detoxification treatment program lasting from 3 to 5 days and a residential treatment program lasting a minimum of 28 days.

Four Winds also provides an outpatient program designed to run from 10 to 12 weeks, as well as an aftercare service for 6 months following treatment.

COTTONWOOD NEW MEXICO

804 Blythe Road
P.O. Box 1270
Los Lunas, New Mexico 87031

(505) 865-3345

Director: David Briick, Executive Director; Jeanne Rigaud, Treatment Director

Average Patient Census: 32
Minimum Duration of Treatment: 30 days
Cost: $4,950 for 30 days; $165 for each additional day. Insurance eligible.
Detoxification Offered: Yes
Accreditation: JCAH

Cottonwood is an intensive residential treatment center for people afflicted with alcoholism, medication addiction and other chemical dependencies. Two adjoining estates have been combined to form this delightful 20-acre oasis in the Rio Grande green belt.

A professional staff, personally and professionally familiar with addiction, supervises each patient's restoration and growth through an individualized program of recovery. Emphasis is placed on the acquisition of skills suggested by the program of AA.

Daily therapy includes groups, private counseling, lectures, films, AA and NA meetings and homework. A pool, volleyball court, track and gym area add to the medically sanctioned exercise program. A licensed physician and around-the-clock registered nurses ensure appropriate medical care and supervision.

Length of stay varies with the strengths and motivations of the patient. Eight weeks of aftercare and monthly alumni meetings, at no charge, are included.

PECOS VALLEY LODGE

1600 East Tilden
Roswell, New Mexico 88201

(505) 622-8360

Director: Thomas Tutor
Average Patient Census: 16
Minimum Duration of Treatment: Detox plus 14 days; can be extended on advice of attending physician

Cost: $1,200 for 14 days, approximately. Insurance eligible.
Detoxification Offered: Yes
Accreditation: Licensed by the State of New Mexico

The program at Pecos Valley Lodge is a structured one of lectures, films with discussions afterward, individual counseling, group therapy and regular attendance at AA meetings. Nurses are on duty 24 hours a day, and counselors are on duty from 8:00 A.M. to midnight, 7 days a week, for the program of detoxification and rehabilitation. Counseling for families is offered and encouraged.

Pecos Valley Lodge is a small facility with a homelike atmosphere and has been in operation since 1954. The facility is associated with the Health and Environment Department of the State of New Mexico and is open to anyone in whose life alcohol is causing a problem. Cross-addiction is treated only if alcoholism is the major problem.

AMETHYST HALL

P.O. Box 32
Velarde, New Mexico 87582

(505) 852-2704

Director: Rocky Hill
Average Patient Census: 12
Minimum Duration of Treatment: Adults, 30 days; adolescents, 45 days

Cost: $7,240 for 30 days, includes payment for aftercare in patient's home community. Insurance eligible.
Detoxification Offered: Yes
Accreditation: JCAH pending. New Mexico state-certified

Amethysts were said to have been worn by the Greeks to maintain sobriety, and for Amethyst Hall the name symbolizes recovery through awareness of the nature of the disease and by working through the Twelve Steps of AA.

Amethyst Hall, a chemical-dependency program for adults and adolescents, is committed to the Twelve Steps of AA and the healing process of personal surrender. The serene, rural setting, on the banks of the Rio Grande River, lends itself to this surrender process and to the realization that nature itself can provide insight into individual uniqueness and oneness.

Patients enter intermediate care when they are physically chemical-free. It is during this phase that the patient is asked to look at and to experience the emotional, attitudinal, behavioral and spiritual realities of his dependencies and their effect on his own life and the lives of those closest to him.

Treatment includes education, individual and group counseling, recreation, relaxation therapy and discussions. Amethyst Hall emphasizes treatment for the whole family, and aftercare includes planning for continuing support activities for the alcoholic as well as the family. During the third week of the inpatient's stay, the family is included in the treatment process. Their daily schedule begins early in the morning and ends late at night.

Through the application of massage therapy from a licensed massage therapist, sessions in progressive relaxation, yoga and autogenic training, the center demonstrates to the patient that emotions can be positively affected by means other than the ingestion of chemicals. Rigorous daily exercise participation is emphasized.

Amethyst Hall will develop and pay in part for an aftercare program in the patient's home community for both the patient and his or her family.

Velarde, New Mexico, is located 35 miles north of Santa Fe and 37 miles south of Taos.

Oregon

B and H STUMP RANCH INC.

18624 Highway 36
Blachly, Oregon 97412

(503) 927-3955

Director: Eric James
Average Patient Census: 35

Minimum Duration of Treatment: 60 days
Cost: $300 per month (sliding scale). Insurance eligible.
Detoxification Offered: No
Accreditation: State of Oregon Mental Health Division

The Stump Ranch is a long-term, low-cost treatment center located in the country in a 35-acre setting. The program is centered primarily on AA, with a minimum of 13 AA meetings per week required.

A major facet of the program is work therapy. Cooking, auto maintenance, wood for heat and all maintenance of the ranch is done by clients. These activities have proven beneficial in restoring self-worth to clients, with the further benefit of maintaining the ranch for those who need its services in the future.

The staff of the Stump Ranch believes that the peaceful environment, removed from the temptations of the city, gives clients a chance to learn about themselves and to find a new and better way of life.

TURNAROUND
Forest Grove Community Hospital

1809 Maple Street
Forest Grove, Oregon 97116

(503) 357-0774

Director: Gary Dries

Average Patient Census: 24 beds
Minimum Duration of Treatment: 28–32 days
Cost: $130 per day. Insurance eligible.
Detoxification Offered: Yes (in hospital)
Accreditation: State of Oregon

TurnAround at Forest Grove believes that just as willpower doesn't work on other major health problems, it doesn't work on alcoholism either, and that this complex disease calls for professional treatment like any other.

The team of professionals at TurnAround are specialists in all the areas in which alcoholism affects people—physical, emotional and spiritual—and are dedicated to the proven success of the principles of AA and the Twelve Steps. They also believe that these steps can be personalized to meet the patients's life-style, for continued sobriety and personal growth.

Prior to admission, each patient is required to obtain medical approval, as well as a history and physical, through either the family physician or the medical director. When the patient is stable, treatment begins with interviews by counselors, clergy and psychologist, who meet with the medical staff to plan an individualized program.

The program stresses mutual assistance and personal responsibility and includes daily lectures and films, quiet time for reading and group therapy twice daily. Counselors meet with patients on a regular basis to talk about particular problems and how best to deal with them. Weekly evaluation of progress is also part of the program.

The continued involvement of families, employers and others important in the patient's life is recognized as an integral part of recovery, and these persons are invited for conferences with the staff.

After discharge, TurnAround continues to provide one-to-one counseling and support groups, as well as AA contacts for each patient and a 2-year follow-up program.

SWEATHOUSE LODGE, INC.

48085 Santiam Highway
Cascadia School Building
Foster, Oregon 97345

(503) 367-6146

Director: Raymond C. Leatham, Ed.D.
Average Patient Census: 23

Minimum Duration of Treatment: 30 days (maximum 90 days)
Cost: Sliding scale fee schedule. Insurance eligible.
Detoxification Offered: No
Accreditation: State of Oregon Mental Health Division

The program at Sweathouse Lodge is designed to deal with the needs of Native Americans in the Northwest who are afflicted with the disease of alcoholism.

The residential program offers a blend of Native American culture concepts and standard alcoholism treatment approaches. Emphasis is placed on offering a wide-ranging Native American cultural education in order to help residents achieve self-awareness and spiritual growth during recovery.

HARMONY HOUSE, INC.

1925 S.E. Taylor
Portland, Oregon 97214

(503) 232-3448

Director: Frank Smith
Average Patient Census: Portland facility, 15 men; Oregon City facility, 13 men

Minimum Duration of Treatment: Varied, but program is structured for 3–6 months
Cost: $52.50 per week. Insurance eligible.
Detoxification Offered: No
Accreditation: State of Oregon Mental Health Division

Harmony House was originally developed by a small group of recovered alcoholics with the intention of helping others so afflicted. From the early struggles to keep the organization alive and together, it grew into a unique program of recovery based on the proven principles of community living and guided study in an environment of love and understanding.

From this early volunteer movement, Harmony House became chartered as a private, nonprofit corporation in 1970. The volunteer members of the board of directors comprise a cross-section of the community—representatives from the professional arena, business sector and lay community.

Today, Harmony House, Inc., operates two residential care facilities for alcoholics. Harmony House I is located at 2270 S.E. Thirty-ninth Street, Portland, Oregon 94214. Harmony House II is located at 1510 Division Street, Oregon City, Oregon 97045. Both facilities are AA-oriented.

Criteria for admission are that the client be alcohol-free for at least 5 days and employable or employed, or in pursuit of job training or education. The candidate must have a sincere desire to work on his alcohol problem. Admission procedure is initiated by contacting the administrative offices at Taylor Street in Portland.

Program elements include individual and group counseling, alcohol education, employment, training and education assistance, an in-house Twelve Step AA study group, attendance at regular AA meetings in the community, recreational activities and nutrition education.

Staffing consists of an executive director and secretary-bookkeeper. Each facility has a house manager, head cook and relief cook-maintenace worker. An alcoholism counselor devotes half-time to each facility. Volunteers also assist in program elements.

Other community services offered by Harmony House, Inc., are information and referral, intervention and community education, including presentations to schools, church groups, service organizations and civic groups.

HOLBROOK RESIDENTIAL TREATMENT CENTER

17645 Northwest Saint Helen's Road
Portland, Oregon 97231

(503) 621-3201
1-800-533-5664

Director: James P. Steave

Average Patient Census: 48 beds
Minimum Duration of Treatment: 28 days
Cost: Adults, $3,000; adolescents, $3,500. Insurance eligible.
Detoxification Offered: No
Accreditation: State of Oregon Mental Health Division

Believing that the recognition and willingness to seek help with the disease of chemical dependency is essential to recovery, Holbrook sees its primary function as providing this help and guidance in a nonjudgmental environment.

Examination and evaluation by the medical staff are followed by the design of an individualized treatment plan by the multidisciplinary team of physicians, counselors, psychologist and clergy. The family is also assisted in beginning their recovery through individual counseling and group experiences facilitated by the family counselor.

Program philosophy is based on learning and practicing, on a daily basis, the Twelve Steps of AA, and each patient is guided through the steps and given written and reading assignments, lectures and audiovisuals.

Aftercare, a weekly participation in group experiences for a minimum of 12 weeks, is encouraged, but is an adjunct to, not a substitute for, patient and family attendance at AA, Al-Anon or Alateen.

Holbrook also offers a specialized short-term program of 14 days, with a direct transfer to aftercare or AA. The cost of the Adolescent Program includes 16 weeks of intensive aftercare. There is also an Alumni Program and workshops, seminars and continuing education for citizens and community resources.

Located a few miles northwest of Portland in a rural country setting, Holbrook offers a relaxing atmosphere of understanding, care and concern.

SERENITY BY THE SEA

321 South Prom
Seaside, Oregon 97138

(503) 738-3388

Director: Marsha Morgan, Ph.D.

Average Patient Census: 24–35
Minimum Duration of Treatment: 28–35 days
Cost: $3,500 complete. Insurance eligible.
Detoxification Offered: Social
Accreditation: State of Oregon Mental Health Division

Serenity by the Sea is a freestanding treatment facility, located right next to the Pacific Ocean, offering a Minnesota-model treatment program and a complete family program. The staff includes intervention specialists. The treatment program is planned for chemically dependent persons age 13 and older.

Serenity by the Sea offers treatment in a relaxed, quiet setting designed for recovery.

Utah

CHEMICAL DEPENDENCY TREATMENT CENTER
Utah Valley Regional Medical Center

1034 North 500 West
Provo, Utah 84604

(801) 375-4357

Director: Eugene Buckner, Ph.D.

Average Patient Census: 20 beds
Minimum Duration of Treatment: 21 days
Cost: $4,100 includes 2 weeks of transition treatment. Insurance eligible.
Detoxification Offered: Yes
Accreditation: State-licensed. JCAH

The Chemical Dependency Unit (CDU) at Utah Valley Regional Medical Center offers treatment for men and women who are experiencing problems with mood-altering substances.

The program typically consists of a 21-day inpatient phase that includes evaluation, treatment planning and rehabilitation. This is followed by 2 weeks of transition phase, when the patient returns for nightly sessions to continue the therapy begun during the first phase. The final phase is aftercare or extended care; this continues for 1 year and is characterized by weekly meetings with a particular emphasis during the first 6 months on relapse-prevention training.

The philosophy of the CDU is that chemical dependency is a primary illness and is best treated through a multiphasic, multidisciplinary approach. This means that the patient progresses from one level of treatment to another and that there are a variety of professionals whose disciplines and backgrounds are brought to bear in the problem. Physicians, psychologists, nurses, counselors, and clergy are all necessary to interrupt this disease process and to assist the patient on the road to his or her recovery. Self-help recovery groups, such as AA, form an additional philosophical foundation for the CDU. Ongoing involvement in such groups is stressed upon the completion of treatment.

ODYSSEY HOUSE OF UTAH, INC.

68 South Sixth East
Salt Lake City, Utah 84102

(801) 322-1001

Director: Glen R. Lambert, M.S.W., L.C.S.W.
Average Patient Census: Adults, 60; adolescents, 16
Minimum Duration of Treatment: Adults, 12–24 months; adolescents, 6–9 months

Cost: Substance abuse program, $800 per month (sliding fee scale available); adolescent program, $1,317 per month; alternative school (adolescents and adults), $130 per month. Insurance eligible.
Detoxification Offered: Not available on site; referrals to local detoxification facilities.
Accreditation: JCAH. Licensed by State Division of Alcohol and Drugs and the Department of Youth Corrections.

Odyssey House is a psychiatrically oriented, therapeutic community for the treatment of substance abuse (drugs and/or alcohol) and antisocial behavior in clients over 18 years of age.

The goal of the program is to deal with the many underlying problems resulting from substance abuse and to return the individual to the community a drug- and crime-free contributing citizen. The group process teaches the individual to confront his problems openly and to take responsibility for his behavior. At the same time, the individual is exposed to many challenging job experiences where he is encouraged to actualize his talents and abilities.

Odyssey House is involved in prevention, child-abuse counseling and concerns of children. There are also special groups for the intellectually gifted, addicted professionals, women in treatment, Native Americans and veterans.

A newly developed alcoholism program has been incorporated into the therapeutic community at Odyssey House, based on the findings that 65% of the individuals who had primary drug abuse actually had secondary and primary alcohol problems. Included in the alcohol program are prevention and education, medical aspects of alcoholism and a group process to aid residents in dealing with this problem.

The Odyssey Adolescent Treatment Program treats youths with histories of neglect, physical/sexual abuse and delinquency, as well as substance abuse. It is also a therapeutic community for youths 14 to 18 years of age, which uses group therapy and positive peer pressure to help effect changes in client attitudes, values and behaviors.

Odyssey has a licensed Alternative School available for adults and adolescents who have not completed high school. A variety of approaches to individualized learning are available, including tutors, teaching machines, lectures and individual educational plans. Both the G.E.D. and the high school diploma are available.

SALT LAKE ALCOHOLISM TREATMENT CENTER

667 East South Temple
Salt Lake City, Utah 84102

(801) 355-8536

Average Patient Census: 30 men
Minimum Duration of Treatment: 60 days
Cost: Sliding scale. Insurance eligible.
Detoxification Offered: No

Director: Phil Quigley

The Salt Lake Alcoholism Treatment Center is an inpatient facility that offers comprehensive psychotherapy for alcoholism. The program includes individual and group counseling, milieu therapy, Antabuse therapy and a full program of alcoholism education offered through lectures and films.

Intensive inpatient therapy for approximately 60 days is followed by an inpatient phase, in which the client begins working and reintegrating himself into the community. This is followed by outpatient treatment that lasts as long as needed. Family counseling is included in the treatment regimen whenever possible and appropriate.

The client must be detoxified for 24 hours prior to admission, have no mental illness and have a primary problem of alcoholism. The Salt Lake Alcoholism Treatment Center is sponsored by UAF, the Utah Alcoholism Foundation. This facility is for males only.

UAF operates eight other facilities, including one for women in Salt Lake City. There are also facilities in Ogden, Provo, Cedar City, Logan and Price. Information about these facilities is available at the Foundation office: Suite 210, 2880 South Main Street, Salt Lake City, Utah, 84115. Doug Dinsmore is Administrative Director and Craig Christopherson is Program Coordinator.

Washington

OLYMPIC CENTER—BELLINGHAM

1603 East Illinois
Bellingham, Washington 98226

(206) 733-9111, Scan: 738-2169

Director: John Rietz, M.Ed., J.D.
Minimum Duration of Treatment: Adult, 28 days; youth, 42 days

Cost: Adults, $3,780; youth, $5,390. Treatment grants (scholarships) available based on need. Insurance eligible.
Detoxification Offered: Yes
Accreditation: DSHS license

Detoxification at Olympic Center may take up to 3 days and is supervised on a 24-hour basis by the medical director, R.N.'s and L.P.N.'s.

The 28-day Adult Program includes individual and group counseling, nutritional diet, exercise at the YMCA (pool, gym, weights), alcoholism/drug education classes and workshops, recovery training and AA/NA meetings nightly, five of the Twelve Steps to be completed before discharge. The Family Program involves group and individual counseling and takes place on Monday, Tuesday, Wednesday, Thursday and Sunday. Ten weeks of aftercare are also part of the treatment.

The 42-day Youth/Young Adult Program at Olympic Center for the treatment of chemical dependency takes place separately from the Adult Program. Youth abide by a "point system" concerning rules. There are monitored halls and outdoor area with camera surveillance. The structured, well-supervised program includes group and personal counseling, lectures and workshops relevant to young people. Exercise at the YMCA, hikes and excursions are part of the program, and youths can receive a G.E.D., or receive credits if in school. Tutors hold class every day. The program is for persons 13 to 21 years of age, with a Family Program the same as above and 6 months of aftercare.

MILAM RECOVERY CENTER

14500 Juanita Drive N.E.
Bothell, Washington 98011

(206) 621-9636

Director: Charles Kester

Average Patient Census: 45
Minimum Duration of Treatment: 21 days
Cost: $2,875. Insurance eligible.
Detoxification Offered: Yes
Accreditation: State of Washington

Milam Recovery Center is a freestanding facility for the treatment of alcoholism, cocaine and other drug addictions. It is located on a 50-acre wooded hill near Lake Washington, 20 miles from Seattle.

MRC recognizes that alcoholism and other drug addictions are primary, progressive, physical diseases that interfere with all life processes and cause physical, nutritional, psychological, social and spiritual deterioration. It is further recognized at MRC that with an effective treatment sequence most patients can and do make full recovery from both the primary addiction and its many complications.

The basic treatment sequence includes a minimum of 3 weeks of inpatient care and 10 weekly outpatient follow-up group counseling sessions. Patients with dual addictions or other complications may be advised to stay longer than the 3-week minimum.

A high staff-to-patient ratio provides for the highly structured program and maintains a powerful treatment milieu. The medical director and various other consulting physicians, together with the counseling staff, make up the primary treatment team.

MCR believes nutritional therapy to be a vital factor in the healing process and in long-term control of addiction. Education in this area, as well as a full explanation of all aspects of the disease process, are important parts of the therapy. Other treatment activities include individual and group counseling, AA and NA meetings, physical exercise and programmed relaxation.

Both treatment and follow-up are focused on continuous total abstinence from alcohol and all other mood-altering drugs as the cornerstone of full recovery.

CAREUNIT HOSPITAL OF KIRKLAND

10322 Northeast One Hundred Thirty-second Street
Kirkland, Washington 98033

(206) 821-1122

Director: Dennis Harrington
Average Patient Census: 83 beds (adults, 53; adolescents, 30)

Minimum Duration of Treatment: Adults, 21–28 days; adolescents, 45–60 days
Cost: Approximately $300 per day. Insurance eligible.
Detoxification Offered: Yes
Accreditation: JCAH

CareUnit Hospital is a facility specializing in the family treatment of alcohol and other drug dependencies for adults and adolescents. Patients undergo a complete physiological and psychological examination, as well as detoxification under the supervision of the medical director of the facility. The treatment program is personalized to fit individual needs and consists of individual and group therapy, participation in specific activities, lectures and films designed to increase the patient's understanding of his or her disease and appropriate ways to enjoy life free from chemical dependency. Families are invited to join in the treatment program, which is designed to free family members from the effects of the disease in areas such as behavior, attitudes and life-styles.

The recovery continues following the patient's discharge from the hospital. Patients return to the CareUnit for aftercare 2 evenings a week for a specified period following discharge. Family units participate once weekly in the aftercare program. Patients and their families are encouraged to explore other resources, such as AA, Al-Anon, Alateen, NA and others, which they were introduced to during their inpatient stay. Aftercare is free to all patients—for a lifetime, if desired.

CAREUNIT OF MONTICELLO MEDICAL CENTER

600 Broadway
P.O. Box 638
Longview, Washington 98632

(206) 636-7363

Director: Robert Nelson
Average Patient Census: 18

Minimum Duration of Treatment: 21–28 days
Cost: $5,500–7,500, depending on length of stay and physical condition of patient. Insurance eligible.
Detoxification Offered: Yes
Accreditation: JCAH

The Monticello Medical Center CareUnit is an acute-care hospital based on an inpatient treatment program, utilizing the team approach to the treatment of alcoholism and other chemical dependencies. A staff of physician, psychologist, social worker, state-certified alcoholism therapist, R.N.'s, and L.P.N.'s work with the alcoholic and the family during the 21 to 28 days of inpatient treatment.

Twelve weeks of aftercare are offered to facilitate sobriety and the well-being of the patient and family. Also, AA and an active alumni group act as excellent support for continued sobriety. The CareUnit's "Gold Card Program" offers free life-long aftercare in any CareUnit across the nation.

SOLBERG HALL
VALLEY GENERAL HOSPITAL

14701 One Hundred Seventy-ninth S.E.
Monroe, Washington 98272

(206) 794-7497

Director: Jack Hayes

Average Patient Census: 40
Minimum Duration of Treatment: 28 days
Cost: $155 per day; average total cost $4,850. Insurance eligible.
Detoxification Offered: Yes
Accreditation: JCAH

Each new patient at Solberg Hall receives a complete physical examination. A complete plan of treatment designed for the individual is established at that time. The plan of treatment includes, but is not limited to, the physical condition and needs of the patient, his social and cultural needs, and his psychological, educational and vocational needs.

The program includes lectures, assigned reading, group therapy, individual and group counseling and AA meetings. This facility provides a detailed brochure listing the full range of structured activities throughout the day, including relaxation therapy, emotional and spiritual explorations and AA rap sessions.

One or more interviews with the patient's spouse and other family or community members are held, as appropriate, and the counselor will involve the family in discharge planning and referrals to community, including AA and Al-Anon as applicable. In addition, while the patient is in treatment, the spouse is expected to attend four 2-hour sessions during the 4-week period to help in an understanding of alcoholism and the alcoholic patient.

Solberg Hall stresses the importance of follow-up care and assigns a counselor through the Community Alcohol Centers, who continues one-to-one counseling for a period of 10 weeks, with extension when appropriate. The Solberg Hall Alumni Association meets at 1-month intervals, and all patients in treatment attend these meetings, as well as alumni ex-patients and their spouses.

OLALLA GUEST LODGE

12851 S.E. Lala Cove Lane
Olalla, Washington 98359

(206) 857-2026, 857-6201

Director: Elaine Kaufmann
Average Patient Census: 34

Minimum Duration of Treatment: 28 days, stays of 6 weeks can be arranged
Cost: $2,800 covers all services including 10 aftercare visits and family program involvement. Insurance eligible.
Detoxification Offered: No
Accreditation: State of Washington.

The program at Olalla Guest Lodge is presented in graduated stages, yet is open-ended, allowing for entry at any time. The staff takes a pragmatic approach to rehabilitation, stressing the principles of AA. Other therapies include assertiveness training, territoriality, reality therapy and achievement motivation. Each client receives approximately 1 hour per week of individual counseling. Family counseling is available and strongly encouraged. Lectures on proper nutritional practices for alcoholics and their families and aftercare services are also available.

The center is located in a peaceful setting on a 12-acre site that overlooks Puget Sound's West Passage.

NORTHWEST TREATMENT CENTER

9010 Thirteenth Northwest
Seattle, Washington 98117

(206) 789-5911, 24-hour number

Director: Jack Mahler

Average Patient Census: 30
Minimum Duration of Treatment: 21 days
Cost: $2,475. Insurance eligible.
Detoxification Offered: Yes, at Waldo Hospital
Accreditation: State of Washington

NTC has an integrated and comprehensive program consisting of orientation, lectures, films, intensive workshops, individual and group therapy, AA and NA study groups, meetings and group discussions. Diet, vitamins, rest and exercise are stressed.

Sensitive to the needs of women and adolescents, the Center offers special groups and classes when indicated. Extensive grounds allow full use of outdoor activities, and indoor recreational facilities as well as occupational therapy are available. The staff of professionals utilizes a multidisciplinary-team approach, and continuing education and in-service training are important to the provision, by this staff, of the highest possible level of care.

The family program supports the addict's recovery by helping the family and/or close associates recover from the secondary effects of alcohol and drug abuse and is an integral part of the services at NTC. The program includes family orientation, education, individual and group counseling, children's play therapy, Al-Anon, Nar-Anon, Alateen and referrals as needed.

Each resident leaves treatment with an individualized aftercare plan that may include counseling, referral for vocational planning or other specialized services. The addict and family may attend 12 weekly small-group sessions as transition from treatment to community, and the Alumni Association provides an open-ended group for socializing and continuing education. Participation in AA/NA, Al-Anon and Alateen is encouraged and recommended. Admission to NTC requires that alcohol/drug abuse is the primary problem, and screening is done on an individual basis.

SAINT CABRINI RECOVERY PROGRAM
Saint Cabrini Hospital

Terry and Madison
Seattle, Washington 98104

(206) 583-4344

Director: Brendan Coleman

Average Patient Census: 34 beds
Minimum Duration of Treatment: 21 days
Cost: $165 per day. Insurance eligible.
Detoxification Offered: Yes
Accreditation: JCAH

The program at Cabrini may begin with a 2- to 4-day detoxification if this therapy is required. The 3-week intensive treatment program that follows is designed to permit the patient to learn to understand chemical dependency as a disease, take part in group therapy sessions and receive individual counseling.

During treatment, all patients complete a course in progressive relaxation therapy and learn to use other techniques for coping with daily stress. Patients also learn the importance of diet to total recovery, and classes on nutrition help them to develop good eating habits that will continue after treatment. AA and NA are studied in depth, and patients are introduced to the fellowships of AA and NA through meetings both in the hospital and in the community. All patients graduate from the program with a personal plan for sobriety after their return to home and job. Aftercare involves attendance at weekly meetings at the hospital for at least 12 weeks, weekly group therapy for 6 weeks and individual counseling sessions with their inpatient counselor.

Family members are strongly encouraged to meet with the patient's counselor during treatment and attend the public lectures and special family group sessions.

Cabrini staff members conduct free public lectures on alcoholism each Saturday at 11:00 A.M. in the hospital and are available to community groups on request to offer lectures and seminars in community education concerning chemical dependency.

SCHICK SHADEL HOSPITAL

12101 Ambaum Boulevard
Seattle, Washington 98146

1-800-426-5065
(206) 244-8100

Director: James W. Smith, M.D.
Average Patient Census: 40–50

Minimum Duration of Treatment: 10 days plus detox; 2 years aftercare
Cost: $5,800 approximate, includes physician's fees; detox, $340 per day. Insurance eligible.
Detoxification Offered: Yes
Accreditation: JCAH

The Schick Shadel Hospital treats alcoholism as a medical disease using counterconditioning, aversion therapy and narcotherapy. In addition to detoxification, if necessary, the patient's program includes a complete physical examination, a physician as the patient's treatment team leader, a psychiatric evaluation, individual aftercare counseling, family counseling, relaxation training, education about alcoholism through lectures, small group discussions and audiovisuals, and referral to community support services.

Aftercare services are provided for 2 years after treatment, and the original counselor contacts are made while the patient is in the hospital. At least two reinforcement treatments are scheduled.

The hospital will be happy to provide a more detailed description of the multitherapeutic methods employed. Patients may be admitted 24 hours a day by self, family or friends, as well as by physicians, lawyers or court. Telephone first to ensure bed space availability.

Treatment program reports, including medical follow-up reports upon request, are available to court referrals. An intervention service is also available to assist in getting the problem drinker to accept the need for treatment.

Schick Shadel does not actively recruit patients with addictions other than alcohol, but will address these addictions as they occur in a polydrug abuse situation.

TAMARC
Thurston and Mason Alcoholism Recovery Council, Inc.

1625 Mottman Road, S.W.
Tumwater, Washington 98502

Mailing address:
P.O. Box 1216
Olympia, Washington 98507

(206) 943-8510

Director: Lois Parker
Average Patient Census: Detoxification Unit, 4 beds; Recovery Unit and Weeknight Program, available on request

Minimum Duration of Treatment: Weeknight Program, 5 evenings per week for 5 weeks; Family Program, 2 evenings per week for 5 weeks
Cost: Weeknight Program, $1,200 including family and aftercare; Aftercare Group, $180. Payment due on entering program. Insurance eligible.
Detoxification Offered: Yes
Accreditation: State of Washington

TAMARC, Inc. (Thurston and Mason Alcoholism Recovery Council, Inc.) offers three categories of rehabilitation service: (1) a four-bed Detoxification Unit; (2) halfway house, which is a residential Recovery Unit for men and women; and (3) a structured intensive outpatient treatment 5 evenings each week for 5 weeks, a Family Program that meets 2 evenings per week for 5 weeks, and an Aftercare Group that meets once a week for 12 weeks.

Funded through public funds, private donations, United Way and charges for services, the facility provides 24-hour crisis-line intervention service from its Community Alcoholism Center.

The program in the Recovery Unit is based on a "bridge back" concept, providing a structured "halfway" environment to help men and women get back into the community. It offers group therapy, individual counseling, and involvement in AA and emphasizes the client's resumption of responsibility as he or she begins a new life. TAMARC treats alcoholism only.

ALCOHOLISM TREATMENT CENTER
Saint Joseph's Community Hospital

P.O. Box 1600
600 N.E. Ninety-second Avenue
Vancouver, Washington 98663

(206) 256-2170

Director: Dennis W. Malmer
Average Patient Census: 48

Minimum Duration of Treatment: 28–35 days
Cost: $132 per day room and board plus $120 history, physical and lab fees. Insurance eligible.
Detoxification Offered: Yes
Accreditation: JCAH

The Alcoholism Treatment Center, occupying the entire fourth floor of Saint Joseph's Community Hospital, is dedicated to the treatment and recovery of chemically dependent men and women—those addicted to or harmfully dependent on the use of mood-altering chemicals such as alcohol.

The facility includes fifty single and semiprivate beds in two treatment units plus detoxification and medical services unit. The primary treatment period generally lasts about 4 weeks, but will vary depending on patient's condition and attitude. Staff includes hospital administrators, doctors, registered nurses, psychologists, counselors on alcoholism, clergy of various denominations, plus personnel in admission, transportation, consultation, training and education.

Saint Joseph's experience indicates that alcoholism is a complex, progressive, multifaceted illness, affecting the alcoholic in many ways and interfering with the individual's ability to manage his or her life. Therefore, the patient's physical, mental, emotional, social and spiritual state's are taken into consideration in the treatment program. The inpatient treatment program, as well as the aftercare program, emphasizes self-assessment measures and positive attitudinal changes as suggested by AA.

Other elements include an 8-week Family Program, a 2-day Family Program, a Marital Communication Workshop and Family Conferences. Families, employers and significant others are usually invited for a conference with patient and staff. Consultation services, in-hospital and on-site seminars to industry and business interested in establishing employee assistance programs, and training programs for students and workers in the field of chemical dependency, are available.

SWARF ALCOHOLISM PROGRAMS

Fourth Plain Boulevard at O Street
P.O. Box 1738
Vancouver, Washington 98668

(206) 696-1659

Director: William J. Streur

Average Patient Census: 35
Minimum Duration of Treatment: Stated program is 21 days, but duration may be less or more
Cost: $78 per day. Insurance eligible.
Detoxification Offered: No
Accreditation: State of Washington

The program incorporates education and training concerning alcoholism and recovery. It includes individual and group counseling, the principles and practices of AA, physical conditioning, a controlled living situation and nutritional counseling. Aftercare planning and activities are also an important part of the program. Counseling for families is offered.

The qualifications for admission include a need for alcoholism rehabilitation, voluntary admission, freedom from the need for the medical services of a hospital and the ability to pay for cost of treatment.

Information is also available on SWARF's intensive outpatient treatment program (12 weeks, 2 nights per week), which is offered in Vancouver, Chehalis and Kelso, Washington.

SUNDOWN M RANCH

P.O. Box 81
White Swan, Washington 98952

(509) 874-2520

Director: Merrill W. Scott

Average Patient Census: 49
Minimum Duration of Treatment: 21 days
Cost: $70 per day. Insurance eligible.
Detoxification Offered: Yes
Accreditation: State of Washington

Sundown M Ranch is a freestanding, nonmedical treatment center with a program that consists of a basic 21-day intensive course of therapy based upon intensive therapy, education, self-understanding and relearning.

The intensive-therapy program includes the following modalities: three lecture meetings each, three days a week, individual counseling, twice-daily small-group therapy, audiovisual materials and a thorough review of the philosophy and program of AA.

Inpatient family treatment is a necessary adjunct to the patient's treatment, and aftercare services are also offered.

Sundown M Ranch, the oldest and most experienced center in the state, is a private, non-profit corporation.

Wyoming

CHEMICAL DEPENDENCY CENTER
DePaul Hospital

2600 East Eighteenth Street
Cheyenne, Wyoming 82001

(307) 632-6411, ext. 264

Director: Victor J. Lisek

Average Patient Census: 12–15
Minimum Duration of Treatment: 28 days
Cost: Available on request. Insurance eligible.
Detoxification Offered: Yes
Accreditation: JCAH

The Chemical Dependency Center at DePaul Hospital provides treatment for alcoholism and other dependencies related to drug use.

Initial medical attention is given to detoxification and any other withdrawal complications. The general atmosphere is informal, but all hospital facilities are available to patients. During the 28-day program the patient is motivated, directed and supported in the process of learning and gaining understanding of himself or herself in relation to surroundings without alcohol/drugs. Treatment focuses on the individual, his failures at managing his affairs, his personal relationships, his identity, and his return to a respectable life-style within the community.

Aftercare programs include support for the development of a personal rehabilitative aftercare plan, recommendations for AA involvement, family counseling and opportunity for continued therapy through CDC's weekly group sessions and open-door policy.

The 3-day intensive Family Treatment Program is designed to help individuals other than the patient deal with the extensive problems caused by alcoholism and is open to all families and persons interested in learning about the disease.

Patients must be 19 years old to be admitted. Upon request, CDC staff will assist in admissions by contacting employers, judicial personnel and other social agencies in behalf of the patient.

CHEMICAL DEPENDENCY CENTER
West Park Hospital

707 Sheridan Avenue
Cody, Wyoming 82414

(307) 527-7501, ext. 261

Director: Dean Gard
Average Patient Census: 8–12

Minimum Duration of Treatment: 21 days, maximum of 45, not including detox
Cost: $172.50 per day. Insurance eligible.
Detoxification Offered: Yes
Accreditation: JCAH

The Chemical Dependency Center is operated in West Park Hospital with a capacity for thirteen residents. Planned individual and group therapy gives each patient the opportunity to explore and confront his or her own addictive process. Chemically dependent men, women and young people, and their families, will learn new behavior to help them reach their own personal goals without the use of mood-altering substances.

The program structure includes medically supervised detoxification, as well as physiological and psychological evaluation when indicated. The 30-day residential treatment program that follows is made up of such modalities as group therapy, individual therapy, family counseling, educational films and lectures, AA orientation and recreational therapy. Each patient is considered as an individual, with an individually designed plan completed after an intensive evaluation and social history workup.

Aftercare treatment involves the implementation of the client's plan for sobriety, as well as family education and the utilization of all applicable helping agencies, such as AA, Al-Anon and Alateen.

Outpatient services, such as therapy, counseling and education, are also available, and the Chemical Dependency Center also offers a professional counseling service to local industry and employee assistance programs on alcohol and drug abuse.

Appendix

NATIONAL ASSOCIATIONS, ORGANIZATIONS AND GOVERNMENT AGENCIES

Alcoholics Anonymous (AA)
General Service Office
468 Park Avenue South
New York, New York 10016

Family Group Headquarters (Al-Anon)
Box 182
Madison Square Station
New York, New York 10010

Alcohol and Drug Problems Association (ADPA)
1101 Fifteenth Street, N.W.
Washington, D.C. 20005
or
444 North Capital Street
Washington, D.C. 20001

American Medical Society on Alcoholism (AMSA)
12 West Twenty-first Street
New York, New York 10010

Association of Labor/Management Administrators and Consultants (ALMACA)
1800 North Kent Street
Arlington, Virginia 22209.

Children of Alcoholics Foundation
540 Madison Avenue
New York, New York 10022

Narcotics Anonymous (NA)
Box 622
Sun Valley, California 93352

National Association of Alcoholism and Drug Abuse Counselors (NAADAC)
951 South George Mason Drive
Arlington, Virginia 22204

National Association for Children of Alcoholics (NACOA)
P.O. Box 421691
San Francisco, California 94142

National Federation of Parents for Drug-Free Youth
1820 Franwall Avenue
Silver Spring, Maryland 20902

National Council on Alcoholism (NCA)
12 West Twenty-first Street
New York, New York 10010

National Clearinghouse for Alcohol Information (NCALI)
Box 2345
Rockville, Maryland 20852

National Clearinghouse for Drug Abuse Information (NCDAI)
5600 Fishers Lane, Room 10A53
Rockville, Maryland 20857

National Institute on Alcohol Abuse and Alcoholism (NIAAA)
Park Lawn Building
5600 Fishers Lane
Rockville, Maryland 20857

National Institute on Drug Abuse (NIDA)
Department of Health and Human
   Services
5600 Fishers Lane
Rockville, Maryland 20857

STATE ALCOHOL AND DRUG AGENCIES

You may wish to use the following list of state agencies to get information on the state-operated treatment facilities available in your area. There are many excellent programs, both inpatient and outpatient available. A call to the agency listed for your area should produce helpful information on available programs, sometimes offered at no cost or at lower cost than private centers.

Be persistent. Be patient. Continue to call or write until you reach someone who can give you the information you need. Tell them that you are seeking referral information, and be prepared when you do reach the appropriate person to provide the information they will need, such as sex, age and type of dependency.

If you are a veteran, important sources of help are Veterans Administration Medical Centers. There is at least one VA Medical Center in each state, and many, if not all, have outpatient and/or inpatient treatment programs available at no cost to veterans.

For information, call the office of the Associate Director for Alcohol and Drug Dependency in Washington, D.C. Telephone (202) 389-5193.

ALABAMA
Department of Mental Health
200 Interstate Park Drive
P.O. Box 3710
Montgomery 36193
(205) 271-9209

ALASKA
Office of Alcoholism and Drug Abuse
Department of Health and Social
   Services
Pouch H-05-F
Juneau 99811
(907) 586-6201

ARIZONA
Office of Community Behav. Health
Arizona Department of Health Services
1740 West Adams
Phoenix 85007
(602) 255-1152

ARKANSAS
Arkansas Office on Alcohol and Drug
   Abuse Prevention
1515 W. Seventh Avenue, Suite 300
Little Rock 72202
(501) 371-2603

CALIFORNIA
Department of Alcohol and Drug Abuse
111 Capital Mall
Sacramento 95814
(916) 445-1940 or 322-8484

COLORADO
Alcohol and Drug Abuse Division
Department of Health
4210 East Eleventh Avenue
Denver 80220
(303) 320-6137

371 | *Appendix*

CONNECTICUT
Connecticut Alcohol and Drug Abuse
  Commission
999 Asylum Avenue, 3rd Floor
Hartford 06105
(203) 566-4145

DELAWARE
Bureau of Alcoholism and Drug Abuse
1901 North DuPont Highway
Newcastle 19720
(302) 421-6101

DISTRICT OF COLUMBIA
Health Planning and Development
1875 Connecticut Avenue, N.W.
Suite 836
Washington 20009
(202) 673-7481

FLORIDA
Alcohol and Drug Abuse Program
Department of Health and Rehabilitative
  Services
1317 Winewood Boulevard
Tallahassee 32301
(904) 488-0900

GEORGIA
Alcohol and Drug Section
Division of Mental Health, Mental
  Retardation and Substance Abuse
GA Department of Human Resources
47 Trinity Avenue, S.W.
Atlanta 30334
(404) 656-7310

HAWAII
Alcohol and Drug Abuse Branch
Department of Health
P.O. Box 3378
Honolulu 96801
(808) 548-4280

IDAHO
Bureau of Substance Abuse
Department of Health and Welfare
450 West State Street
Boise 83720
(208) 334-4368

ILLINOIS
Illinois Department of Public Health
160 North LaSalle Street, 11th Floor
Chicago 60601
(312) 793-2799

INDIANA
Division of Addiction Services
Department of Mental Health
429 North Pennsylvania Street
Indianapolis 46204
(317) 232-7816

IOWA
Iowa Department of Substance Abuse
505 Fifth Avenue
Insurance Exchange Building, Suite 202
Des Moines 50319
(515) 281-3641

KANSAS
Alcohol and Drug Abuse Services
2700 West Sixth Street
Biddle Building
Topeka 66606
(913) 296-3925

KENTUCKY
Alcohol and Drug Branch
Bureau for Health Services
Department of Human Resources
275 East Main Street
Frankfort 40621
(502) 564-2880

LOUISIANA
Office of Prevention and Recovery from
  Alcohol and Drug Abuse
655 North Fifth Street
Baton Rouge 70821
(504) 342-2557

MAINE
Office of Alcoholism and Drug Abuse
  Prevention
Bureau of Rehabilitation
State House Station #11
Augusta 04333
(207) 289-2781

MARYLAND
Alcoholism Control Administration
201 West Preston Street, 4th Floor
Baltimore 21201
(301) 383-2977

Maryland State Drug Abuse
 Administration
201 West Preston Street
Baltimore 21201
(301) 383-3312

MASSACHUSETTS
Massachusetts Division of Alcoholism
150 Tremont Street
Boston 02111
(617) 727-1960

Division of Drug Rehabilitation
150 Tremont Street
Boston 02111
(617) 727-8614

MICHIGAN
Office of Substance Abuse Services
Department of Public Health
3500 North Logan Street
Lansing 48909
(517) 373-8603

MINNESOTA
Chemical Dependency Program Division
Department of Human Services
4th Floor Centennial Building
658 Cedar
Saint Paul 55155
(612) 296-4610

MISSISSIPPI
Division of Alcohol and Drug Abuse
Department of Mental Health
Robert E. Lee Office Building, 11th Floor
Jackson 39201
(601) 359-1297

MISSOURI
Division of Alcoholism and Drug Abuse
Department of Mental Health
2002 Missouri Boulevard
P.O. Box 687
Jefferson City 65101
(314) 751-4942

MONTANA
Alcohol and Drug Abuse Division
State of Montana
Department of Institutions
Helena 59601
(406) 499-2827

NEBRASKA
Division of Alcoholism and Drug Abuse
Department of Public Institutions
P.O. Box 94728
Lincoln 68509
(402) 471-2851, ext. 415

NEVADA
Bureau of Alcohol and Drug Abuse
Department of Human Resources
505 East King Street
Carson City 89710
(702) 885-4790

NEW HAMPSHIRE
Office of Alcohol and Drug Abuse
 Prevention
Health and Welfare Building
Hazen Drive
Concord 03301
(603) 271-4627

NEW JERSEY
New Jersey Division of Alcoholism
129 East Hanover Street
Trenton 08625
(609) 292-8947

Division of Narcotic and Drug Abuse
 Control
129 East Hanover Street
Trenton 08625
(609) 292-5760

NEW MEXICO
Alcoholism Bureau
Behavioral Health Services Division
P.O. Box 968
Santa Fe 87504
(505) 984-0020, ext. 493

Drug Abuse Bureau
Behavioral Health Services Division
P.O. Box 968
Santa Fe 87504
(505) 984-0020, ext. 331

NEW YORK
New York Div. of Alcoholism and
 Alcohol Abuse
194 Washington Avenue
Albany 12210
(518) 474-5417

Division of Substance Abuse Services
Executive Park South, Box 8200
Albany 12203
(518) 457-7629

NORTH CAROLINA
Alcohol and Drug Abuse Section
Division of Mental Health and Mental
 Retardation Services
325 North Salisbury Street
Raleigh 27611
(919) 733-4670

NORTH DAKOTA
Division of Alcoholism and Drugs
North Dakota Department of Human
 Services
State Capitol
Bismarck 58505
(701) 224-2769

OHIO
Bureau on Alcohol Abuse and Recovery
Ohio Department of Health
170 North High Street, 3rd Floor
Columbus 43215
(614) 466-3445

Bureau of Drug Abuse
170 North High Street, 3rd Floor
Columbus 43215
(614) 466-7893

OKLAHOMA
Alcohol and Drug Programs
Department of Mental Health
P.O. Box 53277, Capitol Station
4545 North Lincoln Boulevard
Suite 100 East Terrace
Oklahoma City 73152
(405) 521-0044

OREGON
Mental Health Division
2575 Bittern Street, N.E.
Salem 97310
(503) 378-2163

PENNSYLVANIA
PA Department of Health
P.O. Box 90
Harrisburg 17108
(717) 787-9857

RHODE ISLAND
Department of Mental Health, Mental
 Retardation and Hospitals
Division of Substance Abuse, Substance
 Abuse Administration Building
Cranston 02920
(401) 464-2091

SOUTH CAROLINA
South Carolina Commission on Alcohol
 and Drug Abuse
3700 Forest Drive
Columbia 29204
(803) 758-2521/2183

SOUTH DAKOTA
Division of Alcohol and Drug Abuse
Joe Foss Building
523 East Capitol
Pierre 57501
(605) 773-3123

TENNESSEE
Alcohol and Drug Abuse Services
Tennessee Department of Mental Health
 and Mental Retardation
James K. Polk Building
505 Deaderick Street
Nashville 37219
(615) 741-1921

TEXAS
Texas Commission on Alcoholism
1705 Guadalupe Street
Austin 78701
(512) 475-2577

Drug Abuse Prevention Division
Texas Department of Community Affairs
2015 South IH 35
Austin 78741
(512) 475-2311

UTAH
Division of Alcoholism and Drugs
150 West North Temple, Suite 350
P.O. Box 2500
Salt Lake City 84110
(801) 533-6532

VERMONT
Alcohol and Drug Abuse Division
103 South Maine Street
Waterbury 05676
(802) 241-2170, 241-1000

VIRGINIA
State Department of Mental Health and Mental Retardation
P.O. Box 1797
109 Governor Street
Richmond 23214
(804) 786-5313

WASHINGTON
Bureau of Alcoholism and Substance Abuse
Washington Department of Social and Health Services
Mail Stop OB-44W
Olympia 98504
(206) 753-5866

WEST VIRGINIA
Division of Alcohol and Drug Abuse
State Capitol
1800 Washington Street, East, Room 451
Charleston 25305
(304) 348-2276

WISCONSIN
Office of Alcohol and Other Drug Abuse
1 West Wilson Street, P.O. Box 7851
Madison 53707
(608) 266-3442

WYOMING
Alcohol and Drug Abuse Programs
Hathaway Building
Cheyenne 82002
(307) 777-7115, ext. 7118

GUAM
Department of Mental Health and Substance Abuse
P.O. Box 8896
Tamuning 96911

PUERTO RICO
Department of Addiction Control Services
Box B-Y, Rio Piedras Station
Rio Piedras 00928
(809) 763-5823

Suggested Reading List

A bibliography or reading list on the subjects of addiction, alcoholism and chemical dependency can fill volumes. The following are a very few of the multitude of books that are available from your local library, are listed in *Books in Print* or are available from the catalogs of various associations and specialized publishing groups.

Bissell, LeClair, M.D., and Paul Haberman. *Alcoholism in the Professions.* New York: Oxford University Press, 1984.

Brecher, Edward M. and the Editors of Consumers Reports. *Licit & Illicit Drugs.* Boston: Little, Brown & Co., 1972.

Cohen, Sidney. *The Substance Abuse Problems.* New York: Haworth Press, 1981.

Crenshaw, Mary Ann. *End of the Rainbow.* New York: Council on Alcoholism, 1956.

Jellinek, E. M. *The Disease Concept of Alcoholism.* New Haven: Hillhouse Press, 1960.

Johnson, Verne. *I'll Quit Tomorrow.* New York: Harper & Row, 1980.

Meryman, Richard. *Broken Promises, Mended Dreams—An Alcoholic Woman Fights for Her Life.* Boston: Little, Brown & Co., 1984.

O'Brien, Robert, and Morris Chafetz. *The Encyclopedia of Alcoholism.* New York: Facts on File, 1982.

O'Brien, Robert, and Sidney Cohen. *The Encyclopedia of Drug Abuse.* New York: Facts on File, 1984.

Reilly, Patrick. *A Private Practice.* New York: Macmillan Publishing Company, 1984.

The following organizations have catalogs of their own, along with other publications:

National Council on Alcoholism
12 West 21st Street
New York, New York 10010

Alcoholics Anonymous Central Service Headquarters
468 Park Avenue South
New York, New York 10016

Al-Anon Family Group Headquarters
Box 182
Madison Square Station
New York, New York 10010

Narcotics Anonymous
Box 622
Sun Valley, California 93352

Hazelden Educational Materials
Box 175
Center City, Minnesota 55012
(Narcotics Anonymous literature also
  available from this source)

Glossary of Terms

AA The standard abbreviation for Alcoholics Anonymous, the self-help organization whose approach to recovery has a profound and continuing effect upon almost all rehabilitative programs in this country.

aftercare Centers use this term to describe the continuing monitoring of patients who have "graduated" from their programs; it will continue for from 1 to 2 years. These programs are usually outpatient, though some centers offer "refresher" weeks of residential aftercare. All aftercare programs involve commitment on the part of the patient, and their availability should influence the geographic choice of the center to be attended.

Al-Anon and Alateen These organizations offer support, education and the opportunity for self-esteem for relatives and friends of alcoholics. Emphasis is on treatment of their specific disease of co-alcoholism, and involvement in these programs is encouraged regardless of the alcoholic's involvement with AA. Al-Anon provides help for spouses, relatives and friends of alcoholics, and Alateen is designed for teenagers, from the age of 12 to 20, who have been affected by someone, usually a parent, who has a drinking problem.

CA Cocaine Anonymous, a self-help organization for those addicted to cocaine.

chemical dependency An all-purpose term for addictive disease of any kind involving the abuse of alcohol or drugs.

detoxification The procedure, offered by many of the centers, through which a chemically dependent individual, alcoholic or drug abuser, is withdrawn from alcohol or drugs under supervision. It is designed to ensure that the patient, prior to involvement in the ongoing rehabilitation program, is no longer physically dependent upon the alcohol or drugs to which he or she has become addicted. Medically supervised detoxification is usually performed in a hospital setting, and the patient is sometimes given an appropriate sedative to control withdrawal symptoms. "Social detoxification," when the term appears in the text (it may also be called "subacute" detoxification), does not include sedatives, but does offer evaluation of the condition of the patient in withdrawal and supervision of his or her progress.

EAP The acronym for employee assistance programs. It is often the EAP group who identify those employees affected by chemical dependency and recommend treatment for them.

family programs Almost all residential programs, in acknowledgment of the accepted truth that chemical dependency is a family disease, offer family programs that range from educational lectures and films offered on weekends, evenings or near the end of the patient's stay at the center to residential week-long visits that also include group and individual therapy for family members. Some centers offer family programs even though the alcoholic is not himself enrolled in the residential program.

intervention A process through which a chemically dependent individual is faced with one, two, or more of his family members, friends or business associates who report to him their individual observations of his behavior. The effectiveness of the process comes from the fact that such factual and unemotional reports on behavior, coming from several different individuals who are important to him, prevent his denial. Intervention is best staged by a local professional or by staff members of those centers who offer this service, although it can be arranged by a family member. It can be an effective method of accelerating the realization on the part of the victim of addiction that the time has come for him or her to get help, and that help is available. No intervention process should be initiated unless clear understanding of available programs is ready at hand.

JCAH This designation, when it appears in the center's listing under accreditation, indicates that the center has made a voluntary application to the Joint Commission on the Accreditation of Hospitals, has received their evaluation and has been approved. It is a national standard in the health field. Individual states also offer accreditation evaluations, and those centers who have been awarded state approval are also noted in the text.

NA Narcotics Anonymous, a self-help organization with a Twelve Step program similar to the program used by AA.

Twelve Steps References to the Twelve Steps within the text refer to the basic AA philosophy, which is based upon adherence to these tenets; the Steps are used as guidelines to sobriety.

Glossary of Terms

Index of Treatment Centers with Programs for Specific Groups

ADOLESCENTS

EAST COAST FACILITIES

CONNECTICUT
Natchaug Hospital Inc., Willimantic, 12
Parkside Lodge of Connecticut, North Canaan, 9
The Institute of Living, Hartford, 7

FLORIDA
Bayshore on the Gulf, Dunedin, 21
CareUnit of Jacksonville, Jacksonville Beach, 26
CareUnit of Tampa, Tampa, 35
Charter Glade Hospital, Fort Myers, 23
Horizon Hospital, Clearwater, 19
Koala Center, Bushnell, 18
Palmview Hospital, Lakeland, 28
The Cloisters at Pine Island, Pineland, 32
Twelve Oaks, Mary Esther, 29

GEORGIA
Charter Brook Hospital, Atlanta, 36
Charter Lake Hospital, Macon, 40
Charter Peachford Hospital, Atlanta, 37
CPC Parkwood Hospital, Atlanta, 37
Ridgeview Institute, Smyrna, 42

MAINE
Eastern Maine Medical Center Alcohol Institute, Bangor, 45

Kennebec Valley Comprehensive Alcoholism Treatment Program, Waterville, 48
Merrymeeting House, Bowdoinham, 45

NEW HAMPSHIRE
Spofford Hall, Spofford, 61

NEW JERSEY
Carrier Foundation, Belle Mead, 64

NEW YORK
Arms Acres, Carmel, 71
Conifer Park, Scotia, 80
Four Winds Hospital, Katonah, 74
New York Hospital–Cornell Medical Center, White Plains, 83
Regent Hospital, New York City, 77
South Oaks Hospital, Amityville, 70

NORTH CAROLINA
Charlotte Treatment Center, Charlotte, 86
Charter Northridge Hospital, Raleigh, 88

PENNSYLVANIA
ARC/The Terraces, Ephrata, 95
Bowling Green Inn–Brandywine, Kennett Square, 96

Clear Brook, Inc., Laurel Run, 97
Today, Inc., Newtown, 98
White Deer Run, Allenwood, 91

RHODE ISLAND
Butler Hospital, Providence, 105
High Point, North Kingstown, 104

VERMONT
Brattleboro Retreat, Brattleboro, 109

VIRGINIA
Alcoholism Treatment Program, The Arlington Hospital, Arlington, 114
Charter Westbrook Hospital, Richmond, 121
Mountain Wood Ltd., Charlottesville, 115
New Beginnings/Serenity Lodge, Chesapeake, 116
Peninsula Hospital, Hampton, 118
Springwood Psychiatric Institute, Leesburg, 119

WEST VIRGINIA
Koala Center, South Charleston, 125

SOUTHERN/CENTRAL FACILITIES

ILLINOIS
ARC-Chicago, Hoffman Estates, 149
Chicago Lakeshore Hospital, Chicago, 141
Ingalls Memorial Hospital, Harvey, 148
Lighthouse, Bloomington, 139

INDIANA
CPC Valle Vista Hospital, Greenwood, 158
Fairbanks Hospital, Inc., Indianapolis, 159
Koala Adolescent Center, Indianapolis, 160
Koala Center, Lebanon, 161
Renaissance Center for Addictions Treatment, Elkhart, 157
Saint Mary's Medical Center, Boonville, 155

IOWA
Gordon Chemical Dependency Center, Sioux City, 167
Powell III, Des Moines, 165

KANSAS
Alcoholism Treatment Unit, Saint Joseph Medical Center, Wichita, 173

KENTUCKY
Charterton Hospital, LaGrange, 175
Goodman Hill Hospital, Paducah, 177

LOUISIANA
Baton Rouge Chemical Dependency Unit, Baton Rouge, 179
Bowling Green Inn of Saint Tammany, Mandeville, 183
Charter Forest Hospital, Shreveport, 187
Chemical Dependency Unit of Acadiana, Lafayette, 181
CounterPoint Center of New Orleans, New Orleans, 184
Koala Center, Opelousas, 185
La Maison, Equilibria, Baton Rouge, 180

MICHIGAN
Henry Ford Hospital Maplegrove, West Bloomfield, 193
New Day Center, Battle Creek, 189

MINNESOTA
Alcohol and Chemical Dependency Treatment Center, Saint Cloud Hospital, Saint Cloud, 203
Golden Valley Health Center, Golden Valley, 196
Hazelden Pioneer House, Plymouth, 200
Jamestown Adolescent Treatment Program, Stillwater, 206
Parkview West Youth and Family Center, Eden Prairie, 195
Pine Manors, Inc. #1, Pine City, 200
New Connection Programs, Inc., Saint Paul, 203
Saint John's Chemical Dependency Treatment Center, Saint Paul, 205
Saint Mary's Chemical Dependency Services, Minneapolis, 199

MISSISSIPPI
CDC Mississippi Baptist Medical Center, Jackson, 210

MISSOURI
CareUnit Hospital of Saint Louis, Saint Louis, 217
CPC Weldon Spring Hospital, St. Charles, 216

NEBRASKA
Eppley Chemical Dependency Services, Omaha, 221
Independence Center, Lincoln, 220

NORTH DAKOTA
Heartview Foundation, Mandan, 226
United Recovery Center, Grand Fork, 226

OHIO
Adolescent Alcoholism Treatment Program–Talbot Hall, Columbus, 231
Alcoholism Treatment Center, Toledo Hospital, Toledo, 234
CareUnit Hospital of Cincinnati, Cincinnati, 230
Lakeland Institute, Lorain, 233
The Campus, Westerville, 235

OKLAHOMA
Raleigh Hills Hospital, Miami, 240
The Oaks Rehabilitative Services Center, McAlester, 239
Valley Hope Alcoholism Treatment Center, Cushing, 239

TENNESSEE
Charter Lakeside, Memphis, 247
Koala Center at University Medical Center, Lebanon, 246
Parkview Tennessee, Harrison, 244

TEXAS
Brookwood Adolescent Center–Westgate, Denton, 253
Brookwood Recovery Center–Chocolate Bayou, Liverpool, 260
Brookwood Recovery Center–Katy, Katy, 258

CareUnit Hospital of Dallas–Fort Worth, Fort Worth, 255
CPC of Sunrise Hospital, Arlington, 251

WISCONSIN
Alcoholic Treatment Unit, Bellin Memorial Hospital, Green Bay, 265
De Paul Rehabilitation Hospital, Milwaukee, 269
Kettle Moraine Hospital, Oconomowac, 270
R.O.A.D. Winnebago Mental Health Institute, Winnebago, 271

WESTERN FACILITIES

ALASKA
Charter North Hospital, Anchorage, 275

ARIZONA
Westcenter Adolescent Program, Tucson, 281

CALIFORNIA
CareUnit Hospital of Los Angeles, Los Angeles, 301
CareUnit Hospital of Orange, Orange, 306
Charter Pacific Hospital, Torrance, 321
Memorial Coastview, Long Beach, 298
New Beginnings Program, Lakewood, 295
Starting Point, Orangevale, 307
The McDonald Center, La Jolla, 294
Tustin Community Hospital, Tustin, 321

COLORADO
Addiction Recovery Unit, Saint Luke's Hospital, Denver, 326
Mount Airy Psychiatric Center, Denver, 328
Personal Development Center, Wheatridge, 331
The Centre, Inc., Denver, 327

HAWAII
Salvation Army Addiction Treatment Facility, Honolulu, 332

IDAHO
Pine Crest Hospital, Coeur d'Alene, 336
Port of Hope West, Caldwell, 335

MONTANA
Rimrock Foundation, Billings, 339

NEVADA
CareUnit Hospital of Nevada, Las Vegas, 341
Truckee Meadows Hospital, Reno, 342

NEW MEXICO
Amethyst Hall, Velarde, 349
CareUnit Hospital of Albuquerque, Albuquerque, 343

OREGON
Holbrook Residential Treatment Center, Portland, 353
Serenity by the Sea, Seaside, 354

UTAH
Odyssey House of Utah, Inc., Salt Lake City, 356

WASHINGTON
CareUnit Hospital of Kirkland, Kirkland, 360
Northwest Treatment Center, Seattle, 362
Olympic Center, Bellingham, 358

WYOMING
Chemical Dependency Center, West Park Hospital, Cody, 369

BLACKS

Ebony House Inc., Phoenix, Arizona, 279
Healthquest, Trinity Lutheran Hospital, Kansas City, Missouri, 215

GAYS/LESBIANS

Alcoholism Treatment Service, Pomona Valley Community Hospital, Pomona, California, 310
ARC/The Terraces, Ephrata, Pennsylvania, 95
DELPHOS Alcohol and Drug Treatment Center, Key West, Florida, 27

HEARING-IMPAIRED/DEAF

CCAIRU Project for the Deaf, West Falmouth, Massachusetts, 57

HISPANIC

CareUnit Hospital of Los Angeles, Los Angeles, California, 301

IMPAIRED PHYSICIANS AND HEALTH PROFESSIONALS

Brattleboro Retreat–Ripley Center, Brattleboro, Vermont, 111
Chemical Dependency Unit, Antelope Valley Hospital Medical Center, Lancaster, California (Nurses' Program), 297
DELPHOS Alcohol and Drug Treatment Center, Key West, Florida, 27
De Paul Rehabilitation Hospital, Milwaukee, Wisconsin, 269
Gulf Shores Retreat Centers, Inc., Gulf Shores, Alabama, 131
Henry Ford Hospital Maplegrove, West Bloomfield, Michigan, 193
Ridgeview Institute, Smyrna, Georgia, 42

MEN ONLY

Beacon House for Men, Greenfield, Massachusetts, 56
Decision Point, Springdale, Arkansas, 137
Denton Center, Greenwood, Mississippi, 208
Equilibria, Baton Rouge, Louisiana, 180
Harmony House, Inc., Portland, Oregon, 352
Men's Twelfth Step House, Long Beach, California, 299
Salt Lake Alcoholism Treatment Center, Salt Lake City, Utah, 357
Sand Island Halfway House, Honolulu, Hawaii, 333
Serenity House, Laurel, Mississippi, 211
The Pines Alcohol Rehabilitation Center, Columbus, Mississippi, 207
Warm Springs Rehabilitation Center, Castaic, California (see program description for Acton Rehabilitation Center, Acton, California), 284

NATIVE AMERICANS

Odyssey House of Utah, Inc., Salt Lake City, Utah, 356
Sweathouse Lodge, Foster, Oregon, 352

OLDER ADULTS

Bridgeway Center, Minneapolis, Minnesota, 197
Golden Gate for Seniors, San Francisco, California, 316

PRIESTS, NUNS, BROTHERS

Saint Luke Institute, Inc., Suitland, Maryland, 53

RETREAT CENTER FOR ADDICTION WORKERS

Gulf Shores Retreat Centers, Inc., Gulf Shores, Alabama, 131

WOMEN ONLY

Alcohol and Drug Abuse Center, Phoenix General Hospital, Phoenix, Arizona, 278
Alcoholism Center for Women, Los Angeles, California, 300
Amethyst Women's Recovery Program, Cerritos, California, 287
Beacon House for Women, Greenfield, Massachusetts, 56
Casa de las Amigas, Pasadena, California, 308
Crossroads, South Windham, Maine, 47
F.A.I.T.H., Inc., Worcester, Massachusetts, 59
La Maison, Equilibria, Baton Rouge, Louisiana, 180
Salt Lake Alcoholism Treatment Center, Salt Lake City, Utah, 357
The Gables, Rochester, Minnesota, 201
Women's Alcohol Treatment Center of Hawaii, Honolulu, Hawaii, 334

Special Index